# MAYOR ROB FORD: UNCONTROLLABLE

# MAYOR ROB FORD: UNCONTROLLABLE

*How I Tried to Help the
World's Most Notorious Mayor*

MARK TOWHEY
and JOHANNA SCHNELLER

Skyhorse Publishing

Skyhorse Publishing books may be purchased in bulk at special discounts for sales promotion, corporate gifts, fund-raising, or educational purposes. Special editions can also be created to specifications. For details, contact the Special Sales Department, Skyhorse Publishing, 307 West 36th Street, 11th Floor, New York, NY 10018 or info@skyhorsepublishing.com.

Skyhorse® and Skyhorse Publishing® are registered trademarks of Skyhorse Publishing, Inc.®, a Delaware corporation.

Visit our website at www.skyhorsepublishing.com.

10 9 8 7 6 5 4 3 2 1

Library of Congress Cataloging-in-Publication Data is available on file.

Cover design by Brian Peterson

ISBN: 978-163450-042-5
Ebook ISBN: 978-1-63450-048-7

Printed in the United States of America

Quotations attributed to various individuals have been recreated from the author's memory, and are not verbatim transcripts of what was said. In every instance the author has endeavored as much as his recollection will allow to convey the sense and import of the speaker's words. However, human memory is fallible, and there may be some cases where the speaker recalls differently his or her comments.

To all who served with me in the Office of the Mayor, especially:

Adam Howell

Adrienne Batra

Amir Remtulla

Andrew Gillis

Brendan Crosskerry

Brian Johnston

Brooks Barnett

Carley McNeil

Cathy DeMarco

Chris Fickel

Dana Cochrane

Earl Provost

Emily Thompson

George Christopolous

Isaac Ransom

Isaac Shirokov

Jennifer Dwyer

Kia Nejatian

Michael Prempeh

Nick Kouvalis

Nico Fidani

Olivia Gondek

Pina Martino

Sheila Paxton

Sunny Petrujkic

Tina Arvanitis

Tom Beyer

# Contents

# Foreword | Why?

WHY AM I writing this book?

On May 23, 2013, as I was escorted out of Toronto City Hall surrounded by a swarm of news cameras and reporters, they asked me the same questions, over and over again: What did I say to the mayor? What advice had I given him? Why was I leaving? Did he have a drinking or drug problem? In every case, I responded with essentially the same answer: "My advice for the mayor is confidential."

Since that day, I've kept my counsel. I have not spoken directly to the media or the public about what my advice was, or what my experience was behind the scenes in Rob Ford's office. I spoke twice, under oath, to the Toronto police as part of their investigation into criminal activities that had implicated the mayor and people around him. Some of that testimony subsequently made its way into court documents that were released, through a slow, painful process, to the media. But the bits of my counsel that have been made public were never done so by me. Until now.

Why speak on the record now? Why write a book that opens the curtains on the backstage of Rob Ford's rise, rule, and fall? It took me a year to decide that writing this book was the right thing to do. I have three main reasons.

First, the most salacious episodes already have been revealed, partly by Toronto journalists who've done an excellent job digging up the puzzle pieces and fitting them together, and partly by the Information to Obtain (ITO) search warrant documents filed with the courts by Toronto police and released publicly. So much of the gist of what happened is already in the public domain. What's missing is the context, the connective tissue between the events, the manner in which things unfolded, the import of some events, and the insignificance of others. In some cases, the publicly reported details are wrong. In other cases, the public version of events has mixed up the timeline of who knew what when. At this point, I feel it is important that there be an insider's narrative on the public record. I recognize this may harm my hard-won reputation for discretion. But I think the importance of setting the record straight outweighs the risk.

Second, Rob Ford hurt a lot of good people. The political staff in the mayor's office worked long hours and produced impressive results, under the most difficult conditions imaginable. Whatever you've heard, whatever you've imagined, working there was worse. And at the end of it, their names were sullied. Some of them quit on principle after I was fired, leaving well-paid jobs and suffering the consequence of a long—in some cases continuing—period of unemployment. Many others simply couldn't afford to escape. Working for Rob Ford took a toll on the health and well-being of most of them. Their work and their sacrifices have gone unrecognized. I hope to rectify that.

Finally, I need to tell this story for myself. The day I left City Hall began a long, scary year of depression and self-doubt. This book is part of my healing process.

There is a great story to tell about how and where we succeeded, and why and where we failed. There are lessons to be learned about how to get things done politically that, I believe, are applicable in every democracy. And there are lessons to be learned from my experience of trying to manage a boss who was often right, but too often very wrong. The particulars of my story may be crazy, but its themes are universal.

# Prologue | His First Addiction

*September 2010*

I PULLED UP outside Rob Ford's house about ten minutes early. It was September 15, 2010. A Wednesday. I'd told him we should leave at 4:30 to be across town for the 6:30 p.m. debate. I was always early, because he was always late.

Both Rob's beat-up, filthy Chevrolet Uplander van and his wife Renata's blue Ford Escape were in the driveway, so he was home. That was a good sign. The curtains were closed. That was normal. The Fords were a private family, and their home was a place few staff or outsiders ever entered. Even glimpses through the windows were rare, usually only when one of his two kids was peeking out.

His house was a modest bungalow with a roof that needed repair. It was the first, and by far the cheapest-looking, house on a street that was now lined with much bigger, nicer homes that quickly escalated into the multimillion-dollar range. If you Googled his address, you'd assume the Ford home was on millionaire's row—which it was. But as I sat looking at it from my truck across the street, where he could see me if he glanced out the window, it looked like a place your minimum-wage gardener might live in if you were really rich. I popped the lid open on my Tim Hortons Double Double coffee, and waited.

Getting a politician into the zone for a public appearance, especially an all-candidates debate, was a lot like getting a comedian pumped up before a gig. Politicians are performers, after all. Massive egos. Always craving positive feedback. And Rob was especially tricky. For a politician, he was surprisingly shy. Show most politicians a camera, and they'll automatically turn into the light to get on TV. Not Rob. He dreaded public speaking and felt he was terrible at it. He told me his words got jumbled up and never came out the way he'd intended. He was only comfortable in small groups of constituents, or one-on-one on the phone.

Although there were over forty other candidates for mayor, there were really only four serious contenders: Ford; George Smitherman, who had been the early race leader and was still the pundits' favorite; Rocco Rossi, who was the establishment's second (and more conservative) choice; and Joe Pantalone, the only hope for the city's large left-wing constituency. All but Ford were polished public speakers who loved attention and would speak until they were cut off. They prided themselves on being smart, well-spoken, and able to answer any question with a thoughtful, articulate response tailored to the unique nature of each audience. Ironically, that would be their downfall.

Two other candidates, City Councillor Giorgio Mammoliti and Sarah Thomson, publisher of *Women's Post* magazine, were also covered by City Hall media, but were never serious challengers.

I didn't knock on Rob's door. I didn't phone the house. None of us knocked on the door, except as a last resort. None of us ever called the house. Never. Only his closest, longest-serving, and most trusted staffers had ever been inside the house. In the three years I would ultimately work for Ford, I would step inside his home exactly twice. Both times during a crisis.

Rob said Renata didn't like people coming to the door. She didn't like people calling the house. She must have hated the fact that, every day, Rob gave out his home telephone number on hundreds of fridge magnets. He handed them out to people on the street, pressed them into the hands of TV and radio interviewers, distributed them throughout the corridors of Toronto's City Hall, which perched like a spaceship on a plaza at the corner of Queen and Bay streets. But Renata couldn't stop him. No one could. It was a Rob Ford thing, another of the eccentricities I was learning about as the campaign went on.

I glanced through the debate book I'd prepared for the evening. It was a debate at Burrows Hall Community Centre in Scarborough—a former suburb amalgamated into the megacity that was Toronto, this one to the east. Hosted by a local residents' association, the event was scheduled to go three hours. It was hot. It would be grueling. There would be too many repeat questions from residents, about the same issues important to residents in every other debate. Each candidate would roll out the same answers they'd practiced for months.

We'd done dozens of debates already and there were over fifty to go in the remaining weeks of the mayoral campaign. Rob was a difficult politician to brief. It had taken a great deal of trial and error to figure out how to get him prepared. He had no real interest in policy beyond his broadly stated goals, which he repeated over and over. Lower taxes. Cut the vehicle tax and the land transfer tax. Cut the waste. Cut the size of Council. Cut councillors' budgets. It was his mantra, and he intoned it like a Zen master.

I also wondered if he had attention deficit disorder—it was an ongoing struggle to keep him focused on debate prep for more than a few minutes at a time. We'd started by doing prep in his office at the family business at 28 Greensboro Drive, a nondescript building in an industrial strip running alongside one of North America's busiest highways, Highway 401, through north Etobicoke. But within a minute of beginning, he'd invariably be answering his phone; or remembering some trivial detail he wanted Enzo, the company handyman, to take care of; or running old bills and junk mail through the shredder beside his desk (man, he loved that shredder), and I'd have to guide him back. (Surprisingly, Enzo's family would factor into Ford's downfall some three years later.)

During the six and a half months I'd been working for him, however, I'd come up with a system that seemed to work. I would always chauffeur him to the debates so I could squeeze in prep along the way. I'd bought a fancy-looking, leather-bound, three-ring binder at Staples and filled it with plastic slip-in sheets. For each of the debates, I'd work with the event organizers, get a list of the questions they would ask (if they were willing to share), or the topics they were interested in (if not). I'd prepare a standard package in the binder he could take on stage with him.

**First page:** List of the place, time, name of the group hosting the debate, and names of key people he'd meet.

**Second page:** List of his key campaign messages.

**Pages 3–5:** List of the questions they'd ask and three or four talking points for each, bridging back to his key messages.

**Back pages:** any background material that might be useful, including copies of his campaign literature he could hold up as props.

The final ingredient was Rob Ford's secret weapon—his security blanket, without which he was unsettled and unfocused. He'd misplaced it often enough that I'd learned to make multiple copies and stash them everywhere. There was one tucked into the front of the binder. There was one in a slipcase at the back of the binder. There was one in his pocket and two or three in my suit pockets as well as an envelope of twenty in my truck.

The security blanket was a double-sided printout of every motion he'd put forward in his ten years as a city councillor, how much money it would have saved, and what the vote count was. For example, he'd put forward a motion to save $77,000 by having councillors water their own plants in City Hall, and another to save $80,000 by discontinuing the handout of free cigarettes and booze in homeless shelters. While other politicians focused on the $9 billion operating budget, Ford drew people's attention to the small-scale waste that enraged voters, like eliminating free golf passes for city politicians. Nobody could conceive of a billion dollars—it was a number with too many zeroes. No one knew whether $9 billion was too much or too little to pay to run a city. But everyone knew exactly how much they were paid each year and how hard they worked to earn it. So when they heard Ford say that someone was getting almost $80,000 to *water plants,* they were outraged. When one of his opponents corrected his numbers, it only got better.

"Rob, you know you're wrong," Joe Pantalone would say. He'd go on to explain that the woman who waters plants in councillors' offices was a botanist who also cared for the plants in Nathan Phillips Square—City Hall's main public plaza—and she only made $55,000.

The audience would howl: *$55,000! To look after plants? That's ridiculous!* Rob Ford was the only candidate who agreed with them. From that moment, they'd be his.

"This is gold, buddy. Gold," he'd told me on many occasions. Rob called almost everyone "buddy." He had no real friends and was awkward with strangers, so maybe it was his way of deputizing people around him, building a bond with them. And it worked. Tens of thousands of people in Toronto felt they had a personal relationship with Rob Ford. Calling people "buddy" also helped when you forgot someone's name.

At 4:30, there was no movement in Rob's house, so I called his cell phone. It went straight to voice mail. Not good—that meant it was switched off. Was he ready? Was he even awake? Ford was a nocturnal creature, so he would often nap during the afternoon. I waited a few minutes and called again. Still off.

At 4:40, I got out of the car to knock on the door. This was a last-ditch measure and not something I looked forward to. On my way across the street, I called again. Reprieve: This time he answered.

"Yeah?" Typically curt, when he was on the receiving end of a staff call.

"Hi, boss, I'm parked outside," I said. "Boss" was my version of "buddy." I didn't want to call him Rob, which he preferred. He was a client, not a friend. He was an elected councillor, but calling him "councillor" felt awkward in private. So I'd settled on boss. "We should get going, it's after 4:30."

"OK. I'll be out in ten minutes." Click.

About eight minutes later, the door opened and Rob walked out to his van. He was wearing his usual: dark blue suit with a blue shirt and patterned tie. He didn't look great. His shirt was wet where he'd brushed his teeth and splashed water on his face. The collar was splayed wide, the shirt clearly too small. Pretty much everyone who ever saw Rob had suggested that we get him better-quality suits. But the suits weren't the problem: They were always high-end, from posh retailer Harry Rosen, $1,200 to $2,000 each, and tailored. But stuff a quart-sized bottle of root beer into one jacket pocket, five hundred business cards and fridge magnets in the other, with Rob Ford in the middle, and there's only so much any suit can do.

I pulled my red Ford Explorer around in a U-turn and stopped behind Rob's van on the edge of his driveway so he could hop into my truck without walking through the dirt on the boulevard. I jumped out and stood behind him as he rustled through a pile of papers in his van. There were always papers in the van. Everything Rob did was on paper: schedules, printed out two or three times a day. Call lists, produced daily. These were scattered around under the usual piles of crumpled McDonald's wrappers and orphaned Happy Meal toys.

"Where's my call sheets?" he asked. His precious call sheets. He never went anywhere without them. We spent a few minutes locating them in a manila folder on the floor under the front passenger seat, then climbed into my truck. I reminded him to take off his suit jacket and hang it on the back of his seat to avoid wrinkles. (Later, I learned to carry a spare coat hanger.) By now it was nearly 5:00.

"I need to stop at Esso," Rob said. Another part of his pre-debate routine. I pulled onto the road and drove 150 yards up the street and into the Esso gas station parking lot. There was a Tim Hortons coffee and donut counter inside and Rob always bought a French vanilla coffee and a copy of the *Toronto Sun*.

While he was inside, I phoned Nick Kouvalis, the de facto campaign manager, and told him we were moving and that we'd be cutting it close. I'd also call ahead to alert our advance team (already at the site to scout it out for us) when we were nearby, so that they'd be standing outside when we pulled up, to walk Rob in and help him glad-hand the crowd until I could park and catch up. Rob always wanted to walk in on his own. He was not used to being handled or managed by staff. But I was an ex-army officer and Nick was ex-military and an experienced campaign manager, and we insisted on planning and protocol.

Rob heaved himself back into my Explorer and rolled down the window. Although I'd put his seat all the way back, the car was always a tight fit for him. No matter how hot or cold it was outside, he'd roll the window down so his elbow could rest on the sill, giving him some breathing space. By the time I turned onto Scarlett Road, he was already on the phone. Everywhere we went, any time of the day or evening, no matter what else I'd be trying to communicate to him, he was always working that damn call sheet.

It didn't look like much—just an 8 ½ x 11-inch sheet of plain paper, with phone numbers scribbled in two columns on each side. The numbers were taken, by hand, from his home phone's caller ID window. When constituents would use those magnets Rob gave out and actually phone his house, they'd leave a message. There could be anywhere from twenty to two hundred calls a night, depending on what he had been doing the day before. No one at the Ford house ever listened to the voicemails, but every call logged into the caller ID would be written on a plain white piece of paper by Rob himself, or by Katie, his executive assistant (EA), who was one of the few staffers trusted enough to enter his house. Twenty-five numbers per side. Fifty per sheet. And every one of those calls, he would return. Personally. That was his trademark, his brand—his promise. People loved it; he was sure of that.

As we drove, he'd sit with the paper in his left hand, and his flip phone and a pen—usually my pen—in his right. He'd stab the numbers into the phone with his chubby index finger and wait.

Usually, he got voice mail. "This is Rob Ford, returning your call," he'd say. "If I can help you, please call my office at 416-397-9255. That's 416-397-9255. If I'm not there, you can talk to one of my staff and they'll help you out." He'd put a big check mark next to the number, and then dial the next.

When there was no answer and no voice mail, he'd get annoyed. "Who doesn't have a machine?" he'd grumble. "How am I supposed to call you back if you don't have a machine?"

I'd give him time to make a few calls before beginning the briefing. At the first red light, I'd hand him the binder to go over the gist of the debate:

who was sponsoring it, where it was, who would be there, and what the issues were. Often, they were small: residents upset about too much traffic turning onto their street because there was a new no-turn prohibition on a neighboring road, that kind of thing. We'd get through a few details, then he'd clear his throat and spit a large hunk of phlegm out the window. He'd done that so often that I'd gotten over the grossness of it. But you really didn't want to be sitting in the seat behind him when he did it. Afterward, he'd punch out another number on the phone and I'd have to wait for a few more calls before continuing the briefing.

About one out of every five numbers, he'd connect with someone. Often, they had no idea who he was. I'd only ever hear half the phone call; "Hi, this is Rob Ford, I'm running for mayor of Toronto, how can I help you?" He'd spit it out quickly, followed often by a long beat. Then, "I'm returning your call." Beat. "Well, someone from this number called me. Is this 416-555-5555? Well, then someone called me and left a message." Beat. "Okay, well, if I can help you out in any way, let me know. Have a good night."

But then, every tenth call or so, he'd strike gold. He'd connect with someone who was thrilled to hear his voice. Someone who loved him and would tell him so.

"Yes, this is really Rob Ford. It's me," he'd say, a big grin on his face. They'd explain their problem and he'd promise to help.

"Is it your tree or your neighbor's tree? Uh-huh," he'd say, scribbling a note on the call sheet. "Do you know if it's privately owned or if it's on city property?" Then he'd pull his paper calendar out of his breast pocket and unfold it on my dashboard. Squinting, he'd look at the week ahead. "Will you be home Thursday?" he'd ask. "Thursday at, say, ten o'clock?" Beat. "Good. I'll be at your house on Thursday at ten o'clock with city staff and we'll sort it out. No problem. I'm happy to help. I don't mean to be rude, but I gotta let you go now. Bye."

He'd hang up, scribble a note on his calendar, and stab his phone to reach his own office line, where he'd get his assistant's voice mail. "Katie, it's Rob Ford," he'd say—his full name, every time, like he had to remind her of who he was. "I need MLS [the Municipal Licensing and Standards enforcement officers] and Forestry at (address) on Thursday at 10:00 a.m. Set it up." He'd then check the number off his call sheet, and move on to the next.

Every time that happened, he'd say to me, "Ten votes, right there." He'd sound happy, sure of himself. "That's all there is to it, man," he'd tell me. "Returning people's calls. That's what you gotta do. They tell their family. They tell their friends. That's ten votes. It's gold."

After a few weeks of this, I learned not to fight the calls. I learned to work between them. As we closed in on the venue, after every third or fourth call, I'd interject and draw his attention back to the binder. We'd cover one talking point, or one way to deflect an opponent's assault, and then I'd wait while he dialed another few numbers.

By the time we pulled up to the community center that evening, I'd covered all the critical points for the debate, while he'd dialed thirty numbers, left ten messages, talked to six people, and soaked up some love from three or four of them—just enough to build up his enormous yet eggshell-fragile ego for the clash of the debate. Later, I'd observe that whenever he was pressed or cornered, or there was a crisis in progress, he'd default back to his call list. Madly dialing. Looking for positive reinforcement in the praise of strangers. He called it his "ground game." I called it "dialing for love."

Much later—after he'd won the election, after his first year as mayor, after his behavior had become increasingly unpredictable—I'd watch as he struggled with other, more dangerous addictions. But from the beginning of our time together, his first addiction was love.

# PART I | HITTING THE CAMPAIGN TRAIL: FEBRUARY–OCTOBER 2010

# 1 | What Am I Doing Here?

*January 2010*

Rob Ford wasn't the first boss I'd have to stand up to. In the autumn of 1989, as an army captain in Kamloops, British Columbia, I witnessed a superior officer drive while drunk, damaging a military vehicle in the process. It was late, and I was the only one around with any authority.

I spent fourteen years as an army officer, serving across Canada and in Europe, the Middle East, and Africa. I learned about problem solving, leadership, and ethics, often in crisis situations. I learned that the mission comes first, and that good teams are brutally honest with one another. I expected my troops to push back on my ideas as hard as I pushed back on my boss's ideas. That's how we tested them.

There was no point sitting silent if the bus was heading for a cliff. You spoke up and argued your case. If you were right, the plan usually changed. If you were wrong, you usually found out why. Sometimes, though, the plan didn't change and you didn't know why. Sometimes, there were factors you hadn't been told about. You trusted your boss not to tell you to do something stupid or suicidal unless it had to be done. But you also knew that someday, something just like that might have to be done.

Once the plan was decided, however, the debate was over. From that point on, you executed with excellence. You sold the mission to your troops as if it were your own idea and never apologized for it. You never said, "Yeah, it's stupid, but it's orders." You owned the plan, for better or worse. That was loyalty, and it worked both ways. When your troops screwed up, you owned that too. You'd wear the shit from up top, and not blame your team. In return, they'd move mountains to protect your back.

When you join the army, some of your first lessons are about military law. Military law dictates that a soldier must obey all lawful commands;

you may be court-martialed for disobeying one. But the key word is "lawful." It's your responsibility to know what's lawful and what's not. If the command is unlawful, it's your responsibility to disobey it. Good soldiers obey the laws. And they set examples for those who follow them.

So when I witnessed my superior officer driving drunk, I arrested him, and later testified against him at trial.

I haven't always been popular with my bosses—but I never thought any of them hired me to be popular. I thought they hired me to get difficult jobs done, by doing the right thing. Later, I would learn that this principle doesn't always carry over to politics. But I tried.

\*\*\*

In 2007, about ten years after I left the military, I accepted a challenging job in Badakhshan, Afghanistan, a hard-to-reach northern province on the frontier with Tajikistan, as part of a small European Union project dedicated to improving the capabilities of the Afghan border police. I had been recruited by the United Nations Development Programme that had been hired to deliver the EU program. They were looking for someone with a freakishly unusual mix of skills and experience. They needed an experienced management consultant with an MBA, crisis management skills, and at least ten years' service as an infantry officer with experience in conflict zones. They found me.

The job came at a perfect time. I needed to make some cash, pay down some debt, lose some weight, and figure out where I wanted to go next, both professionally and personally. I'd run my own consulting business for the previous ten years, and had wound it down from ten employees at its peak to just me while I figured out my next step: either find some way to grow capital and stick with it, or give it up and join a bigger firm.

My marriage was in a similar state of flux. My wife, Carol, and I had been married for twelve years; our two boys, Hunter and Jonathan, were nine and four. Carol and I got along well, but we'd grown apart; we weren't in love anymore. When the job in Afghanistan came up, we both saw it as a good opportunity—or perhaps an excuse—to take a break from one another and get some perspective.

By the end of 2008, I'd wrapped up my piece of the border management project and had found a further opportunity with International Finance Corporation, the private sector investment banking subsidiary of the

World Bank Group. In December 2009, I finished my last reports for them and headed back to Toronto.

So there I was, living in the basement of my home—which seems ironic now, given the highly public roles so many basement-dwellers would eventually play in Rob Ford's fall from grace—with my two terrific children, a wife whom I'd agreed to divorce, a stale network of business contacts, some savings, some debts that would soon eat through the savings, and a decision to make: How was I going to make money?

It was an interesting political moment in Toronto, a city that was growing faster than its infrastructure, but not as fast as its tax rate. A dozen years earlier, six smaller cities—downtown Toronto, plus five former suburbs—had been amalgamated into one "megacity." But the projected efficiencies had failed to materialize. The size of government had grown, not shrunk, increasing the burden on taxpayers.

Don't get me wrong: Toronto was (and remains) one of the best cities in which to live. Crime is low; health care is universal. Gay marriage has been legal and celebrated for over a decade; people from diverse cultures live together peacefully. Arts, culture, finance, tech, and academia thrive here. But it wasn't utopia. No city is.

Unlike most US cities, Toronto pays its bills almost exclusively through property taxes, receiving no portion of the income or sales taxes that go to the federal and provincial governments. In 2006, the city was allowed to introduce limited new taxes and did so with a vengeance: vehicle registration tax, municipal land transfer tax, new user fees for water, sewer, and garbage services. At the same time, services were being cut; potholes went unfilled; water mains burst. Minor City Hall scandals—politicians using tax dollars to buy espresso machines for their offices or bunny suits for their parties—drove people crazy.

In 2006, transit workers went on an illegal wildcat strike; in 2008, they went on strike again, legally this time, but without any notice to the public. Millions of commuters ride Toronto's buses, subways, and streetcars daily, and these disruptions cost the city's economy an estimated $50 million per day.

Then, on June 22, 2009, the city's employees went on strike, and stayed out for over a month. Local parks turned into makeshift garbage dumps. The city stank—though not in Etobicoke, where Rob Ford was a councillor. That western borough had privatized its garbage pick-up before it was amalgamated into the megacity. After a month, Toronto's mayor, David Miller, gave in to the union's demands. A city that had suffered through a long strike saw his capitulation as treason. His popularity never recovered. On September 25, he announced that he would not seek reelection. The race for mayor in 2010 would be wide open. It was a rare event in an electoral system that normally heavily favored the incumbent.

Temperamentally, the megacity wasn't working either. There was a growing divide between the former city (the downtown) and the former suburbs (that now had more voters). City Hall was downtown, where residents often worked, went to school, and shopped within a ten- or twenty-block radius of their homes. Many didn't own cars. They made frequent use of the city's urban libraries, community centers, pools, and amenities. They hung out in funky cafes and went to art galleries, museums, and theaters.

But the population of Toronto was swelling with immigrants who found affordable housing in the city's outer reaches. Their Toronto experience was not the same. They typically traveled for miles—meaning hours—between home and work. Their transit options were fewer and less reliable. And they felt City Hall was deaf to—perhaps even disdainful of—their concerns.

It was in this climate that I reached out to some friends in the political world to see if they could connect me with any of the mayoral campaigns. It was this climate that led me to Rob Ford.

*** 

By January 2010, leading candidates had begun to stake out their turf. The race favorite was George Smitherman. A successful Liberal Party politician, he was bright, articulate, and gay, a perfect fit for Toronto's left-leaning electorate. (A quick primer: Ontario is the most populous province in Canada; Toronto, its capital, is the largest city in Canada. The political head of a province is called a premier.) Smitherman had been successful at the provincial level, as the elected member of Provincial Parliament for Toronto Centre. He had been deputy premier, as well as minister of health and long-term care and minister of energy and infrastructure. But he'd resigned his provincial seat, and was all-in for the mayoralty campaign, where he was considered a centrist.

Further left was Deputy Mayor Joe Pantalone, a tiny, popular, and charismatic politician who'd represented a downtown ward at City Hall for almost thirty years. Closely aligned with the incumbent mayor, David Miller, it seemed that he would either become mayor himself, or retire from politics. Then there was former Liberal Party fundraiser Rocco Rossi—a tall, bald, experienced businessman who'd been the head of the national Heart and Stroke Foundation for four years, and was as close to a conservative as most Toronto politicians get.

Rumored to be running was John Tory. At the time, Tory was a popular afternoon radio show host on Newstalk 1010, Canada's largest talk radio station. But from September 2004 to March 2009, he had been the leader of the Progressive Conservative Party of Ontario, the province's official opposition to the government. He'd tried and failed to form his own government—his downfall was advocating for financing religious minority schools, such as Jewish and Islamic schools, on an equal basis with Catholic and secular public schools that are financed by taxpayers, an idea the voters rejected. Tory was a respected lawyer and business executive who had first run for mayor of Toronto in 2003, losing to David Miller in a close race. He was considered then by many in the city to be honest, fair, a nice guy, and, in some circles, "the best mayor (or premier) we never had." Would he run again for mayor? Political channels were awash with rumors.

Rumors were also swirling around a loud-mouthed, heavy-set councillor from Ward 2 named Rob Ford. Ward 2 was in the northwest corner of Toronto—far, far from City Hall. Many residents there lived on welfare or disability subsidies in social housing complexes. Others were hardworking blue-collar families, many of which had immigrated to Canada between 1950 and 1970. Ward 2 also included acres of semi-industrial and industrial land.

Ford was a hard-right conservative with outspoken, often outlandish views. He believed the best social program was a job, and that criminals should be locked up without bail. He opposed harm-reduction programs for drug addicts and felt the city should scoop homeless people off the street and force them into treatment or jail. He opposed any and all tax increases and almost any city spending not targeting roads or core services. He was a big booster of the police service and the city's former, tough-as-nails police chief Julian Fantino.

Ford had a cult-like following in his own district, which he'd represented in Council for ten years. In fact, he was so famous for responding personally to constituent complaints that he'd begun getting them from all over the city. He would slide into his van and drive across the city to meet with citizens who were angry at their own councillors. Predictably, the other councillors were not impressed. They asked repeatedly for city staff to find a rule that would keep Ford locked up in his own district.

Ford routinely pushed the same motions every year at budget time, calling for Council to reduce city budgets, slash costs, and end perks for councillors. In the forty-five-member Toronto City Council, he routinely lost those votes by 44 to 1. But he had become the flag-bearer for taxpayers tired of waste and arrogance at City Hall. They would come to be known as Ford Nation.

My friend John Capobianco, a longtime conservative activist, was backing Rocco Rossi. He set up a meeting for me with Rossi's campaign manager, Sachin Aggarwal. Meanwhile, another friend, Dean French, who had succeeded me as president of our local Conservative Party association, called me about Rob Ford.

French asked my opinion of Ford, and I was honest: I thought he was good at getting mentioned in the press, but rarely in a positive way. I thought conservatives respected his "always say no to spending" approach, and his consistent railing against new taxes and civil service bloat. I thought if Ford could tone down his bellicose antics, people might like his fiscal conservatism. But I also thought he was a bit of an oaf, with a penchant for getting himself in shit. To me, Rossi was a better bet. When French asked me if I thought Ford could be mayor of Toronto, I said no.

French insisted Ford wasn't as bad as he looked in the press. He also had a huge power base in Etobicoke, which tilted further right than the rest of the city. He was serious about running for mayor, but he needed staff— and he'd never hired anyone but administrative assistants before. French, who was informally helping Doug Ford assemble a campaign team for his brother, asked if I'd come on board and help run the campaign.

I asked who the campaign manager was, and French answered, "Rob's brother Doug." I asked if they had money. They did. The family owned and operated Deco Labels & Tags, a specialty printing business with operations in Etobicoke, Chicago, and New Jersey. Rob's father, Doug Ford Sr., had launched the business with a partner in 1962 and bought him out years later. Deco had found a profitable niche printing labels for everything that needed labels—and that, apparently, was a lot of things. I said I'd take the meeting.

***

In mid-February 2010, I met with Sachin Aggarwal at Rocco Rossi's campaign headquarters on the edge of the city's fashionable Yorkville area. It was full of signs, six-foot folding tables, and metal chairs. New computers were being unpacked. Upstairs was another long meeting table and a quiet zone at the end of the room, overlooking Avenue Road. It looked every inch a campaign office for a major contender. Aggarwal was smart and on top of things. We discussed how Rossi might eat into Smitherman's vote. But there were no paid positions available, and I needed to be paid.

Then on February 23, 2010, French and I met with Doug Ford. Not at a campaign office—at a Perkins restaurant near the Toronto airport. The back booth that Doug chose was in a closed section near the kitchen, but no one objected. One, the Fords were regulars. And two, there was little upside to arguing with Doug Ford.

Doug looked like a cleaner, smarter, fitter, better-dressed, and more successful version of his younger brother Rob. His blonde hair was carefully arranged and his suit fit him well. He had perfect teeth, a blinding smile, an easy laugh, and a piercing gaze I could feel drilling into my forehead throughout our conversation. Rob was nowhere to be seen.

Dean introduced me and established my conservative bona fides. I'd been a board member and a president of the local Conservative Party of Canada Association. I'd been the director of communications for John Capobianco's 2004 and 2006 federal election campaigns. I began to run through my CV: MBA from Western University, Canadian army officer for fourteen years, a detour into banking from 1996 to 1998, then consulting and Afghanistan.

Doug cut me off. "That's exactly what we need," he said. For the next hour, he launched into a near-soliloquy about Rob's strengths and the core of his platform, pausing only to answer the few questions I managed to slip in. He spouted phrases like "stopping the tax-and-spend mentality at City Hall," and "getting the city back on track" to attract business. He vowed to ax Toronto's landmark red and white streetcars, which rumbled along the surface of main arteries, and build more subways instead. He talked about the Ford family's hold on Etobicoke, their experience running their father's successful 1995 campaign for provincial office and Rob's City Council campaigns, and the huge on-the-ground team they could put into place.

He talked about Rob's longstanding appearances, every Thursday morning for six years, on *The John Oakley Show* on AM640 radio, in a segment called, "What's Eating Rob Ford." The segment had a populist bent and had built a loyal following for Ford. Listeners across the Greater Toronto Area had embraced Ford's plainspoken, "call a spade a spade" approach to politics. Doug said that Rob planned to announce his candidacy on the March 25 segment, followed by a formal launch at a wine and cheese party his family had already planned to celebrate Rob's ten years on Toronto City Council.

Somewhere in there, I threw out an idea: As a councillor, Rob could organize a "Subway Summit," inviting experts to talk about different ways to build and finance subways. It would link Rob's name with transit (one of Toronto's most pressing issues as its population exploded) and position him as an activist committed to moving the city forward. Doug loved it. He asked me to start on it right away.

We talked money. Doug wanted me full time. I was hesitant. I didn't want to commit to full time as I was flirting with another private client and needed to develop more if I was going to get back into the consulting world. We agreed it made sense to be flexible. There would be days I worked two or three hours and days I worked twelve or more. On average, I expected the job would be three or four hours a day, four or five days a week until Ford was out of the race. I didn't think he would catch up to Smitherman or Rossi.

The amount of money any Toronto mayoral candidate can spend is limited by law. In 2010, the spending limit for the near-eleven-month campaign would be around $1.3 million. For everything: staff, advertising, offices, signage, database, call centers, the whole gamut. It was tight. They couldn't afford to pay anyone big bucks.

Doug and I agreed on a $30,000 flat fee, open to renegotiation if the job required more work than I expected. He gave me Rob's cell number, and promised Rob would call me later that day. I figured I'd put in my time and be finished by the end of May. The Toronto mayoral campaign is a bit like a US-style primary and election merged together. Many early candidates drop off as the race progresses and the bills pile up. I expected Rob would be out by summer.

I was way off. Rob never called me. In fact, we didn't even meet until early March. I ended up working sixteen- to twenty-hour days, six to seven days a week, until election day on October 25. I'd taken the job to earn a few bucks while I found other work, but I got hooked on the adrenalin of succeeding against long odds. I never was able to negotiate more money; frankly, I didn't really try. It was a horrible business deal. It almost drove me into bankruptcy. But it turned out to be one hell of a ride.

# 2 | Who Are These People?

I DROVE UP to Diane Ford's red brick house at the very end of Weston Wood Road, a quiet cul-de-sac in central Etobicoke, about eight miles northwest of Toronto's downtown. This is not the Toronto of sleek glass high-rises, reclaimed factory lofts, museums, and concert halls. This is a former suburb of commercial strip malls, mostly modest houses, and leafy streets. The people who live here are more likely to be concerned about their block having a pothole than the Toronto City Hall having a "green" roof.

Weston Wood Road leads east off the local north–south artery, Royal York Road. Across from the cul-de-sac is Royal York Plaza, a tired, 1970s-era commercial strip mall with a grocery store, a gas station, and a number of small shops, including a Chinese takeout shop called Mayflower, which made Rob's favorite takeout dinners, and a dingy pub called Sullie Gorman's. Four years later, the pub would be the setting for one of Ford's notorious racist rants, which would be recorded and leaked to the media, prompting him to finally enter rehab. But on this day, the neighborhood was quiet.

Diane Ford, Rob's then seventy-five-year-old mother, was the matriarch of the Ford clan, which included Kathy, then forty-nine; Randy, forty-eight; Doug, forty-five; and Rob, forty. A bright, no-nonsense woman, she was the widow of Douglas Ford Sr., who died from cancer in 2006 at the age of seventy-three. Ford Sr. was a tough-talking, no-bullshit conservative businessman who parlayed a mediocre sales career into a multimillion-dollar business, and served one term, from 1995 to 1999, as a Progressive Conservative backbencher in the Ontario government. (He reportedly kept the bar in his Queen's Park office well-stocked, and MPPs—Members of Provincial Parliament—of many political stripes would gather there after the legislature adjourned for the day.) One of his compatriots, Jim Flaherty, would go on to become Canada's minister of finance.

Diane's three-story house, dominated by a cedar-shake roof, is the house Rob grew up in, and it remains the Ford family headquarters. It's the venue for most of the Fords' major social gatherings, and when enemies are attacking, it's where the family gathers to regroup.

Inside, the decor is eclectic—Oriental rugs, vases, statuary. Outside, the half-acre backyard boasts a swimming pool, fountains, and several bronze statues, including a bare-breasted nymph, a kangaroo, a baboon, and a naked boy peeing into the water. A rock garden climbs a hill, dividing the main pool area from a more private family garden. A large play area with a children's swing set occupies the farthest corner of the yard, against a chain-link fence and vehicle-sized gate that lets out onto the wooded parkland beyond.

Annual "Ford Fest" gatherings—community parties the family throws for "everyone in the city"—took place here until 2013. While working for Ford, I would attend four of them, along with about five thousand other people who came for the free hamburgers and beer, to listen to live music from local cover bands, and for the chance to meet, shake hands, and pose for a photo with Rob and Doug Ford.

Serious business, however, happens downstairs, in a large rec room equipped with a full wet bar and wide-screen TV. This is where the clan would gather on election night in 2010; it's also where Ford's council allies would confront him in a mini-intervention in 2012. On this day, it was the site of my first Rob Ford campaign team meeting.

A dozen of us, including Doug Ford—not Rob, though; he was late— gathered around a jerry-rigged boardroom table comprising a card table, a four-foot folding table, and a round dining table, with an assortment of kitchen and folding chairs jammed in wherever they fit. We took turns introducing ourselves and explaining our roles as we saw them. Many referred to themselves as "volunteer organizers." Most were veterans of Rob's previous council campaigns, and some had worked on his father's 1995 provincial campaign. Except for Doug's daughter Krista, they were middle-aged, white, and largely unimpressive.

The exception was Tom Beyer, a volunteer who was working on social media for the campaign. He seemed eager and knowledgeable. But my inner alarm went off when he listed the number of websites already running or being prepared: There was Rob's Council page, his personal site, and a campaign site; there was a personal Facebook page, plus a fan page managed by Rob's niece, Krista; and there were a number of Twitter handles. It seemed like too much to keep track of. I'd already studied the campaign websites for Smitherman and Rossi. Both were professionally developed and slick. Too slick for Rob Ford, I thought. He was a Chevy, not a Mercedes. He was Everyman's candidate. His web presence should be effective, but appear low-cost, almost homemade, but still highly effective; it would require a fine balance.

Overall, no one at the table seemed to understand that a campaign to be the mayor of one of North America's largest, most progressive cities in the early days of the twenty-first century was in a different league than a campaign for City Council. They believed that if their tactics were good enough to win Ward 2, they were good enough to win a city of forty-four wards. They just needed to work forty-four times harder.

That was naive. The Toronto mayoral race is the biggest political campaign in Canada. The federal and provincial governments are parliamentary systems; political parties run candidates in electoral districts across the country or province. Each district elects one representative to a seat in the legislature, and the party that wins the most seats forms the government. The leader of the winning party becomes the prime minister of Canada, or the premier of the province. Campaigns typically last no longer than thirty-six days.

In Toronto, there were twenty-two federal and provincial districts that elected members to the federal and provincial parliaments. (This number is increasing to twenty-five beginning with the October 2015 federal election due to population growth.) But there are forty-four city wards; generally speaking, each federal district was divided into two city wards, each represented by a city councillor. The mayor, however, is elected directly by everyone in the city.

To put that in context: In the 2011 federal election, Prime Minister Stephen Harper won his seat in the Calgary Southwest district with 42,998 votes. We estimated whoever became mayor of Toronto in 2010 would need over 300,000 votes to win, based on past voter turnout. Not only would that person need to motivate the greatest number of voters of any politician in the country, he or she would also have to survive the longest campaign, almost eleven months. This was a function of a fixed election date in late October and a campaign registration period that began on the first working day of January.

City councillors didn't need to create policy or platforms. They just needed to knock on doors to build name recognition, then get their few thousand supporters out to vote on election day. In 2010, Rob Ford would have to develop policy, a platform, prepare for scores of debates, put up thousands of lawn signs, and persuade over three hundred thousand people to get out, rain or shine, to vote for him. It was far from a council race—it was the biggest political campaign in the country.

From the moment discussion began in Diane's basement, the rhythm was peculiar, as if Ford's campaign were already well underway. Doug declared that Rob (who was still a working city councillor and had been since 2000) would announce his candidacy on March 26, 2010, at the Toronto Congress Centre, a suburban conference facility near the airport. He expected five thousand people to attend—an unlikely number, I thought. Someone asked what color the lawn signs would be. Another said it would be important to get Etobicoke's *Snapd*—a monthly, free-distribution community newspaper—to cover the launch. There was also a lot of bashing of Smitherman and Rossi, which gave me pause. Underestimating one's opponents is never wise. Doug seemed to have an attention deficit problem, finding it hard to stay engaged in the conversation and often steering the talk off into other directions before any conclusions could be reached.

About an hour into the meeting, Rob arrived, to a brief round of applause. Other politicians might shake hands and greet people by name. Rob, however, seemed shy, and avoided direct eye contact when speaking. He pulled a seat up to the table and uttered a few familiar sentences about stopping the waste at City Hall and improving customer service.

When my turn to speak arrived, I posited that winning the election would be a massive undertaking that required a formal structure, a detailed strategy, and a large team. A silence fell. Those who were veteran volunteers from Rob's past council campaigns seemed offended. "It's all about knocking on doors," one said. "That's how you win elections."

I turned to Rob. "Why are you running for mayor?" I asked. A campaign can't only be about how to get someone elected. There has to be a reason why a candidate is running, and a reason people should vote for him.

"Because people want me to," Ford replied. "Everywhere I go, people are always telling me I should run for mayor. I have ten years of experience in the private sector running Deco, the largest label printer in Canada, and ten years on Council. I know the value of a dollar and what customer service is all about."

We'd have to work on that answer. It was the single most important question he'd be asked in the early campaign, and one he'd be judged by.

As it turned out, I would spend much of my next four years trying to figure out why Rob Ford wanted to be mayor. Only later, after I'd been fired, did I finally feel I understood. But I didn't then.

To me, it wasn't enough if people believed Ford would be a prudent fiscal manager—he also had to build a city people wanted. Or was he destined to be a one-term mayor, one who gets the finances in order, then hands it to the next guy, who can afford to have a vision for the future?

I jotted my thoughts into my notebook: How do we mitigate people's fear that Ford may not be ready for the bigger role? He's not an eloquent speaker—could the campaign highlight his actions and accomplishments, rather than his words and vision? What were those accomplishments? What was that vision? It seemed to be, "Toronto is the greatest city in the world, but it's going in the wrong direction." (Of course, those were my words rephrasing his, and we'd need to do some research to confirm people actually felt the city was going the wrong way.) He definitely needed a speaking coach.

After twenty minutes, Rob excused himself, saying he had to get back to work. An hour and a half later, the meeting ending, leaving me with a handful of notes and a head full of doubts. I went for coffee and sketched out the beginning of an assessment of how the public would perceive mayoral candidate Rob Ford, based on what I'd learned so far. I still have it:

I sketched out two columns: I titled the left-hand column "RF's weaknesses" and listed five negative public perceptions I'd seen and heard in the media. They included frequent comments that he was racist due to his "Orientals" comment; that he was a "wife beater" because he'd been charged with domestic abuse once, but wasn't arrested and the charges had been withdrawn; rumors he was an alcoholic fueled by a well-reported episode at a local hockey game; suggestions he was a "rageoholic" because he seemed prone to angry outbursts; and finally, the fact that he talked with his eyes closed—I noted to myself, "Speaking from the heart but can't make eye contact. Nervous?"

I titled the right-hand column "Mitigation" and it was still blank. I didn't yet know how to mitigate these perceptions. But I knew I'd have to try.

*March 11, 2010*

Four days after the rec room meeting, I entered City Hall for the first time, for my first proper sit-down with Rob Ford. Toronto's City Hall, designed by Finnish architect Viljo Revell and opened in 1965, is an iconic space-age building with two clamshell-shaped towers protecting flying saucer-shaped "pearls" set back off a large public plaza, with a skating rink in winter, and space for concerts or craft shows in warmer months. In 1969, it was the inspiration for an alien building in a *Star Trek* comic; in 1988 it appeared in an episode of *Star Trek: The Next Generation*; and it also has shown up in video games and music videos. Unlike many seats of government, it's open to the public—anyone can circulate around the rotunda, and even up on the second floor where the political offices are. The semi-circular Council chamber sits within a domed central "saucer," supported by a single pillar running through the center of the rotunda down to the foundation of the building. I was impressed.

I was dressed like a successful consultant: conservative suit, splashy Thomas Pink shirt, cufflinks, understated tie. Ford wore a dark blue suit, a blue shirt with the top button undone, and a blue and black diamond-patterned tie. His suit jacket was hanging on the back of his leather chair. This was Ford's uniform. He went everywhere and did everything in a suit. He described himself as a businessman more than a politician, and businessmen wear suits.

I sat down at a round table in Ford's office. Every inch of wall space was covered with photos and certificates of appreciation from community groups, as well as framed copies of editorial cartoons, mostly lampooning him. (So he had a sense of humor about himself. That was good.) His desk was covered in papers, and a huge plastic cup of water was leaving rings on the blotter.

Rob sat at his desk and spoke at length, fidgeting most of the time, avoiding eye contact almost entirely. He would look down at the papers on his desk and fuss with them while speaking, or lean back in his leather chair and look up toward the ceiling as if seeking divine inspiration. He was a big man, not quite six feet tall, but easily 330 pounds. His thick, sausage-like fingers were unexpectedly expressive, and I found myself distracted by his sharp, yellowed, mis-spaced teeth. His voice was an octave higher than I would have expected for someone his size, but once he got going he spoke with passion. He was genuinely upset by spending at City Hall and took it personally when money was wasted on things he didn't think important. He laughed easily, though, and shrugged off most of the criticism he'd received in the press and from his colleagues.

Almost by rote, Ford listed the top five things he wanted to do as mayor: Reduce the size of City Council from forty-four councillors (plus the mayor) to twenty-two. Repeal the $60 car registration tax. Eliminate the city's land transfer tax. Make Toronto's transit agency an official "essential service," so workers could no longer strike. And privatize the garbage collection. These were all eye-level things that concerned average residents. There was no "vision for the future of a great city" talk here.

He wanted to tackle other, similar issues, too: make the paramedic service an essential service; eliminate the city's fair-wage policy; reduce the money handed out in grant programs; clean up graffiti across the city; introduce subsidized rent vouchers so that people in subsidized housing could move into private rental units; and add daycare spaces. He knew what the city spent for each service. He pinpointed waste that could be trimmed. He seemed thoughtful, and took pride in his ideas. Rob Ford was not the fool many people dismissed him as.

I zeroed in on his idea to reduce Council by half. He talked about how much money it would save: about $350,000 in salaries for each councillor plus their staff plus about $53,000 in office expenses each, representing about $9.2 million per year. This was small potatoes out of a $13 billion city budget, but it was big money to voters. But could it be done?

To me, it seemed ridiculous. What councillor would vote him- or herself out of a job? His answer floored me.

It's important to know that Ford didn't work to lobby votes for his motions, as most politicians do. He didn't approach fellow councillors for support or offer to horse-trade for something they wanted. In classic Rob Ford style, he just wrote up the motion, submitted it to the city clerk, and waited for the vote to be called at the next council meeting. Yet, when Ford had introduced a motion to cut Council in half a few years earlier, fourteen councillors had actually voted yes. It wasn't the twenty-three he needed, but there were fourteen people willing to risk their own jobs. Why?

Ford's eyes lit up when he answered. "They're politicians, buddy," he said. "They all think they'll win."

Many city councillors aspired to higher political offices at the provincial or federal levels. If a councillor wanted to run provincially or federally in the same area he or she already represented, the person would have to carry his or her own ward, plus the adjacent ward that made up the other half of the provincial/federal district. If, however, there were only twenty-two councillors, each would have the full provincial/federal district. They would already have the volunteers, the voter identification lists, the sign locations, and the relationships essential to a winning campaign. It would make the move up so much easier.

I was stunned. Legally, Council can determine its own size. Ford had figured out how to use the councillors' egos and ambitions to do the job for him.

I spent several hours shaping some of Ford's ideas into a platform that would appeal to voters, and sent a rough draft to Doug the next day. It was a start.

\*\*\*

My more immediate worry was the launch date. Everyone was working toward March 26, but I didn't think Ford was ready. I thought the wine and cheese party scheduled for that night should simply be a ten-year-anniversary celebration, as advertised on the invitations Ford was sending out everywhere. I thought Rob should run a shadow campaign, with some policy announcements, including the subway summit we'd discussed at Perkins. That would build his profile and test the waters to see if he had enough city-wide support to launch a mayoral run. If he did, he would announce. If he didn't, he'd run again for council.

Doug, however, had other ideas. He wanted Rob to make his usual appearance on the *John Oakley* radio show at 7:00 a.m. Thursday, March 25, and publicly announce his intent to run. Then he wanted Rob to lead a contingent of supporters down the street to City Hall, where he'd register in front of the press gallery cameras and take questions from the media. The following day, he'd use his wine and cheese event to make his campaign launch speech to thousands of cheering supporters.

To pull that off, I figured Ford would need speeches, a website, a video crew to tape "what Rob did for me" testimonials, a backgrounder and news release for the media, a handout copy of the launch speech, and a short, punchy tagline that both summed up Rob's campaign and resonated with voters. The good news was, we had five whole days until launch. So much for this being a half-day job, five days a week. I was already pulling sixteen-hour days, every day. It would only get busier.

I pushed Rob to delay. Unless he needed the extra time to raise funds, there was no advantage to launching his campaign early. At some meetings, he'd agree with me. At others, after he'd spoken to Doug, he'd say he'd changed his mind. Later, I would realize this was a trait of his: He'd agree with whatever anyone said to him, while continuing on the course he'd always planned on taking. It wasn't until March 24 that I got a definitive answer: We were launching the next day.

***

Walking into my second private meeting with Ford in his City Hall office, the first person I saw was his EA, Katherine Bee, whom Ford called Katie. She was a slim, attractive brunette who worked hard and seemed able to take Ford in stride. She had a law degree and briefed Rob on council agendas, prepared and filed his motions, and kept track of his schedule and calls. That day, she'd run into a small problem concerning the Rob Ford Football Foundation, a registered charity Ford ran privately to raise funds for football programs in high schools.

Football was one of Ford's great passions. He'd played in high school and at Carleton University in Ottawa. He coached the Don Bosco Catholic Secondary School football team, the Eagles, and was set on leading them to the championship in the fall.

But that day, Bee informed Ford that a citizen had complained about a letter she'd received from the Rob Ford Football Foundation. The woman demanded to know how Ford had gotten her address, and said she didn't think it was appropriate for him to use city councillor letterhead for private foundation business.

Ford didn't see the problem. Bee tried again to explain it, but he cut her off with a gesture I would see repeated a thousand times. He didn't just shake his head. His entire head shuddered left to right, as if he was having a spasm. His arms flew up, bent at the elbows, palms open, as if he were the victim of a stickup. It was his physical reaction to information that simply didn't compute.

I stuck a toe into the discussion. Even though the stationery, envelope, and stamp were all paid for out of Rob's pocket, and not by his City Council budget, the letterhead still read "Councillor Rob Ford" at City Hall. I explained that someone might think that using councillor letterhead was a misuse of taxpayer-funded stationery, the very type of abuse Ford was proud of battling. Maybe they should get some Rob Ford Football Foundation stationery.

"That's crazy," Ford said. He *was* Councillor Rob Ford, whether he was doing council business or private business. It was part of his name. Why shouldn't he use it?

I backed off. He ignored the complaint, and "solved" the problem by ordering that all future mailings should come from Deco, the family's private company, instead of City Hall. None of us imagined that this stationery issue would one day lead to an Ontario Court judge throwing Ford out of office. I had more immediate concerns.

When I signed onto the Ford campaign, Rob was already a controversial figure. Over the years, he'd been involved in a number of incidents that were amply reported and known to many voters. They would certainly be used to disparage his character and undermine his credibility as a mayoral candidate. I had to know what I was getting into, working for this man.

I had clear ground rules: I would always do the right thing. I would do nothing illegal. I would not help anyone do anything illegal. I would not harm someone, or do something I wasn't comfortable with. I wouldn't lie—about anything, for anyone. Not only did this protect me, but it also served my clients. Once people know you'll break the law or lie, no one will trust you. If no one trusts you, you can no longer be effective.

I knew Ford had flaws and had done stupid things in the past, but I needed to hear his side of the stories, however awkward the conversation would be. I needed to learn about his character, and to figure out how to mitigate the negative impact of his past on his campaign prospects.

"Ask away, buddy," Ford said. "I'm an open book."

I cleared my throat and launched in, keeping it conversational and light. I didn't want him to put up his guard. I needed him to open up to me.

I began with an incident that occurred during a Toronto Maple Leafs hockey game at the Air Canada Centre on Saturday, April 15, 2006. Ford reportedly was intoxicated, and got into a shouting argument with a couple sitting near him. His language was obscene and offensive, and eventually security escorted him out of the building. When a reporter for the *National Post*, one of Canada's two national newspapers, asked him about it, he denied being there. A few days later, after another newspaper picked up the story, he told the *Toronto Star*, "I wasn't even at the game, so someone's trying to do a real hatchet job on me." Days later, he finally admitted he'd been there, and called it a "huge mistake."

"I reflected on it last night and talked to my family," he told the Canadian Broadcasting Corporation. "I came forward and admitted it. That's all I can do. I mean, I'm not perfect." It was a refrain the world would eventually hear repeated many, many times—but I didn't know that then.

Ford's explanation sounded genuine. He claimed the *Post* reporter had asked him about the wrong game. When the reporter corrected that mistake, Ford admitted his own. While it seemed to me that Ford was using the reporter's mistake to avoid an unpleasant truth, I took him at his word. There was something uncannily likeable and believable about the guy; he admitted to so many flaws, it was easy to believe he wasn't hiding any more.

Next, I asked about some of the remarks he'd made in Council that had gotten him into hot water. He had called fellow councillor Giorgio Mammoliti, who is Italian Canadian, a "Gino boy" in the heat of an argument on the council floor. He'd described councillor Gloria Lindsay Luby as a "waste of skin."

Ford asked me if I'd ever been to a council meeting. I hadn't. "Then you don't know what it's like," he said. "You have no idea. No idea. You should hear what people call each other when the microphones are off." (Councillors' microphones are turned on only when they have the floor to speak.) So yes, he'd said those things—but other councillors had said worse to him. His mistake had been to say those things when his microphone was turned on.

I then asked him about his comments about gays and Asians. He'd taken contrarian positions at Council against city funding for the annual pride parade, which brings millions of tourist dollars into the city each summer, and in 2006, he'd opposed spending $1.5 million on an HIV/AIDS awareness program. In a Council speech, he'd infamously said, "It is very preventable. If you are not doing needles and you are not gay, you wouldn't get AIDS probably. That's the bottom line." He was pilloried for these comments.

I asked Ford if he had a problem with gay people. He said he didn't care if you were "straight, gay, black, white, or purple," but he didn't believe taxpayers should pay for parades. Not for the gay community, not for the Santa Claus parade, not for anyone. He also said taxpayers shouldn't fund disease awareness programs. "My heart bleeds for people with AIDS," he said. "But we can't pay for every disease. How do we choose? Why just AIDS? Why not cancer? My dad died of cancer and it was horrible. We don't spend money on that." His argument didn't make much sense, but I figured we could build a reasonable argument for his position.

My litany of questions continued. On March 6, 2008, during a council debate on allowing retail shopping on holidays, Ford said, "Those Oriental people work like dogs. . . . They sleep beside their machines. The Oriental people, they're slowly taking over. They're hard, hard workers." When I asked him about that, he still didn't quite get what he'd done wrong. He said he was trying to pay Asians a compliment.

"I didn't know 'Oriental' was wrong," Ford said. "I visited China with my dad. We went through the factories there and workers were literally sleeping beside their machines. They work so hard." He confessed that his ideas often came out jumbled, and he hated that. He knew he needed help with public speaking. I told him that was what I was there for.

I saved my toughest question for last: In March 2008, Ford had been arrested and charged with assaulting and uttering a death threat to his wife, Renata. When the charges reached the courts in May of that year, the Crown prosecutor withdrew them, saying there were inconsistencies in Renata's story.

Here's the story Ford told me: When he arrived home on March 25, Renata had been drinking, and was angry. "She was screaming about something and wouldn't calm down," he said. She called 9-1-1, and police came to the house. Ford said he was charged by police because all allegations of domestic abuse had to be charged, but that police hadn't arrested him. Instead, they suggested he take his kids and go somewhere else to spend the night.

That last point struck me. If the police let him leave with his children, they must have believed his side of the argument. It helped to defend his actions without having to impugn his wife's character. It's one thing to publicly admit your own failings. It's quite another to publicly out someone else's. It was something we could use to blunt this charge when it was leveled at him. Though Ford's version was notably different from the version in the press, he and his wife had remained together, and no further problems had been reported. Defending Rob without criticizing Renata was a fine line to walk. It was a challenge we would face many times over the next three and half years.

Despite these missteps, Rob struck me as good-hearted; a meat-and-potatoes guy in a low-fat, gluten-free town. He preferred standing ankle-deep in the mud on the sidelines of a high school football game over schmoozing at $500-a-plate dinners. He worried about filling potholes, not the hole in the ozone layer.

I knew he didn't look dashing. I knew people looked down their noses at him. I knew he was a lousy speaker—often because he didn't always understand *why* he believed what he believed. Rob wanted subways because people told him they wanted subways, and it was his job to represent them. In that regard, he was like any other client I'd consulted for. Clients know what they think they want. But it often takes some digging to find out what they really need, and some verbal acrobatics to get them to want that. Rob Ford struck me as a humble guy who wanted to focus on the things that the people he knew wanted, and to waste less money on bells and whistles so average people could afford to continue living in his city. I didn't see any problems in that.

I asked Ford if there were any other issues that could come back to bite him. Had he ever been arrested? Did he have a drinking problem? Had he ever used drugs? Did he frequent prostitutes? Were there any other skeletons in his closet?

"There's nothing left in my closet, man," he answered. After everything we'd just discussed—heaven help me—I believed him.

# 3 | This Guy Could Win

THE CAMPAIGN LAUNCH event turned out to be the hook that pulled me all the way in.

Despite my fears and warnings, the Ford campaign was going ahead with the wine and cheese party as our official launch. The political rule of thumb was, book a small room and cram it full of people to make the crowd seem larger. The Fords didn't work that way. Doug booked a cavernous space in the Toronto Congress Centre and hired an audiovisual and staging company. He figured five thousand people would come, so he told the world they were expecting ten thousand and booked a space big enough to handle more than that. Not for the last time, I was sure we had the makings of a disaster on our hands. I stepped in and made sure the space would be curtained off at about fifteen hundred seats. If we needed more tables, we could pull back the curtains; if we didn't, the hall wouldn't look empty.

As for the refreshments—somebody at some meeting asked what kind of cheese they should have. The answer, I recall clearly, was "both kinds"—meaning, white and orange cheddar. Plus "that marbled one," to spice things up. On the day, enough cheddar showed up to feed an army regiment. I wasn't crazy about serving wine, but that was a Ford family tradition. So Randy Ford, the eldest brother—whose trademark "Crocodile Dundee" wide-brimmed black hat would earn him the nickname "Blackjack" among campaign staff—negotiated a bulk order of cheap wine from a local supplier. Cheese. Wine. Done. •

Meanwhile, I was working to pull Rob's policy ideas together into a rough outline of a platform, as well as writing a speech for him to give at the launch event. Lorne Honickman, a lawyer, communication consultant, and media personality whom the Fords trusted, and who appeared on AM640 on Thursday mornings with Rob, helped us find a speech coach to help polish Rob up for the reveal. Doug was keen on the idea, and Rob had agreed—but he didn't want anyone to sit in on the coaching session. He was too nervous. He wouldn't tell me this himself, however. Instead, I got a call from Doug the night before the coaching session telling me not to go. I wasn't keen about that, since I'd written the speech, and wanted to know if the words fit Rob's voice. I didn't like being in the dark about his strengths and weaknesses.

The speech was part rah-rah, pump up the crowd, and partly a hint at what Rob's campaign platform would focus on. I drew heavily from conservative standbys like "putting families at the center of everything we do." People knew Rob Ford as the world's champion penny-pincher, but I wanted to stress what he was willing to invest in. He had clear ideas about how to improve the lot of people trapped on waiting lists for affordable housing, and how to improve childcare services, so I wove some of those themes into the speech, along with his pillars: stop wasteful spending, reduce the size of council, cut the perks councillors enjoyed.

On the morning of the announcement, we gathered early at a café at Victoria Street and Queen Street in Toronto's downtown, across the street from one of the city's busiest trauma centers, St. Michael's Hospital. It was chilly; I kept my topcoat on over my suit and tie, and carried my briefcase, which had copies of notes and platforms, as well as Kleenex and other trappings of political servitude including Ford's business cards, pens, a comb, hand cleanser, gum, and paper towels.

At 6:30 a.m., a bus pulled up and a horde of supporters streamed out, all clad in "Rob Ford for Mayor" T-shirts, and carrying Rob Ford campaign placards stapled to wooden handles. I was pleasantly surprised by the numbers. Tom Beyer and Krista Ford were in the thick of it, vibrating with excitement. As Rob entered the café, he was instantly surrounded by the throng of campaign volunteers. The energy in the air was palpable. Ready or not, here we go.

I pulled Rob aside and went over the plan: We would walk from here to the AM640 radio station in an office tower just off Toronto's Yonge Street, the north/south artery that divides Toronto's west and east sides. The volunteers would wait in the lobby while he went upstairs to the studio. He'd do his regular hit with John Oakley, make his announcement, then come back downstairs. We'd march en masse for three blocks to City Hall, where he'd register as a candidate and give a sound bite to the media, then head up to his council office.

Rob nodded, but I could tell he was only partially hearing me. The long, narrow café was packed with sixty-odd supporters, and Rob was already sweating. I got him a bottle of water and some paper towels to mop his face, and reminded him to smile. Tom and Krista herded the crowd outside, distributed signs, and lined everyone up. For a moment we looked around, confused about which way to go.

Tom Beyer—who also liked to wear hats, on this day a pork-pie number that made him look like a background player from the movie *The Blues Brothers*—suggested we walk north along Victoria, which would take us past the City TV studio at Yonge-Dundas Square, a tamer version of New York's Times Square. The studio was glass-walled on street level and their *Breakfast Television* show, morning news and entertainment, was broadcasting live. We could snag some free media exposure. It was a brilliant idea—I was embarrassed I hadn't thought of it myself.

We set off. The day had warmed up, and a few news photographers who'd been tipped off to the event buzzed around Rob like flies, snapping shots of the big march. I still have one iconic photo: me in my overcoat, sweating up a storm, walking beside Rob Ford, followed by a horde of sign-waving supporters.

We hit Yonge-Dundas Square at the perfect time. Rob's march to City Hall followed by "hundreds" of sign-waving supporters outside the TV studio was carried live across the city. (Our supporters took a few laps around the glass studio to make them seem more numerous.)

At AM640's studio, in an office tower high above Toronto's Eaton Centre mall, Ford was welcomed by the station staff, who shared his politics, as a returning hero. We squeezed the campaign staff and a number of volunteers into the reception area, while Rob and Doug sat down in the studio with Oakley. The producer asked if we could make some background sound for the announcement. Krista Ford, who'd been a competitive cheerleader for years, led a chant, "Ford for Mayor! Ford for Mayor!" and the crowd joined in, filling the airwaves with what sounded like hundreds of Rob Ford supporters demanding he run for mayor. I took note of Krista and Tom's skills. I would call heavily on them as the campaign wore on.

The media followed us from the radio station to City Hall, where a dozen more reporters waited in the city clerk's election office. They crowded around while Rob signed his papers and counted out his $200 entry fee, bill by bill, onto the counter. Shutters clicked, flashes blinded, TV cameras bumped people out of the way. Shades of a future yet to come.

\*\*\*

*March 26, 2010*

I arrived early at the Toronto Congress Centre and found my way to the large ballroom. It was set up with round tables of ten, with seating for about three thousand. The curtains were being strung across the center of the room to cut it in half. A massive, professional stage and lighting rig was in place with a banner backdrop that featured a Toronto skyline with the words "Rob Ford Mayor" emerging in a super-hero style script. It was hideous. The tagline we'd settled on for the time being, "Turning around Toronto," was too low on the banner and was unreadable from the floor. No matter. I'd soured on it already.

There were exactly four people in the room, middle-aged women under the harsh direction of one particularly dictatorial volunteer who'd run Rob's campaign offices during past council runs. They were inflating balloons. They had about twenty done, and about two thousand to go. I found the manager, and together we set up a green room stocked with a coatrack with hangers, water, soft drinks, and ice, and he gave me a key so I could keep it secure. I then spent half an hour wandering through the building, learning where the bathrooms, exit doors, and fire escapes were. Old habits die hard. Tom Beyer and I set up reception tables just outside the main hall door. Doug Ford arrived. Now all we needed was a candidate.

Soon, Rob and his wife, Renata, entered the hall through the main door, and were immediately swarmed by supporters, whose numbers had grown. It was the first time I met Renata. She was a slightly frail-looking woman who clung to Rob's arm as if she might blow away if she let go. She wore a glittery gold dress and looked like she had put a great deal of effort into looking good. I slipped in beside Rob and suggested we go to the green room for a quick briefing. Rob came, but he didn't stay long—he wanted to work the room.

He stationed himself in front of the reception tables, chatting with each person who registered (we wanted their contact information, so we could reach out to them during the campaign for support, donations, and lawn sign locations) and posing for pictures. It was like an old home week. Everyone seemed to have a story to reminisce about.

I'd cooked up a plan with Tom to pull supporters out of line to videotape testimonials about why they loved Rob Ford. It was working, but it was also getting late. We needed to get the main event on stage. Rob didn't want to disengage; I had to convince him to give up his spot and walk quickly down the reception line instead, shaking hands. The second we reached the end, I dragged him and Renata into the green room to get them in the zone for the speech.

I left Rob alone to practice while I did a quick tour of the venue. Most of the fifteen hundred seats were now full; hundreds more people stood around the edges. It wasn't the five thousand Doug had expected, but two thousand was a pretty damned impressive number.

I told Rob that number as I lined him and his family up behind a bagpiper. We entered the hall to cheers. Suddenly, it was mayhem. The crowd surged forward to shake Ford's hand. There were TV cameras and photographers everywhere. I had to run ahead to make a hole in the crowd for Rob to pass through. As he reached the foot of the steps leading up to the stage, I leaned into him and put my hand on his shoulder, whispering into his ear. "There's a fresh glass of water for you on the small table. Your speech is ready on the podium. You look great, people love you. Give 'em hell."

He climbed up on the stage and waited for the room to settle. "There are over five thousand people here tonight, folks," he said. "That's amazing!" I closed my eyes and smiled. Rob's penchant for exaggeration was fast becoming a trademark.

But as he spoke, I watched the crowd. I'd never seen anything like it at a political event before. Every conceivable age. Every imaginable skin color. People in wheelchairs and with canes. People in track suits and Hugo Boss. People wolfing down free wine and cheese like they hadn't eaten all week. Others, turning up their noses at the cheap wine and shuddering at the cheddar buffet. All of them, though, erupted in applause whenever Rob mentioned reducing the size of council, getting control of wasteful spending, and returning the power to the little guy. He spoke well—just enough polish to sound good, just enough halting discomfort to come across as a regular guy who hated giving speeches. People could identify with that. His lack of polish helped him build a bond with the audience.

After the speech, as music played, Rob continued working the floor. I moved to the back of the hall and watched. The size and jubilation of the crowd took me by surprise. I talked with many of them, including an elderly black woman who'd spent two and a half hours riding buses from the farthest reaches of Scarborough, on the opposite side of the city, to get to this event, because she "wouldn't miss it for the world!"

Ford had a magical, incomprehensible relationship with these people. It was palpable. It was how I imagined a church revival might be. It was . . . populism, I guess. I'd never seen it firsthand before.

John Mykytyshyn, a hardcore Conservative Party organizer whom I'd met on John Capobianco's failed federal campaign, appeared out of the crowd and we watched together for a moment. "It looks like you've got yourself a candidate," he said. "This guy could win."

For the first time, I thought so, too.

# 4 | What Do We Believe?

THE POST-LAUNCH PERIOD of organization and planning I'd hoped for never came. Instead, we had to assemble a team and a plan on the fly. As a result, two things happened. First, I learned a great deal about Rob's leadership style and that of his brother Doug. Second, we were forced to mold a winning campaign team from a collection of second- and third-string political veterans and rookies. The former was to be a continuing handicap throughout the Ford years. The second was the secret ingredient in Ford's success.

Rob was a big-picture guy—Expand Transit! Cut the Waste! The only place he micromanaged was in customer service. Rob knew exactly how to deal with constituent calls. First and foremost, he took enormous pride in saying he returned every call. Second, he had a litany of tried-and-tested customer service axioms he'd learned at his father's side.

"I work for the taxpayer," he'd say. "They're my boss. When they say, 'Jump,' I ask, 'How high?'"

That was often too true. After he was elected mayor, Ford would regularly come into his office in the morning in an angry mood. He'd pull whoever his chief of staff was at the time—Nick Kouvalis, Amir Remtulla, or me—into his private office, and attack.

He'd complain by name about some junior staffer who was just "not making it." He'd accuse the staffer of not returning calls, despite repeated warnings. When asked to explain, he'd talk about a call he'd made or received the night before from a constituent who insisted he'd never heard back from the mayor's office. Rob would be livid, his face brilliant red, his tie askew. "I have no idea what people are doing all day down here," he'd complain. "How long does it take to return a phone call?"

The task of talking Mayor Rob Ford off the ledge would often fall to me or to Earl Provost, who had joined the team near the end of the campaign and became the director of stakeholder and council relations in the mayor's office. Earl was uniquely able to calm down the mayor with humor and measured doses of ego boosting. Almost without exception, we'd learn that the offending staffer had, indeed, returned the call—often numerous times. There were a number of "frequent fliers" who called regularly to complain about the same unfixable thing. When they didn't get satisfaction from the mayor's staff, they'd call the mayor. Ford would always take their word over that of his own staff—which was frustrating to the staff, but cemented the love these citizens had for their "friend," Mayor Rob.

The other axiom he'd repeat ad nauseam was, "My father told me there are two rules in business. The first rule is, 'The customer is always right.' The second rule is, 'Reread the first rule.'"

Neither of these sayings was originated by Doug Ford Sr., but I'm not sure if Rob knew that. It didn't matter. His father occupied a mythic space in Rob's life and his words of wisdom were unquestionable.

So Rob was extremely hands-on with retail campaigning. *This* is how you return a call. *That* is how you put a magnet or a canvass card on a door. But with policy or other big picture city-running stuff, he was hands-off. He'd explain what he wanted, then assume somebody would make it so. Doug Ford had a similar leadership style. But Doug loved the big picture, economic or political strategy discussions. He'd proselytize and give his opinion, make a judgment, then leave the meeting. I soon realized that, after the meeting, he wasn't taking action on anything. He just assumed it would happen. Somehow.

I kept pushing Doug, as the campaign manager, for a team structure. As early as March 15, 2010, I'd drafted a structure, written a memo to Doug and Rob, and walked them through it on the phone and in person. Now, a month into the campaign, we still hadn't formalized a team structure. We needed organization. We needed role definition. Too many things— websites, media stories, debates—were happening without a plan. One day I wandered into Deco, the family business, to find a graphic artist proofing a piece of candidate literature that was going to print in the afternoon. I was the only one on the team who was in any way responsible for platform, policy, and communication strategy. Yet I'd never heard there was literature in production. Doug had asked for it—but no one had decided what it should say. So the artist took Rob's old council campaign stuff and did up a piece. If I'd wanted to know which charities Rob Ford had donated money to in 2006, it would have been fine. But it did nothing to advance Ford for mayor. I spent the rest of the afternoon at her computer, rewriting the copy in the desktop layout program so the piece at least mentioned some of Ford's platform objectives. And in four bullet points, rather than five hundred words.

In the absence of a proper campaign manager, I began to fill the vacuum. I reached out to volunteers who'd identified themselves at the launch event and began interviewing people with communication skills. I asked Tom Beyer's wife, Janet, a natural, gifted manager, to coordinate the volunteers; we were going to need hundreds if not thousands, and they all needed to know what to do, how to do it, when, and where.

In the meantime, we wanted to capture supporter data and build a voter identification database. Doug arranged a meeting at Deco with Campaign Research, run by Richard Ciano, a prominent federal conservative organizer, and he wanted me to be there. Before Ciano arrived, Doug met with me in the small boardroom just off the tiny reception area in Deco's office. The room was small, with a nice table and seating for six. It had two doors, one opening onto the reception area and the other leading into the office area. The main door from reception to the work area was normally locked and controlled by a receptionist seated behind a sliding glass window partition. When she wasn't there, the small boardroom became a thoroughfare for people bypassing the locked door. At night, though, the office was quiet. Doug and I were alone.

Doug laid out his plan for the meeting. He was suspicious of Ciano, describing him as one of those "big city operators" who thought they'd come to Etobicoke and teach the "country bumpkins" how to do politics. Well, the Fords had been doing politics for years, and quite all right too, thank you very much. He suspected Ciano was coming to sell him another $50,000 computer database that wouldn't work, and polling that would cost him a fortune to confirm what they already knew. Doug was wise to his routine, but wanted to hear him out.

Doug asked me to play bad cop to his good cop, so we could see what Ciano was really about. I found it amusing that he used those exact words to plan our roles for the meeting. But hey, he was my client.

Ciano began by saying he thought Rob had a good chance at winning the race and becoming the first real conservative to plant a flag in Toronto politics in years. Doug loved him up, while I grilled him about cost and value. At the end of the meeting, I told Doug that Ciano seemed fine; he nodded slowly and excused himself to smoke a cigarette. The meeting was over.

Our campaign team had moved from Diane Ford's basement to an underused space on the second floor of Deco's satellite building, next to the main office. We set up a number of folding tables to create one long meeting table. At our next team meeting, I was ready to introduce the new organizational structure I'd prepared and the people I'd identified to play key roles. In the absence of leadership from Doug, I'd decided to step in and get it done, and he told me to "go ahead." As I called the meeting to order, Doug walked up the stairs with Richard Ciano. Before I handed out the organization diagram I'd prepared and began to explain it to everyone, I asked Doug if he wanted to kick off the meeting. I'm glad I asked.

Doug introduced Ciano as the new campaign manager and turned the floor over to him. I stifled my surprise, tucked my charts back into my notebook, and began taking notes. This impulse decision by Doug Ford turned out well for the campaign. But it would prove to be a standard Doug move that recurred many times, both during the campaign and after the mayor was in office. In the end, moves like this one would cause us more trouble than they solved.

Under Ciano's leadership, the campaign team took shape. It was a team of second-stringers and political rookies. The rival campaigns, which had launched earlier, had already bought up the town's top-tier political organizers.

So Ford formed his team around Ciano and Nick Kouvalis, one of Ciano's business partners. Kouvalis was a thin, swarthy Greek Canadian from Windsor with thick dark hair, a mustache and goatee, and eyes that seemed always to be watching, assessing, calculating. He had a quick smile and an easy way with people. I stayed on in a role that changed often, but focused on policy, strategic communication, and debate preparation. We reached far afield, to Winnipeg, to bring in Adrienne Batra, a hardcore conservative whom Nick knew from the Canadian Taxpayer Federation. She was a new face in Toronto and not someone who'd ever been a director of communication on a major campaign. She became ours.

The rest of the team was made up of Rob Ford camp followers, local conservative activists, and "the kids"—recent university grads who were keen, ambitious, and inexperienced. We worked them hard and paid them little, but most came from wealthy Toronto families and didn't rely on the money. They were loud and fun; they loved to party; and they wasted time on gossip and petty feuds. But they got the work done, and by the campaign's end, many had matured into hard-working, reliable young adults.

The other mayoral campaigns had experienced campaign managers who could turn around and pull binders off their office shelves and rerun successful campaigns from years past. They knew that the summer was a shakeout period, that the real campaign started after Labor Day. We didn't have a binder with a winning formula in it. We didn't even have anyone on the senior staff who'd worked on a Toronto mayoral campaign before.

So we made it up. And that, I believe, was a key part of why we succeeded.

We knew what our candidate's strengths and weaknesses were, and just translated what was politically obvious into what was pragmatically possible when it came to what we would have Rob say and do. We started with a simple, mathematical estimate of how many votes we'd need for him to win. Then we figured out where in the city we could find those votes. We didn't make assumptions. We built everything from scratch. And we planned to have the race pretty much won by Labor Day. The experienced A-listers managing the other campaigns didn't see it coming.

At first, Nick focused on building the database, but his rough edges quickly earned him the respect of the Fords and he developed an effective rapport with both brothers. Nick and Richard shared my concerns about the campaign's finances. One of the first things they did was to seek a legal opinion on how Doug had financed the first few weeks of the campaign. They wanted to make sure they corrected anything that had been done incorrectly. The last thing anyone wanted was a long and painful campaign audit after the election.

Ciano focused on the broad campaign strategy, figuring out a fundraising plan, planning a budget, and dealing with the Fords. It was the last task that finished him, I think. Ciano is a planner. He's logical. Every decision is based on fact. He's used to dealing with reasonable, rational professionals. Nothing in his life, I suspect, had prepared him to deal with the Fords: two brothers who insisted on doing things their way and didn't care much for "proven political practices." Everything was new to them. And everything new resulted in pushback. Simple things could be ridiculously hard.

We wanted Rob to make a campaign announcement at City Hall; he'd read a prepared text from a podium and take questions from the press. It was going to cost us $300 to rent a podium for the half-hour event, but when the Ford brothers found out, they vetoed it. It was robbery! Our budget for the campaign was $1.3 million and the argument over a $300 podium raged for days. On the day of the event, Rob spoke from a beautiful wooden podium that magically appeared. I asked Nick who'd won the argument. He smiled and told me Randy and Doug had been up all night building it from supplies they bought at Home Depot. I laughed.

Within a few weeks, Ciano went back to Campaign Research, and turned over the Fords to Nick. Nick was not only more patient with them, but also more confrontational. When they were being stupid—falling back on "tried and true" Ford campaign tactics that worked for one small ward, but clearly wouldn't scale up to a city-wide mayoral race, or refusing to pay people to do fundraising—he'd call them out. He spent a lot of time in screaming matches with Doug, and occasionally Rob. They weren't used to people telling them "no." I can't remember how many times Nick packed up his car and headed home to Windsor, a three-and-a-half-hour drive away. He'd call me from the highway, saying he was going home—a game of brinksmanship—and the Fords would buckle.

Between dramas, Nick and I would find a few precious moments to discuss strategy. His polling had, shockingly, confirmed Rob's gut instincts about what was important to people in Toronto: transit; City Hall spending; waste; mismanagement; taxes. Together, the latter four vastly outweighed the importance of transit. So we looked for ways to put them together.

If you believed waste and mismanagement were the key issues, well hey: there was only one candidate in the race who had done nothing else in his entire political life except rail against waste and mismanagement. That was Rob Ford's brand. Working with Ciano, Nick had refined the message down to "respect for taxpayers" and "stopping the gravy train." I thought the first one was too unwieldy and the latter one was too cartoonish. Shows what I know.

We never defined "gravy train." We never had to. The beauty of it was that it meant something different to everyone, but was always something to be despised. Who didn't want to stop a gravy train? Which taxpayer didn't think she was paying too much but not getting enough?

We whittled Rob's messages down until every question was answered with some version of stopping the gravy train and respecting the taxpayer. People attending debates and media asking questions quickly grew frustrated with Rob repeating the same mantra. But absolutely everyone who voted in October 2010 knew what Rob Ford stood for.

Meanwhile, the other campaigns were pushing transit, releasing costly improvement plans, and trying to steer discussions to that issue. Only Rob kept talking about respect for taxpayers and stopping the gravy train. We knew that if we were right, Ford's numbers would take off quickly, and then the other campaigns would figure out what Ford had known instinctively: It was about money. We figured that would happen around Labor Day. We were ready.

We recognized there would be an inflection point, when the others would begin to mimic Ford. At that point, we planned to pivot. Once everyone else had admitted that the real issue was respect for taxpayers, Rob would shift to "Who's tough enough to stop the gravy train?" and "Who do you trust to finish the fight?" Ford was known as a penny-pincher who stood on his principles even when he knew he'd lose. There were hundreds of 44-to-1 votes to prove it. Instead of making him seem crazy, those votes would now make him seem tough. We followed that strategy right through to Election Day.

Meanwhile, Rob was keeping busy with debate after debate. One of the first big ones was hosted by the Toronto Real Estate Board at the Toronto Congress Centre in Etobicoke, where Rob had held his launch party. Five candidates were on stage, in front of an audience of about one thousand realtors from all over the Greater Toronto Area, as well as the major TV networks and newspapers.

Rob owned the audience. He was the lone candidate who was committed, in no uncertain terms, to repealing a new land transfer tax that the real estate industry loathed. Others said, "I'll look into it." Only Ford stood up and said he'd kill it. The room erupted into cheers.

George Smitherman, then the race leader, was not amused. When it was his turn to speak on a question of character and the qualities that make a good mayor, he turned to Ford and let loose a well-planned assault. He reminded the audience of the comments Ford had made opposing the city's AIDS prevention program. It was one of the weak spots Ford and I had talked about in our first meeting.

"I'd like you to explain to people how your character, and especially these comments, is justifiable now that you present yourself as someone who wishes to be mayor of Toronto, one of the most diverse places to be found anywhere in the world?" demanded Smitherman, who is him-self gay.

I watched Rob, who was looking up at the ceiling while Smitherman worked himself up into a fine stage rage. When Smitherman finished, Rob looked at him, then at the audience. "Let me tell you what Rob Ford's character is about," he said. "It's about integrity. It's about helping kids get off the street. Helping thousands of kids." He then went on—as we had coached him to—to explain his Rob Ford Football Foundation and the work he did as a volunteer coach for a local high school football team. The room loved it, but the media smelled blood. The post-debate scrum focused entirely on Rob's stance on gays.

While driving Ford back to Deco, I called Richard, and via speakerphone we agreed that Ford had to get in front of the gay issue. It was textbook PR crisis management. Call a press conference, issue a statement, admit to being wrong. Apologize profusely. Find some gay people who supported him, and move on.

"Okay, buddy," Rob grunted at Richard. "Whatever. You're the boss." He was exhausted from the debate, sweaty. But he was even more silent than usual. So, after Richard hung up, I asked Rob what he'd like to do.

His answer: Nothing. He still believed what he'd always believed: Funding an AIDS awareness program wasn't the city's fight. The provincial government was responsible for health care. AIDS prevention was health care. He didn't want to apologize because he didn't understand how anyone could be offended by his telling the truth.

I told him people interpreted his remarks, and his opposition to Pride Parade funding, as proof he was anti-gay. "I'm not anti-gay," he said. When people called him and asked for help, he helped them. He didn't ask if they were gay or straight. He said the idea of gay sex "creeped him out," but he didn't care what people did behind closed doors. He was convinced he could ignore the issue. What was new? He'd answered all those questions years ago. "What are they going to do?" he asked. "Ask me all over again?" I said yes, that's exactly what they're going to do. "Ridiculous!" he exclaimed.

When we got back to Deco, Rob went into his office and I talked it over with Richard and Nick. Maybe we should let him do it his way, I proposed. This is how he thinks. He didn't want our politically correct, damage-control message. He didn't feel sorry. He believed his remarks were true, and he didn't want to withdraw them.

Richard knew that if we continued with the standard mea culpa strategy, Ford's apology would be on that night's evening news and in tomorrow's papers, then it would be finished. But Nick agreed we should let Rob be Rob. People knew he put his foot in his mouth; they knew about his past transgressions. People didn't care. Those who did—who thought Ford was a fat, uneducated redneck from the boondocks—were never going to vote for him anyway. So why should we waste time trying to change Ford to satisfy them? We knew his base. Christians, Muslims, Sikhs, and others, many of them recent immigrants, most of them socially conservative.

So we ignored the issue. And it almost worked. Until the Night Shift convinced Doug to change the plan.

# 5 | The Night Shift

WHAT I HAD expected to be a few days a week and done by May had turned into a sixteen- to twenty-hour daily grind. But I could taste victory and the opportunity to affect change beyond that, so I was hooked. We were all-in.

During the campaign, an unhealthy pattern formed that would eventually spill into the mayoralty. During the day, Nick and I would work on strategy with Rob and Doug. We'd go over things until both brothers agreed. They'd go home. Nick and I would head out to a bar near Deco on the airport strip, Arizona B-Bar & Grill, that was either too loud for us to be overheard, or too empty for anyone to be near us.

We'd arrive sometime between 11:00 p.m. and midnight. I would pull out the three-by-five-inch index cards I took notes on at debates and events and bring Nick up to date on what I'd noticed: how Smitherman was defining an issue, or what Rossi was using to attack Ford. Nick would go over what was happening on the broader campaign: new polling information, for example, and how we could use it to shape our message. We'd leave when we were confident everything was in place for the next day.

By 10:00 a.m., it would all be blown to hell.

Rob and Doug loved nothing more than calling Nick early—or better yet, coming into the office—with a brand new plan. A great idea. A fresh direction. Overnight, they would have figured out what we were doing wrong, and instruct us to undertake an immediate, corrective, entirely counterproductive new action. Invariably, their fix was something we'd already considered and rejected. Often, we'd spent an hour talking with them—just the night before—about why it wouldn't work. But Rob and Doug wouldn't listen. They'd spent the night on the phone with, or in the company of, an invisible, too-powerful group of characters we dubbed the Night Shift.

We didn't know who they were at first, but over the years we developed a list. They were Ford regulars, people the brothers had accumulated since high school. We believed Doug's Night Shift included old high school buddies like David Price, who was then a sales executive at a Bay Street financial firm; business associates; the local police superintendent; the police union boss; former politicians who'd known Doug Ford Sr.; old City Hall politicians trying to build lobbying careers and hoping for a big comeback someday; and current lobbyists trying to build relationships. We thought Rob's Night Shift included acquaintances (he really had no close friends), including former football players and coaches who still looked up to him; a retired judge friend of Diane's; a trusted reporter or two; dozens of people who called him regularly and who considered him a "friend," although the relationship was entirely one-sided; and—as we learned much later—probably some of Rob's drug-culture associates.

Everyone on the Night Shift was an amateur political strategist who would read the tabloids or listen to talk radio and recognize a brilliant opportunity we'd missed or a gaping flaw in our plan. They'd prescribe some course of action—either stupidly simplistic or breathtakingly complicated—and the brothers would be sold on it. With the dawn, the Night Shift would recede into the shadows and those of us on the Day Shift would begin to clean up the damage.

After the Toronto Real Estate Board (TREB) debate, where Rob had been slammed by George Smitherman on the gay issue, we'd all agreed to let Rob be Rob—to ignore it and to move forward. He didn't feel compromised, and his base was happy. But after the Night Shift got hold of Doug, he suddenly realized we'd done it all wrong. We needed to get ahead of the story and show the world that Rob didn't hate gay people. So he concocted a better plan.

About a week after the TREB debate, Rob and I were at an all-candidates prayer breakfast hosted by the city's interfaith leaders. *Toronto Star* reporter David Rider told me about a reader who'd contacted him: Dieter Doneit-Henderson was an HIV-positive gay man who lived with his husband in Rob's ward and liked his platform enough to volunteer for him. But he wanted to speak with Rob about his views on gay people. He claimed to have emailed Rob's office and received no response. David wanted to know if Rob would get back to the guy and what he'd say. On the drive to the next event, I mentioned the story to Rob. Rob told it to Doug. Doug shared it with the Night Shift.

Far too early on the morning of May 11, 2010, I woke up to the shrill ring of my cell phone. It was Nick. He wanted to know if I'd set up a meeting between Rob, the *Toronto Star*, and a gay couple. I didn't know what he was talking about. Nick said, "Go look at the *Star*."

The *Star* had a big picture of Rob, in his suit and tie, sporting a campaign button, sitting uncomfortably on a tiny couch with Doneit-Henderson, who was stickman-thin. Doug had orchestrated this brilliant crisis management coup without telling anybody on the campaign team. He'd gone directly to Rider, who'd arranged a meeting, complete with a photographer, between the Ford brothers and Doneit-Henderson and his husband in their living room. "I apologize if I offended you or your husband in any way. That's not my style," Rider quotes Rob as saying, referring to his 2006 comments about gay men and AIDS prevention funding. The same apology he insisted he didn't mean and wouldn't give when it was Plan A.

The story continued from there: Doug jumped into the conversation to assure Doneit-Henderson that Fords don't discriminate against gays or anybody else. "I've had gay friends come and visit me in Chicago," Doug reportedly said. "Gay men have slept in my bed."

Yeesh.

Doneit-Henderson and his husband had just moved to Etobicoke from Ottawa and were having trouble finding a family doctor who'd take them. Rob promised to call the provincial minister of health and try to help. We didn't know it then, but with that offer, Rob had opened Pandora's box. Trying to close it would almost cost Ford the campaign.

The gay issue, which we'd effectively put behind us, was back on the front page. Every news outlet needed to cover this new angle and dredge up Rob's old comments for context. Later that day, when Nick confronted him, Rob said Doug made him do it. Doug claimed none of us on the campaign staff knew what we were doing. He had talked to lots of "experts" who'd told him so. He had no idea what we did all day, so he did what needed doing.

The next few days were a flurry, with multiple new story angles: Does the gay community accept Rob's apology? Is an apology enough? Has he truly changed his spots? As well, the campaign took scores of irate phone calls from die-hard Ford supporters upset that Rob had apologized. We referred them to Doug. Doug began to realize he might not have handled the crisis as much as he had kindled it. For a brief period, we all agreed that no one would set up media interviews without Nick knowing about it first. By "no one," most of us meant Doug. I don't know what Doug thought we meant.

Doug left on a business trip to Chicago the next day. Nick drove him to the airport and handed him a box of condoms—"For the next time you decide to have a gay man in your bed," he said, underlining the point that Doug had to stop freelancing. Soon enough, however, the Night Shift was back.

Throughout his term as mayor, Rob routinely would defer to the Night Shift, no matter what his professional staff had said. With Doug, it was even worse. Once Rob was mayor, Doug was more readily accepted into social circles he'd previously been excluded from. His Night Shift seemed to expand to include former premiers and high-powered political operatives—none of whom had ever worked in a mayor's office, with City Council, or with Rob. Doug's Night Shift had all kinds of inspired initiatives. And Doug had an uncontrollable influence on Rob.

It was the Night Shift, for example, who conceived the ridiculous, embarrassing weight-loss challenge that turned the mayor's office into a carnival game. It was the Night Shift who developed the plan—which was universally hooted down—to build a Ferris wheel on Toronto's waterfront. And it was the Night Shift who ultimately cost Rob his dream of finishing a half-built subway line for the eastern borough of Scarborough, which he'd promised to build for his strongest supporters. (More on that later.) The Night Shift was a Nightmare.

# 6 | Money and Power

RIGHT FROM THE beginning, it was obvious that fundraising was going to be a challenge. It was a major priority for Richard Ciano when he came on board, and remained a major headache until well after the election was won and Rob was mayor. In fact, it would continue to dog us until well after Rob took office.

Corporations and unions can't contribute money to Toronto election campaigns. Only individuals can donate, and the amount they can give to a mayoral campaign is limited to $2,500 per donor. Expenses are also capped in Toronto elections. For the 2010 race, candidates for mayor were allowed to spend about $1.3 million and no more. The intent of these rules is to provide a level financial playing field for all candidates—so no one can buy an election—and to ensure no candidate is beholden to any single donor or interest group.

To raise $1.3 million under the Toronto campaign rules would require at least 520 donors paying the maximum allowable of $2,500 each. If Rob was a conventional candidate, that would have been relatively easy. He could have reached out to some political fundraisers who could be counted on to find five hundred donors among the city's most successful capitalists, host a few dinner parties at which he would speak and schmooze, then collect the $2,500 checks. Though no one expected to hold influence over the candidate in exchange for a donation, many wealthy people liked to imagine they were influential by making political donations. The real power brokers, however, were the fundraisers. They would find some way to profit from their relationship with the mayor in a legal fashion. Knowing the mayor personally, understanding what he or she thought on issues, being able to arrange a meeting, could be parlayed into lucrative client retainers without anyone breaking any laws.

But Rob was not a conventional candidate. None of the usual fundraisers knew him. In fact, the Ford family was not part of the city's capitalist establishment. Doug Ford Sr. had started out poor and clawed his way into a lucrative business, seizing opportunities when he found them. The Fords, though wealthy, were new money. A working-class family from the "countryside" of Etobicoke, they had found a profitable niche and dug in. Almost every product in every store needs a label, after all, and Deco Labels & Tags produced a steady churn of cash to keep the family in comfort. Not private-jets rich, but Florida condos and three-months-a-year-holiday wealthy. They didn't travel downtown much, they hadn't gone to school with the political and business power set, and they didn't know a canapé from a canopy.

George Smitherman and Rocco Rossi had connections to the establishment. But Rob didn't seem to care that he wasn't part of the country club set. He lived in a small, isolated world of close family, label making, constituent politics, and football. Doug, however, struck me as a guy who hungered to find a home in the establishment. But he, like his clan, was a suburb-mouse out of place in a growing city.

As Rob's poll numbers grew, I felt a strong sense of spreading concern among the establishment, followed by outright panic as it became clear he really could win. None of the traditional power brokers had backed Rob. None of them could be said to know him or be a close confidante. What happens if a mayor is elected who owes nobody anything? That was not good for business. Not at all.

Near the end of the campaign, the fundraisers were flocking to the Ford camp—rats swimming toward the rising ship. They were gracious in their offers of help, magnanimous in their praise in the news media. They were "backing Ford all the way." That they had done nothing but despise Ford for the entire campaign and had done nothing to help him get elected mattered not a whit. They needed to be seen to have a relationship with him. In their world, relationships meant money.

One of the things I most liked about Rob was that he didn't play that side of politics. He was blissfully immune to it. Nobody in the power set had helped him get elected, and he didn't care.

On the other end of the political spectrum were the unions. They could not directly write checks any more than the corporations could. Like the corporations, though, they could facilitate hundreds or thousands of voluntary donations from individual members to meet the campaign's financial needs. Naturally, union leaders might be forgiven for expecting a friendly ear from the candidate if he became mayor. Perception is valuable in the political world.

Rob, however, was not a union supporter either. The Ford family's shop was non-union, and they worked hard to keep it that way. So the unions were acting as fundraisers for Joe Pantalone, the de facto progressive in the race.

Rather than finding support from those two traditional camps, Ford had built up a large but disorganized base of populists. The largest concentration was in Etobicoke, but they could be found across the city in nearly every ward, community, and neighborhood. They came from every walk of life, from rich bankers to homeless addicts. But most of them were hard-working, low-paid citizens just trying to get by. If they were going to donate to a campaign, it was going to be in $10s and $20s, and it was going to mean switching from beef to noodles for a week. Even at an average donation of $100, the campaign would need thirteen thousand donors.

The Ford family had bankrolled the first phase of the campaign, but they weren't ready to write a $1.3 million check to make Rob mayor. Normally, campaigns would borrow money from a bank, then repay it before or after the election with money raised for the campaign. But the Fords didn't do "normally." They patently refused to take a loan. The Ford family, and possibly the family business, didn't do debt. Ciano had his work cut out for him.

Doug Ford undertook his own fundraising initiative. He was certain he could pull it off. No, he didn't have the big money connections that the other campaigns had. But he'd always been able to raise money for his brother's previous council campaigns and his father's provincial campaign. Never mind that those campaigns were much smaller (they were limited to about $30,000 in spending based on the population of each ward, so the Ford family could handily pay any shortfall in their fundraising). Doug had the answer: parties. Big ones.

The family's annual summer "Ford Fest" BBQ attracted thousands of attendees. The launch party drew in two thousand. Again, it didn't matter to Doug that, though he'd rented some credit card point-of-sale devices and set up donations tables in order to turn the free launch event into a fundraiser, the donations didn't come close to the $10,000 price tag for the event. He was convinced that more fundraising parties would do the trick.

For each one, Doug would begin by selling tickets, the conventional way to raise funds at an event. Then the family would start to worry that the turnout would be embarrassingly low. So Doug would do media to announce the event and invite "everyone" in the city to attend—albeit with no mention of cost. Just before the party date, the family would start stuffing mailboxes with invitations and handing them out to everyone they met, inviting them all to come. Of the hundreds that would end up attending, some had paid in advance, but most had not. After all, the Fords were known for their free parties.

Naturally, people who had paid for tickets were pissed that everyone else was getting in free. It would be chaos at the door. Then a decision would be made to let everyone in free. So the "fundraiser" would wind up costing the campaign tens of thousands of dollars. Doug was not a stellar fundraiser.

Nick Kouvalis came up with an alternative plan. First, he organized a data capture process, so that every person attending Doug's events, and any subsequent campaign event, would provide us with their contact information. The campaign then developed a follow-up direct mail/email campaign to solicit funds from those who had attended the free events. It was a new idea in campaign fundraising, but it worked reasonably well with Ford's supporters, who could afford to write checks for $20 to $200. Every mailing brought in a small but predictable flow of cash. Thanks to the mailings, plus a small team of commission-based, full-time fundraisers, the revenue was coming in fast enough to keep up with spending. Eventually, after Ciano had solicited legal advice on how to bring the campaign into compliance with the law, and Rob had finally agreed to let the campaign take a bank loan, the campaign had enough money to carry Rob through to Election Day at the end of October 2010—barely. The campaign had raised about $900,000, from thousands of (mostly small) donations. But it had spent about $1.7 million (the extra $400,000 was attributed to fundraising expenses that were excluded from the $1.3 million spending cap). So, the campaign finished the race owing the bank about $800,000.

The campaign finally paid off its debt in January 2011 by joining forces with two other mayoral candidates, Rocco Rossi and Sarah Thomson, who also still had election debt. They threw a joint "Harmony Dinner" for the city's bigwigs. George Smitherman, who had raised more than enough money from traditional sources to fund his second-place run, was gracious enough to participate in the dinner and help bail out his competitors. The dinner raised $1 million in one evening, with tickets selling from $250 to $2,500 for a VIP experience. Sometimes you need friends in high places.

Less than four months later, two private citizens filed a complaint with the city's Compliance Audit Committee, alleging that Rob's campaign had broken election finance laws. An audit was ordered. One of the issues in dispute was whether the direct mail campaign constituted fundraising under a financing law that hadn't contemplated the idea of holding free events, then soliciting funds from the participants afterward. The complainants questioned if those events—for which few if any tickets were sold—were "fundraisers" and should therefore be excluded from the spending limit.

The audit was a long, expensive, and painful process that didn't conclude until February 2013—three years into Rob's four-year term. The auditor ultimately reclassified a number of the campaign's expenses, causing the final financial reports to show it had overspent the $1.3 million expense limit by $40,168, or about three percent. The biggest problem the auditor found was the way Doug had financed the early part of the campaign—something that had concerned me from the beginning.

My very first invoice had been paid, not by a check from the campaign, but by one from Doug Ford Holdings Inc. When I'd asked Doug about it, he told me not to worry, that Stephen Chan, Deco's comptroller and the campaign's chief financial officer, had said it was okay. I'd met Chan and he seemed to be pretty squared away. In any case, Doug was the campaign manager and it was his concern, not mine. Campaign finance was not my area of expertise, but I found Doug's method odd enough that I pointed it out to Richard Ciano after he became campaign manager. That was what had prompted Ciano to get the legal opinion.

The Compliance Audit Committee accepted the audit results and decided not to prosecute the campaign any further. Their audit, however, cost the taxpayers $181,469.44. That is $140,000 more than Rob's overage. Isn't politics a beautiful thing?

# 7 | Building Ford Nation

A S THE CAMPAIGN progressed, we were learning how to capitalize on the appeal of Rob Ford. He wasn't the brightest candidate, though he was far smarter than most people credited him for. He wasn't a great speaker, though he was the most effective communicator in the race—he didn't speak eloquently, but everyone knew what he meant, even if he flubbed the words. He wasn't a sharp dresser or particularly attractive; not a day went by without somebody approaching me to help with his image or clothing. But he was uniquely able to connect with people and have them remember and like him. We soon discovered that was a goldmine.

One morning, I got stuck at a traffic light on University Avenue at King Street. University is a thoroughfare running north–south through the heart of Toronto's downtown, with a majestic boulevard down its center featuring leafy trees, seasonal flower beds, war memorials, flagpoles, and fountains that never seemed to function. As the light was turning red, I realized I was stuck in a crosswalk, and so I eased my car backward. (This was well before I'd been described as #evil.)

The driver behind me began honking furiously. I checked my mirror—I was nowhere near him. Next thing I knew, he was at my door. Shit.

But I was mistaken. "I love you, man!" he exclaimed, a huge smile splitting his face. "My mom loves you, my whole family loves you." I did not know this man.

"You helped my mom with the flooding in her basement ten years ago, she still talks about that," he went on. "You're going to be a great mayor!"

*He thinks I'm Rob Ford. Do I look like Rob Ford? Fuck. I really need to lose some weight.*

"Do you have any buttons I can have . . . or bumper stickers?"

I had bumper stickers. In fact—lightbulb—I had one pasted to the back of my car. He must have seen it. I reached into my back seat, grabbed a handful from a box and shoved them out the window. The light turned green.

"You're awesome, man. Thank you! My whole family is voting for you!"

"Uh . . . thanks," I said as the man raced back to his car.

I drove away, mind whirring. Rob Ford was some kind of weird folk hero.

Earlier in this book, I've written about what I described as Rob's cell phone addiction, about how he dialed for love. Each day, he'd set out with a fistful of letter-size sheets of plain white paper covered with handwritten telephone numbers. No names. No messages. His EA, Katie, would give them to him. After he'd returned a call, he would put a big, clumsy checkmark next to the number, and when he finished a sheet, he'd give it back to Katie. The previous day, he'd finished two sheets, handed them to me, and asked me to make sure Katie got them. That's why I was in that crosswalk, being mistaken for Ford—I'd just come from City Hall; I'd just given Katie the sheets. She'd opened a drawer in her desk and dropped them inside. The drawer was full of call sheets, with the numbers checked off.

"Wow," I said. "You've got a lot of those."

I asked her what happened when the drawer was full. She said, "I put them in here." "Here" was a banker's box, nearly full, of nothing but checked-off call sheets. Hundreds of them. Wow again. And that was only a few months' worth, she said. When the box was full, it went to Deco for storage.

That night, at Arizona for our regular debrief, I told Nick the call sheet story. His eyes lit up. The next day, he went into Rob's office at Deco and pulled the lid off one of the half-dozen banker's boxes stacked against the wall. More call sheets. A storage room somewhere held even more.

"This is gold, buddy," Rob had told me many times when he was making calls to constituents. He was right. But not only in the way he'd thought.

Those numbers, those hundreds and thousands of numbers, were a database. Nick hired a bunch of people to begin calling them. Many were disconnected; others led to people who had no idea who Rob Ford was. But a lot of them—I mean, a lot—were answered by people who remembered Rob clearly, and loved him for caring. He'd been the first and only "important person" to ever return their calls. And he'd been doing it, steadily, for ten years.

Here in our hands was a list of over one hundred thousand supporters who loved Rob as much as the guy at the stoplight did. They all said they'd walk through hell to vote for him, and so would their families and friends.

Ford Nation was born.

***

During the campaign, the Ford family organized two of their popular "Ford Fest" celebrations. I'd never heard of anything like it. For the past fifteen years, the family had hosted an annual barbecue in their backyard. Doug Sr. had started it and after he died, the family continued it. It wasn't a private affair. It was open to the public—all of the public. In 2010, during the election campaign, the family printed up invitation cards and distributed them en masse all over the city: "Burgers, Hot Dogs, Beer, and Pop. Everything is Free!" Rob talked about Ford Fest on the radio, on TV, and at every public speaking event. He invited everybody. They expected about five thousand people to attend, maybe even ten thousand. *Yeah, sure,* I thought.

A ridiculous amount of the campaign's time and effort went into organizing Ford Fest. The party needed people to order food and beer. People to set up chairs and tables. People to decorate it. People to hand out stickers and, at Nick's insistence, people to record the names and contact information of everyone who attended, as they entered. I was convinced it was a waste of time. Nick wasn't happy, but he put up with it because it kept Doug busy and out of his hair.

On the day of my first Ford Fest, I helped set up, then headed home to spend time with my kids. By the time I got back, a couple of hours later, I had to circle the parking lot in the strip mall across from Diane's street three times before I found a space. As I stepped out of my car, I could hear music thumping the air; and as I approached Diane's house, I saw about two hundred people crammed onto her front lawn. I soon found out why: The backyard was full. They couldn't get in. At that moment, the music stopped. Doug's introduction for Rob rang out—loudly—over the sound system. I stood in the crowd and listened to Rob deliver the speech I'd written for him. The attendees—about five thousand of them, all told—ate it up.

No one stayed long at Ford Fest, but the flow of people was continuous. I eventually made it to the backyard, which was sardine room only. The media hadn't seen anything like it either; I don't think reporters had paid it any heed while Rob was a councillor. With Rob running for mayor, though, it got phenomenal coverage.

So we did it again, later that summer, at a private home in North York. It was much smaller, but equally successful. And Nick gathered thousands of new names to add to the Ford Nation database.

Eventually, thousands of Ford Nation members reached into their pockets and gave us donations, $10 here, $200 there. And three thousand of them worked for us on Election Day, for free.

\*\*\*

Throughout the time I worked in the mayor's office, people would come in and ask to see Rob. The receptionist would offer to set up a meeting, but they'd insist that Rob was a friend; he'd instructed them to just drop in if they were downtown. If Rob happened to be passing by, he would invite them inside, give them a tour. Hosting everyday citizens in his office was the part of being mayor that he liked best.

Many of these "friends" would ask Rob to be a guarantor on their passport applications. I would explain that he couldn't do that because he hadn't known them for two years. Often, they'd get upset—they had known him for more than two years. They called each other at least once a month. I believed them. It felt like Rob called every person in the city once a month. But I also knew that Rob would have no recollection of this person, or what they'd talked about. They were one of, literally, over one hundred thousand. In their minds, the friendship was real. But it was entirely one-sided.

Still, to the members of Ford Nation, Rob was a pal, a member of their extended family, a beloved Uncle Buck, so they stuck by him. When someone attacked him, they would fight back for him. Later, though Rob admitted to smoking crack cocaine, he was still family to them. And you don't turn your back on family.

\*\*\*

Ford Nation wasn't dubbed "Ford Nation" until very close to the election in 2010. We didn't call his supporters that. I was adamant that Rob shouldn't, and he agreed. It sounded arrogant. It sounded presumptuous. It sounded entitled. It didn't sound like Rob.

Doug loved it.

After the election, we began using the term internally, but never for public consumption. When Doug used the phrase publicly once or twice, Nick took him to task for it. As we began the battle to gain control of the city's spending, the media and the members of the public who hated what we were doing used the term as a pejorative. "Ford Nation" was a horde of illiterate, mouth-breathing, redneck, racist homophobes who wanted to destroy everything that made Toronto great. Being called a member of Ford Nation was a put-down, a slam.

But Rob's supporters loved the label. They described themselves as Ford Nation. As Rob started to lose his battle with serious addiction, he and Doug began using it publicly. Soon there were T-shirts, bobblehead figures. Even a short-lived TV show. *Ford Nation* aired one time only on the right-wing Sun News Network, the closest thing in Canada to Fox News in the United States. It aired in the fall of 2013 at the peak of Rob's drug-fueled fall from grace and was, I have been told, the network's highest rated show ever. It never aired again. The problem was cost—not so much in money, as in time. Sun News is a small cable station and producing the one-hour show, I am told, occupied their main studio for an entire eight-hour day. All their other shows air live without rehearsal.

The *Ford Nation* program continued, for a few episodes, as a YouTube series produced by the Ford brothers themselves, including an episode featuring a Skype appearance by Jimmy Kimmel.

Immediately after the election, Nick and I began thinking about how we could leverage Ford Nation. A large segment of Torontonians prized good fiscal management and wanted the city to focus on the basics of municipal governance, rather than the globe-trotting, save-the-world causes championed by the previous administration. These people loved Toronto, too, and wanted to be able to afford to live here.

Canadian politics doesn't have the Political Action Committees (PACs) that exist in the United States. But the political left in Canada had pioneered the concept of building "nonpartisan" action groups that supported partisan causes under the guise of "everyday citizens concerned for (fill in the blank)." These were, in many ways, cheaper, more limited knock-off PACs.

The far-left New Democratic Party had big labor unions on its side, as well as the "Council of Canadians"—a so-called nonpartisan voice that, coincidentally, aligned with the NDP platform. But the NDP rarely was able to form a government at the federal or provincial level. Modern unions, though historically supportive of the NDP, began looking for another horse to bet on that could deliver on promises made. Labor partnered with the Liberal Party (the NDP's ideological competition) to create the "Working Families Coalition," a largely union-backed group that campaigns year-round and spends big dollars during federal and provincial elections to help Liberal candidates win.

Why wasn't there a conservative PAC-style group in Canada? Perhaps because Canadian conservative politicians lack the charisma and evangelical appeal of US politicians. Most Canadian politicians looked and sounded more like pharmacists than Baptist preachers. Until Rob Ford. Ford was that rarity in Canadian politics—a populist. We wanted to use his die-hard following to build a movement that would not only keep him in office forever, but also pave the way for conservative politicians across the country.

The problem was, the movement had to be bigger than the Fords. It had to be independent of Rob's personality, for legal reasons (related to campaign finance and election laws) as well as pragmatic ones. In the end, it never happened. For better and worse, Rob Ford is one of a kind.

Ford Nation continues, and remains loyal. As Rob's addictions became public in 2013, the Nation shrank to a tenacious core. But it survived. Ford Fests continued through Rob's tenure as mayor, and he's said they'll continue beyond it. Many people have reasons to love Rob or Doug. Rob made sure of that, one call at a time.

# 8 | Go Ahead, Take Me to Jail

"I THINK ROB did something stupid."

Nick and I were debriefing at Arizona after another sixteen-hour campaign day in mid-June 2010, about four months before the October 25 election. Our internal polling had Rob slightly ahead of Smitherman, and on June 11, a publicly released Nanos poll agreed: 29 percent for Ford, 26 for Smitherman. The earth shook under us. The establishment, truly worried now, sought ways to burst Rob's bubble.

In the heat of the campaign, we analyzed every move made by the competition, preparing countertactics for their tactics and expecting that they were doing the same. It's possible we strayed into paranoia, but politics is a blood sport and an election campaign is politics at its most visceral. Everything is on the table. One candidate wins. All others lose.

We knew Rob had a controversial past. But we believed it was now out in the open. He'd assured me there was nothing left to hide. But none of that protected us from fresh fuck-ups.

Nick took a swig of his vodka and orange juice. "I think there may be a tape of him saying something stupid," he said.

"What did he say?" I asked. "To whom?"

Nick wasn't sure, but Rob clearly had done something bad. We were beginning to recognize his "tell:" He was on his best behavior and avoiding conflict. He'd stopped pushing back against Nick. He was saying things like "Whatever you want" and "You're the boss." Like a child cleaning his bedroom to distract you from the fact the cookie jar was smashed and hidden in the kitchen cupboard. We just weren't sure how bad Rob had been. We could see he was nervous. And he was complaining a lot about Dieter Doneit-Henderson.

Since meeting with Rob in his living room, Dieter had become Rob's loudest gay cheerleader—and a bit of a media whore. He called into talk radio shows saying he was Rob's gay friend and that Rob was "totally misunderstood"; Rob absolutely loved gay people and was doing amazing things to help him and his husband.

The campaign staff wasn't pleased. We wanted to put the gay issue behind us, but Dieter was keeping it in the news. I wondered aloud if he was working for someone. Maybe the *Toronto Star*? They'd introduced him to us. Or, perhaps, Smitherman's camp? Dieter's media campaign rankled everyone: Rob's base didn't want to think of him as gay-friendly. Progressive voters were convinced it was a sham. The fact that neither was true just complicated matters. For us it was lose-lose.

. Dieter also had grafted himself onto the Ford family. I didn't have to deal with him—in fact, I don't recall ever meeting him. But he became a bigger and more problematic piece of the conversation every day.

He'd initially asked Rob to help him find a doctor, and Rob had tried: He called the provincial minister of health and the local member of Provincial Parliament. I think Doug even took Dieter to his family doctor, but that didn't work out. Doug's daughter Krista had somehow been instructed by the family to drive Dieter around the city shopping for doctors. Reportedly, Dieter didn't seem to like what they were telling him.

Through Nick, I heard that Krista was freaked out: Dieter had asked her to drive him to get his medicine. But instead of directing her to a pharmacy, he had taken her to a shady house in a bad neighborhood. Krista had refused to help Dieter any further. Doug was livid and fighting with Dieter. Rob was fed up.

As we distanced ourselves from Dieter, he grew angry; he was demanding more and more time from the Fords, more and more help to find a doctor willing to write him a prescription for powerful pain medication. There were stories of him calling the campaign office and threatening people, threatening Doug and his family, calling Rob incessantly. He was posting negative things about Rob on his blog and directing people to them with wild, accusatory tweets.

Rob had begun feeling out Nick with "what if . . ." questions about Dieter and their relationship—and dropping hints of what he might or might not have said to him on the phone. The things he admitted to saying didn't seem problematic, but he was so nervous, he must have said something more. Something stupid.

Over the next week, as the campaign ground on, rumors bubbled up on the Internet (through Twitter, blog postings, Facebook, and from our media contacts) that there was a tape of Rob Ford talking to Dieter, and it was bad. Nick confronted Rob again, and Rob assured him there was nothing bad on the tape. *What tape?* Well, Rob seemed to feel that maybe he'd been taped. *How would you know you were taped?* Well, it seemed Dieter had told him about the tape and was threatening to release it unless Rob helped him get medicine. OxyContin, to be specific, the highly addictive and often abused pain medication.

Fuck.

Now it was a race against time. We assumed the *Star* had the tape, because they had introduced us to Dieter in the first place. We knew they were endorsing Smitherman, whose politics more closely matched the paper's editorial slant, and we expected that they would hold onto the recording until a critical point in the campaign, and then run a damning exposé. We needed to know what was on the recording, and we needed to manage its reveal to minimize the damage.

Nick charged twenty-four year old Fraser Macdonald, a member of our communication team, with the task of figuring out a way to befriend Dieter online and get him to give us a copy of the recording so we could see how bad it was before it was released publicly. Fraser was ingenious. Much earlier in the campaign, he'd created a false Twitter identity called @QueensQuayKaren. (Queens Quay is a shopping and residential development on Toronto's downtown waterfront, which is left-leaning, George Smitherman territory.) In her Twitter bio, "Karen" described herself as "Karen Philby, a downtown Toronto gal who likes politics, my cat Mittens, and a good book." She had 153 followers and her avatar picture sported a "George Smitherman for Mayor" ribbon.

It's important to remember that in 2010, Twitter was a nascent social medium, being used pretty much for the first time in Toronto municipal politics. I estimated that 90 percent of the people following the campaign on Twitter were journalists or political staffers and volunteers. There were few, if any, "real" people involved in the discussions. At times, it felt as if the entire Twitterverse consisted of about seventeen twenty-somethings, sitting in their basements in their underwear, each pretending to be a dozen different people. There was nothing real about it, and most people used fake names and pictures.

Nick revealed the "identity" of Karen to Kelly Grant, a reporter from the *Globe and Mail* newspaper, for an article she wrote about the campaign on October 29, 2010, and discussed the tactic at a November 5, 2010, post-campaign panel discussion hosted by the Public Affairs Association of

Canada. Despite the commonplace nature of the ploy, it prompted some overwrought breast-beating from a few in the Twitterverse, mostly I think from those who'd been unsuccessful at it themselves.

Over the course of the summer, Karen had sent about 150 tweets, many of them about the mayoral campaign and most of those supportive of Smitherman. In the grand tradition of Kim Philby, the Russian mole inside MI6 at the height of the Cold War, Karen was one of Fraser's sleeper agents, ready when duty called. It called in June.

Karen began engaging with Dieter, commiserating with him over his bad experience with the Fords, and stroking his ego. Within a few days, Dieter had privately shared a link to the recording with Karen. On June 15, Fraser brought it to Nick, and Nick called me.

"How bad?" I asked.

"Bad," Nick said. "It's over. We're done."

I jumped in my car. When I got to Deco, I could see Rob's van and Doug's Navigator in the parking lot. Nick and Adrienne were smoking outside the center building where our war room was located. As I walked up the short sidewalk, Adrienne stubbed out her cigarette and headed to her car. She looked livid.

"Well?" I asked.

"We're fucked," she said.

Nick took me up to the war room and turned his laptop toward me so I could listen to the recording. Then he left me alone and went over to the main office to talk with the brothers. I sat and listened to the recording, hunched over the tinny speakers to catch the poor-quality audio. The recording was just over fifty minutes long. It had been made on June 4, 2010; the Toronto Star later revealed they'd received the recording from Dieter the following day.

Nick and Adrienne were right. It was bad.

As I listened to the recording, I stopped it frequently and rewound parts of it to listen again. I took detailed notes of the potentially damaging statements Rob had made.

The overall impression the recording gives is of a frustrated Rob Ford, trying frequently to end a phone call without offending Dieter. Dieter sounds manipulative, as if he's trying to walk Rob into a trap. He starts out by complaining that someone with a campaign or City Hall email address has sent him emails he didn't like. Rob is concerned about this and apologizes. He asks Dieter if he's "sure it's our campaign doing this? It couldn't be Smitherman?"

Dieter responds with, "I wouldn't put it past him." He goes on to say, "Somebody here is fucking you around with communications." Then, more threatening, "This is going to cost you something. This is no good."

Throughout the call, Ford tries to disengage or steer the conversation to the fundraising event Doug was organizing in Scarborough that week. That appears to be Rob's primary concern. Doug had booked a huge hall and, as with Ford Fest, the family were terrified nobody would show up. They were desperately encouraging anyone and everyone to attend. Rob invites Dieter and his husband to the event numerous times during the call.

About thirty-nine minutes into the conversation, after trying multiple times to get Rob to promise to buy illegal drugs for him, Dieter explodes in laughter, then says in an exasperated tone, "Fuck, can you find OxyContin for me, Rob?"

"Huh?" Rob grunts.

"Can you find OxyContin for me so I can get on the medication?" Dieter puts it out there, bluntly.

"I'll try, buddy, I'll try," Rob responds in his usual constituent sympathy voice. "I don't know about this shit, but I'll fucking try to find it."

At forty-two minutes, Dieter says, "It's all recorded." Then, "When we go to the media, we have major, major evidence. We've recorded all of this." He's talking about his interactions with doctors who've refused to write him prescriptions for OxyContin. He goes on, "I recorded the entire face-to-face conversation with doctor number nine. David Rider [the *Toronto Star* reporter who introduced Rob to Dieter] has the recording." As the call finally ends, at fifty minutes, Dieter says, "I have a sneaking suspicion that this could have been contrived by Smitherman."

After listening to the whole conversation, I went back and replayed key sections. Rob said a lot of stupid things on that call—things a normal person wouldn't say. But he never actually said he would do something illegal. (He came close, though. Too damn close.) He certainly never said what a politician should say: "You're out of your mind if you think I'm going to buy drugs for you. Goodbye!"

I found Nick outside, frustrated after a battle with the brothers. Apparently Doug was screaming at Rob for being so stupid. Nick was ready to head back to Windsor (again). I asked him to hear me out.

I didn't think the tape was fatal. Rob was stupid, but anyone listening to the whole tape would plainly hear that Dieter was trying to set him up, leading him to say something incriminating. They'd also hear Rob trying to be nice, trying to end the call a half dozen times. Although Rob had said some pretty idiotic things, he never actually said he'd do anything illegal. The crucial thing was to get reporters to listen to the whole recording. Bits and pieces out of context would be damning.

It was a crisis, but I thought we could manage it. Yeah, I'm that hopeful. Rob was well known as a politician who went the extra mile to help people; Dieter was not a credible accuser; and I believed the facts could point to Ford as the victim of a scam, if not an outright extortion attempt. I was confident enough in my crisis management ability to give it a shot.

Dieter had been threatening the family and the campaign. He was behaving erratically and saying slanderous things on the Internet. At one point in the taped conversation, he mentioned he could see Rob's house from where he was. Rob was afraid of this guy; so was the family.

While we talked, I went through the tweets Dieter had sent to see how ominous they were, and to take screenshots of them in case they were erased. I noticed something that sent a chill down my spine. Something I hadn't noticed before. The tweets were geotagged with Dieter's location when he sent them. The location read "Edenbridge Drive." That was where Rob and his family lived. This guy was at or near their house when he sent these threatening tweets.

That was all we needed. We spoke to the brothers and I told them they had to call the police and lay a complaint. This was going to become public and it was important that Rob be the victim, not the villain. Adrienne and Nick arranged an exclusive interview about the threats and the phone conversation with a friendly newspaper journalist. She listened to the entire recording. That interview produced three consecutive days of negative columns about how stupid Rob had been. The brothers were livid with the reporter, but it was exactly what I wanted—although I'd have preferred one column, not three.

The morning the first column appeared, we held a press conference at Deco and made sure the media got copies of the recording. We didn't want to use the campaign office, because we didn't want the campaign branding in the picture. No "Ford for Mayor" signs. No buttons. Adrienne and I wrote Rob's comments—he expressed concern for his family, and sympathy for Dieter, a man he'd only been trying to help and who, clearly, needed more help than Rob could offer. The rest of it was political jujitsu. Nick coined it the "wind in our sails" tactic. That is, everything they threw at us was just wind in our sails. This episode just showed how far some people would go to prevent Rob from going down to City Hall to stop the gravy train and bring back respect for taxpayers.

"All I have ever done in my ten years of politics is return people's calls and try to help out every single person," Rob told the assembled reporters. "Unfortunately, this is a good deed that has gone horribly wrong.

"I began to fear for my family. [Dieter] clearly said on the tape that he could see my house. In my opinion, this person needs help."

Then Rob delivered the positioning line.

"There are people out there that will do everything in their power to make sure that I'm not mayor of this great city.

"Who tapes phone calls?"

Wind in our sails. It worked.

***

The OxyContin tape was the first major crisis of the campaign, but far from the last. It helped forge our leadership group into a cohesive, effective, and confident crisis management team. It also helped reassure Rob and the Ford family that we knew what we were doing. It encouraged them to heed our counsel about future crises and strategic decisions. It didn't, however, motivate Rob to be honest with us in all things. His attempts to withhold key facts from us would continue to handicap our ability to avoid some crises. It took a while for us to fully understand this.

We followed the OxyContin model for the crises that followed: buy time without making things worse; unearth all the facts and assess the risk to Rob's brand; make a plan to minimize or contain the damage while moving as quickly as possible to safer ground; execute the plan aggressively; then get back on the path to victory as quickly as possible, review the results, and learn from the experience.

This approach worked reasonably well for some of the crises that followed. The *Toronto Star*'s football assault story, for example (more on this later), was easy to deal with from a crisis-management perspective— but it had long-lasting strategic consequences that would help shape Rob's successes and failures as mayor. Other crises were tougher, like the one that blindsided us in August, when the *Toronto Sun* broke a bombshell story that Rob had been charged with possession of marijuana ten years earlier.

Either way, we quickly learned not to trust Rob's version of events and to always look for corroborating evidence. This slowed us down, of course—we had to take an incremental approach to crises that we would have wanted to manage in one fell swoop. But that was life with Rob Ford.

Here's how the August story played out: While in the campaign RV driving back from an event, Nick overheard Rob answering his cell phone. After a couple of sentences back and forth, Rob grunted "no" a few times, then a few times more. Then he got angry.

"I'm dead serious. When I say no, I mean never. No question. Now I'm getting offended. No means no."

Alarmed, Nick grabbed the cell phone from Rob's hand and hung up. Rob told him it was *Toronto Sun* reporter Jonathan Jenkins, and he'd alleged that Ford had once been arrested for drugs. Rob was steaming.

Nick ordered the driver to pull over and tugged Rob out of the bus onto the shoulder of the roadway. Over a few minutes, Nick dragged a story out of Rob, who seemed to have trouble remembering the details. Jenkins had been reading from a police report that said Florida police had charged Rob Ford with possessing marijuana in 1999. Rob denied it. Then he slowly began admitting to parts of it. In what we would later come to recognize as a classic Rob Ford delaying tactic, he would begrudgingly confess to the minor details first, then more over time as he was backed further and further into the corner. I'd specifically asked him about arrests or drugs at the very beginning of our relationship. *No—never,* had been the answers then. Not "never" now.

Eventually we got the truth: Rob had been pulled over by Miami police on Valentine's Day after a dinner out with Renata, who was then his fiancée. The police found a joint in his back pocket. He was drunk enough, apparently, to goad the police officer with his hands outstretched together as if waiting to be handcuffed and blurting, "Go ahead, take me to jail." It wasn't the last time he'd challenge police to arrest him.

Nick got Jenkins back on the phone and Rob copped to the charge, apologized for getting angry with him, and said he had forgotten about it.

Nick called me at home to tell me what happened, and I warmed up my computer. As the night passed, Rob's family lawyer worked the phones to Florida and got more details about the incident. As they came in, I talked with Adrienne and Nick and we planned another morning news conference in front of Deco. We would again use the "wind in our sails" tactic—it was a ten-year-old episode that just showed how far some special interests would go to prevent Rob Ford from derailing their gravy train.

Honestly, it was one of my favorite crisis statements. There was more to the story than what Jenkins knew, and we were going to put everything out on the table in the morning, to take our lumps all at once, rather than in dribs and drabs over the next week.

"The reason I forgot about the marijuana in my pocket, is because I was being arrested for drunk driving at the time." We never used that line in the statement, but I actually wrote it in the first draft. It was the essence of Rob's mea culpa for saying "no" to Jenkins when first asked. The marijuana charge had been dropped, and Ford had been convicted of failing to provide a breath sample, which is the same offence as driving drunk.

The local papers pulled Rob's arrest mug shot from the Miami-Dade police and it ran on the front covers of every major Toronto newspaper on the same day. I would argue it was great publicity for Rob, if only because most people simply don't have the bandwidth to consume much news. The average voter in Toronto sees the newspaper cover in the sidewalk box at the bus stop. It was a good picture of a younger, fitter-looking Rob Ford. Only some read the headline. Even fewer read the article. I imagine thousands of conversations like this:

"Who's that?"

"Rob Ford."

"Who's he?"

"He's running for mayor. Wants to stop the gravy train."

That's how some elections are won.

# 9 | Those Damned Debates

THE TORONTO MAYORAL campaign is unlike any other election campaign in Canada. It's almost eleven months long, by far the lengthiest campaign in a country where the average federal or provincial election lasts thirty-six days. Typically, the winner must accumulate over 300,000 votes to win, compared to the 20,000 to 50,000 to win in most provincial or federal districts. Candidates must create high-level policy platforms for a government that manages a $13 billion budget to provide roads, water, sewer, police, firetrucks, ambulances, public health, social housing, welfare services, and parks and recreation to almost 10 percent of Canada's population, and manage the most booming construction market in North America. Meanwhile, campaign teams must knock on thousands of doors, plant thousands of lawn signs, and organize thousands of volunteers to get three hundred thousand-plus voters to the polls on Election Day. It's the Super Bowl of Canadian politics, part US-style primary and part presidential election.

There are no political parties at the municipal level in Toronto, so each candidate runs as an independent. The left-wing candidate, however, is almost always a member of the NDP, and benefits from that party's organization in terms of skills, expertise, and thousands of volunteers. Unions typically support the left candidate with donations and volunteers. One of the other candidates will normally win the backing of the city's business establishment, which can help ensure that his/her campaign is fully financed. Everyone else is on his or her own.

The system has its strengths and weaknesses. One of the most common complaints is that the campaign is too long. I used to think that, but watching the 2014 mayoral campaign from the outside, I now believe that the long campaign serves a purpose. Without a party system, there is no process of vetting or validating candidates. Anyone who is eighteen years old or older, who can legally vote in Toronto, and who is willing to put down a $200 deposit can run for mayor. In 2010, there were over forty candidates on the ballot. In 2014, there were sixty-three vying to replace Rob Ford. Maybe four or five of them are capable of mounting a credible campaign. The rest are fringe candidates in it for vanity reasons, or to protest something or other. How is the voter to tell the difference?

The answer is by closely observing the first eight months of a grueling campaign. Quickly, the flakes float away; only a few candidates are serious enough to assemble a proper team and finance the early part of a one- to two-million-dollar campaign before fundraising kicks in. As well, only a few can survive the hundreds of events and interviews they must attend over the primary period. By Election Day, there may be sixty names on the ballot, but people won't recognize most of them; the process will have winnowed down the contenders to two or three.

A big part of that winnowing occurs in the debates. They're a unique and terrifying part of Toronto's municipal democratic culture, and they are exhausting. In a Canadian federal election, the party leaders competing to become prime minister will debate each other twice: once in English and once in French. In the last Ontario provincial election, the party leaders . debated just once.

But in the seven months Rob Ford campaigned in 2010 (he registered March 25, three months into the campaign period), he participated in almost one hundred debates. (There were more; he skipped some.) A dozen were televised or broadcast on radio. The rest were in churches, community centers, school gymnasiums, public libraries, lecture halls, movie theaters, and corporate meeting rooms. Every TV and radio station in Toronto, every newspaper, every community group, residents' association, rate payers alliance, arts club, theater coven, professional association, service club, church, and bowling league hosts its own debate. They begin in January or February just to squeeze them all in.

Typically, the organizers send out an email to however many leading candidates there are at the time (more may join after the first debates; many will withdraw before the last), saying that all of the candidates have been invited *and have confirmed*—"Will you join us, too?" It's a white lie, but it works.

Early on, nobody wants to be left out. Later, as the process becomes exhausting, no candidate wants to be the first to skip a debate. The others pounce on any opportunity to say, "He's afraid to debate me!" or "She doesn't care about the (fill in blank) community like I do!" Eventually, somebody has to miss one for an unavoidable reason, and accept his or her pillorying. But the spell is broken. From there on in, candidates will decide which debates they can skip. They can't miss too many, however, or that will become the message track.

The media runs out of interesting stories to write early in the campaign, but they doggedly attend each debate in case something crazy happens. When Rob Ford was involved, they were all Just. Waiting. For. Him. To. Blow. Since they were there, they reported who attended, who had the most volunteers, who had the best one-liners, who looked tired. And especially who wasn't there. Candidates who skipped debates became the story of the day. That's not what candidates want. So the debates never end.

In 2010, the media, the competitors, and the political elite of Toronto couldn't wait to see Rob Ford in the debates. They'd watched him for years at City Council, where he'd stand up and rail on and on. He'd head down a rabbit hole or off on a wild tangent, get frustrated with the Speaker's attempts to get him back on track, then lose his temper when the heckling got vicious. He was notorious for throwing fits during Council debates.

No one thought Ford was smart enough to survive the debates. No one thought he understood how the city operated, or any of the election issues—especially transit, the alleged key issue. Ford-haters were plentiful, and the prospect of seeing him take on smooth, experienced operators like George Smitherman and Rocco Rossi had them salivating.

Within days of announcing his campaign, Ford attended his first debate, March 29, 2010. It was held at Mary Ward Catholic Secondary School in Scarborough, the city's fast-growing eastern borough, which often felt forgotten by City Hall. We hadn't yet formulated Rob's campaign platform, but he knew what he believed in.

Our pre-debate brief was simple: *Don't lose your temper. Don't fuck up.*

All he had to do was come out of the debate looking calm, collected, and in good humor. People expected him to be belligerent. They expected a bully. They expected a loud, pugnacious fighter. We wanted them to see none of those things. It turned out better than we could have hoped.

The main candidates at the time were Smitherman (the race leader, who all assumed would win); Rossi (the main challenger); Joe Pantalone (the left-wing champion); Giorgio Mammoliti (a city councillor and a long-shot, but always entertaining); and Sarah Thomson (a fringe candidate and the lone woman in the crowd). And, of course, Rob Ford.

Smitherman made a case for a bold new vision of a city full of "mature conversations." The others took turns bashing Smitherman for his eHealth fiasco (a billion-dollar failed attempt to build an electronic database for personal health records) as health minister and his record in provincial politics. Ford stayed out of the fray. He followed the game plan. He reiterated his simple, straightforward message to the audience of mostly high school kids: your parents pay too much tax; it takes you too long to get downtown on a lousy bus service that always goes on strike. He didn't join in the Smitherman-bashing. He didn't even use all his opportunities to speak. He was happy to sit quietly and let the others beat up Smitherman, to let the others look mean and angry.

During the question and answer period, one of the students asked what the candidates would do to ease youth unemployment. Many of their brothers and sisters had graduated and couldn't find jobs. Smitherman had a great plan to engage communities and employers along with the province in a high-level dialogue to create a new integrated employment strategy. Or something like that. Pantalone touted all the things he and the former mayor had already done, the things that hadn't provided jobs for these kids, and he vowed they would continue on the same path. The others had similar lofty plans.

Ford was different. At that debate, I saw for the first time how he could work his magic. When it was his turn to speak, he leaned forward in his chair and made eye contact with the crowd. His face lit up. He loved talking with students and he knew their language.

What they really needed, he explained, were more part-time jobs. When he was a kid, everybody had a job after school. They made their own money and went to the mall to buy clothes and music and other things they wanted. But there weren't many part-time jobs for students anymore. The room hummed with agreement.

Rob said he was a businessman, and knew how businessmen thought: that they needed to make more money so they could hire more people—students included—to grow their businesses. But the city taxed the businesses too much. And residents paid too much tax to the city, so they didn't have money to spend in stores—money that would create jobs. He finished by saying that if anyone needed a job, give him a call. He couldn't promise anything, but he would be happy to send their resume out to business owners he knew. He added that if they wanted to get work experience, they might want to volunteer on a political campaign—his or one of the others. The room cheered.

The other candidates and the media mocked Ford. He wasn't a serious contender; he didn't understand that job creation is more complex than cutting taxes and forwarding resumes. But Ford understood the audience, and they understood him.

At debate after debate, Rob would show his exasperation with picayune questions. He would answer them with an exhausted, sour expression on his face. I would coach him as he headed to the stage, "Talk to these people like you talked to the kids at Mary Ward, like they're your football team. Less swearing, but as much passion." He'd do his best and it was good enough.

At every debate, I would sit in the front row, directly in front of Rob, or stand at the back or on the sides of the room where he could see me. I reacted to what he said. If he was looking angry, I'd stare at him with a ridiculous shit-eating grin on my face. He'd chuckle and leer back at me with a terrifying horror-movie crazy man grimace. But he'd smile more. If he was going too hard, I'd use my hand to signal him to soften up. If he was coming across cold, I'd mime throwing a football to remind him to connect with the audience like they were his team.

I'd also take notes. I'd learned early on to carry a pocket full of 3-by-5-inch index cards, held together with a rubber band. Every time Rob or anyone said something I wanted to remember, I'd jot it down. After each debate, as we drove to the next event, I'd pull out my note cards and go through them with Rob. I'd show him where he could have answered a question better, or used it to pivot to his key messages. I'd keep reminding him to adjust his neutral position; when he wasn't talking, he'd often tilt his head back and stare at the ceiling, looking totally bored. Once, he cleaned his fingernails during a debate.

"But it's so boring!" he'd protest. Instead of looking up, I wanted him to look down at his binder. "Put a pen in your hand. Take notes about what the other person is saying, or just doodle. It looks better." He'd listen. He'd try. Contrary to what I'd feared before I joined the campaign, he was coachable and eager to improve. And he did.

Our strategy throughout the early debates was simply to defy expectation. People expected angry Rob. They never got that. No matter how much the others poked him and prodded him, he refused to lose his cool on stage. Our plan wasn't to have Rob win the debates. He didn't need to win. He didn't need to get in the best zinger. As he moved up in the polls, he became the subject of the others' attacks in debates. Before every debate, I'd whisper in his ear, "You're fifteen points ahead. They want to get you angry so you blow up on TV. Don't take the bait. Don't say more than you have to. Stick with your message." He grew to be good at it.

While every other candidate was trying to look smart, sound cool, and win the argument, Ford let the barbs bounce off his back, and stuck to his message. "I'm going to City Hall to cut the waste. To keep your taxes under control. To stop the gravy train down there. It's time City Hall showed a little respect for taxpayers."

His opponents—and often the audiences, frankly—didn't like that, because they never got specific answers to their questions. (In fairness, they rarely got answers from the other candidates, either.) Pundits and columnists mocked Rob as a one-line pony. But as they laughed at him, Ford's polling numbers went up. People were bored with him, they were frustrated, but they knew what he stood for. And what he stood for was resonating with them.

George Smitherman, on the other hand—many people didn't understand what he was saying. Asked about, for example, inclusionary housing policies, he would respond that they could "enliven each (development) to produce a quantum of units." Voters who didn't know what "quantum" meant were left scratching their heads. Ford knew that people didn't like to feel intellectually inferior, and he played to that. At a debate late in the campaign, Smitherman answered one question with a long, complex, poetic construction. Rob stared at him, then mouthed to me, "What the fuck did he say?" At a debate a few days later, he decided to ask it aloud. After Smitherman spoke, Ford looked out at the audience and said, "I don't know about you, but I have no idea what he just said." The room loved it.

The televised debates were another concern. An error on TV is magnified a thousand-fold compared to an error in a church basement. But Rob's attitude was always, "Bring it on." We'd agreed to a series of debates to be held in the studio of a twenty-four-hour news channel, CP24, and hosted by a popular personality and former politico named Stephen LeDrew. Our plan was, as always, to stay calm and stay on message.

We arrived early for the first debate. I parked a few blocks away, and we waded through a crowd of T-shirt-wearing, placard-waving campaign volunteers from every camp, who were jockeying for front-row positions outside the glass-walled studio, so their signs could be seen by the cameras inside. Rob sat in the makeup chair while they powdered his face and hair. We then found a quiet area in the back of the studio—it was under construction, and dusty—and did a quick prep.

Rob began to sweat and wheeze heavily. I found him some cold water, but his breathing got worse. He thought he was having an allergic reaction to the makeup; I thought the dust, heat, and his poor physical condition were bringing on an asthma attack. (I'd learned he had asthma a few weeks before. I've had it since I was a kid.) He didn't have a Ventolin inhaler. I feared he might drop dead right in front of me.

"Wait here," I said. "I have a puffer in my car." It was four minutes to airtime. My car was three blocks away. I ran.

I needed a few blasts on the puffer myself by the time I got back. I found Rob, bright red and wheezing, in his chair on the set, being fitted with a microphone. The countdown was starting. I ignored the floor director's protests, zipped up to Rob, and gave him the inhaler. He took three or four drags and handed it back to me. The debate began.

When the moderator introduced Rob, a few seconds after he had complained he couldn't even breathe, he smiled wide, leaned back and opened his arms in a welcoming gesture as if it were the best day of his life. He was a performer. Over our time together, I'd witness him whine and exaggerate an ailment to get out of doing his job on more than one occasion. But in public, he was always "great!"

From that debate onward, he refused to use makeup on TV. As a result, he always looked red and sweaty. Because he never got his own asthma inhaler, he suffered frequent respiratory illnesses and was hospitalized twice while mayor for complications related to it. His disregard for his own health had us wondering, even before he'd won the election in 2010, whether he'd survive to the end of his term.

The TV format turned out to be perfect for Rob. The segments were short and punchy. There was very little time for five candidates to say much. The host would throw to a reporter on the street who talked with passersby, then to another pretty host who would read an email or tweet, then to a commercial. During the commercials, I'd approach Rob, place my hand flat over his microphone to block the sound, and whisper advice in his ear. Rob did wonderfully. The other candidates fought like angry kids. Rob watched silently, smiling and shaking his head. Perfect.

At each subsequent CP24 debate, the field of candidates got smaller, like some weird form of musical chairs or reality TV competition. This meant the amount of time allotted for them to speak got longer, and the producers became more guarded against allowing political staff on or near the stage. We ignored them.

Throughout all of the debates before October, we'd kept Rob on a short leash. We wouldn't let him hit Smitherman too much over his connection to public scandals over waste and mismanagement at eHealth. Nick and I kept telling Rob: *Not yet. Let the others beat him up. Keep your cool. There will be a time, near the end, when he's not expecting it. Then you can whack him hard.*

That time came in one of the last CP24 televised debates. It was pretty much a two-man race at that point. Rob was raring to go. During a commercial break, Nick went up to Rob, covered the microphone, and whispered in his ear. Rob grinned. Now.

In the next segment, Rob blasted Smitherman with a prepared line about eHealth. Smitherman wasn't expecting it, and he bungled his response, sounding defensive and looking guilty. Rob was thrilled.

At each subsequent local debate, Rob kept hitting Smitherman with eHealth. Once per debate, but always at a different point. Soon Smitherman was flinching each time Rob spoke, wondering if this was the time he'd get smacked. Rob got bolder and wanted to branch out by hitting Smitherman with other failings he'd been accused of. The Night Shift was trying to brief Rob about a wind turbine scandal, or some other perceived grievance. We kept him focused with a simple analogy.

"When a boxer opens up a cut over his opponent's eye, he doesn't start hitting him in the kidneys. He keeps working the eye, making it bleed more and more." That's what we wanted Rob to do with eHealth. Simple. Effective. Rob got it. He hit hard.

At the final CP24 debate, I put a folder full of papers on the table beside Rob when he sat down. We made sure George saw it there, and Rob made sure George saw it when he moved it to the floor beside his chair as the camera lights came on. During the debate, we watched Smitherman's eyes repeatedly glance downward, looking at the folder. I imagined him wondering, "What's in there? When will Rob reach for it?" It had Smitherman squirming.

Ford never did reach for the folder, by the way. It was full of scrap paper.

***

Despite Rob's successes, by the middle of September, all of us were exhausted. Debates had focused on waterfront development, small business, accessibility for the disabled, seniors' issues, black community issues, building developers, realtors, church leaders, social housing concerns. We had to develop a policy position for each issue, then figure out how to bridge back to taxpayers' rights and the gravy train.

Organizers would build in three to ten minutes for opening and closing statements. The fact is, politicians are a lot like comedians: They have about three minutes of material. If you give them ten minutes, they'll usually keep talking, but you'll just hear the same thing three times. And if they can't make their point in one minute, they're in the wrong business. The bald truth is, smart politicians don't care what your question is. They're there to deliver their message.

By mid-September, the debates had answered every question the voters had about what the candidates stood for. They started to become a cheap evening of live theater. People would come to hoot and holler, cheer their favorites, and boo the villains. It was more professional wrestling than politics. In my opinion, Torontonians would be better served if mayoral candidates agreed to a half-dozen debates, all televised. Candidates could then spend some actual time *thinking* about their policies and platforms. Guys like me could spend time *developing policies and plans*. But this was the system, so we went with it, and made it work for us.

There was a problem, though: Rob wasn't sleeping.

The last debate or event of his day would normally finish at 10:00 or 11:00 p.m. It was rare that he got home before midnight. His wife Renata's aging parents looked after Rob's two children during the day. But they didn't do much housework, and they let the kids sleep all day. So Rob would stay up and clean, do laundry, and take care of his wide-awake kids. According to Rob, Renata wasn't much help around the house.

We kept trying to get Rob to go home during the day and sleep, or check into a hotel. He refused. "I'm okay, buddy," he'd say. But he wasn't okay.

One morning, during a debate about the city's waterfront development plans, hosted by residents and businesses on the lakeshore, Rob's performance was awful. He had two more debates that day; the evening one was going to be televised. Afterward, in a nearby parking garage, I told him I was going to pull him from the afternoon debate so he could get some sleep. He insisted he was fine. I insisted he wasn't. I told him he hadn't mentioned his message, that his answers hadn't made sense, that he'd stopped in the middle of sentences. At one point, when pushed, he'd even told people not to vote for him.

"Bullshit," he growled.

"You said it twice," I countered.

We exchanged a few more choice words and he got angry. It was the first time he'd gotten angry with me. He turned his back on me, climbed into my truck, and started returning calls. We drove in silence back to his house. I dropped him off and called Nick. Somehow, Nick got Rob to go to a hotel. I withdrew him from the afternoon debate.

Later, after Rob had admitted to a drug problem, I often wondered if he'd been using anything during this part of the campaign. I never thought so at the time, and I still don't. I've had a lot of experience with sleep deprivation from my years in the army, and Rob's behavior was classic. I think he was sober. But he was practically brain-dead from exhaustion.

Rob did speak during the campaign and afterward about others in his life who had struggled, or were still struggling, with drug addiction, but he did so with disgust and disdain. His behavior then was completely different from how it was later, when I began to suspect he was abusing alcohol, and later drugs.

# 10 | E Day

O N ELECTION DAY—OR E Day, as it's known among political operatives—I met Rob outside his house just after the polling stations opened at 10:00 in the morning. October 25, 2010, turned out to be a comfortably cool 64 degrees with no rain—ideal conditions for people heading to the polls. That was good news for us—we felt a higher turnout would only help us.

Adrienne Batra, our director of communication, and Isaac Shirokoff, Ford's body man, piled into the back of my SUV, while Rob wedged himself into the front passenger seat for the short drive to his neighborhood polling station. As soon as the door was closed, he was on his cell phone, telling Renata to get to the polling station, and to make sure her parents voted, too. (She was supposed to have come with us but apparently hadn't been ready when Rob wanted to go.) Then Rob called his mom, Diane, to see if she'd voted yet.

That short drive came at the end of a long road. Ford's team had been working toward this day for seven months, since the campaign formally began on March 25, 2010. This day's efforts, though, would be coordinated in large part by Earl Provost, then a forty-six-year-old longtime Liberal operative who'd worked for many federal, provincial, and municipal campaigns over the years. He had joined the campaign a month before just to plan and manage the E Day operation.

We'd recruited over three thousand volunteers and trained them specifically to work on this day. Each one needed to know where to go, when to go there, what to do, and how to do it. Before everyone identified by our Voter ID program as a Ford supporter woke up in the morning, volunteers had hung a door card reminding them when and where to vote. Every single polling station—and there were about fifteen hundred—had Ford volunteers in place from the minute it opened until the minute the ballot counting was complete. They were there as "scrutineers" to observe the process and see that only qualified voters cast ballots. Anyone not qualified was challenged. Each scrutineer had a list of Ford voters, and as they voted, the volunteer would strike their names off our lists. At regular intervals, the inside scrutineers would pass the names of those identified supporters who had not yet voted to outside scrutineers, who would knock on their doors and offer them a ride to the polling station. Scrutineers didn't need to attend the ballot counting—in Toronto municipal elections, ballots are counted electronically. But they observed the handling of the data cards from each ballot reading machine to ensure that nothing was changed or switched during the process.

Earl had set up and run dozens of training sessions so that every volunteer knew exactly how to do his or her job, and how to handle every "what if" that could conceivably happen during E Day. What if the polling station doesn't open or close on time? What if people try to vote twice? What if unqualified voters try to vote? It's a long day. My job was to be with the candidate, make sure he was ready for his speech, win or lose, and manage his movement through the post-election party.

The polling station in Rob's neighborhood was at the elementary school his daughter attended. It was mid-morning, not long after the polls had opened, when we parked up the street, got out, and did a quick body check. Adrienne adjusted her hair and sunglasses in the window of my truck while I straightened Rob's lapel pin and brushed some lint off his jacket.

Rob was nervous. He asked, "What do you think?" We assured him—it's done; you've won. "You think so? I don't know. Smitherman is close, man. I don't know."

We started walking down the sidewalk. As we came into sight of the front doors, a half-dozen shoulder-held news cameras plus a handful of photographers turned and charged.

"How do you feel, Rob?"

"Are you going to win?"

We continued walking, turning up the stairs and toward the school doors. Rob smiled and kept it light. "I feel good. It's up to the people of this great city."

The TV cameras stopped at the door, barred from entering the polling place. I stood back as Rob entered the polling area, walked up to the election official, and showed his ID. "I know who you are," the man said, smiling. Rob laughed. He wanted to do everything right.

He cast his ballot and we ran the gauntlet of media again on the way back to the car. I took him to the campaign office and dropped him off, then took off with Adrienne to do some advance work for the night's party.

The E Day party was set up at the Toronto Congress Centre—the same room where Rob had launched his campaign exactly seven months prior. Early in the morning, the parking lot was empty. But inside, the whirlwind of activity knocked me sideways. I'd been to a federal Conservative party convention where Prime Minister Stephen Harper had given a rousing speech to the party faithful, which was covered live by national news networks. And I was at the party leadership convention where Harper was crowned leader of the party. Both of those convention halls paled in comparison to what I saw at the Congress Centre.

The room set-up was massive. The stage against the far wall was a reasonable size, but there were risers being built all around the room for every imaginable TV network. It was far bigger than the federal party conventions. My first thought, after seven months beside Rob Ford, was *How much is this costing?*

Someone from the campaign team, I forget who, walked me through what was going where. In addition to the main stage, there were four or five media risers, plus a consolidated platform for journalists who didn't need live camera sets. I walked up onto the stage to check out the view, then walked behind the stage and through the curtain to find a back door. There was one that led directly out to an outside parking lot, and I made note of the door number that led into the backstage area.

Adrienne and I walked the floor and talked about how we would move Rob around after his speech: Exit stage left. Start with the CTV riser, which was set off to the side, then move clockwise to the other TV risers in the center of the room. We'd work him along those, then over to the radio lineup. Finally, we'd let him loose to work the room.

All the campaign staff, myself included, had voted in the advance polls, so we could focus on work during E Day. Rob kept busy doing a bit of mainstreeting—working selected locations, meeting people, shaking hands, and posing for pictures—and some media interviews, and went home early in the afternoon to be with his family. I dropped Adrienne at the campaign HQ, then sat down to drink too much coffee and go over the speeches one last time. Nick had asked for three: one if we lost, one if we won, and one if we won big. I'd spent most of my time working on the last one. In fact, I only really wrote two—I figured any win would be a "big win" as far as Rob was concerned. But I had also written a concession speech. It's bad luck not to have one.

Around 6:00 I went to the campaign office, where I met up with Sajid Rahman, a campaign volunteer and reserve army officer I called Saj, and three off-duty Ontario Provincial Police officers who'd been hired to provide close protection for Rob during the evening. Saj, Nick, and I also planned to stick close to Rob throughout the evening. Based on our other public events, we knew it was going to be a loud, boisterous crowd; it would take some effort to keep things calm around Rob. I suggested to the three OPP officers that we head over to the conference center for a walk-through. I'm pretty sure they thought I was nuts. They'd done this type of thing hundreds of times for VIPs, including foreign premiers and presidents, rock stars, and the pope. They were confident enough just to wing it. I, on the other hand, was a former infantry officer who'd had the adage, "Time spent in recce (reconnaissance) is seldom wasted," beaten into my skull by a succession of instructors, commanders, and real-life experience. I insisted.

We headed to the conference center and parked next to the back door behind the stage. The door was open. We walked in through the backstage area and right through the entire building to the front door, along the route I'd planned. The cops humored me.

They planned to do a standard box—one guy in front of Ford, and one on each side. Saj would bring up the rear, while I followed the lead officer, to guide the whole group. My plan was that Ford and his family would step off the campaign bus out front, go through the main doors, and turn left into a small room we'd set up as a greenroom, where he could do a final read-through of his speech and get himself sorted.

I made the OPP officers do the whole thing with me: Front door to greenroom. Greenroom to ballroom, via a long hallway. Ballroom door to the right side of the stage. Downstage left, around the loop of media risers. I made them walk the whole route, up and down the stairs to the stage, up and down the stairs of the risers. I pointed out where the washrooms and exits were and said our plan was to let him mingle for a while, then exit the same way we came in, when he was ready to go. If there was a problem, we'd extract him through the back door behind the stage and into my car and out of the area. They followed along, talking casually, straggling a bit. Not taking it too seriously. Another day on the job. I'm sure they thought I was a weekend warrior asshole cop wannabe.

I left my car where it was—outside the back door—and rode to Diane Ford's house with the police. In the basement rec room, where I'd attended the very first campaign meeting in mid-March, there was a spread of cold cuts laid out. This time, there was a nervous electricity in the air as the Ford family and friends gathered and talked nervously about how the election might go. Around 7:30, Rob arrived with Renata and the kids. He was dressed in a good suit and looked sharp. His mother fussed over his tie and collar points, which were always askew. He brushed her off.

Everyone was nervous. Rob chatted with friends and occupied himself with his two kids. Adrienne had handpicked some media to sit with the family. There were a couple of TV cameras and a number of photographers from the daily papers. (Not the *Toronto Star*, which we were shunning at the time.) As time ticked toward eight o'clock, when the polling stations would close, the family settled onto the overstuffed couches facing the large screen TV. Somebody changed the channels so each TV news cameraperson could shoot B-roll of the Fords watching his station. The kids pushed at each other and climbed all over Rob, who sat directly in front of the TV.

At eight o'clock, the polls closed. Rob called out, "Where's Renata? Come over here." She squeezed through the crowd, under the TV cameras, and sat down on the couch, pulling their daughter, Stephanie, onto her lap. The couch was full of family, fidgeting, trying to look confident for the media. Somebody called for the volume to be turned up.

Behind the couch stood a row of family friends and a few Ford staffers, including me. A few minutes after eight, the first results started scrolling across the screen. Some well-known councillors were reelected within minutes; others looked like they were in trouble. The first results appeared showing Doug Ford leading in Ward 2. The room cheered.

Then a banner appeared on the screen. I read it aloud: "Rob Ford Elected." It was only 8:08 p.m.

The nail-biter that everyone had expected, based on late polls that had Smitherman running neck and neck with Rob, never happened. It took only eight minutes for enough ballots to be counted electronically to declare Ford the sixty-fourth mayor of Toronto.

I had to say it a second time before people heard me. Rob had won.

The room went crazy. Ford stood up, embraced his wife and kids, then his mother, brothers, and sister. Cameras flashed. TV cameras streamed the reaction live to their networks. We watched the live shot of ourselves on television. It was surreal. Eventually, I made my way through the crowd and shook Rob's hand. He was beaming. Beaming and sweaty.

My phone rang: it was a staffer for Dalton McGuinty, the premier of Ontario, who wanted to speak with Rob. I handed him the phone.

Smitherman and Pantalone called next and conceded, politely and briefly. The room was loud and I could barely hear Rob speaking on the phone. It wasn't yet clear how big the win had been, but the media were reporting it as a commanding win. We would later learn Rob had won just over 47 percent of the votes cast; Smitherman took 35 percent.

I called Nick, still at the campaign office, who was jubilant, and we talked about when Rob should go to the hall. We didn't want him to go too soon, because the other candidates hadn't made their concession speeches yet, and most of the E Day volunteers were still in transit from their polling stations. In fact, many of them spent the next hour making their way back to campaign HQ to hand in their scrutineering records. Some using transit, others in cars not listening to radio, only learned about the victory when they arrived. The election was settled that quickly.

The speed caught everyone by surprise. Pundits on TV and radio stations across the city had expected to fill an hour or more of airtime with theories and speculation. Instead, by minute ten, they were out of material.

Adrienne shooed the media out of the house and the family spent some time absorbing the magnitude of what had just happened. Somebody took the kids home, and Rob, Renata, and the rest of the family prepared to go to the hall. It was well after 9:00 p.m. when we piled into the campaign RV and headed to the party. I stopped the vehicle about five hundred yards short of the front doors and reminded everyone, once again, what was going to happen. The three policemen, Saj, Nick, and I would exit first, then Rob and Renata, and we'd head into the hall. The rest of the family would follow on and make their way to the stage. Adrienne would meet us at the front door. That was the plan. They all thought I was nuts.

Tom Beyer put the RV in gear and we started moving forward again, to the front door of the hall—or rather, as close to the front door as we could get. We had to stop about forty feet away because of the mayhem outside. We opened the bus door and I stepped out into chaos.

As soon as my feet hit the ground, we were hit with a wall of sound—supporters cheering, reporters shouting questions. It was deafening. The lights of about two dozen TV cameras blinded me. All I could see was an inferno of light and the feet of the camera people. People piled out behind me and we formed up around Rob and Renata as we'd rehearsed. I pointed to an open door—not the main door; one I'd spotted earlier—and shouted at the cops that we were going in that way. Rob was already sweating profusely, blinded, and blinking rapidly. I grabbed him by the arm, yelled, "Follow me!" and we pushed forward into bodies.

The cameras didn't give way. Instead, they enveloped us, blinding us further. I could smell the bodies of the camera operators as our protective circle tightened around Rob and Renata until we were almost touching each other. Slowly, we inched forward and through the door. The route to the greenroom was blocked with people, so I tapped the lead sergeant on the shoulder and yelled at him that we were going straight to the ballroom. He turned right and our pod followed, accumulating more media and supporters as we moved, getting bigger and slower with each step.

During our rehearsal, it had taken us about one minute to walk from the front door to the ballroom entrance. Surrounded by the screaming horde, able to see only the lower legs of the camera operators in front of us, and the black live-feed power cables they trailed, it took ten. I yelled for the people behind me to watch their step as the camera cables uncoiled and snaked beneath our feet. I looked over my shoulder and saw Rob, holding Renata close, both dazed and disoriented. We pushed ahead.

We had planned to stop at the ballroom doors so Adrienne could cue Rob's entrance music. That was no longer an option. If we stopped, we'd never get started again. As we reached the ballroom, we oozed through the doorway, a mob of people squeezing tight around the nucleus of our pod and then expanding out into the cavernous room. Except the cavernous room wasn't cavernous anymore. It was full of people. Thousands of people. All not only standing in our way, but also surging toward us. Yelling. Pushing. Cheering. Shoving.

The pressure of the crowd squeezed in on the media. The media squeezed in on us. Our progress slowed to a crawl. It was like pushing through a mudslide. I slid my left foot forward. Braced. Moved my right foot up. Repeat. Rob and Renata were crushed together. We'd lost the Ford family a while back. I was pressed against the lead policeman and Nick. It was getting hard to breathe.

I started pushing back on the crowd with all my strength. They didn't move. It was worse than the riots I'd experienced in Africa. I elbowed somebody to get them to move and they eased away a few inches. We lurched forward an inch. I stomped down hard on someone's foot and he pulled it back. We pushed forward another inch.

The people around our pod were smeared against us as we passed them. I could feel my suit jacket being pulled behind me as it caught on arms and elbows. I was worried for my phone and my wallet in my jacket pocket. I saw the policeman in front of me fighting the same battle. I wondered if he was armed and thanked God I wasn't a soldier anymore. I'd be freaked out about losing my weapon in a mob like this.

At one point, my head down, I caught sight of a baby stroller behind the legs of a cameraman in front of us. "Baby!" I yelled. Somehow, the camera guy avoided falling backward over the baby carriage and we oozed around the stroller. I never saw if there was a child inside.

It took us about thirty more minutes to get Rob onstage. We were all panting. Rob was dripping in sweat. Renata was completely frazzled. It had been terrifying. It had also been exhilarating. It was a physical engagement. Like running a race or finishing a workout. In the middle of a hurricane. We had literally pushed hundreds of people ahead of us out of our way.

The stage was packed with dozens of cheering people. I had no idea who they were. We'd planned to have some family, friends, and volunteers up there as a visual backdrop for Rob's speech, but there were dozens more. I got Rob up on the stage and found water for him. There was no time for him to collect himself. Over the din of the crowd, I could vaguely hear Rob's victory theme song, "Eye of the Tiger" by Survivor, wrapping up.

The speech was folded in half inside my jacket pocket. I pulled it out, checked that it was in order, and placed it on the podium. Rob followed me to the podium. I headed for the exit stairs.

"Thank you, thank you, thank you very much!"

"Toronto now is open for business, ladies and gentlemen. Seven months ago, we began this journey together right here at the Toronto Conference Centre. We fought a long, hard campaign. We were disciplined. We were creative. We were tireless. Tonight we celebrate victory."

"But this is not just my victory . . . this is a victory for every single person that lives and works in this great city of Toronto."

A few sentences in, some jackass reached over Rob's head from behind and put a multicolored lei around his neck. Rob looked startled and I was off like a shot. Video coverage of Rob's speech shows me crossing the stage like a bullet, in front of the podium, to grab the guy and scream at him to back off before he put a second string around Rob's neck. Randy, who was standing a row or two behind Rob, reached forward and pulled the guy back. Rob was startled, but he just adjusted the lei and continued reading.

As Rob resumed speaking, I tapped the uniformed policeman at the foot of the stairs and yelled, "No more up here!" He started pulling people off the stairs. There were way too many people on the stage; I could feel it swaying and trembling under us as the crowd of people behind Rob jumped and cheered.

Near the beginning of the speech, I'd included a reference to Rob's dad, Doug Sr., because I knew Rob would want to thank him. I also knew it would make him emotional, soften him so that he didn't look like he was gloating. It worked well. As he thanked his father, he looked up to the heavens and his voice wavered, his eyes watering. He looked humbled. He looked human.

After the speech we formed up again and made the same mad, slow-motion crawl through the crowd. Everyone in the building wanted to shake Rob's hand, give him a hug, and have a private moment with him. They were mostly volunteers and hardcore Ford supporters who'd worked tirelessly through the campaign. Rob wanted to talk with them, but the scene was too manic. We had to push on, get to the TV risers for media interviews.

By the time we'd worked through the TV stations, which took the better part of an hour, Rob was physically and emotionally spent. Then the first TV crew asked us to go back because their audio hadn't recorded properly. Looking over the sweltering, writhing sea of humanity between us and the first riser, the answer was obvious: No way.

Rob's eyes were dull with exhaustion. I asked if he wanted to work the crowd, or get out of there. He wanted to go. I tapped the lead cop on the shoulder: "Door 2—back door." We began the slow push back to the main stage, behind the curtain, and through the back door into sudden cool silence. We all stopped outside the door and caught our breath.

The senior cop looked at me and said, "That was nuts." He and his two colleagues had worked protective details for years, through the craziest rock concerts, VIP protection, and even the Toronto G20 summit, which had occurred a few months prior, complete with violent street protests, millions of dollars in property damage, and torched police cars. "I've never, ever seen anything like that," he added. I hadn't either. Not in Africa. Not in the Middle East. Not in Afghanistan.

But that was the Rob Ford factor. Later, during his term as mayor, everywhere he went, the crowds were the same. He was like a rock star, or some magical totem. Everyone felt they knew him. Everyone wanted to touch him, to take a picture with him, to have a moment with him. From the steel and stone Bay Street financial district to the social-assistance apartment towers that housed the city's impoverished families, it was the same: Ford was greeted by name and quickly surrounded by a sea of normal people going nuts. Even before Jimmy Kimmel. Even at the beginning. If you saw it, you might better understand how he hung on so long.

# PART II | THE EARLY DAYS: OCTOBER 2010–MARCH 2012

# 11 | A Cherry on Top

THE MORNING AFTER the election, I woke up around eight. It was October 26, 2010. Rob would be sworn in as mayor on December 1. We had thirty-six days to learn how to run a city, hire an office staff, figure out who the mayor would appoint to key positions in his administration, get a handle on the city's $13 billion budget—which had to be approved early in the new year—and work out a legislative calendar that would translate the campaign platform into actions to produce results on a one hundred-day, one-year, and four-year basis. (Media loved reporting on major milestones such as the "first one hundred days" of an administration.) Campaign days were long and exhausting. The next month would see even longer days, but they would be exhilarating.

During the campaign, I had precisely one conversation with Rob about what would happen during the transition if he won. It was about 10 p.m., two weeks from the election; we were driving back from an evening debate in the east end of the city, and things were looking good. In a quiet moment, I said I was going to start working with Nick on what the structure of the mayor's office would look like. We'd have to figure out what positions we needed and how many people would be required.

"David Miller [the outgoing mayor] had twenty-five staffers," Rob said. "That's ridiculous."

He admitted that Miller had always been well-briefed, though. Miller had two or three executive assistants; Rob figured he'd need two or three EAs as well. Rob didn't seem to have any idea what Miller's other staffers did—he just knew there were too many of them. At some point, he decided to have eighteen staff members in his office. He somehow intuited that this was the right number—demonstrably fewer than Miller's twenty-five.

The previous council had approved an increase in the mayor's office budget—which covered all its expenses including salaries, benefits, office supplies, and transportation—from $2 million to $2.7 million. Rob was determined to reverse that increase back to $2 million. Of all the mistakes we made in the Ford administration, under-resourcing the mayor's office was the first—and the biggest. Slashing the budget and staff size was consistent with the Ford brand. But it severely impaired our ability to effectively lead the sixth-largest government in Canada.

To make matters worse, Rob never actually approved hiring eighteen people, and the office always ran below strength. We peaked at seventeen during Amir Remtulla's tenure as chief of staff. During my tenure we never had more than fourteen. As well, Ford personally vetoed many of the office expenses that would have made our team more efficient and capable, and always under-spent the budget—even after reducing it by 26 percent.

Two days after the election, Nick and I found our way to the sixteenth floor of the west tower at City Hall. It may be an iconic building, but as a practical workspace it leaves much to be desired. The sixteenth floor, like all floors in the towers, was shaped like a banana. The elevators arrived mid-banana on the outside curve, where a glass door required a security pass. Just outside the door was a small desk staffed by a friendly receptionist. She ushered us through the doors into a small meeting room near the entrance.

The sixteenth floor "banana" was about 100 yards from tip to tip, with floor-to-ceiling windows lining the inside curve, which looked down onto the roof of the flying-saucer-like council chamber and beyond to the broad concrete expanse of the city's central public square. A chain of decent-sized cubicles lined the windows, providing about two dozen workstations. The longer outside curve of the banana was windowless and punctuated by four private offices, a small boardroom, a kitchenette, washrooms, and fire stairs.

We sat down in the small boardroom and were introduced to the city's senior staff: Joe Pennachetti was a professional-looking, silver-haired accountant who had been running the city, as city manager, since 2008. He had three deputy city managers reporting directly to him: Sue Corke ran "Cluster A"—the city's soft services, including shelters, housing and social services, parks and recreation, and emergency medical services. Richard Butts managed "Cluster B"—the city's hard services, including transportation, fire services, water and sewers, and solid waste. Cam Weldon was the third deputy city manager and the city's chief financial officer.

We also met that day with Ulli Watkiss, the city clerk, who didn't report to the city manager; she and her staff worked directly for City Council, managing and supporting the city's legislative process.

We were provided with three blue binders—plus one red one, for urgent issues requiring decisions before December 1—as well as a sheaf of spreadsheets and notes. The first order of business was to schedule a series of briefings for the mayor and transition team.

The rest of the transition team was still being identified. I was happy to be part of it. After the conversation I'd had with Rob, where he said he wanted three EAs, I'd told him I'd enjoyed working with him on the campaign and hoped I'd be able to help him put his policies into action. I'll never forget his answer.

"I can't make any promises," Rob said, in the tone of voice he used on the telephone with strangers. "I've got a lot of people asking for jobs and we'll have to see."

Even after working alongside Rob Ford for seven months at that point, I was still surprised. I didn't say anything, but I took it up with Nick that night during our regular Arizona debrief. "I haven't gone through hell with this guy just so he 'can't promise me anything,'" I said. Fact of the matter was, I was so underwater financially at that point that if Rob didn't hire me, I'd probably wind up homeless.

Nick laughed. "You'll be on the transition team," he assured me. "We've asked Case Ootes [the outgoing deputy mayor] to chair it." Ootes was a good choice. A staunch conservative voice on previous councils, he had chosen not to run for reelection in 2010 and was widely respected as a calm, straight shooter by everyone at City Hall.

The rest of the team included Doug Ford, because he was Doug Ford; Gordon Chong, a former municipal and regional politician who'd been out of politics for a while but had conservative leanings and knew a lot about transit; Amir Remtulla, who had once been Ootes's EA and was now a public affairs manager at a major Canadian beer company; Claire Tucker-Reid, a management consultant who had spent six years as an executive in the city's civil service; and from the campaign team, Nick Kouvalis and me. The whole team met almost daily—often with senior civil servants to brief us on specific issues, sometimes without them to brainstorm strategy or discuss the political side of the equation.

Well, almost the whole team. Rob and Doug were wildcards. Rob attended some of the meetings, but not many—and mostly toward the end, when we needed decisions on political appointments. He was busy attending events as the mayor-elect and still-sitting councillor for Ward 2. We were receiving about one hundred invitations each day, and simply reviewing them, deciding which to attend, and scheduling them was a Herculean task that required us to bring on two administrative staff earlier than expected. I imagined that Rob was also reconnecting with his wife and children after a grueling seven-month campaign of twenty-hour days, but I was never sure what he was up to.

Doug popped in and out randomly. When Doug came to a meeting, it was normally twenty minutes after it had started, and he expected us to go back to the beginning to bring him up to speed. This would take at least ten minutes. Then he'd tell us who he'd been talking with on his own, and he'd make suggestions related to those conversations that often had nothing to do with the meeting we were having. He'd participate in the next ten or fifteen minutes of the meeting. Then he'd step out to make a phone call or have a cigarette and we wouldn't see him again until he popped into another meeting later in the day, or the week.

Nick and I were accustomed to this and barely noticed it. The others, however, quickly grew exasperated. They wanted to meet without telling Doug when we were meeting. Nick ensured that didn't happen. We'd learned during the campaign that to manage Doug well, we had to keep him apprised as much as possible.

Another challenge in working with Doug: He was chatty. With everyone, including his new media "friends" who were investing valuable time developing buddy relationships with him. More than once, information that we considered secret, including people under consideration for key appointments, made its way into the news. Our suspicions that Doug was the source were confirmed one day in the middle of November, when we were discussing one key appointment and had almost settled on a recommendation, then realized we couldn't do it because it conflicted under the complex rules surrounding who could sit on which board. So we had to change course and select someone else. But Doug had left the meeting before we made the change. As far as he knew, Person A was our choice. And that's what the newspapers printed the next morning. There was only one person who knew we had discussed her, but who didn't know we had "unchosen" her: Doug Ford.

We began to guard our conversations around Doug. It wasn't like he was trying to leak information; I'm convinced he was unable to help himself. When he was talking to "friends," information just dribbled out like spittle from a baby's mouth.

Near the end of transition, Nick and I were discussing sensitive plans to adjust the 2011 budget with the city manager, CFO, and budget director Josie La Vita. It was important that the information not leak out until we could present the whole story. Otherwise, the opposition would have time to mobilize and make the changes much more difficult. The civil servants expressed concern that our transition team was leaking information and were worried about sharing a surplus projection with us. I explained that we knew who our leak was and, "without naming names, we'd like to suggest we change the topic if Doug Ford joins the meeting."

They were incredulous, but when Doug entered the meeting midway, I quietly flipped over the projection document we were discussing and slid it under my notebook, and everyone else did the same. We chatted with Doug for ten minutes about a number of off-topic subjects he brought up. After he excused himself and left, we pulled out the sensitive document and continued our conversation. That information never leaked.

That month didn't seem to have enough days, and I often found myself leaving City Hall after 10:00 or 11:00 at night. Normally, the only person on the transition team still working that late would be Nick. He and I would walk out together through the empty rotunda, avoiding the custodian who rode around on a small floor-polishing machine, buffing to a high sheen the Carrera marble floor that had been specified by the building's Finnish architect and imported from Italy, then hand-cut into strips in Canada and laid down. The only other souls at work in the building were cleaners who'd come by the sixteenth floor to empty trash baskets. I made a point of saying hello to them every night—not only because they deserved my respect, but also because they had access to all of our offices after hours. Likewise, I made a point of always stopping to chat with the officers at the security desk just inside the main door of City Hall. Maybe it was the ex-army officer in me—or maybe I was just being shrewd. But it made sense to me to earn the trust and respect of the security staff. I had no doubt they would be valuable allies throughout our time at City Hall. Though even I couldn't have imagined how big a role they'd play once Ford was mayor.

Once we moved into the mayor's office, I could have taken the elevator directly outside my office right to the parking garage. Instead, I almost always walked around the mezzanine and down the stairs so I'd pass the security desk. It was important to be seen as working hard. I have no doubt they noted that the mayor's staff were almost always the last people out of the building every day. Leadership by example.

***

I was late to a budget meeting with the city manager, CFO, and budget director one afternoon near the end of the transition. It was a rare full house, with the entire transition team there, including Rob seated at the head of the table, looking uncomfortable as usual. I squeezed into the room just as the meeting began and took a seat jammed in the corner against the wall.

The staff was going to brief us on the latest budget surplus projections. At every meeting, the projected amount of money from the 2010 budget that would be unspent by year-end kept growing and growing. Its abundance had already caused us to consider changing our fiscal strategy going forward in 2011.

"Tell me you've found us more money," Nick said, smiling at the CFO.

Cam adjusted his glasses and looked down at his spreadsheet, which he held in both hands. Squaring his shoulders, he began.

"Well, we've found you more money," he said, with his slightly lopsided grin.

"If it's $240 million, I'll kiss you," I proposed. That was the amount we needed to allow the mayor to freeze taxes for a year, something he hadn't promised, but had just recently decided he wanted to do.

"The new projection for the surplus, which I think is about 99 percent final, is about $270 million," Weldon said.

"*I'll* kiss you," Nick laughed.

"Awesome," I said. "You, sir, can stay!"

Conversation stopped. The room fell silent. The silence became awkward. I was confused.

For years, whenever someone on one of my teams had done something exceptional, I'd often replied by joking, "You can stay!" As if I would, or could, get rid of everyone else for less than stellar performance. It always got a laugh. Slowly, it dawned on me that the city staff didn't know I was joking. Apparently, neither did the transition team. I realized that, as far as everyone was concerned, we might be able to fire people. Certainly, there were many City Hall observers who'd predicted that Rob Ford would begin his reign as mayor by firing senior managers by the truckload. Oops.

"I was joking," I said, trying (but failing) to ease the tension. Regardless, the meeting continued, and I stopped trying to be funny for a while.

Rob just shook his head and plowed ahead. "So this means I can freeze taxes next year?" he asked.

The staff groaned.

***

Many nights, as we walked out of the building, Nick and I would discuss Rob's future as mayor. Nick believed Rob could be a multi-term mayor if he didn't screw up. I still felt he was likely to be a one-term, turn-around mayor. We were both concerned about his health. It had never occurred to me that he was abusing drugs or alcohol, and I'm convinced he wasn't then. But he never looked well. He was at least 330 pounds. He was forever out of breath and horking gobs of phlegm into wastebaskets or out of car windows. I knew he had asthma and wasn't doing anything to manage it. He ate crap and didn't sleep. He was a mess.

From the midpoint of the 2010 campaign on, Nick and I talked openly about whether Rob would survive to the 2014 election. For me, the odds of his living out his first term were never better than 50/50.

***

There are two processes by which city councillors are selected for various committees, boards, commissions, and other appointments in Toronto's government. Newly-elected councillors are each provided with a survey that asks them to indicate what they want to do. By law, they must each sit on at least one of Toronto's seven standing committees, so they are asked to provide their first, second, and third choice for those committees. They are then also asked to indicate which of about four dozen other committees, boards, or commissions they are interested in.

The city clerk receives the completed survey forms from councillors and collates them into one master document listing the choices and preferences of all the councillors. This document is then submitted to the Striking Committee, which decides who goes where and makes a recommendation to the full City Council, which ratifies the appointments.

That's the official process. But that's not how it actually works. It takes hours to go through the councillors' preferences and come up with a plan that gives most, if not all, of them some satisfaction. The process is complicated because many committees and boards have unique rules. The chair of the Toronto Transit Commission, for example, cannot also be the chair of a standing committee. No one who sits on the Audit Committee may chair a standing committee or sit on the Budget Committee. Members of the Striking Committee can be appointed to only one of the Police Services Board or the board of the Sony Centre for the Performing Arts, but not both.

Add to this the fact that some appointments are more popular than others, and it becomes a dog's breakfast. No councillors, for example, ever want to sit on the pension boards, and few are interested in the Audit Committee. Some of them will inevitably be required to accept appointments they don't want.

So it's a good thing that a mayor's transition team has about half a month to go through all the councillors' responses to figure out how best to satisfy the greatest number of councillors. The transition team then drafts a recommended slate of appointments, which the committee chair (who is the mayor or the deputy mayor, at the mayor's discretion) can propose at its first meeting. They normally approve that slate without much discussion and it goes on to Council, where it is generally ratified without change. Why does the slate get such easy passage through the Striking Committee and Council? Politics.

In the Toronto municipal government, the mayor has some powers and many responsibilities beyond those of a normal councillor. But like a councillor, the mayor only gets one vote on any matter. So to pass something through Toronto's forty-five-member council—for example, a key part of the mayor's campaign platform—the mayor must woo twenty-two councillors to vote with him.

One of the most critical priorities of the transition team is to build a coalition of councillors who will support the mayor's key agenda items. In 2010, I developed a complicated spreadsheet to build a solution to the appointment puzzle, ensuring that all the rules were followed, that as many councillor requests as possible were fulfilled, and that the mayor was able to build a trustworthy coalition that could pass his agenda through Council. To build that coalition, we color-coded councillors: blue, yellow, and red. "Blue" councillors were those we believed would be ideologically aligned with Ford and support most of his key mandates. "Red" councillors were those most opposed to Ford's ideas, whom we expected would form the de facto opposition and fight Ford on every item. Those councillors in the middle, who might support some but not all of Ford's priorities, were the "Yellow Team," and we'd have to woo their support on an issue-by-issue basis.

By the end of transition, we felt Ford could count about twenty-three councillors on his Blue Team, leaving fifteen on the Red Team and about seven on the Yellow Team. But it didn't start that way.

This is where politics comes in. To assure the mayor twenty-three votes on his key items, it was necessary to extract allegiance from councillors.

That allegiance could be influenced by rewarding councillors with their preferred appointments—and by bestowing certain choice appointments the mayor could dish out at will.

For example, the mayor could directly appoint the deputy mayor and each of the chairs of the seven standing committees. In exchange for these high-profile positions, councillors got no extra pay, staff, or perks; they were expected to work longer hours on harder files. Their boon, however, was the high profile that came with these positions—and in Toronto, profile means reelectability. So Rob could reward those who'd already supported him and secure obeisance from others in exchange for one of these appointments.

After Doug won his seat as councillor for Ward 2, he expected to be appointed deputy mayor. He seemed to believe that Toronto had elected him co-mayor, and he saw himself running the city at his brother's side, filling in for him when he wasn't available. But because Rob could be assured of Doug's vote on any issue, handing him a prime appointment would be a wasted opportunity to secure someone else's allegiance. Doug wasn't happy about it, but he recognized Rob needed every bit of leverage to build a coalition.

With Rob and Doug Ford's votes assured, plus those of the appointed deputy mayor and seven committee chairs, the Ford administration could count on ten votes. Thirteen more to go.

Other key appointments included the Speaker and Deputy Speaker of Council and the chair of the Toronto Transit Commission (TTC). We decided to reward Councillor Frances Nunziata, who had been a long-standing friend and ally to Rob, with the Speaker's role—it was the only thing she wanted and she'd had direct discussions with Rob about it during the campaign. As Deputy Speaker, we selected John Parker, an articulate lawyer and early convert to Ford. We thought he'd be a stable, even-handed counterpoint to Nunziata, who could get a little worked up at times.

We had long discussions about the role of TTC chair. It was both a high-profile position and one of the few that came with additional staff and budget flexibility. It would also be a critically important role in the execution of Ford's subway strategy. We batted around a number of ideas. Councillor Denzil Minnan-Wong was a stalwart fiscal conservative who had been critical of TTC management. Where did he stand on subways? Councillor Karen Stintz was a well-respected fiscal conservative who seemed ready to take on a leadership role. If she was willing to spearhead the subway file, she could add a much-needed female voice to Ford's leadership team.

Rob, however, vetoed both Stintz and Minnan-Wong, because "they'll use it as an opportunity to campaign for mayor in 2014."

I pointed out that all forty-four councillors would be thinking about running for mayor in 2014. Especially after Rob had proved that the right long shot candidate could win. "They all want to be mayor," I explained. "But you are *the* mayor. If voters like what you've done in 2014, they'll reelect you—not them. Why would they want someone who'd been close to Ford, when they can have Ford?

"And if voters don't like what you've done," I added, "the team that's been close to you will go down with you. So keep them close."

In the end, we nominated Stintz for TTC chair. I still think it was the right decision. But it didn't work out as we'd hoped.

We added two rookie councillors, both bright women new to politics, to the mayor's executive committee. We needed more women on the team and we also thought it would be helpful to have some fresh perspectives on the Executive. Everyone else was a veteran politician. We were not, however, able to achieve the geographic balance we wanted.

For matters of extremely local interest—adding stop signs, pedestrian crossings, local building issues, etc.—Toronto City Council is subdivided geographically into four Community Councils. Each city councillor sits, with his neighboring councillors, on one of these Community Councils. Together, they deal with those local matters so the entire forty-five member City Council doesn't have to. At least, that's the theory. I'm not sure it ever worked as well as intended.

We wanted to include councillors from each Community Council on the executive committee, to provide geographic representation from the entire city. But the hard truth was, no councillors from the downtown community would support Ford's agenda. We couldn't afford to waste a position for tokenism.

At the end of the process, we had a coalition of up to thirty councillors, including twenty-three we considered Blue Team members (though some of those were soft), and seven Yellow Team councillors whose votes we could get on a case-by-case basis for important issues. We then balanced the membership on the committees to create strength in the areas where we needed it. Rob was most concerned that he be able to control the big money committees—those that managed significant budgets: the Government Management, Public Works and Infrastructure, and Planning and Growth committees. We ensured four of the six members on each of those committees were Blue Team councillors and balanced out the rest. We made a conscious decision to sacrifice the Community Development and Recreation committee to the left and loaded it up with Red Team councillors who would never support Ford. To spend money, they would have to get the Budget Committee to approve their budgets, and we made sure that committee was loaded with fiscal conservatives.

Along with reviewing the city clerk's official survey, Nick and Case Ootes met with every councillor to ask them what they wanted to do and to find out what parts of the mayor's agenda they supported. Nick developed a four-stage ask: Would they support the elimination of the $60 vehicle registration tax; would they support making the TTC an essential service; would they support reducing councillors' office budgets; and would they pass a slate of candidates nominated by the Striking Committee without amendments if they were reasonably happy with their appointments?

We promised nothing in return, but took scrupulous notes of their bottom line asks. *What did they really want to do in this four-year term?* From that we looked for areas of alignment with the mayor's agenda. Rob Ford, who should have been leading this process—meeting personally with each and every councillor—wanted no part of it. It was the first indication that he simply wasn't interested in the leadership responsibilities that came with being the head of the council in Canada's largest city.

***

One of the least important tasks of the transition team was to select a special guest who would drape the Chain of Office on the mayor at the formal First Meeting, which served as the council's de facto inauguration. In the United States, the president is sworn into office by the chief justice of the Supreme Court. In Canada, the prime minister is sworn in by the governor general of Canada. In Toronto, there is no formal rule about who invests the mayor. The official oath would be administered in private by the city clerk, a commissioner of oaths and the officer of the city responsible for overseeing and validating the election results. The public inauguration of the mayor was traditionally done by a dignitary such as a senior judge, cleric, or other VIP of importance to the city. But Rob Ford was not a traditional mayor.

We wanted to kick off Rob's term with a different flavor, so we spent some time considering who to invite as the mayor's special guest. We didn't want a judge or cleric. The premier was a Liberal and Rob, a die-hard member of the Conservative party, didn't want a Liberal. The prime minister would never accept, lest he be obliged to do the same for every other mayor in the land.

As a joke, I suggested Don Cherry. Cherry is a household name in Canada; he's a colorful and frequently controversial hockey commentator known for his loud fashion sense and his louder, opinionated "Coach's Corner" segment on every episode of the CBC's *Hockey Night in Canada*. A former professional hockey player and coach of the NHL's Boston Bruins, Cherry exemplified Canada's blue-collar everyman. Born in Kingston, Ontario, he lived in Mississauga, a suburb west of Toronto.

After going around the horn and back again on a dozen high-caliber candidates, we kept coming back to Cherry. Would it work? Would he do it? Doug got Cherry's number and asked him. Cherry loved the idea. If nothing else, we thought anything Cherry said would likely be more controversial than anything Rob would say, so if Rob made an error, no one would notice.

I called Cherry to arrange the details. Although he's infamous as a no-nonsense, tough-talking, insensitive bruiser of a commentator, on the phone he sounded like a sweet, hesitant grandfather. His main concern was driving into the city and where he'd be able to park. I assured him we would send a car to get him and to take him home.

On inauguration day, I was excited to meet Cherry. He arrived on schedule in a car driven by one of our staff members—right up onto the main square, normally out of bounds for vehicles. He stepped out of the car in front of City Hall's main doors resplendent in his trademark peacock clothes: eye-dazzling pink suit jacket, oversized collar, and a white silk tie.

I told him I loved his suits. He shook my hand, shot me the look I'd seen a thousand times on television, and, in the voice he used to berate a lackluster on-ice effort, said, "I don't wear suits. I wear jackets."

After draping the gold chain of office around Rob Ford's neck, Cherry addressed the assembled crowd of newly elected and reelected city councillors, their families, senior city staff, and media. He had refused to provide us with a copy of his remarks, though he'd allowed us to suggest some general topics he might choose to cover: Rob Ford as a new kind of mayor, fighting for the little guy. In any case, he spoke off the cuff. It certainly proved to be a distraction from anything Ford said that day.

"I'm wearing pink for all the pinkos out there that ride bicycles and everything," he began.

Apparently, Cherry felt the need to defend his appearance at Toronto's City Hall. His selection as the special guest for the investiture hadn't pleased the city's news media.

"You know, I am befuddled, because I thought I was just doing a good thing, coming down with Ron—Rob—and I was going to do this here, and it was going to be nice and the whole deal. I've been being ripped to shreds by the left wing pinko newspapers out there. It's unbelievable. One guy called me a jerk in a pink suit, so I thought I'd wear this for him too, today.

"This is the kind of thing you're going to be facing, Rob, with these left-wing pinkos," Cherry continued. "They scrape the bottom of the barrel. I was asked 'why' [was I going to do this today] and I asked Doug, 'Why?' And he said, 'We need a famous, good-looking guy.' And I said, 'I'm your man, right?' Right off the bat."

Cherry concluded his brief remarks with, "That's why I say he's going to be the greatest mayor this city has ever, ever seen, as far as I'm concerned. Put that in your pipe, you left-wing kooks!"

I thought he'd gone a little over the top, but I was sure no one would be talking about any mistakes Rob might make during his speech. I didn't realize it then, but the left-wing cohort on Council, and within the city's political activist community, interpreted Don Cherry's presence and his speech as a declaration of war. We would be under siege from day one. In a matter of days, lapel buttons reading "Pinko" appeared on the jackets of bike riders all over the city.

*\*\**

To my surprise, we had almost no interaction with the outgoing mayor's staff. Rob Ford and David Miller never met. Miller hadn't named a chief of staff, but he had two senior EAs who, together, fulfilled much the same role. Nick met with one of them, Bruce Scott, once or twice. I met once each with Scott and with Stuart Green, Miller's other senior EA, essentially his communication director. The meetings were brief. And that was it.

We had one tour through the offices after hours, before the handover date, and were provided with a blueprint of the office space. I did up an office plan and we waited patiently to get into the suite so we could be set up and running before the official first day. That didn't happen. Miller's staff didn't move out of the mayor's office until close of business on the last day—leaving us to operate the mayor's office out of the transition team space on the sixteenth floor for a number of days while city staffers repainted the walls and cleaned the carpets.

The handover of city government from one administration to another was unlike any other handover I've ever had, in the military or in business. Normally, continuity of operations would be a primary concern. Not so in politics. When the new guard marches in, it starts fresh, as if there had been no administration before it.

When we finally moved into the mayor's office suite, the filing cabinets and desk drawers were empty—save for a half dozen packets of gravy mix, a tribute from Miller's staff to Ford's "Stop the Gravy Train" election mantra. We took it in the good humor with which we assumed it was intended.

\*\*\*

December was a mad month of twenty-hour days and rapid-fire successes. We were all looking forward to taking a few well-deserved days off over the Christmas period. There wouldn't be many days of rest, as we had a budget to put together, but we all wanted to squeeze every ounce of rest we could from each of them.

During his first Christmas season as mayor, Rob was obsessed with shift schedules. While I was working daily with the city manager and CFO on how to balance the city's $13 billion budget, which would be launched in early January, Rob was worried about who was going to answer the office phone on Christmas Day.

With Doug and Nick out of town on a joint family vacation, mending fences after a long and often fractious campaign, I was in charge of the office and Rob was in charge of the city. As usual, Rob focused on the picayune details of which phone calls had been returned and which hadn't. He hung around the office with little to do except find things to be dissatisfied about. He was driving us crazy.

He wanted the office staffed on Christmas Day and Boxing Day—the day after Christmas and a statutory holiday in Ontario. I explained they were holidays and the office should be closed. He insisted they weren't and we had to stay open.

"What if there's a major snowstorm?" he asked.

"What would the City Hall staff do if there is?" I responded.

"Answer the phones," he replied. His mantra.

On Christmas Eve, City Hall closed down at two o'clock. Rob insisted that the mayor's office stay open until 5:00. I didn't argue. I arranged for a skeleton staff.

As City Hall grew empty and quiet around us, I suggested to Rob that he walk around the office suite and wish the staff a Merry Christmas. "Hunh . . ." he grunted. "You think?"

"It's Christmas Eve, they've been working sixteen- to twenty-hour days for the past month, and they're staying late to make sure we're ready to serve the public," I said. "I think they'd appreciate it."

I walked with him as he made the circuit. At the first desk, he fished around in his pants pocket and produced a roll of cash an inch and half thick. He peeled a twenty dollar bill from it and handed it to the staffer, wishing him Merry Christmas. Ford's idea of a gift. As we went from desk to desk, Rob gave each staffer twenty dollars. He or she thanked Rob, they chatted awkwardly for a few minutes, and he moved on to the next person. When he was done, he went back to his office to return more constituent calls.

At 3:30, I let all of the staff go home except Rob's EA and body man, and took over the reception desk myself. I was hoping the phones wouldn't ring, because I had no clue how to answer or transfer a call. They didn't. The good citizens of Toronto had better things to do on Christmas Eve.

Around four o'clock, Rob came out and found me at the reception desk. He looked startled. Then he grunted and reached into his pocket. As I stood up from the desk and walked around the chest-high counter to say goodnight, he pulled out a twenty dollar bill. He flung his hand out toward me and the bill slipped from his fingers and fluttered to the floor between us.

We stood for a brief moment, each of us looking at the other, then at the twenty dollar bill. "Merry Christmas," Rob finally wheezed.

"Uh . . . thank you," I replied. I didn't want to bend over and snatch up the bill like it was going to blow away. But I also didn't want to ignore what he obviously intended as a generous gift. Slowly, awkwardly, I leant down to pick the money off the carpet. "Merry Christmas to you too, Mayor," I said. I put the twenty dollars in my pocket.

Rob grabbed a fistful of Dubble Bubble gum from the large pink bucket he kept on the reception desk and padded out the door, into the empty second floor mezzanine, and onto the elevator. As soon as the elevator doors closed, I sent Kia, Rob's EA, home and sat back down to wait out the clock at the reception desk.

Alone in the building. The phones didn't burp. Not a creature was scurrying. I heard not a chirp. I waved to the guard doing rounds on the floor; he looked at me oddly and continued his chore. When the clock ticked to 5:00 p.m. on the dot, I turned out the lights and was off like a shot. Merry Christmas to me, and to Rob, a good night.

# 12 | The Bulldozer

ROB FORD IS a bulldozer of a politician whose greatest political asset is his personality. It attracted a legion of loyal supporters and motivated them to volunteer during his campaign, and to rally around him when he was ridiculed by the public. It also insulated him from self-doubt and allowed him to be the best rope-a-dope politician I've ever seen. Like Muhammad Ali, he would lean against the metaphorical ropes of a Council debate or public scandal until his opponents grew exhausted from hitting him with an endless series of counterarguments and shameful allegations. They'd "prove him wrong" over and over until they grew hoarse with their own rhetoric. Once they were spent, he'd shake them off and plow forward to achieve his goal.

Most politicians are masters of nuance and "on the other hand." They preach careful study and moderation; they love "mature conversations" about "complex issues" with "no easy answers." After all of this careful contemplation, however, little gets done. That's fine if you live in a society where everything is pretty much as you like it. If you think the situation needs a serious reboot, you don't want most politicians. You want a Rob Ford.

A Rob Ford never hedges his bets. When he's in, he's all in. There are no gray areas and no "one of the best" efforts. There is only black, white, and "the best ever"—or the "unprecedented" "worst ever." This approach has obvious flaws. Most things in life are comparative, not superlative. Many things require balance—often a complicated balance that must be adjusted constantly as the situation evolves. Simple yes/no, all/none approaches are limiting and make enemies.

But this approach also has its strengths. Little energy is wasted in consideration, leaving more energy for execution. Quick decisions lead to rapid action. Which is a great thing, if you agree with the decision. Once he became mayor, Ford began implementing his plans before his opposition even had time to consider most of the "other hands."

The official First Meeting of Toronto City Council after a general election is a ceremonial one where the new Council is formally presented to the public. The next is the first real working meeting. Even then, most of its time is taken up with routine statutory issues and city planning matters that were on hold during the election period. Very little substantive new business normally occurs. This gives the new mayor and Council time to gel, get to know each other, and ponder the "balance" required to "find consensus."

On December 16, 2010, Rob Ford accomplished three of his key campaign promises at the first working Council meeting of his term as mayor. We had done the leg work during the transition period, lining up the votes, and in quick succession he knocked off three key items. He got thirty-nine of forty-four councillors to agree to slash their own office budgets from $50,445 to $30,000. He passed a motion, by a vote of twenty-eight to seventeen, to request the provincial government declare transit an essential service. (The province quickly acceded to this request—a vote of the legislature made it law.) He also abolished the much-hated $60-per-car vehicle registration tax, one of his core election promises, by a vote of thirty-nine to six. It was a breathtaking start for a mayor whom many had thought wouldn't be able, as one wag said, to pass gas without the permission of Council.

The rookie mayor and his rookie office weren't passing gas—they were cooking with it.

***

Outside the council chamber, we were closely watching the situation at Toronto Community Housing Corporation (TCHC) go from bad to worse. The city-owned corporation managed all of Toronto's government-owned social housing. With almost fifty-nine thousand low-income rental units in twenty-two hundred buildings housing about 164,000 tenants, TCHC is North America's second-largest social housing provider, after New York City.

No one thought TCHC was doing a great job. Ford had made hundreds of visits to TCHC properties, responding to resident calls and advocating for repairs to their units, for pest control, and the like. He had built a huge base of support among low-income residents in city housing, and they had turned up to vote for him by the thousands.

Toronto's auditor general released two damning reports about the housing authority in February, pointing to examples of inappropriate purchasing, inadequate records, missing contracts, and millions of dollars in waste. One finding, that the corporation had spent $93,000 on two staff Christmas parties in 2008 and 2009, was particularly galling. It found TCHC had spent $1,000 on staff gift chocolates from luxury retailer Holt Renfrew and $800 for a masseuse at a staff picnic. This was gold for Rob Ford. He immediately demanded the board of directors and the CEO resign.

When they refused, Ford was left with a standoff. He had publicly demanded the resignation of the thirteen-person board, despite having just installed four city councillors as new members of it two months prior at Council's inaugural meeting. They clearly hadn't been party to the failings and had been chosen for this role, in part, because they were committed to cleaning the place up.

Although Ford had spoken in haste, he wasn't wrong. The entire city had lost confidence in TCHC and its ability to manage a $6 billion real estate portfolio owned by the taxpayers, and to operate the almost $800 million-per-year corporation in the best interest of both its residents and the city as sole shareholder.

The thirteen people on the board included the mayor (or his designate), three city councillors, seven members of the public selected by City Council, and two tenant representatives selected by the tenants. Few of the incumbent directors had experience managing, or sitting as directors for, large corporations. They tended to be housing advocates or people who had worked in the social housing sector. None had the skills we felt necessary for managing an $800 million corporation effectively.

City Council had already installed four new councillors on the board, including Councillor John Parker, the mayor's designate. It would have an opportunity to replace the seven citizen members when it got around to appointing civic appointments sometime in the late summer. But immediate action was required. And Rob was an immediate action kind of guy.

We continued to encourage the board to resign. They continued to not resign. In the meantime, I made an alternative plan. We could introduce a motion at the next Council meeting, scheduled for March 8, to fire the board. Problem was, it was much easier to fire the entire board. Crafting a motion to solely fire the non-councillor members of the board would be complicated, and complicated motions were easy to unwind on the council floor. So I proposed we fire the entire board on March 8 and replace it with a single managing director until a new board could be appointed. We would talk with the four councillors on the board and promise to support their reappointment if they agreed to the plan.

Who would the managing director be? It had to be someone we already knew and trusted, who could start immediately, with the competence to manage a large corporation, and get it stabilized before the new board took over. He or she would have to assess the competency of the CEO and determine whether she was part of the solution or the problem. Finally, it had to be someone the public would respect and whom Council would approve.

Amir, Earl, and I started bouncing around names. Quickly, we realized we didn't have enough time to reach out to many prospects. We settled on the one name we felt confident met all of our criteria: Case Ootes, who had chaired the mayor's transition team. By the time we arrived at this solution, we'd missed the deadline for adding new items to the council agenda—but that was okay. We didn't want to telegraph our intention and provide an opportunity for left-wing councillors to organize an opposition.

On March 8, 2011, the deputy mayor stood on the floor of Council to introduce a motion prepared in the mayor's office to reconstitute the board of directors of TCHC. Like any other item introduced from the floor, it required a two-thirds vote to be placed on Council's agenda for debate, without first going through the committee stage. When the vote to introduce was called, we came up four votes short of the thirty we needed to waive referral to committee. Two of the four councillors who were already on the board, and who would have been reappointed, voted against. Three councillors whom we expected to support the motion were absent. As a result, the item was automatically referred to the next meeting of the executive committee for consideration there. Left-wing councillors cheered.

We'd been foiled. Rob was pissed. Amir was red-faced that "he" had lost a vote. I was angry at the no-show councillors and those who'd changed their minds. I wasn't ready to accept defeat. There had to be another way.

During a quiet time in Council business, I asked John Elvidge—the director of the city clerk secretariat that ran Council meetings and the definitive expert on Council rules and procedures—if we could schedule a special meeting of the executive committee to deal with this item. Why, yes, we could. The rules required twenty-four hours' notice, so the mayor called a special meeting of the executive committee for the following afternoon, during Council's two-hour lunch break. As the notice went online and was distributed in writing to Council—still in the middle of its

March 8 meeting—opposition councillors howled and the media buzzed. The battle was not over.

As I sat at my desk in the council chamber, just two rows behind the mayor, I watched the councillors who'd opposed the TCHC board item leave the chamber one after another. My staff, roving the second floor, reported that the councillors were meeting and then returning to their offices to make phone calls. We quickly learned that they were sounding the alarm and putting out an APB to every social activist in the city to have them descend *en masse* on the next day's special executive meeting. I'd forgotten that members of the public could make deputations at committee meetings. Clearly, the left was hoping to fill up the room with residents, who have the right to make presentations to the committee, who would use their five minutes to rail against the plan—weakening councillors' resolve and running out the clock so the meeting would have to be adjourned when Council resumed.

I reconvened with Elvidge to discuss how we might avoid the deputations. There was no way. Then I had an epiphany. Elvidge knew all the rules, and he was both impartial and discreet. Why not just ask him? I leveled with him: We wanted the item back to Council as soon as possible. We had twenty-six votes, which was not enough to introduce it without notice, but was enough to adopt the item if it could be introduced. Elvidge provided the solution. I smiled. "Perfect!" I said. "Let's do that."

Just as the opposition councillors were returning to their seats in the council chamber, having called out their legion of supporters for the next day's special executive committee meeting, the city clerk circulated two new notices around the floor. The first was a notice of cancellation of the special executive committee meeting. Eyebrows shot up around the room. What were we up to?

The second notice made it clear. It was a notice from the mayor as Head of Council convening a special meeting of the whole City Council for 5:30 the following afternoon. Elvidge had pointed out that the mayor can bring any matter directly to Council with twenty-four hours' notice.

The left-wing councillors erupted in fury. They would now have to call all their activists back to cancel their orders and ask them to attend a different meeting. Also, no deputations are allowed at Council meetings, so they'd have to sit silent. Pity. (As I said, I've never cared about being popular.)

Councillor Gord Perks rose on a point of order to protest the "slick political maneuvering from the mayor's office." I wrote the phrase down in my notebook and shared it with the team afterward. It was high praise indeed.

Rob Ford was exactly what TCHC needed. Where other politicians would have wasted months, maybe years, testing the waters, assessing the options, and building consensus for change, Ford understood the situation needed firm leadership and swift change. The situation at TCHC was very bad. (It's still not very good.) But more of the same wasn't going to make it better.

When Ford called for the ouster of the board, he demonstrated that he was willing to do something few politicians are willing to do: fail. In my opinion, however, his actions worked. The managing director got appointed and fired the CEO, and we reconstituted the board with experienced leaders who'd managed large corporations and nonprofits. It wasn't filled with political hacks; it was filled with people who knew how to solve problems and lead organizations. It was the most successful board we assembled during the Ford term.

*\*\**

Then came the island airport issue. Toronto's main airport is Lester B. Pearson International, commonly known as Toronto Pearson, located in the northwest corner of Toronto, about a forty-minute drive from downtown. But there's a second, much smaller commuter airport located on Toronto Island in Lake Ontario, directly opposite downtown. The island is man-made; it's separated from mainland Toronto by a navigational channel that's less than 100 yards wide in places, and is accessible via a five-minute ferry ride. The airport is a bone of contention. Residents of the island (there are about three hundred shanty homes) and many downtowners don't like the airport, and don't want to see it grow. But the Port Authority wanted a bridge.

In a previous mayoral election (2003, David Miller vs. John Tory), the bridge had been the wedge issue: Tory supported it, Miller vowed to kill it. Miller won handily. So one of the first issues Ford faced in 2011 was a renewed request by the Toronto Port Authority to build a fixed link from the city to this island. Not a bridge this time—an underwater pedestrian tunnel, with a price tag of $50 million. In 2003, Ford had been pro-bridge. In 2011, he still was.

In the early weeks of Ford's term, I met with Geoffrey Wilson, CEO of the Toronto Port Authority, and offered to reopen the discussion of a bridge. But the TPA was adamant: They preferred a tunnel. That seemed odd. To me and to Rob.

The federal government had appointed Finance Minister Jim Flaherty, the senior minister after the prime minister, as the minister responsible for the Greater Toronto Area. Although the TPA was an independent agency, it was a creature of the federal government and worked closely with the federal Ministry of Transportation. I asked Flaherty's advisors, based at the ministers' regional office in downtown Toronto, if they really preferred a tunnel to a bridge. They did.

Ford even brought up the issue himself, twice, during his first official meetings with Flaherty and Prime Minister Stephen Harper. He said he was willing to fight for a bridge—but Flaherty and Harper both confirmed they preferred a tunnel.

Discussions between the city staff and the TPA progressed well through the spring of 2011. I received regular updates from the city manager about details as they were worked out. At one point, there was a dispute between the TPA and the city over the value of a detail: in exchange for granting the TPA the right to access the mainland through the city's dock wall (which would save the TPA millions of dollars), the city wanted to be able to run its water and sewer pipes through the TPA's tunnel. When the city offered to pay for any additional construction costs the pipeline might incur to make this happen, the two sides struck a deal, which they were ready to take to Council.

Just before that scheduled Council meeting, however, a problem arose. Mark McQueen, the chairman of the TPA—a part-time patronage position appointed by the federal government—vetoed it. He demanded the city pay millions more dollars to include its pipes in their tunnel. The agreement was scuttled.

City Manager Joe Pennachetti was furious. He was adamant the city should not pay a "fee" to the TPA for the use of their tunnel. The city provided water and sewer services to the island from its mainland connections, he explained. The current pipes would eventually have to be upgraded, and the city had earmarked money in its ten-year capital plan to do this work in about five years' time. By including the pipes in the tunnel, the city would save about $10 million in costs, but would have to accelerate the expense to the current year. That was a good deal for the city and it cost the TPA nothing. In exchange, the city was saving the TPA millions by allowing it to land its tunnel on the city's dock wall at no cost. It was a win-win.

But McQueen wanted the city to fork over $10 million in order for him to sign off on the deal. Pennachetti thought that was absurd. If the city wasn't going to save money by doing the work earlier than it had budgeted for, we might as well just wait the five years. I agreed and told him I'd ask the mayor.

When I briefed Ford on the situation, explaining the tunnel the federal government wanted might not happen if we didn't give in to this demand, he shook his head. "No way we're going to pay them anything," he said. Clear direction. The truth was, we were having a difficult time whipping up support in Council for the tunnel. No one, including the mayor, had campaigned on the issue, and everyone remembered the political poison the bridge had been.

I passed Ford's message to Pennachetti and told him we'd help in the negotiation in any way we could. I also reached out to Flaherty's Toronto staff to warn them that McQueen was scuttling the deal.

Pennachetti arranged a last-ditch meeting with the TPA and city staff in the mayor's office. Amir and I attended on Ford's behalf. He'd reiterated to us what he'd said to me: He was backing Joe, don't pay a cent. If it kills the deal, it kills the deal. He preferred a bridge anyway. Amir and I decided that, if the need arose, I'd speak to the details. Amir was new in his role as Rob's chief of staff and I'd been handling the file since Christmas.

Pennachetti was already in the room when we entered, along with some of his staff. Also present were McQueen and Geoffrey Wilson. McQueen dressed the way you'd expect a wealthy investment banker to dress: expensive suit, French-cuff shirt, gold cufflinks, flashy watch. He was well-spoken and made a good argument why the city should pay the $10 million, quoting from Rob Ford: "There's only one taxpayer," so the city should contribute its savings to the TPA to help defray the cost of the project. Except, the TPA was already going to save millions because the city was granting access to the dock wall, and it was going to pay for the project not with tax dollars, but with user fees. Eventually, Joe looked at Amir for help. Amir looked at me.

I said the mayor supported Joe's position. The city wouldn't pay. He was happy to support the deal that was negotiated in Council and work the floor to get it passed.

McQueen argued with me. To him, the deal made sense his way and his way only. He seemed to be one of those guys who's genetically programmed to be a hunter-killer. Even if he's surrounded by food, he'll instinctively fight for more. Like the scorpion in the fable, who stings the frog that's carrying him across the river, he just couldn't help it. It's what scorpions do.

I stood firm: Take it or leave it. "If the tunnel doesn't happen, it's no skin off our nose," I explained. "In fact, it would make our jobs a whole lot easier."

McQueen steamed. The meeting ended. But a few days later the TPA relented and agreed to the deal as Pennachetti had negotiated it with Wilson—the form I said the mayor would support.

The matter went to Council for a vote late in the day on July 14, 2011. Although we had rounded up enough support to pass the agreement, the opposition had filibustered through the day, pushing the vote later and later. It was almost 7:00 p.m. when it was finally called.

I had learned the conservative councillors were fair-weather voters. They didn't stay late and were quite content to miss votes. Earl and I stationed our staff members at every exit from the council chamber in order to keep our voters on the floor. A councillor would wander to the exit, intending to leave; one of us would intercept him/her and repeat that the vote was about to be called.

"I need a coffee," the councillor would say. "I'll be back in time."

"How do you take it?" our staffer would ask. "We'll bring one to you right away."

In addition to staff on the doors, we had rovers in the hallway outside councillors' offices rounding up stragglers and pushing them into the elevators for the council chamber. When the vote was counted, the tunnel was approved by a vote of twenty-four to thirteen. Despite our vigilance, four of the councillors who'd promised their support had slipped our net and gone home.

It was important to Ford to get the tunnel approved, because he had assured the prime minister he'd get it done. But it was more important that he not renege on his deal with taxpayers to respect their interests. He wasn't about to give away the farm to get the tunnel. When he was sober, Ford could keep his eyes on the prize.

\*\*\*

One of Ford's other big campaign promises was the privatization of residential garbage pickup. Toronto was one of the last Canadian cities to rely on unionized city workers to collect garbage. It cost the city a fortune and most of the public supported privatizing it. So, early in the transition period, we asked city staff how we might accomplish it. The news was good. City staff had been advocating internally for privatization for many years, but the Miller administration hadn't listened.

We were concerned, however, about the city's draconian collective agreements. To buy labor peace, peace with the unions, previous mayors had signed away many of management's rights to manage. In the process, they'd introduced the concept of a "job for life," which made it virtually impossible to lay off any of the city's unionized employees. Fortunately, city staff had the critical elements of a privatization plan in place, waiting for a political leader to champion it. They certainly found one in Ford.

For years, whenever a permanent city garbage worker had retired or quit, he had been replaced with a temporary employee. Temporary employees did not have the same "job for life" protection that permanent employees had. Over time, the city had accumulated enough temporary employees in the solid waste division to staff one of its four districts. This would allow the city to privatize one district without laying off any permanent employees. They'd simply transfer the permanent employees in the affected district into one of the remaining districts.

What this would produce was a city divided down its center, along Yonge Street, into two roughly equal halves. The western half with private garbage pickup, and the eastern half with city pickup. This would set up the perfect test kitchen. We could compare side-by-side performance and cost between identical city and private pickup operations. And we could do it quickly. It wasn't the full privatization that Ford had promised. But once he saw the wisdom in it, he took ownership and championed it in public and in Council.

The popular myth about Ford is that he didn't listen or learn on the job, but that's not true. Before he began losing his battle with addiction, he regularly accepted advice and compromised on issues that weren't critical to him. Of course, the Bulldozer also recognized the political attractiveness of the two-step approach to garbage pickup. "We'll do this now and people will love it," he said to me. "I'll campaign on doing the other half in 2014."

Given the alcohol- and drug-fueled circus that Ford's term as mayor became, it's easy for people to forget that in his first year in office, he was a force to be reckoned with. I remember storming into his office to get a critical decision on a major program. He'd been avoiding a decision for days, and when I finally cornered him behind his desk, he was on the phone, speaking patiently with a woman who was in obvious distress.

When he hung up, he started reading me her address and telling me to get Municipal Licensing and Standards over there. I cut him off.

"Rob," I said, exasperated, "we don't have time for this. We need to focus on the important things."

Rob glowed red. "That woman," he hissed at me, "has been living without heat or electricity in her apartment for two weeks. There is nothing more important than that right now."

He was right. People had elected him to make their lives better. For a time, he was able to do that.

# 13 | The Shunning

THE OXYCONTIN TAPE could have cost Ford the election, but his team saved him using what I call *political jujitsu*: You see your opponent's line of attack, but rather than directly opposing it, you move with it, giving it just enough of a boost so he overshoots his target. He lands on his face. You remain standing.

We tried to use that same technique with the media. We never saw the press as objective purveyors of facts and information. We saw them as scrappers engaged in a street war for readers and advertisers—not only globally, but especially in Toronto, one of the few cities in North America with four major daily newspapers.

Our primary enemy was the *Toronto Star*, the largest-circulation daily paper in Canada. (Its Saturday edition is typically about two inches thick.) It was molded by one of its early editors, Joe Atkinson, who took the helm in 1899. He believed the newspaper shouldn't be a dispassionate observer of the world around it; it should be a force for good. That is, "good" as Atkinson defined it. By 1913, the *Star* was Toronto's largest paper and Atkinson had become the controlling shareholder.

The *Star* remains, to this day, an active player in city politics. It doesn't just report the news; its editors consciously try to shape events. From the beginning, they didn't like Rob Ford.

On the other side of the political spectrum is the *Toronto Sun*, a tabloid that caters to working-class people who read it on the subway, love sports, enjoy the scantily clad daily "Sunshine Girl," do not favor long stories, and adore Rob Ford. Still, Ford had not been the *Sun's* first choice for mayor; Rocco Rossi had seemed the smarter bet early in the campaign. They were conservative, sure, but Rob was also an embarrassing candidate to champion. Their senior management squirmed at the thought of him as mayor.

Back at the tail end of the campaign, Rob and I, along with a few others, attended a *Sun* editorial board meeting just before they were to endorse a candidate. It was an unorthodox affair. We arrived at the *Sun* offices at 333 King St. East in Toronto, and were greeted at the door by then-editorial page editor Rob Granatstein, who ushered us through the newsroom and into a boardroom. At least, he tried to usher us through the newsroom. Rob Ford is a retail politician. About two dozen people were working at desks and cubicles in the center of the room, and in the small offices along its sides. Rob pinballed back and forth across the room, introducing himself to everyone. They all got a handshake and a business card. And they clearly loved it—no other candidate had stopped to talk to the staff on their way in.

In the boardroom, Rob sat on one side of the table, facing a small video camera set up to record the interview. Doug sat on his right side, Nick Kouvalis on his left, and I sat to Nick's left, close to the end of the table. The room was crowded with every editor and columnist on the paper's masthead.

They led off with the usual questions and Rob provided the usual answers. They then started to push him for details, corroboration of his statements, and campaign promises. When they got too pushy, or ventured into areas we didn't want to discuss, Nick or Doug would jump in. When they asked for details about the financial or subway plans, Rob looked at me, and I provided a response.

One of the lines of discussion we wanted to avoid: Rob's position on a controversial business deal City Council had approved for a boardwalk restaurant on Toronto's eastern beachfront. Rob had opposed it, and had publicly complained that the in-camera discussions leading up to the decision had been scandalous. The *Sun* reporter pushed him, asking him if he was saying there was corruption.

"These in-camera meetings, there's more corruption and skulduggery going on in there than I've ever seen in my life," Rob said. I tapped Nick's foot under the table and looked at him. He nodded. Rob was straying close to dangerous, possibly even libelous territory. Nick redirected the line of inquiry.

One of the *Sun* editors complained that Rob's staff was talking too much. None of the other candidates had brought handlers, he said. The other candidates had the confidence to handle the questions themselves. "Jesus," I jumped in. "You beat the shit out of him in your newspaper because you don't think he can work with a team. Now he's got a team here, and you're complaining about that too?"

The editor looked startled. He said they were trying to decide who to endorse in this campaign and they wanted to hear from the candidate, not his handlers. I leaned into the table and looked him straight in the eye. "You and I both know you're going to endorse Rob Ford," I said. "Your readers love him. If you don't endorse him, you'll lose fifty thousand readers the day after you print."

That pretty much wrapped up the *Sun* editorial board meeting. Rob pressed the flesh and chatted with more people on the way out. On October 17, the *Sun* endorsed Rob. Five days later, so did the *National Post*, the other conservative Toronto paper. The *Globe and Mail*, which considers itself "Canada's National Newspaper," and is slightly left of center politically, begrudgingly endorsed Smitherman as the better of "two flawed candidates." To no one's surprise, the *Toronto Star* also endorsed Smitherman.

\*\*\*

Before the election, on June 16, we'd leaked Dieter's OxyContin tape in a controlled release, and survived. A month later, on July 13, the *Star* published a damning story about Rob Ford under a banner headline that stretched across its front page. Reporters Rob Cribb and Kris Rushowy quoted anonymous sources claiming that, while Ford was a volunteer football coach for Newtonbrook Secondary School, he "went berserk" after a bad play during a football game at Appleby College, a private school in Oakville (a wealthy bedroom suburb just west of Toronto). The story said Ford had run onto the field, where he "shook" and "slapped" one of his players.

The same anonymous source told the *Star* reporters, "It is outrageous that a person in a position of trust and responsibility, such as a high school football coach, could beat up a player in front of many witnesses and walk away with impunity."

As well, the story quoted an anonymous former student, who said he'd witnessed Ford grabbing a player by the throat. More anonymous sources said Ford frequently yelled at and lost his cool with the players.

Ford, also quoted in the story, said the allegations were false; his friend and fellow coach Ron Singer corroborated Ford's statement. Chris Spence, who at that time ran the Toronto District School Board as director of education, was quoted, too—he was noncommittal. As director of education, Spence was the school board's top official and reported only to the elected board of trustees, through Chairman Bruce Davis—who happened to be the campaign manager for Rob's chief rival, Smitherman, at the time. (Spence resigned in disgrace in 2013 after it was revealed he had plagiarized a number of articles he'd written while running the school board.)

To say that Ford was furious underplays his response by several orders of magnitude. Coaching football was his only consistent pleasure, and this was a direct attack on it. He threatened to sue the *Toronto Star*. His lawyer (and family friend) Dennis Morris even issued a notice of libel.

The *Star*, however, would not back down. Not even when the *Globe and Mail* tracked down the allegedly abused former player, Jonathan Gordon, on a Canadian military base on the East Coast two weeks later and ran a story that said the event never happened. (Our director of communication, Adrienne Batra, had tracked him down, and connected him to the *Globe*.) Gordon hated Ford, but that only added veracity to his denial. "That's completely untrue," he said. "Trust me, if he had slapped me, I would have beat the crap out of him. No word of a lie."

Ford's response was to blacklist the *Toronto Star*. Though they were arguably the most influential of Toronto's four major dailies, with the largest City Hall bureau, Ford refused to talk to them. The campaign stopped sending them backgrounders, advisories, briefing notes, and news releases. Rob wouldn't give them interviews and Adrienne tried, as much as possible, to call on other reporters in press conferences.

I asked how long we were going to keep this up. Adrienne rolled her eyes and replied, "Until the *Star* runs a front-page apology for the football article, above the fold. That's what he wants."

"That's never going to happen," I pointed out. Adrienne rolled her eyes again. I excel at stating the obvious.

A few days into the shunning, Nick, Adrienne, and I sat down at Deco to discuss the *Star* situation. We all knew it couldn't continue. They were the city's paper of record. They had more City Hall reporters than the other papers combined. They broke the most stories and had the most in-depth election coverage. TV and talk radio, even the other papers, often followed their front pages. Nick and Adrienne had run past Ford everything they could think of—would he accept a lesser apology inside the paper? What if the *Star* wrote a positive piece as contrition? Could Doug talk him out of this? But Ford wasn't budging.

After a minute of silence, I started to think out loud. I do that a lot. Sometimes I even remember to remind people that I'm doing it, which helps to diminish the weird looks I get. A little.

*What if we run with it? The same jujitsu we used before? The* Star *hates Ford. Ford hates the* Star. *Let's play it up so everyone in Toronto knows they hate each other. If there's more bad news to come, chances are the* Star *will break it first. But if everyone knows the* Star *hates Rob Ford, maybe they won't believe it as much. Maybe we can make it permanent wind in our sails.*

That's what we did. Rob not only didn't talk to the *Star* for the remainder of the campaign, he made a point of telling people he wasn't talking to them: "They would do anything to make me lose," he implied.

After Ford became mayor, we asked if he wanted to change his approach to the *Star*. His answer was the same: Not without an apology. So the shunning continued.

The *Star* was outraged. They complained to Janet Leiper, the city's integrity commissioner, that this was an egregious offence. She investigated at length, including detailed interviews with Adrienne, who by that time had left the mayor's office, and with me. I spent some time explaining our view of the world to Leiper. She eventually concluded that the mayor and his office were doing nothing wrong. More livid *Star* sputterings followed.

Behind the scenes, of course, we were ensuring that *Star* reporters were aware of the events and information they needed to do their jobs. At least, the events and the information we wanted them to have. We left them off our electronic distribution lists, but included their subsidiary newspapers, who shared it with them. Often, Adrienne would walk a printed copy down to them in the press gallery, a small rabbit warren of offices one floor below ours. Or she'd just drop in and tell them what was up. Rob was aware of most of this and never took issue with it.

As director of policy and strategic planning (which was my title in the early days of Ford's mayoralty), I provided a number of technical briefings on background for all the media, including the *Star*. I'd also sit in the common area of the press gallery and talk to reporters, answering questions, the *Star*'s included.

The *Star*'s City Hall reporter, Robyn Doolittle (who later wrote the book *Crazy Town*, centered around Ford's infamous crack video), invited me down to a social event her paper was hosting for its new interns. She expressly wanted to introduce me to her boss, Michael Cooke, the *Star*'s editor. I met and chatted with him in a corner of a Fionn MacCool's pub in downtown Toronto. He asked me what it would take to end our feud. I told him an above-the-fold, front-page apology. He said that would never happen. I replied, "I know."

Then we both admitted something. The boycott was working for Ford, I said. "Nobody believes anything you write about him. He could murder someone in the public square outside City Hall and, if the *Star* wrote about if first, many would think you made it up."

Cooke said it was working for them, too. They were breaking stories and had a whole lot more to break. He intimated that I had no idea what they had coming. He would stop at nothing. He was going to destroy Rob Ford forever. "Wind in our sails," I replied. We both toasted that and our conversation moved on to other topics.

Over the next months, Cooke and I ran into each other a few times. One of us would ask, "Is it still working for you?" The other would reply, "Yep, is it still working for you?" "Absolutely."

Publicly, the shunning became a standing joke in Rob's speeches: "I read in the newspaper—well, not in the *Star* . . ." It always got a big laugh.

Shunning the country's major newspaper is not exactly recommended as a public relations move. But it was classic Rob Ford. And for a long time it worked. In 2013, two weeks after the *Star* and the website Gawker had run their first stories about Rob's crack video, a published poll found that while 96 percent of Torontonians had heard about the crack tape, only 50 percent believed it existed, despite the nation's largest newspaper proclaiming it true on its front page.

Of course, the shunning and the vendetta between Ford and the *Star* had unintended consequences. I am not a media scholar, but in my opinion, the *Star*, in its quest to bring down Ford, sacrificed some of its journalistic standards. In the race to beat the *Star*, some other news outlets did the same.

In May 2013, the *Globe and Mail* published an exposé on Doug Ford, alleging he'd sold drugs in high school. The story was woven from unattributed anonymous sources and, to my mind, failed to be convincing. We'd known the *Globe*'s investigative team had been working on this story for months, and we'd been waiting for it with apprehension. I suspect they took so long to publish it because they didn't have enough corroboration— until the *Star* lowered the bar for everyone.

I don't know if our shunning strategy and the *Star*'s response did any permanent damage to the credibility of mainstream journalism in Toronto. But it certainly didn't help.

# 14 | Taking Care of the Pennies

"ONE OF THE things my father taught me," Rob Ford told me—as he has told thousands of listeners in person, at debates, on the radio, and on TV—"is if you take care of the pennies, the dollars will look after themselves."

Rob's approach to budgeting was straightforward. Less is more. Worry about the small expenditures. Never start with the final offer. I watched him hammer that home time and again, often to my exasperation.

Toronto's 2011 annual budget was about $13.3 billion. This included about $9.4 billion for operating expenses—the part of the budget that got the most public attention. The money to pay these expenses came from three main sources: property taxes, user fees, and flow-through funding from the provincial and federal governments for joint programs.

The rest of the $13.3 billion included a rate-supported budget of $1.2 billion and an annual capital budget of about $2.7 billion. The rate-supported budget funded water, sewer, garbage, and parking services, which were paid for by direct user fees. The capital budget was funded by borrowing—and a transfer of current funds from the annual operating budget. Interest and principal payments on the capital debt were funded from the operating budget.

Unlike many US cities, Toronto is prohibited by law from borrowing to fund operating expenses. It can use debt only to finance long-term capital investments, such as road, bridge, and subway construction, building of libraries and community centers, and water and sewer works. This means the city is legally required to balance its operating budget every year. In theory, this makes it virtually impossible for Toronto to ever go bankrupt, as many US cities have done.

Instead of borrowing from lenders, the City of Toronto routinely borrowed from the future to balance its current operating budgets. At the end of a year, city staff would discover the city had under-spent its operating budget by a certain amount—usually due to unexpected events that reduced the city's costs on a one-time-only basis. The city would call that a "surplus" and then use it to justify additional new spending in the next year—spending that would recur year after year. Good luck and increasing the tax rate every year had resulted in these pretend surpluses for a number of years, and Council had counted on them continuing to grow, ballooning its spending as if the money would always be there.

Imagine budgeting $1,000 a year for food, then discovering at the end of the year that you'd under-spent your budget by $200 because you'd taken a temporary job with free meals for a couple of months. What should you do with the extra cash? Well, if you were Toronto City Council, you'd assume next year would be the same, budget another $1,000 for food, and increase your entertainment budget by $200 for a three-year commitment to a digital sports package on TV. All in the hope that you'd magically save $200 in food again in each of the next three years—despite the fact that you now had a different job that didn't provide free meals.

What Ford wanted to accomplish was simple: He wanted to provide some tax relief to citizens by eliminating the $60 per car registration tax that brought $64 million each year into the city's coffers; eliminating the city's land transfer tax that was supposed to bring in about $300 million per year; and keeping property tax increases at or below the rate of inflation. He also wanted to begin paying down the city's debt load. My job was to figure out how to do that.

I had spent weeks during the campaign extracting budget information from City of Toronto public sources to understand how the city spent its money, and how it earned it. I'd compiled complex spreadsheets that allowed me to run various budget scenarios over a four-year term. My expensive MBA was being well exercised. I built a financial plan for Ford's campaign platform that would allow him to reduce spending by about $2.8 billion aggregated over four years, allowing him to pay down some of the city's debt and to fund his transit expansion plan.

One of the key assumptions underlying my financial model was a published statistic that said the city's rate of employee attrition was six percent each year. In other words, six percent of city employees quit or retired each year. The city's biggest expense was labor, so we developed a plan to reduce the size of the city's workforce. I proposed we reduce the workforce by only replacing, on average, half of the people who departed. We would still hire for key positions and promote from within, but as less important roles went vacant, we'd eliminate them. I built a financial model that assumed we'd shed about three percent of our labor costs each year. The compounding effect of this was dramatic. It would save the city about $1.1 billion over the four-year term. I also proposed we target modest annual reductions in operating spending of 2.5 percent, 2.0 percent, and 1.5 percent in each of the first three years of the term. This would save about $1.7 billion over four years.

There is a truism in the military that no plan survives first contact with the enemy. Turns out, it's true in government as well. Our plan for financial reform didn't survive our one-month transition period.

Very early in the transition briefings with city staff, they reported the city's actual attrition rate was about one percent, not six. Obviously, this was a problem. There went our pot of money. Yet each successive briefing from the finance folks revealed a growing annual "surplus." As the surplus grew over $300 million, Nick and I settled on an alternative financial plan.

Rob wanted to impose arbitrary cuts to program spending. He talked frequently about $50 million in grants the city disbursed each year, mostly to community arts groups and social services groups. He saw these as wasted money. Nick and I understood, however, that arbitrary cuts would be nothing short of a declaration of war on the city's well-organized left wing establishment. That war was coming, but we weren't yet ready for it. We needed time to prepare. So we planned to use the 2010 pretend surplus to buy some.

Instead of wrestling the city's budget down to size right away, we decided to delay the battle until the 2012 budget. Essentially, we would follow in the footsteps of previous administrations and apply the entire 2010 surplus to balance the 2011 budget. That would allow us to keep Council happy and afford us the better part of a year to analyze the changes we wanted to make without materially affecting the services residents received from the city. Of course, this approach was as unsustainable as it had been for the previous mayor, and it was something Ford had consistently railed against as a councillor. So it would take some fancy selling to get him to agree.

Rob had promised to eliminate the vehicle registration tax right off the top, in the first working meeting of the new council. I felt it was important to do so. Not only would it keep his promise, it would also put pressure on city staff to find the efficiencies we needed them to find. I knew they'd never cut costs without feeling fiscal pressure to do so. So we planned to turn the money tap off at the beginning of the year. I hoped the pressure of knowing they were going to be $64 million short the following year would be enough to motivate the bureaucracy.

Rob listened and eventually agreed to our plan, with two big caveats. First, if he wasn't going to cut the budget in his first year, he sure as hell wasn't going to increase it. It had to be flat—spending the same amount as the year before. More importantly, he wanted no increase in property tax rates. Residents had grown accustomed to annual three percent tax hikes under David Miller. The least Ford could do, he said, was freeze the property tax rate for a year.

During the election, Rob hadn't promised to forgo tax increases. All he'd promised was to keep them "at or less than inflation." This would be better than promised. City staff freaked out, but we knew there was enough money in the 2010 surplus to pay for any inflationary increases and the loss of the car tax revenue.

So we decided to balance the 2011 budget the easy way. And Council, by and large, approved. Of course, this created an even larger budget pressure for the next year. Essentially, we were going to start the 2012 budget process $774 million in the hole. Against popular expectation, we felt this was a good thing.

Just as we used the car tax cut to put pressure on city staff to get serious about finding efficiencies, we intended to apply even more pressure to force Council to think outside the box. We applied our energies to shaping a public narrative around a "$774 million gap." Rob spoke at length about how he was handed a budget with a $774 million gap. Media reported on how foolish it was to spend the surplus and be left with an impossible $774 million gap to fill. Eventually, all the councillors were talking about the $774 million gap as a beast that had to be slain. By the time we started talking about the 2012 budget, pretty much everyone in the city realized we had a $774 million gap to fill and tough decisions were going to be necessary. Focus achieved.

The other key part of our strategy was the acceleration of the city's budget process. Traditionally, Toronto would approve its annual budgets in April or May. But we planned to approve 2011's two months early, in February. We'd then immediately embark on the most comprehensive Core Service Review the city had ever seen, identifying opportunities for major waste elimination and service restructuring that would unlock hundreds of millions of dollars in savings. We'd use this process to draft the 2012 budget, which we wanted passed by the end of 2011—before the 2012 budget year started.

It was an aggressive plan and we knew we would have to drive the councillors in our coalition mercilessly. We figured we could whip them hard through the 2012 budget, at which point they'd be exhausted and sick of us. But by then we'd have done all the heavy lifting required for the entire four-year term. We'd be able to loosen up and begin to focus, not on "fixing the fiscal foundation," but on "building for the future." This would provide much more palatable choices for the councillors. Once they'd saved money and gotten the city out of its dependency on pretend-surpluses, there would be money available to fund service improvements. Councillors could be heroes just in time for the 2014 election.

Passing a City of Toronto budget was a gruesome process. Toronto's "open and transparent" government rules notwithstanding, budgets are like sausages: best seen only in final form by the consumer. That's how it works at the provincial and federal levels of government. All of the wrangling over what's in and what's out and how things will come together is done ahead of time. On Budget Day, the finance minister stands up in the legislature, makes a speech, and *voila!* There's a fully-cooked budget looking all delicious on the shelf. In Toronto, not so much.

One of the challenges we had with our first budget was that Council rules weren't quite what people believed them to be. Rob Ford and his budget chief, Councillor Mike Del Grande, initially believed there was a rule in place that Council couldn't move motions to "unbalance" the budget: if a councillor moved a motion to add $50 million in spending for a pet project into the budget, she'd have to also move to reduce $50 million in spending somewhere else to offset her initiative. Unfortunately, this rule doesn't actually exist. The city clerk explained that we could move a procedural motion at the beginning of the budget meeting to introduce that as a rule, but it would require two-thirds majority support because it would change normal Council procedure.

That was problematic. We had a bare majority coalition to pass most items on the mayor's agenda. To win two-thirds support, we'd have to count on the unaligned councillors who occupied the middle ground (who became known as "the mushy middle" in the press), and they were a skittish lot. I wasn't convinced we could win the vote. I was also concerned that if we moved the motion and lost, we would telegraph our concern to an opposition who might not have thought about screwing with the budget that way. (They might also have thought the rule already existed.) When I briefed Amir and Rob about my concerns, they agreed: It was too risky.

Before every Council meeting, the mayor would be briefed in his boardroom on the meeting's agenda. The long, narrow room that looked out onto Nathan Phillips Square was packed for those meetings. The beautiful softwood boardroom table was a historic artifact from the former Metro Toronto Council chamber. It was far too large for the room, as were the comfy executive chairs arranged around it. The room heated up quickly and could be a miserable place during long meetings.

Rob sat at the head of the table, with a ten-page listing of the item numbers and titles for the meeting. Everyone else in the room would have huge binders and folders with hundreds of pages of the meeting agenda and supporting documents crammed onto the table in front of them. I'd sit next to Rob with my agenda binder. The deputy mayor and Speaker of Council often attended, as did the budget chief for the special budget meetings. Beside me would be the city clerk, her two senior staffers, and the city solicitor. The city manager and his senior staff would take seats along the table opposite me, around the end, and back up the near side. Earl Provost occupied the chair at the end of the table opposite the mayor and our council relations and policy staff sat on the window ledge behind him.

The mayor would suck water through a straw from a plastic 7-Eleven Big Gulp cup and flip through the pages of his summary while plucking wet pieces of fresh grapefruit from a Tupperware container and feeding them into his mouth. He was always on a diet.

"Okay, EX 3.1," he'd say, kicking off the meeting with the first item on the council agenda. He'd go through the entire agenda—often two hundred or more items—and be briefed on each one by staff.

The budget meetings, scheduled to begin on February 23, 2011, were expected to last at least two days. Past budget meetings had lasted for a week or more. As we went through the items, Rob brought up the idea that there should be an "offset" rule to prevent unbalanced motions from being passed. The city clerk explained, again, that this was not the case. City staff were as concerned as we were about the possibility of councillors unbalancing the budget. Any changes they made to the spending would change the tax rate, and it was a complex calculation that normally took half a day to complete. They didn't want to be calculating the tax rate on the fly. The mayor, of course, didn't want anything to happen to the budget that would affect his zero-percent tax increase plan. It was important to all of us that we somehow prevent councillors from moving malicious motions to unbalance the budget. But there wasn't a way that didn't require a two-thirds majority.

As the staff continued briefing the mayor, I'd ask questions and solicit details on various issues that either I was curious about or, often, that I knew the mayor didn't fully understand. I'd ask for an explanation so he didn't have to. We were a good team. When the discussion got detailed, or Rob had a question, I'd flip my briefing book around for him to see the tables or spreadsheets. He was good with numbers and could read a table of figures and city financial statements pretty well. Sometimes, I'd whisper into his ear about a particular tactic or concern we'd discussed in private but didn't want the staff to hear.

During the mayor's first budget meeting briefing, I began to form a plan that might help us ensure no one could hijack our budget. After we wrapped up the main discussion, I asked some questions. "The mayor can designate any item he chooses to be his Key Items, is that correct?" I asked—knowing the answer, but wanting to walk people through my plan.

"Yes," replied the city clerk.

"And his Key Items are automatically done first, there's no vote required to change the order. Council can't prevent that?"

"That's right."

There were five budget items to be dealt with by Council at the budget meeting. The last item on the agenda involved setting the tax rate. "So, if the mayor was to designate Item Five, the tax rate, as his Key Item, then it would be debated first, correct?"

"Yes," said the clerk.

"But we can't do that," interrupted the city staff budget director. "We can't set the tax rate until Council has passed the budget, because the budget drives the tax rate."

I asked her to bear with me.

"And it takes a two-thirds vote to reopen an item that Council has passed, right?" I asked.

"Yes, unless a year has passed," replied the city clerk.

"So, if we debate the tax rate item first and adopt it, then it's basically locked in. Then we debate the operating budget . . . and any amendments that are proposed that would increase spending in one area, without an offset to decrease it in another area, would either result in an unbalanced budget—or require a tax rate increase. Correct?"

The finance people nodded, so I continued.

"But it's against the law to pass an unbalanced budget," I said, and everyone nodded . . . "And, since we would have just adopted the tax rate, we can't change that without a two-thirds vote, right?"

"Hmmm . . . Just a minute." The clerk had a quick side-discussion with her senior staff. "Yes, that's correct."

I could see the city manager and the CFO knew what I was thinking.

"So, any amendment to the operating budget that would have the effect of throwing it out of balance would have to be ruled out of order, because they would create a condition that cannot be created. Is that right?"

More quiet discussion amongst the clerks. Finally, they nodded.

"Thank you," I said. "I think that's all the questions I have. I'm not sure what the mayor will decide to do, but I would ask all of you to please keep our discussions in confidence—as I know you will anyway."

So the mayor named the tax rate as his Key Item—moving it to the top of the agenda. Council complained a bit about this being unorthodox, but the order change happened and the tax rate passed easily after some debate. That locked in the tax rate at a zero percent increase, exactly as the mayor had promised. Any attempt to change the operating budget after this point would be ruled out of order unless there was a two-thirds vote to reopen the tax rate. We knew we could count on the support of more than one-third of the councillors, so we knew we were home free.

Immediately after the tax rate item passed, Rob rose and went to speak with the reporters. He had his tax freeze and nothing could change that. Where the money got spent was less important, so we planted our flag in the ground and declared victory. Rob decreed it was a "great day for taxpayers." I don't think most of the councillors had even realized, at that point, that the day was won. Rob had won another convincing council showdown with the left who'd vowed to stop him. They hadn't seen it coming.

We used the same "tax rate first" approach again for the 2012 and 2013 budgets. Council grew to accept it as normal, because it made sense. The tax rate is what everyone cares most about, and doing it this new way prevents councillors from throwing months of work into chaos with an ill-considered motion from the floor in the heat of a debate.

\*\*\*

With our first budget passed, we continued on with the next phase of our plan: the most comprehensive review of city services ever undertaken. This was how we planned to identify efficiencies and savings to trim the

2012 budget. The Core Service Review process kicked off immediately after the 2011 budget was passed. The city manager hired an outside consulting company, KPMG, to go through the city's programs and services and identify which were mandated by law; which were necessary services a city must provide even if they were weren't legally mandatory; which were services the city traditionally provided, but were not actually necessary; and which services were totally discretionary. Next, they identified hundreds of things the city could consider eliminating, reducing, or reorganizing to save money. We hadn't paid them enough, nor given them enough time, to assess which of these options were advisable—so there were no recommendations. The timeline was short so the review could feed into the 2012 budget that we wanted to have all but completed by year-end. So the report was really a list of "could considers." Many of the options were clearly impossible or undesirable. However, KPMG identified a number of areas the city could explore for service efficiencies.

That's what Rob wanted: a list of things he could change to reduce spending. After delivering an un-promised tax freeze for 2011, he'd already decided he wanted a tax increase in 2012 of no more than 2.5 percent. He figured staff would want 3 percent and he'd insist on 2 percent, but he'd settle for 2.5 percent after pushing them as hard as we could. How did he arrive at 2.5 percent as the "right" number? That was his gut feel of what people would accept as a win. Over two years, it would average out to 1.25 percent (since 2011 had zero increase).

The 2012 budget was hard fought. People were concerned that Ford would attempt the most draconian of KPMG's possibilities, or go after their most beloved services—that he would, for example, close libraries. Toronto is justly proud of its library system with one hundred branches serving 2.8 million residents. (New York City, in comparison, has eighty-eight public libraries serving 8.4 million residents.) To my knowledge, Ford never intended to reduce the number of libraries. But libraries became a major flash point in the core service review and budget debates anyway, thanks to a media battle between Doug Ford and Margaret Atwood, one of Canada's most famous authors.

It's reasonable to assume that Atwood did not support Rob Ford. I was impressed by her entrepreneurship when I learned that Canada's largest bookstore chain, Chapters Indigo, was offering steep discounts on purchases of Atwood titles to anyone presenting a Toronto Public Library card. When I asked the cashier at my local store what the promotion was about she replied, "Because the mayor is closing libraries." He wasn't. But who says authors can't be canny marketers?

When asked what he thought about Atwood's campaign to "save the libraries," Councillor Doug Ford did not say, "There is no plan to close libraries." Nor did he say, "You should ask the mayor what his plans are, I'm just a councillor."

What Doug Ford did say was, there were "more libraries than Tim Hortons" in his ward. When asked by the *Globe and Mail* if he'd close a library in his own ward that he'd described as underused, he replied, "Absolutely, I would. In a heartbeat." On a roll, Doug went on to tell the *Globe*, "Good luck to Margaret Atwood. I don't even know her. She could walk right by me, I wouldn't have a clue who she is. She's not down here. She's not dealing with the problem. Tell her to run in the next election and get democratically elected." The battle with Toronto's literati was engaged.

Rob was exasperated with Doug. At this point in the review process, Rob was disciplined and on message. Doug was shooting from the hip and picking fights we didn't need. We appealed to Paul Ainslie, Doug's council seatmate, who'd become our de facto babysitter for the mayor's brother. He was the chair of the Library Board. But even he couldn't get Doug to understand that he wasn't helping us.

"He's an idiot," was all Rob would say when confronted with the need to get his brother to shut up. "You tell him. I've tried. He won't listen to me." But neither Amir nor I was reckless enough to get between the mayor and his brother. Nothing good would come from that.

More than 340 people signed up to make presentations to the executive committee as part of its consideration of the Core Service Review report. Normally, they would each be permitted five minutes to speak, and then each councillor present could ask them questions for three minutes. Even without questions, the public deputations alone could take twenty-eight hours. While the mayor was committed to hearing what people had to say, the fact is that after the first dozen presentations on any topic, you've pretty much heard all the opinions there are on the subject. The rest are just piling on. But it's a democratic process. And Rob is passionate about democracy.

We decided to reduce the speaking time to three minutes and to run the meeting all through the night, if necessary, to fit everyone in. It was not a popular choice with city staff, but we knew that if we suspended the meeting and spread it over a number of days, we'd run out of days. There were other council committees that had to meet, and business to get done. We couldn't allow one committee meeting to hijack the entire city agenda.

We also recognized that, by running the meeting all night, many people wouldn't show up to claim their speaking slot. That would shorten the list. I also refused to move the meeting out of the small committee room and into the main council chamber. Although the chamber would be more comfortable for the audience, it isn't designed for committees. Committee work is better done in the committee room. We also didn't want a big crowd feeding off its own energy. The fact that the committee room would get stuffy quickly and could be uncomfortable was, for me, a bonus.

As it was, the event turned into a watershed for civic engagement in Toronto. People showed up in their pajamas and held potluck parties in the spare committee rooms set aside for overflow audiences who couldn't fit into the main room.

The meeting began at 9:30 a.m. on July 28, 2011, with a presentation from KPMG and the city manager. Then the deputations began. Shortly after midnight, we were just halfway through the list of names, and I decided to head home for a couple of hours' sleep, a shower, and a change of clothes. I'd just ironed a new shirt and drifted off to sleep when the ring of my BlackBerry woke me up. It was Earl. The mayor was acting weird. He needed me to come back.

When I got back to City Hall, Earl told me the mayor was acting as if he'd been drinking. He was getting punchy with the crowd and making mistakes. The crowd was laughing at him. I'd seen on Twitter that a few regular critics were speculating he was drunk. Rob had been in the committee room nonstop since the lunch break, aside from one or two trips to the restroom. It seemed impossible for him to be drunk, but during the campaign I'd seen him act dopey when he was exhausted. At this point, we'd never seen Rob drink, nor worried that he had a drinking problem. It didn't matter, though. This was not good.

I walked up to Rob and knelt down beside him, motioning for him to turn off his microphone. I leaned in so I could whisper into his ear, with my face turned away from the crowd. I could smell too much cologne, but no alcohol.

"Hey boss, why don't you take a break and let the deputy mayor have the chair for a while?" I suggested.

"I'm good, buddy," he replied.

I watched the speaker's countdown clock reach three minutes and stepped back while Rob thanked the deputant who was speaking and called for the next one. Once the new speaker had begun, I moved back in beside Rob. I told him he looked tired and was sounding tired, making mistakes.

I said I knew he was okay, but that people on Twitter watching him on TV were saying he looked drunk.

"I'm not drunk," he hissed.

I told him I knew he wasn't, but he was tired. He should take a break for an hour, let one of the other councillors have the chair and put his head down for a bit. Come back fresh. Eventually, he agreed.

Meanwhile, Earl hadn't slept at all and it was showing. He'd become a little paranoid. Around 4:00 a.m., he became convinced that someone was going to pie the mayor. He had visited the overflow rooms and found a number of empty whipped cream cans. He was at red alert, expecting an imminent barbarian invasion. Though it wouldn't have surprised me if Earl were right, I urged him to relax. We had the situation covered. There was security everywhere. I stood in the corner of the room reserved for mayor's staff and Earl took a seat in the audience, looking very jumpy, eyes darting around the room, rocking forward and back in his seat, ready to leap up and stop anyone who charged the mayor with a cream pie. He texted me he was nervous, sure there was going to be trouble. I texted back that I could see only one suspicious-looking person in the room: him.

The meeting finally wrapped in the early hours of the next morning, twenty-two hours after it had begun. One hundred sixty-seven deputations had been heard. The committee moved a number of amendments that we'd spent the night writing, and voted on them. The actual business of the meeting was over in a matter of minutes and the stage was set for the 2012 budget.

Except the 2012 budget became a messy, largely unnecessary battlefield. Strategically, we were hitting our targets. It would be smaller than the previous year's budget—quite possibly an unprecedented accomplishment. But we were getting serious pushback from the Yellow Team ("mushy middle") councillors, who were aligned neither with the mayor's coalition nor with his opposition. They were demanding that a number of small projects that city staff had eliminated be put back into the budget—about a $15 million ask.

We were managing a combined operating, capital, and rate-supported budget package of over $13 billion, an amount that was essentially going to be the same as the year before. For the first time in memory, we were going to stop the ballooning of the city's budget. Against that background, $15 million—about one tenth of one percent of of the total budget package— didn't concern me much. But I felt it was important to fight attempts to add money back into the budget. I'd learned that, often, the best way to get Council to do something was through misdirection. While Council focused on our left hand, which was fighting them on the $15 million in discretionary additions, our right hand was quietly pushing through the rest of the $13 billion package. I was quite pleased with myself, actually.

Rob didn't want to give in on any of the councillors' requests. But we had agreed with the budget chief that we could let the "mushy middle" win this one. In fact, we figured, we could add more than $15 million back in if we needed to and still hit our targets. We didn't want to roll over on the $15 million before the council meeting, though; we knew people would start looking for more things to add back in. So we continued to oppose them—so they wouldn't fight for even more spending.

Unfortunately, I didn't get to feel pleased for long. I should have realized that the process of fighting us was actually bonding the highly individualistic, unaligned councillors into a coalition. Leaders were emerging. I didn't recognize the threat until it was too late.

We could have backed down on the floor of Council and sided with the middle to pass the $15 million additions. That would have produced a near-unanimous vote. Amir and I recommended that Rob do so. But he didn't want to accede to their demands. He didn't believe any of the requested additions were worth spending taxpayer money on. He decided we would stand to the last man, even though I explained quite clearly that we were going to lose. It was a certainty. I even told him the vote count. But he prevailed, so we whipped our coalition to stand with him. Our councillors didn't like that one bit; they didn't want to be seen to lose a vote.

Yet once the decision was made, I felt it was important for them all to go down together. If they stood proud against "spending," our coalition would be stronger than if it fell apart. It would also send a powerful signal to our labor unions, who were at the bargaining table with us as the budget debates were happening. I wanted our chief negotiator, a hard-nosed, battle-hardened veteran named Bob Reynolds, to be able to point at the mayor and say to the unions, "You think he's going to blink? He just faced down a firing squad even though he knew he was going to lose. He's not going to blink before you do."

As the bells were ringing, announcing the vote on the $15 million budget amendment, I was approached in a panic by councillor Michelle Berardinetti followed by Jaye Robinson. Berardinetti seemed desperate. Robinson was wavering. "Are you sure we can win this?" Berardinetti asked. "Are you sure we should vote no?"

I looked at her. We'd had this conversation a half dozen times in the past thirty-six hours. She knew we were going to lose. So did Robinson. They also both knew they had to stand together with the team, or the team would be finished. I knew they wanted to believe we could win. So I lied to them.

With the bells ringing, the Speaker was ordering me off the council floor. Most councillors were already in their seats, pressing their buttons, and the crowd was leaning in, salivating in anticipation of what they hoped would be a victory against the mayor. I looked them in their eyes and said, "If we have your two votes, Councillors, we will win."

They sighed, went back to their seats, and voted with the mayor. If I had that moment to do over again, I don't know that I would do it differently. We needed them to stand with the mayor. But it bothers me to this day that I wasn't able to find another way to win their confidence in the heat of the moment without lying.

When we lost that one minor amendment (23 to 21, exactly as we'd projected), Rob was livid. Despite our explaining our strategy to him throughout the budget process, and getting his approval at every stage, he was angry. Amir, Earl, and I had coached him on seizing the victory. He got his tax rate. He got a budget lower than the previous year's. He hit all the targets he'd promised. The right hand had won the day.

But like the councillors we'd sought to misdirect, all Rob could see was the left hand. All he could think about was the $15 million vote he'd lost. Not the $13 billion vote he'd won. All he could see was failure. When he spoke with the media, he should have declared victory. He read our talking points, but he was half-hearted. He looked like a man who'd lost the battle.

What I didn't understand until later was that the balance of power had shifted in Council. Not only had the mushy middle learned to work together, they'd learned they could succeed. It didn't matter that they were fighting over something we were happy to let them win. They didn't know that. What they did know was that they could win. That would prove to be a problem.

One year later, as we were preparing the 2013 budget, everything had changed. The mayor's office had no time for financial strategies—we were fully consumed by managing the train wreck that Rob Ford had become. We had little capacity to provide much strategic guidance on the budget. We left it largely in the hands of the budget chief, Councillor Mike Del Grande, and Sheila Paxton, a mature, experienced City Hall political staffer with a brilliant mind. I'd poached Sheila from Councillor

Mark Grimes when I became chief of staff. Together, they delivered a 2013 budget that included a two percent tax increase and met our targets without causing mayhem in Council. We had enough mayhem on our hands already.

# 15 | Behind Closed Doors

As FAR AS I know, I'm the only person Rob Ford has ever actually fired. Normally, the chief of staff would be responsible for hiring and firing in the mayor's office—to do the dirty work and to disappoint people, which politicians don't like to do. But as we know, Ford wasn't a typical politician. In his mayoralty, he and he alone could approve new hires. (He approved as few as possible, after delaying as long as possible.) Every dollar of salary was authorized by him. Every office expense was approved personally by Ford. As well, he and he alone could approve someone's being fired. As tough as he talked, though, I don't believe he'd fired anyone until he became mayor. It's a sign of how cornered he felt after the Gawker video story that he pulled the trigger on me.

In addition to the myriad political dramas we managed daily on the second floor and in the council chambers, there were also the routine petty politics of managing an office full of political operatives and trying to keep them all aligned to the same goals. We had a core team that had bonded during the campaign, and integrating new people into the team wasn't always easy. Most of this happened behind closed doors, though it did occasionally erupt loudly enough to draw public attention.

When Rob was first elected, staffing his office was Nick Kouvalis's and my first hurdle. Rob and Doug had no idea how to do it. But they had friends—many of whom were part of their respective Night Shifts—they wanted places for. Nick and I wanted to find as many places as we could for the senior campaign staff who had soldiered with us through eighteen- and twenty-hour days during the campaign—places in our office, or in the offices of councillors, especially the new councillors. (We figured they'd be loyal to us there, and it would be win-win.) And remember, Ford had capped the number of staff at eighteen.

For many municipal politicians, eighteen may seem large. But Toronto, the fourth-largest city in North America, has the sixth-largest government in Canada—it's larger than seven of the ten provinces and all three of the territories. We needed those staffers, and we needed them to be good.

By the time Ford was sworn in, his office was about 60 percent staffed. As the campaign team lacked hands-on experience inside City Hall, we brought in three experienced political staffers who'd worked the second floor at City Hall for years. Andrew Pask and Olivia Gondek had both worked for Rob when he was a councillor. They knew him well and he trusted them. We also brought in Sunny Petrujkic, who'd been executive assistant to Case Ootes, the chair of Rob's transition team and a well-respected retired city councillor and deputy mayor. To this mix, we added Tina Arvanitis, who'd worked in Ottawa for Jim Flaherty, Canada's minister of finance, and understood communication, political branding, and operational planning.

Though Nick was chief of staff, Doug also insisted on hiring Cathy DeMarco, who managed the Fords' label business in Chicago. He was grooming her to eventually replace Nick—even though she had no prior experience in politics or government. She was under the gun from the get-go. She faced a steep learning curve, compounded by the logistical challenges of relocating. And because she was more Doug's choice than Rob's, she was caught between the two brothers. I suspect Doug saw her as his first mole in Rob's office. I think Rob did, too, and quickly began to reject her. It seemed to me that he was projecting his frustrations with his brother onto Cathy. She worked hard, but didn't stay long.

Tina Arvanitis didn't, either. She came in like an Energizer Bunny, full of ideas and experience, and we used her many talents to help us rebrand some citywide projects that were closely associated with the former mayor, to better reflect Rob Ford's priorities. She was a key asset, but we could never afford to pay her what she was worth, and an industry association looking for someone to help it grow quickly scooped her up.

What we didn't have, and never did get, was a director of communications. Looking back, it was one of our greatest failings. Adrienne Batra, who'd stayed on after the campaign as press secretary, was a brilliant media pit bull, and she knew how to handle Rob. But she wasn't charged with communication strategy and planning. Nick had looked around for an experienced political communications director, but anyone good enough was asking $130,000 or more, which Rob felt was exorbitant. He thought $40,000 was a great income. So that position remained unfilled. As time went on and we immersed ourselves, first in policy and legislative initiatives, then in Rob's personal issues, we felt its lack more and more keenly.

While Tina and Cathy came and went quietly, as you might expect in a professional political office, the departure of Nick Kouvalis was somewhat more dramatic. It was brought about by a standoff with Andrew Pask. Pask had been Rob's EA for seven years when Rob was on Council; he'd left to pursue other opportunities, something Rob considered disloyal. But Nick and I needed experienced people on our Council relations team, to help us manage relationships with the councillors and their staffs. We convinced Rob that Pask was the guy to manage that team. Olivia Gondek and Sunny Petrujkic would report to Pask, and Pask would report to me.

It took a lot of convincing. Rob liked Pask, but called him a traitor for leaving. That was ridiculous. Rob talked often about how he'd never hold anyone back, but he didn't understand what that meant in practice. He expected everyone he hired to remain in servitude to him forever. Eventually Nick and I prevailed—but then Pask didn't work out. He was used to working directly for Rob, and behaved as if he should have Nick's job. He seemed particularly offended that he reported to me, a City Hall neophyte.

The final straw snapped one morning in January, when Nick and Pask got into a shouting match that ended with Nick firing Pask. Pask refused to be fired, insisting that he reported only to Rob. So Nick called City Hall security to escort Pask out. It was an ugly scene.

When Rob arrived, he called both Pask and Nick into his office and played the "what's your side of the story" game. He was infamous for this. He didn't understand organizational structure or team dynamics. He treated everyone "equally"—regularly undermining his chief of staff and city managers by overruling them in front of subordinates.

Nick explained that Pask wasn't performing and that he had fired him. Rob, who thought only he could fire people (even though he never followed through) and didn't want to make a decision, delivered what he thought was a clever ultimatum: "Either you both go, or you both stay."

Nick had planned to stay on as chief of staff until April or May, then hand over the reins to me—or, if Doug had his way, to Cathy DeMarco. He knew he'd have no control over Pask if they both stayed.

"If I go . . . he goes too?" Nick clarified with the mayor. Yes.

So he told Rob, "OK. You need to fire us."

It was not the answer Rob had expected. Or, for that matter, Pask. But Rob went along with it, and Pask stormed out.

By the time Ford asked me to assemble the staff for a meeting, Nick had left, too. Rob made this terse statement: "Nick and Andrew are gone. They don't work here anymore. Mark is the interim chief of staff until we hire a permanent one. Any questions?"

The room was stunned. Me, too—it was the first I'd heard about being interim chief. Both Fords had a habit of making decisions on the fly, without consulting those most affected by them.

Rob returned to his office and I took over the meeting. It was business as usual, I said. There was lots of work to do: constituent issues, policy development, council and committee preparation. No change. No one was to comment on rumors. No one was to speak with the press. Adrienne would confirm that Nick and Andrew had both left the staff and that I was interim chief until a permanent replacement was appointed.

Within an hour, the media was reporting that Ford had fired Kouvalis. There was no mention of Pask's departure. I assumed Pask was the source, managing his reputation, hoping perhaps that if no one knew he'd been "fired" too, he might have a chance to mend fences with Rob and return. That would be bad for the office, and for me. So I told a couple of key City Hall reporters, including one at the *Toronto Star*, that there was more to the story. By the end of the day, the media was reporting that both Kouvalis and Pask had been let go.

Later that day, Rob told me he'd like to keep me as chief of staff, but he would have to look around. He really liked me, he said, but Doug didn't. I wasn't surprised, and I'd hear it often over the next two years. It may even have been true.

Nick's departure chummed the water, and the next month was a political feeding frenzy for every backroom shark who wanted to take over the mayor's office. Nobody in the political establishment respected the Fords. Everyone thought they were idiots who'd stumbled into the vault. The mayor's office controlled a $13 billion budget, and the guy running it didn't owe anyone anything. As a result, since Rob had been elected, no one knew which way the city was going to go. No one knew which initiatives would be funded and which wouldn't. In short, the social circle that counted on knowledge of the political winds to enrich their bank accounts was, for the first time in modern memory, completely without a weather vane.

But here was a chance for them to control the weather. Whoever could put "their guy" in as chief of staff would be able to set their sails before the competition could react. Fortunes could, once again, be made in a predictable and "civilized" manner. Resumes poured in by the dozens. Candidates, all seemingly sponsored by some power broker or another, were advanced.

In the end, the decision came down to me and Amir Remtulla, a political veteran who was well thought of in Conservative party circles. He was highly recommended by Case Ootes, who'd recruited him to the transition team; and he was close with Paul Godfrey, one of Toronto's captains of industry, a political and business "godfather" and highly respected backroom power broker.

On January 27, 2011, the city's elite gathered for the Harmony Dinner—a chance to pay their respects to the new mayor, and to donate funds to erase the almost $1 million in outstanding debt from the Ford, Rossi, and Thomson mayoral campaigns. Just before Rob took his seat at the head table, he pulled me aside and told me he'd hired Amir as chief of staff. Later that night, Doug added that it had been a "tough decision." Naturally, I was disappointed. I considered quitting, but I couldn't afford to. I assumed that Amir would want to bring in his own team, but I didn't think Ford would be willing to fire me. And Ford, as I said, insisted that only he could.

From the day Amir began as Rob's chief of staff in February 2011, however, I was never confident on Monday that I'd still be working there by Friday. Things began to go wrong almost immediately. I don't think it was Amir's fault. I think it stemmed from a growing battle for power between the Ford brothers.

Now that Rob was mayor, he didn't have to acquiesce to Doug's dictates. He had the law on his side (being mayor was a one-person job), as well as the experience (Doug was a rookie and didn't know his way around City Hall politics) and the staff (we frequently reminded him he was mayor, not Doug). But if Rob ignored Doug, Doug would pummel him with endless calls and tenacious harassment. Often, Rob would cry uncle, telling us, "I can't handle one more call from him. Just do it."

Amir's leadership style was different from Nick's and mine. He liked to bellow at meetings. He felt that if he stressed emphatically enough that something *must succeed* that it would, somehow, magically do so. When something didn't work as he'd hoped, he'd harangue the staff until he'd vented his frustration. Still, I resolved to work with him and never undermine him.

The subway wars made everything harder. During transition, both Amir and Case Ootes had argued at length against the mayor's agenda to build a subway along Sheppard Avenue, an east-west corridor to the north of the city. But Rob was adamant: The city needed rapid transit, and the Miller-era light-rail plan—which ran on the surface, not underground—had never been intended to move people quickly. It was intended to move more people.

When Amir came onboard as Rob's chief, he told me point-blank that he needed to be convinced that the new subway was a good idea. I tried, but I was paranoid: I knew he couldn't fire me without Rob's approval. But I also knew he could engineer circumstances where I'd fail on something major and be forced to quit. I vowed to keep my head down and prove my support.

From the beginning of Amir's tenure, the office had a pool on how long he'd last as chief of staff. I didn't participate, but I figured he'd be around a year. That was enough time to leave without it looking like a mistake: He could take credit for one or two successes, say he'd done the job he set out to do, then get the hell out of Dodge. In fact, he lasted about eighteen months. That made him Ford's longest-serving chief. By the end of his four-year term, Rob had had five chiefs and two interim chiefs.

Also from the beginning of Amir's tenure, Doug Ford seemed to be working against him. I think Doug wanted to be Rob's chief. He competed viciously with every one of us. We heard countless stories about him attending various conservative social events, meeting big-shot party stalwarts, and soliciting them to fill Amir's job. Not an easy environment for anyone to work in.

Further complicating matters for Amir, and the rest of us, was that Nick didn't leave when he was fired. Rob had agreed to let him lead the subway file from outside the office, to help protect his reputation by demonstrating he still had influence over the mayor. This, of course, made Amir's job excruciatingly difficult. People outside the office didn't know who was in charge. Nick, Rob, and Doug spoke frequently. Nick regularly told me how tired he was getting of Rob and Doug's constant calls asking his advice and complaining about Amir. Almost daily, Amir would complain that Nick was calling Rob and Doug to badmouth him. Doug regularly complained that Nick called him all the time. I just listened to everyone and nodded.

Amir assumed the whole staff was feeding Nick information. It made him a very nervous cat. He was guarded with me. He frequently had private meetings with Rob, city councillors, civil servants, other levels of government, and external stakeholders. He had regular off-site breakfast meetings with his mentors and political friends and sponsors outside City Hall. This made sense to me—he was, after all, the mayor's chief of staff.

What didn't make sense was that much of the direction I received from Amir didn't seem to come from Rob. On the subway file, in particular, Amir seemed to be creating obstacles that didn't need to be created. On other files, he seemed to be doling out bits and pieces of information on a highly compartmentalized basis. It was a little bit like living in a detective novel. Earl, the other staffers from the campaign days, and I had developed a pretty open approach to information. Because it was often hard to figure out what Rob was doing, we tended to pool our information to build a better picture of what was happening. We used that practice to analyze what Amir was up to as well.

Most of Amir's behavior could be chalked up to skittishness. He knew he was walking into a high-profile job that could make or break his career. His primary mission, from the beginning, appeared to be "Don't fuck up." He was cautious. He assumed everyone on staff was out to get him. He managed a bit like a dictator under siege. A few months into Amir's tenure, I stopped going to morning staff meetings. I think he preferred it when I wasn't there.

Rob didn't help matters—he had a habit of making up tales in order to pit one staff member against the other. I often wondered where he'd learned that behavior. Every other day, I'd have a staff member—from the most junior to senior—in my office complaining about something another staffer had told the mayor. The second they'd pause for breath, I'd interject.

"How do you know this?" I'd ask.

"The mayor told me Person X had said I wasn't doing my job properly and they had to cover for me constantly," he or she would complain.

"And what do we know about things the mayor says?" I'd ask.

The aggrieved staffer would stare at me and take a few breaths, and then I'd see the person's eyes light up and shoulders relax.

"He's full of shit, isn't he?"

"Yep," I'd say.

Rob had done it to me at least a dozen times since I started working for him in March 2010. In a private moment, he'd say something like: *What's going on with you and Amir* (or any of the other staff, his brother, a councillor, supporter, or anyone we were dealing with at the time)? *He's pissed at you and wants to fire you. He says you keep screwing up and he's had it with you. I told him I didn't want to fire you. I think you should talk to him and sort it out.*

He seemed to love winding people up and pointing them at each other. I started to think it was his way of feeling in control, by keeping everyone around him on edge. If everyone else was screwed up, he'd feel better about himself.

We quickly figured out what he was doing, and it became part of the standard briefing I'd give new staffers: "Welcome aboard. Sometimes, the mayor likes to wind people up." I'd urge them to come to me if it happened. Usually they did, and I was able to calm things down. As Rob's addiction problems worsened, though, that would become more difficult.

One of Amir's first orders was to have Earl, Adrienne, and me produce "strategies." I was to produce a policy and legislative strategy. Earl was to write a stakeholder strategy and Adrienne a communication strategy. I recognized the task: When I was vying to be chief of staff, Doug had insisted that I deliver written strategies, so things could be measured. I was sure he would never read a written strategy if one were produced. Clearly, Amir was fulfilling a promise he'd made to Rob and Doug during his interview process.

Adrienne and Earl tried to submit strategies. I wasn't about to. I was already working from 8:00 a.m. to midnight six days a week, and I thought the idea was frankly idiotic. What was the point of writing a four-year, day-by-day strategy, when the challenges were constantly changing? Also, I was concerned if I wrote such a plan, Amir (and probably Rob and Doug) would figure they didn't need me any more.

So on the day I was supposed to present my "plan" I threw together a few PowerPoint slides and delivered an overview of objectives and pathways, complete with pyramid charts and Venn diagrams. I hadn't been a consultant for twelve years for nothing. Amir, Rob, and Doug acted like I'd shown them the key to a secret alphabet. I gave the same presentation a few more times to different members of the executive committee, and each time I was a hero. Every day for the next two weeks, Amir asked for an electronic copy of the presentation. Then every couple of weeks for six months after that. Eventually Amir resigned, and on August 20, 2012, I became Ford's third chief of staff. I never did give Amir a copy of that presentation, though. I'm loyal as hell. But I'm not stupid.

# 16 | The Union Deal

IN FEBRUARY 2011, Doug Ford came out swinging against the city's unionized employees—specifically, against a job security clause known as "jobs for life." "Nobody should have a job for life," Doug told the *Toronto Star*. "I can tell you we'll go after it in every negotiation we can. I can't say we'll be successful, but I can say we'll give it one hell of a try."

The union's response was predictable and immediate: "Employment security is a number one priority for Local 416," Mark Ferguson, the local's president, said in the same article. "It's not a clause that we are going to negotiate out of our collective agreement." The president of the local labor council, John Cartwright, took it one step further: He described the Ford administration's intent as "Coming to kick the shit out of their workers."

And just like that, the stage was set for a bloody labor battle and a protracted strike that could last, analysts and academics predicted, through the summer of 2012. But they were wrong. The union negotiation was one of the things Rob Ford did just right.

Thousands of unionized frontline city workers had voted for Ford. They were the same people who'd slipped Ford envelopes stuffed with evidence of wasteful mismanagement while he was still a councillor. These formed the basis of many of his anecdotes that resonated so well with voters. The employees knew there was waste in the system, and Ford knew there was a difference between the rank-and-file workers and their union leaders. As a result, we were always careful to focus our attacks on the union leaders, not the workers.

\*\*\*

Since Toronto's amalgamation in 1998, the city's unions had steadily gained power through a series of successful labor negotiations. The "jobs for life" provision, which guaranteed job security for all permanent employees, was their greatest triumph. Employees could be fired for cause, but it was virtually impossible to lay anyone off if the city wanted to reorganize a department. Other clauses stripped managers of their ability to set work hours and shift lengths. Unless something changed, the efficiencies that Ford had been elected to realize would be impossible.

The city's collective agreements with the city's two largest unions, Local 79 (representing about twenty thousand indoor workers) and Local 416 (eight thousand outdoor workers in the parks, transportation, solid waste, and water divisions, as well as paramedics), both expired at the end of 2011. Local 416, though smaller, was scrappier, and Local 79 usually followed 416's lead.

If history was the guide, the city would sit down with the unions in January 2012, after the previous three-year agreement had expired. The process would carry on into the spring, and if discussions broke down, the unions would go on strike in the summer, when the weather was nice. In Toronto's most recent major strike, during the blazingly hot summer of 2009, festering mountains of garbage had risen in city parks, choking the city with their stench. No one wanted a replay of that.

We decided early on—as far back as the transition period—to take a different tactic. We wanted to drive union negotiations on our schedule. If there was going to be a strike, we wanted it to happen in January or February, when frigid winter temperatures would curtail both the smell of garbage and any enthusiasm for picket lines. Olivia Gondek, who had a master's degree in industrial relations, became our go-to person on the labor strategy file. We also pushed Joe Pennachetti, the city manager, to fill the long-vacant position of chief negotiator with someone who had a killer instinct, who would battle to roll back some of the more egregious benefits in the unions' contracts.

Amir and I held information-gathering meetings with top labor relations lawyers. My "technique" was to ask questions like a third-grader: "So what happens on January first if there's no new agreement? Does everything just stop?"

Their answer was no: Normally the union keeps working until bargaining breaks down. At that point, we could choose to lock out our employees or they could vote to strike. The strike could begin immediately after a yes vote, or at some point later on.

We didn't want the unions to choose the timing of a disruption. We could control the timing by locking out employees rather than waiting for a strike. But Rob was insistent we not do that. Any labor disruption would hurt frontline workers. If they were going to be out of work and without pay, he wanted it to be the union's fault.

If we locked them out, we also feared losing the moral high ground and public support. If that started to soften, I knew, our councillors would fold like cheap suits and hand the union everything it wanted.

"So if bargaining continues and work continues," I asked, "what do people get paid? What are the terms of their employment?"

The answer: Work normally continues under the terms of the expired agreement until a new agreement is put in place. But technically, since there's no agreement in place, the city could impose new terms and conditions. Of course, that would probably trigger the union to strike.

Bingo! That was the detail we'd been looking for. We'd impose terms that would provoke them to strike in January's dark deep-freeze. Sure, they could choose to wait to strike until summer—but by then they'd have worked for six months under the new terms, and they'd be loath to subsist on strike pay. The lawyers warned us that it's rarely done, and had never been done before in the public sector. But for me, that was good news: Nobody would see it coming.

Amir, Olivia, and I agreed to keep our plan secret as long as possible, and, if necessary, to let people think we were planning a lockout. Rob agreed—as long as we could force them out in the winter. Those heaps of rotting garbage had helped bring down David Miller. He didn't want them crushing him, too.

On June 6, 2011, we met with city staff on the labor file. They needed to know how long an agreement to seek (two, three, or four years?), and what bargaining targets to go for. Our priority was concessions on the "jobs for life" clause and the return of management rights; we'd even yield on affordable wage increases if we had to, to achieve them. But the length question gave us pause. A two-year contract would see us return to the bargaining table in 2014; we could bargain for some concessions in the first contract, then try to extract the rest in 2014. A three-year contract would have us come back just before the Pan Am Games (a major international multi-sport event, basically a minor Olympics) arrived in Toronto in the summer of 2015, but we didn't want that—it would give the unions way too much leverage. We opted for a four-year agreement that would end after the Pan Am Games.

The city staff bargaining team officially received its mandate from a City Council committee known as the ELRC, the Employee and Labour

Relations Committee. The ELRC was chaired by the deputy mayor, and included other councillors whom we'd selected because they were fiscally conservative and discreet. We'd intentionally omitted New Democratic Party councillors, because the NDP was historically aligned with the unions. Still, every councillor could attend ELRC meetings, even those conducted out of public view. So we couldn't discuss our real bargaining strategy there; we'd do that in the mayor's office. The deputy mayor, as chair of the ELRC, would take his instructions from Rob. In the meantime, we geared up for a strike.

At the close of the June 6 meeting, I asked the city staff the same question I'd asked the outside lawyers, but they gave me a different answer. They agreed that, in the event of a strike, work continues under the same terms, but they did not agree that the city could impose terms. So Amir and I pushed the city staff to engage outside legal counsel—not in the event of a strike, but now. Lo and behold, when they did this, they came back to us with a brilliant new plan: *We can impose terms and conditions!* Amir and I smiled.

***

In October 2011, the city served notice of its intent to bargain both Local 79's and Local 416's contracts. They union members were surprised. In fact, Local 79 refused to bargain; they said they wouldn't be ready until January. The city underwent the process of filing the complaints and reports that would set the stage for a lockout on January 19, 2012.

But remember, this is Canada, land of hockey. Though a January strike would save us from reeking garbage, it would jeopardize the amateur hockey season because most teams played in city-operated ice rinks. So city staff also conducted special training sessions for management so they'd be able to drive Zamboni machines on city rinks. Such is the stuff local government is made of.

The Zamboni plan was just part of the city's contingency plan for a labor disruption, be it a strike or a lockout. We thought a protracted strike was likely, and Rob had been quite clear in his meetings with us and with city staff: If the union walked out, we wanted the city to keep operating. Managers must be able to keep city services operating. Where they couldn't, he wanted replacement workers brought in. City staff bristled at this, noting it would enrage the unions. We didn't care. Unless we were going to stop collecting taxes, Rob Ford wasn't going to stop providing services. Staff eventually developed a detailed plan and trained managers on line functions. This readiness plan eventually leaked out to the unions and helped convince them we were planning to lock them out in January.

In the meantime, bargaining continued. A key part of our strategy was to ensure that what we asked for was reasonable. Rob wasn't crazy about that. He would prefer to hold the unions to zero wage increases and complete elimination of the "jobs for life" clauses. But he was willing to listen to reason—especially when that reason was spoken by Bob Reynolds, the man Pennachetti had hired in the early fall to be the city's chief negotiator.

Reynolds was a gruff, plain-spoken, cowboy-like veteran of combative negotiations across Canada and around the world. He always had a twinkle in his eye and a smile about to appear on his face. For every situation, he had a story to tell about a similar time that had ended with a car blowing up or a gun being drawn in some backwater mining town hours from law and order. Rob trusted him immediately.

Ford wanted to reduce job protection coverage from everyone to no one. Reynolds convinced us that was unreasonable. He pointed out that no union leader had ever won reelection after *conceding* rights. Whatever agreements we negotiated would have to be ratified by each union's membership, so the presidents would have to be able to sell it as a good deal. Reynolds showed us that if we rolled back the job protection clause so it only protected workers with twenty-two years' seniority, then 50 percent of the membership would still be protected. And the union president only needed 50 percent plus one to win the ratification vote.

Our next step was making sure the public—including the union members—knew how reasonable our proposals were. We weren't going to let the union own the message. So we engaged Karen Gordon, of Toronto-based Squeaky Wheel Communications, to help shape it. She'd recently worked on the collective agreement between Toronto and its police service, and knew the city well.

Karen and I agreed that Rob Ford couldn't be the face of the negotiation. He was too polarizing a figure. Rob agreed with our assessment. Rather than lead the file, his role was to remain resolute and stubborn on the budget and the subway plan, to signal that he was not going to accept anything less than victory, and he played it to the hilt.

So Deputy Mayor Doug Holyday became the public face of our negotiation team. Doug is a somewhat irascible sweetheart, a then-seventy-year-old former mayor of Etobicoke, who was respected as a straight-talking, well-mannered fiscal hawk with a sharp wit. He and Karen drafted a series of op-ed columns for local papers, which got our message out early. A public opinion poll conducted in late January 2012 proved our strategy was working: 71 percent of Toronto residents felt the unions' "jobs for life" clause was unreasonable.

After the contracts expired on December 31, 2011, the public and the unions expected us to lock out workers on January 19, 2012, the first day we could legally do so. We in the mayor's office were expecting the unions to strike as soon as they learned of our intent to impose terms. (I was shocked that our secret plan was still under wraps.) Bargaining continued. We were willing to give the unions small wage increases, but insisted on concessions on job security. The unions, for their part, offered to accept a wage freeze but were holding firm on job security.

On Tuesday, January 31, a large group gathered in the mayor's boardroom at 3:30 p.m. The room was stuffy and packed to the rafters. Attending were the mayor, Doug Ford, Deputy Mayor Doug Holyday, Councillors Denzil Minnan-Wong and Mike Del Grande, Amir, Olivia Gondek, and me. From city staff there was Bob Reynolds; City Manager Joe Pennachetti; Bruce Anderson, executive director of human resources; Darragh Meagher, director of employment law; and Jackie DeSouza, director of corporate communications. Rounding out the meeting were Craig Rix, a partner from the outside law firm advising us; and Karen Gordon, our outside public relations consultant.

City staff advised us that there had been no substantive progress made in bargaining with Local 416. They were dealing with 416 first because, although it was the smaller of the two main city unions, it was traditionally the most aggressive and 79 often followed its lead in bargaining. The senior city staff recommended a strike/lockout deadline of midnight on Saturday, February 4. We would be ready to lock out employees Monday morning, while the union would have to take a strike vote before they'd be in a legal strike position. Local 79 was watching the aggressive nature of our negotiation with 416 and was, unusually for them, keeping its distance.

The city was ready to begin its contingency messaging on Thursday, advising residents and staff what to do in the event of a labor disruption. On Friday, we would inform the union that we weren't going to lock them out if a deal was not reached by midnight Saturday. Instead, we were going to impose terms and conditions on Sunday. Ford listened unusually closely and asked a lot of questions, but he was ready.

The Office of the Mayor, in early 2011, pose with Governor General David Johnston and his wife, Sharon Johnston. Back row, from left: Isaac Shirokoff, Nick Kouvalis, myself, Brian Johnston, Tom Beyer, Michael Ford, Andrew Pask, Adrienne Batra, Sunny Petrujkic, Cathy DeMarco, Olivia Gondek, Earl Provost, Adam Howell, Pina Martino, Jennifer Dwyer, and Kia Nejatian. (City of Toronto)

Rob flips pancakes at the Calgary Stampeders' Grey Cup breakfast in front of Toronto City Hall, November 2012. (Author's collection)

Rob, Amin Massoudi, Doug Ford, and I celebrate outside the law offices of Lenczner Slaght after learning Rob won his appeal on conflict of interest charges and so would not be removed from office. (Author's collection)

Rob signs documents during a lighter moment in the mayor's office. Amir Remtulla, Adrienne Batra, Jennifer Dwyer, and Kia Nejatian look on. (Author's collection)

Rob's annual Ford Fest, 2014. More than a thousand people attended. (© Victor Biro/
Demotix/Corbis)

Isaac Ransom, Earl Provost, Doug Ford, and Rob preparing for the mayor's weekly radio show. (Author's collection)

Rob and I during a special council meeting on the proposed casino. (Steve Russell)

Rob and Dieter Doneit-Henderson. After Dieter claimed that Rob had not responded to an email, Rob made a point of visiting him in his home. (Rick Madonik)

Rob launching his Cut the Waist Challenge. He said, "Enough's enough. You can't be running the city, you can't be doing all this, at 330 pounds." He abandoned the challenge five months later. (© Carlos Osorio/ZUMA Press/Corbis)

Rob speaks with Global TV news reporter Jackson Proskow behind his home. They are standing next to the cinderblocks that Rob claimed *Toronto Star* reporter Daniel Dale had used to peer over his backyard fence. Rob later apologized to Dale for insinuating the reporter was photographing Rob's children. (Author's collection)

Rob listens to his brother Doug. Doug was one of his closest confidants, but the two often went head-to-head in disagreements. (Associated Press)

The mayor and I after attending a gay rights flag-raising event. Just hours before, the *Toronto Star* and Gawker announced they'd seen a cell phone video of Rob smoking crack cocaine. (© BRETT GUNDLOCK/Reuters/Corbis)

Rob and his wife, Renata, during a news conference. Rob admitted he was receiving professional help for drinking problems and apologized for using obscene language earlier in the day when he denied allegations that he had made sexually suggestive comments to a female aide. (© MARK BLINCH/Reuters/Corbis)

One of many rallies and demonstrations held to evict Mayor Ford. (Danielle Scott)

A photo still from a video of Rob smoking crack cocaine. The video is one of three clips that a self-professed crack and heroin dealer claimed to have shot in the basement of Rob's sister's home. After months of denials, Rob checked himself into rehab the day after this image was published. (*The Globe and Mail*)

My walk out of City Hall after being fired by Rob. (Associated Press)

When the announcement came on Friday, the public and unions were shocked. Imposing terms had never been done in the public sector in Canada before. The unions didn't have a response planned for this scenario. They'd either have to suck it up or go on strike Monday—in the middle of winter, before they were ready.

The city and Local 416 bargaining teams and the mediator were holed up on the top floor of the Sheraton Hotel across the street from City Hall. The city's team was set up in a low-ceilinged, poorly lit, wood-paneled meeting room that might have been the height of luxury in 1972 when the hotel opened, but hadn't been updated since. The team of lawyers, labor relations, communications, and administrative staff had been hunkered down there for weeks. The room smelled of sweat and warm bodies mixed with that morning's muffins, half-eaten sandwiches, and stale coffee.

As the evening wore on, and Amir and I popped in and out to get updates, it seemed clear that we weren't going to reach an agreement before midnight. Reynolds wanted an extension, but he wasn't going to ask for one yet. Rob, hunkered down in his office for the night, agreed.

We extended the deadline by two hours. 2:00 a.m. came and went. Reynolds was in his element: exhausted, but running on adrenalin. He'd already won agreement on everything we wanted—better than we'd hoped to get on many fronts. The union had finally buckled on rolling back the "jobs for life" clause, but was pushing back on limiting it to employees with twenty-two years' seniority.

But as time ticked on, Reynolds proposed to me that we give on the twenty-two years. He thought the union would accept fifteen years as the cutoff point. The mandate he'd been given by the ELRC (with a nod from the mayor) authorized him to go as low as ten years, but he didn't think he'd have to. He wanted to know if the mayor would be okay with fifteen.

I went back to Rob's office. The lights were dimmed and he was stretched out asleep on the big leather couch in his office, shoes and tie off, shirt unbuttoned at the neck, and sleeves rolled up to the elbows. I woke him and he lay there while I briefed him on Reynolds's plan. He listened carefully, scratched his head, and asked if there was any way we could get more. I told him neither Reynolds nor I thought so, and he signed off on it. The deal was done.

We agreed to let 416 announce the deal first and put their spin on it. It was close to complete capitulation on their part, but we were careful to call it simply a victory for taxpayers. At about 5:00 a.m., I sketched out some remarks for Rob and tweeted word of a press conference: The mayor would speak to reporters outside the Sheraton in thirty minutes. At some point the thought crossed my mind that 90 percent of the people who followed me on Twitter were opposition activists who hated me. I hoped the other 10 percent were media.

Rob spoke in the dawn light, with City Hall behind him. He stuck to his message: It was an "absolutely fantastic day for the taxpayers of this great city." No gloating.

In the days that followed, Local 79 and the city's other, smaller unions followed suit. Although the library union went on strike briefly, it eventually settled for essentially the same deal as the others. The labor negotiations proved to be the crowning moment of Ford's term as mayor. He set the stage and provided the political capital and intestinal fortitude that drove the process. Because he was tenacious in the face of criticism, the city staff were able to take a risk on an innovative strategy. They knew he would back them in a fight. And he was content to stay in the background, providing a motivating force. He set the parameters at the beginning, pushed everyone to reach for more, then got out of the way and let everyone do their jobs. If only he could always have been that way.

As Doug Ford had promised off the cuff in February 2011, we'd gone after the "jobs for life" clause as hard as we could. Although Ford hadn't completely eliminated the clause, we'd beaten it back significantly and made Canadian labor relations history in the process. Governments across Canada called on the city manager to teach them what Toronto had done.

It turned out that Doug stayed out of the negotiation process largely because he'd been working on a side project of his own: an ill-fated plan to redraw the city's vision for its multibillion-dollar waterfront redevelopment. He worked on it secretly, keeping it away from Rob and the mayor's office until just before launching it into the public eye at the end of August 2011. The public reaction to his proposal was swift and brutal: Doug was widely ridiculed, and members of the mayor's coalition threatened rebellion. He kept a low profile for many months after that.

# 17 | The Subway Wars

SUNDAY, FEBRUARY 5, 2012 was arguably the highlight of Rob Ford's mayoralty, with his decisive victory over the city's most rancorous union. But the chill was barely off the champagne before the long slide downhill began.

Sunday afternoon, we heard rumors that Councillor Karen Stintz—the chair of the Toronto Transit Commission—had done something no other city councillor had done since the city was amalgamated. She'd secured the signatures of enough councillors on a petition to call a special meeting of Council to debate, and kill, Ford's signature Sheppard Avenue subway plan. By Monday morning, the newspapers, which should have been applauding Ford's victory over the unions, were instead heralding a major defeat on the subways.

I was angry—and worried. Although Nick was supposed to have taken charge of it when he "left" the office, the subway file had become mine; a public failure here would hurt. My days at City Hall seemed numbered. Again. Still.

Rob was frustrated. "They're gonna vote no?" he asked rhetorically, shaking his head. Trying to understand it. "Seriously? They're gonna vote for streetcars? They're gonna get killed in the election."

To him the whole issue was a no-brainer. People wanted subways; they didn't want streetcars. Just ask them, they said so. That's all there was to it. He couldn't fathom how anyone could fail to understand and support this.

At the beginning of the 2010 campaign, all the candidates but Ford had been pushing their transit visions as "the big issue" of the campaign. Ford, by contrast, summed up his transit strategy simply: build subways, get rid of streetcars. We put together a transit plan, but it was so inconsequential to us that we released it near the end of the campaign, at midnight, in a YouTube video.

By February 2012, however, it was considered the defining component of Rob Ford's mandate. And it was all fucked up.

***

As late as February 16, 2007, the TTC had focused on subways as the best form of rapid transit. They'd been working for years to extend a four-stop stub of the city's subway network—running from Yonge Street east along Sheppard Avenue in the former borough of North York—further eastward, to the center of the city's fast-growing but low-income borough of Scarborough. On that day in 2007, the city's budget committee approved $3 million for pre-construction environmental assessments.

One month later, Adam Giambrone, then the thirty-year-old city councillor and chairman of the TTC, issued a press release heralding a new vision for transit, both on Sheppard Avenue and around the city. Subways were out; light-rail transit (LRT) was in. Giambrone branded it "Transit City," and then-Mayor David Miller backed it. Without studies. Without a City Council vote. Just a news release. Scarborough residents were pissed. After waiting decades for a subway connection to the heart of their community, they felt cheated by the city once again.

Facing an election in October 2007, the provincial Liberal government agreed to fund Transit City as part of its signature $17.5 billion "MoveOntario 2020" plan. Politicians loved LRT. It was cheaper than subways; more miles of track could be laid into more voting neighborhoods for the same price. The downside was that the TTC's LRT wouldn't run much faster than the buses it would replace. It was light transit, for sure—but rapid it was not. So nobody mentioned that part.

The Liberals were reelected, and by 2010, plans for Transit City were well advanced, though little actual construction had begun. Scarborough residents, however, remained convinced they'd been swindled out of a subway. As a small plank in his election platform, Ford had promised to halt the LRT plan and build subways instead. An LRT, he said, was just a streetcar by another name. Drivers hated streetcars; Ford loved drivers. Typically, he also wanted to assure taxpayers that they wouldn't have to foot the bill.

The latter point was tough, of course. After months of research, I put together a skeleton plan that included completion of the Sheppard Subway. To pay for it, I developed a complex funding formula involving tax-increment financing, which wouldn't require tax increases or traditional

THE SUBWAY WARS | 155

debt. A few days before the plan's release, I explained it to Rob, in his Deco office, one final time.

When I was done, he regarded for a moment the documents and charts I'd given him, then dropped them on his desk and leaned back in his ratty old high-backed executive rocker. He looked up at the ceiling, laced his fingers together atop his belly, and said, "Buddy, this is way too complicated. How am I going to explain this to people?" (He was right. As I had explained the financing plan to Rob, even my eyes glazed over. The average Torontonian wouldn't grasp it.)

"How much is the subway going to cost?" Rob asked. $4 billion, I answered.

"How much money is Ontario giving us for Transit City?" About $4 billion for Phase One.

"Why don't we just use that money?" Rob asked. I could have replied, "Because it's not our money to repurpose"—but he was right. If the province balked, we could revert to the complex plan after the campaign. In the meantime, Ford's instinct was the classic KISS: Keep it simple, stupid. I rewrote the plan, drafted a new script for Rob, and we shot the video. Critics and reporters hated it, but voters understood it.

***

Immediately after Ford was elected, during the transition phase, Nick and I met with TTC general manager Gary Webster and his right-hand man, Vince Rodo, to get our subway plan going. Webster was a tall, thin, bespectacled engineer who listened carefully and paused before he spoke. He was about seven minutes into a detailed briefing on Transit City when I realized he was going to fritter away the whole meeting telling us what we already knew. I interjected as politely as I knew how. Which, in fairness, is probably not very. I told him the only thing that interested us about Transit City was . . . stopping it.

"Pardon me?" asked Webster, genuinely surprised—whether by my question, or the fact I'd interrupted him, I'm still not sure.

We explained Ford's plan. Webster took notes, in a meticulous script using a fine-point pen. "I see," he said, at last. "Well, that could be a challenge."

Rodo jumped in. He's short, trim, mid-forties. Where Webster dressed like a NASA engineer from the 1960s, Rodo looked more like the guy who counts the money in the backroom of a shady casino in a gangster movie. All he lacked was the green eyeshade. Rodo said the TTC couldn't stop the project; they were merely contractors for Metrolinx, the agency the province of Ontario had created to implement its multibillion-dollar, Ontario-wide transportation plan.

I pointed out that Webster and Rodo reported to the TTC, and the TTC answered to whomever Ford appointed to run it. What if they said to stop providing the service to Metrolinx? "If the Commission were to decide to discontinue support for the project, then the TTC would withdraw its services, yes," Webster said, thoughtfully.

"But we have commitments to Metrolinx that have to be upheld," Rodo said.

I asked for a copy of the contract. Rodo said the master agreement hadn't been signed. How could that be? A hundred million dollars had been spent, without a written agreement? It was so unbelievable that I didn't believe them. Sure enough, a few days later, a lawyer whom Nick enlisted dug up a copy of a signed and executed Memorandum of Agreement between the TTC and Metrolinx, stipulating the work that the TTC was to perform in exchange for the money. I was livid.

*Oh, that agreement . . .* Webster and Rodo said dismissively when next we met. They claimed it had expired. I pressed, feeling like I was cross-examining a hostile witness. Was the TTC still working on stuff for Metrolinx? Yes. Was there a new agreement covering this new work? No. But again, within twenty-four hours, our same lawyer found two subsequent agreements. Now I was not only livid; I was scared.

"Who are these guys?" I asked Nick. "Why do they think they can lie to us?"

"They're civil servants, and they don't want to help us shut down their project," replied Nick.

"But how do they think they can get away with it?" I pressed. "Think about it. In a few days, Rob Ford is going to appoint the new Commission, their bosses. The Commissioners will be loyal to Ford, who appointed them—and they can fire these two guys with a show of hands." I didn't understand how they could feel safe while telling us things that simply weren't true.

Both of us began to wonder what the hell happens inside the TTC. For years, politicians had come and gone as chairs and commissioners of the organization. Even if they argued for major change before accepting the job, within a short period of time, these politicians became mindless spokesmodels for the transit organization—advocating for more of the same old, same old. What mysterious power did the TTC have over its appointed masters? I couldn't believe they could be so goddamned confident as to bald-face lie to us, sure they had nothing to worry about from a board of directors that hadn't even been appointed yet. By the end of my time at City Hall, I still couldn't answer this question. The only theory I have that fits the evidence sounds so paranoid, even to me, that I'm not willing to write about it. Or maybe the mysterious power affected me, too.

\*\*\*

Councillor Karen Stintz wasn't Rob's choice for TTC chair; neither he nor Doug was happy about the idea. But Nick, the transition team, and I argued there was no better option. In 2009, Stintz had championed the Sheppard subway. Nick told me she'd agreed to do so again. Almost immediately after the election, though, she began backpedaling: While she supported subways over LRT, she was concerned about paying for them. The fact was, she wanted the province's money to cover a project in her district, an east-west LRT along Eglinton Avenue, another east-west corridor, but well south of Sheppard. She made it clear that the Eglinton line was her first priority.

By Ford's first day as mayor—December 1, 2010—Webster and Rodo were still balking at our plans. Doug felt we should replace Webster; that wasn't unusual when a new administration came in. But Nick and I both opposed the idea. He'd been in the job for four years. If we could get him on our side, he could get the subways done more efficiently than a new person who had to learn the ropes. Rob agreed to keep him—if and only if we could get him to stop screwing us around and work with us. I told Ford, "You've got to look Webster in the eye and say 'I need a subway champion. I need someone to carry the flag up the hill for subways.' Will you do that?" Rob nodded.

At 7:00 a.m. on the day he took office, as his first official function, Rob Ford met with Gary Webster. (The media, expecting Webster to be fired, was already waiting outside the mayor's office.) Rob asked my question verbatim. Webster answered yes—as long as he could keep going with the Eglinton line. We agreed—if funding it didn't conflict with our Sheppard plans. He volunteered to get rid of the Transit City branding, prevalent on the TTC's website and marketing material, which was a holdover from Miller's administration. Ford and Webster shook hands; Webster spoke briefly to the press; we all sighed with relief.

And then it was Rob's turn in front of the cameras. Day one of the job, and he went off-script. Aggressively. Instead of sticking to the speech

I'd written for him, which included the phrase "building a Transportation City" (my extremely subtle rebranding of Transit City), Ford shoved a sharp stick into the eyes of the TTC and its LRT plan. "Transit City is over, ladies and gentlemen," he asserted. The Subway Wars were on.

Our battlefields were meetings (after all, this was city politics). The key players were the TTC folks, Stintz, Webster and Rodo, plus two Metrolinx execs: CEO Bruce McCuaig; and Chairman Robert Prichard, a prominent Toronto lawyer, highly placed Liberal party rainmaker, personal confidante to Ontario's Premier, Dalton McGuinty, and the real power opposing Nick and me.

Our meetings with them quickly developed a pattern. Prichard would explain the minister of transportation's mandate. Nick and I would outline what Ford wanted. The TTC and Metrolinx would agree to come back with estimates and plans. Instead, they'd come back with lengthy explanations of why what Ford wanted was impossible. We'd push back with our research. They'd agree to come back with a new plan that considered our research. At the next meeting, they'd present a new round of objections. Lather, rinse, repeat.

"Why don't I just call the premier?" Rob would ask after every fruitless meeting. "We need to get the shovels in the ground." Unfortunately, the premier was not the kind of guy who liked to sort things out on the phone. We dutifully asked, but his staff never did provide the mayor with the premier's cell phone number. And phone calls between the two were few, far between, scheduled in advance, and well scripted—at least on the premier's end.

Metrolinx's big objection was financial. It turned out that the province didn't really have the billions it had promised to spend on transit in Toronto. Instead, they planned to borrow the money. This would add to their capital debt, but not show up as an expense on their annual income statement or operating budget. However, for this to work, the province had to be able to claim the asset—the transit line—as its property. It had to own it. If the city owned the line, the provincial accountants would not allow it to be considered a capital asset. Therefore, the entire amount spent in any one year would have to be charged against the annual operating budget—and that would throw the province's books off. I got the distinct impression Prichard was particularly pleased by this obstacle, though somewhat dismayed that we understood it. He seemed to hope we'd be so flummoxed by it we'd throw up our hands and say, "Oh, well. We tried."

We didn't. I said, smiling, that we'd let the province own the subway line. Prichard, smiling back, explained that his accountants wouldn't consider an extension to a system that was owned by the city as a separate asset that was owned by the province. No problem, I countered. We'll sell you the rest of the subway system for a dollar so you can own the entire line. Prichard said he'd take this idea away and see if it would fly. You probably won't be stunned to hear what he said at the next meeting: It wouldn't—

Exasperated, I interrupted Prichard's monologue while he was taking a breath and asked him (a) why Metrolinx seemed to be doing everything it possibly could to ensure that our discussions failed; and (b) why, though we'd all agreed to keep our discussions confidential, the *Toronto Star's* transportation reporter never failed to file a story, mere hours after each of our meetings, that was favorable to Metrolinx/TTC and unfavorable to Ford. "Why are you fucking us around?" I asked.

Perhaps Prichard felt I didn't know how important he was. (If so, he was probably right.) His face turned bright red and he began to foam at the mouth. Literally: White spittle gathered at the corners of his lips. More spittle flew across the table at me as he responded. It was a short meeting.

But it seemed to work. Suddenly the logjam was broken. Metrolinx offered a counterproposal: They could extend the line they were building on Eglinton out to Scarborough center. It wasn't exactly what Ford wanted. But it accomplished pretty much the same thing. I told Prichard I could sell that, and Ford went for it.

It was another month of lawyering before we came to an agreement, but we eventually held a press conference where Ontario Premier Dalton McGuinty, Mayor Rob Ford, Rob Prichard, and Karen Stintz all smiled and shook hands while they announced the agreement. Mayor Ford's transit plan was born.

Still, I couldn't help but note that at those meetings, Stintz, Webster, and Rodo sat on the same side of the conference table as Metrolinx, leaving Nick and me alone on the opposite side. It was not just symbolic. They were holding pre-meetings with Metrolinx to coordinate their stories before joining us for the formal discussion. The TTC was siding with Metrolinx against Ford. And Stintz was sitting with them.

Rob and Doug were furious. They wanted Stintz fired. Again, Nick and I talked them off the ledge. Stintz spent more time with the TTC than she did with us, we reasoned; they're engineers, they have established trust as transit operators. It was natural she'd believe them over us. Plus, Rob had just appointed her. Firing her this early in the administration would reflect badly on him and turn her into a bona fide enemy.

Still, we needed a spokesman. Ford couldn't do it. He was great with championing taxpayers, but not so great at explaining the nuances of transit agencies. So we recruited Gordon Chong, who had been on Rob's transition team, as chair of a new entity, Toronto Transit Infrastructure Ltd (TTIL). I hoped that TTIL would not only develop the Sheppard subway line, but would eventually take over Toronto's transit infrastructure development, allowing the TTC to focus on operations—which they badly needed to do.

The deal we'd struck with the premier, however, was contingent upon City Council's approval. Doug was anxious to put the plan to them. But I knew we didn't have enough votes. Our Blue Team was willing to follow the mayor, but they needed to know how we were going to pay for it. Hard to fault them on that. Time to loop in the federal government.

During the transition period, the (Conservative) federal government had indicated it was inclined to support our subway project. Why wouldn't they? Ford was the first conservative mayor of Toronto in a long time. He could be a conservative ally in the next federal and provincial elections. And, as I've mentioned before, Finance Minister Jim Flaherty was an old family friend of the Fords. Not to mention subways made good economic sense.

On November 19, 2010—in the middle of Rob's transition period—he, Doug, Nick, and I met Flaherty at the Ministers' Regional Office (MRO) in Toronto. The MRO is a local private office suite that federal ministers use when they're in the city. Because Toronto is Canada's financial capital, the finance minister touched down there often; he even had staff posted there. I had armed Ford with an agenda of topics to discuss with Flaherty, the foremost of which was funding assistance for the Sheppard subway.

When Flaherty arrived in the boardroom, he greeted Rob and Doug with hugs. He sat at the head of the table and swapped stories about Rob's father and their trip to Asia many years before. (Apparently, it involved some drinking.) After ten minutes of chat, he was ready to get down to business. He asked Rob what he could do to help him.

I had my notebook open, with facts and figures on the subway and our other agenda items at the ready. But Rob had his own agenda.

He leaned forward in his chair, opened his mouth. "We need some Astroturf," he began. "The field at Don Bosco is horrible. It's so muddy in spring, you can't use it. I know Suzan Hall got $1 million from the feds for artificial turf in her ward. I want it at Bosco."

I have a pretty good poker face. But as I turned toward Nick, I couldn't completely hide the horror in my eyes. I saw the same look in his. Doug, sitting next to Rob, openly gaped at him. Flaherty's staffers looked at all of us. The second-most powerful politician in Canada had just asked the newly elected mayor of Toronto how he could help the city. In other words, the genie had just appeared out of the lamp. The answer should have been on the tip of Ford's tongue: He needed billions of dollars to build a subway he'd promised and dearly wanted. (Not to mention, billions more for roads, social housing, and sewers.) Instead, Ford asked for Astroturf. And not for all of the city's high school football teams. Just for his.

Flaherty didn't miss a beat. He furrowed his brow. Looked at a staffer, asked what programs might cover that. The staffer replied that he'd have to do some research. Rob, oblivious to the fact that Nick and I were mentally screaming "What the fuck?" at him, named a handful of schools that had recently received new fields, bleachers, and scoreboards from a federal program. Bosco needed a scoreboard and new stands too. They talked about that for a while.

Doug tried to steer the conversation back on track. "And subways, Rob," he said. "Ask him about subways." Rob did, eventually, but not until he had a commitment that Flaherty's staff would look into what new programs might bolster sports and recreational infrastructure. "Astroturf" became a shadow file in the mayor's office that I managed to stay completely away from.

Eventually, Amir was able to point the Toronto Catholic District School Board at the right program so they could apply for football field funding themselves. A number of their schools needed refurbishment and Bosco was among them. They asked the mayor for a letter supporting their grant application, and he happily provided one.

By the end of the meeting, though, Flaherty had tasked one of his staffers to find out what the federal government could do about helping build subways and follow up with me.

*\*\**

Unfortunately, Gordon Chong didn't fare much better with TTIL than we had with the TTC. Webster, who had agreed to carry the mayor's flag for the subway plan, still seemed to be working against it at every turn. Our initial push for subways had run out of political steam. So Chong hired Dr. Jo Kennelly, a PhD consultant who'd worked many challenging files through federal funding approvals, to prepare an interim report by the end of 2011. Before she finished it, however, he ran out of money to pay her. I told him to let her go; I couldn't get the $25,000 needed to finish the report. Chong defied me, though: He told her if she finished the report, he'd pay her. And when she finished it, Chong looked to me to find the money. I was furious with him. I knew the public would find out, and that they'd want Rob's blood for the costs.

I couldn't go to Council for the money. The mayor's office should have been able to afford it—when Ford took office, there had been a budget for consultants. But Rob had zeroed it out. He hated consultants, and wanted to show fiscal restraint. We could have easily moved the money around. We had lots. But Rob refused to let me pay for the report.

I got angry with him. On the one hand, he would insist we push on the subway, and he'd badger us about why we hadn't already taken it to a council vote. On the other hand, every time we proposed to do the work required to pave the way to win a vote, he refused to spend money. Now we had the report we needed, and the money was there—we had an office surplus of hundreds of thousands of dollars for the year.

Finally, after I'd brought up the issue twice more, Rob agreed to pay. Under one condition: "I was going to give everyone in the office a year-end raise," he said. "But this means no raise for anyone."

When I told Chong he could pay the consultant, he smiled. "See, I told you it would work out," he said. He delivered the interim report to the mayor's office in January 2012. I never told anyone what that money had cost them.

*\*\*\**

I wanted Council's vote on the subway issue to be as simple as possible: Should Council commit some funds to further study of the Sheppard Avenue subway plan, and to submit a proposal for capital funding to the federal government? I wanted Stintz to lead the vote. But by this point, a year into the process, relations between Stintz and the mayor's office had deteriorated to the point where neither trusted the other.

Back in early 2011, when Rob and Doug were musing out loud about firing Karen, she told the mayor flatly that she didn't think his subway funding plan would work. She said she didn't want to be responsible for a multibillion-dollar disaster that taxpayers would have to pay for, and offered to resign.

Rob didn't accept her offer. He told her he supported her 100 percent and insisted that he we would pay for the subway without it costing taxpayers a dime. He just wanted everyone to pull together to find a plan that worked, and to be open and honest with each other. No more surprises. No more mistrust.

The minute the door closed behind Karen, Rob exploded: "I hate that bitch! We've gotta fire her."

Nick and I calmed him down. Let's see if things improve, we insisted. Then, without telling me until later, Nick met with Andrew Bodrug, Stintz's chief of staff at the TTC. In an effort to build trust, Nick told Andrew that Ford wanted to fire Stintz, but Nick had talked him out of it.

I thought that was a mistake. Andrew was completely loyal to Stintz. He'd deliver the message verbatim. Rob had said to her face that he supported her 100 percent. Nick said Rob wanted her fired. One of them must be lying. Why would she trust us? To make matters worse, Doug Ford repeatedly bashed Stintz in the media. It drove us crazy. We were trying to win her over, and he was portraying her as the Antichrist incarnate.

At one point, Doug approached me with "news" from his "sources" that Stintz had a conflict of interest. He said her husband worked for Bombardier, the company that was building the LRT vehicles, so naturally she didn't want a subway plan. Maybe she was being "paid off." Or maybe her husband was. I pointed out that Bombardier also made our subway vehicles, so they'd profit either way. But Doug was salivating. He wanted the story leaked to the press. He promised to get his spies to put together a dossier.

I, on the other hand, searched that magical thing called the Internet, and quickly found out that Stintz's husband didn't work for Bombardier. He'd once worked for a consulting firm that had done a (long-completed) project for an entirely different division of Bombardier, but that was it. I told our office to ignore Doug and move on. His feud with Karen, however, continued.

Later, as the report dragged on, Stintz called a meeting with me in the small meeting room next to my office. She was tense when she started, talking fast and loud, and quickly got faster and louder. She was certain she was going to be tarred with a disaster. I, equally frustrated with the TTC's undermining us at every turn, told her the TTC was the problem. I told Stintz they were lying to her about what we were doing, and the obstacles they were creating for Chong; I tried to point out examples. She yelled at me. I shouted back. After that, she would have little to do with me, even though I continued to advocate for her with the Fords—right up until the end of March 2013, when even I began to wonder if she wasn't as evil as the Fords made her out to be. By then, I was beginning to believe she was actively conspiring with the left to destroy Rob Ford.

*** 

So in February 2012, when Stintz signed up enough councillors to force a showdown in Council, I knew we had a big problem. We finally had Chong's report, but had not been able to release it in a way that built Council and public support. Stintz and the TTC were in control of the narrative, and it made Ford look terrible. The woman he'd chosen as his transit boss was leading the charge against him on a program that had become synonymous with him.

It wasn't just Rob's problem, either. It was mine, too. Somewhere along the line, the subway file had been passed from Nick to Amir to me. Suddenly, I was the one holding the bag.

Before the Council meeting, Stintz met with Ford in his office and offered a compromise—a compromise that was more like a coup. Essentially, she offered to share credit for the "compromise" if he agreed to do everything her way. She didn't care if the Sheppard line was built, but she wanted everything else to go back to the way it had been before Rob was elected—to continue the plan to put an LRT on Eglinton, with the east end of it emerging from the tunnel and running down middle of the street. Rob accepted. He was most concerned about the Sheppard line. It was bad policy, but good politics, because that's how Council would go anyway. Stintz had the votes. We didn't.

But then something bizarre happened. Shortly after leaving Ford's office, Stintz appeared on television to say she'd offered a compromise to the mayor and he had refused her. Which was precisely the opposite of what had actually happened.

Later I was told that, between meeting with Rob and making her announcement, Stintz had met with left-wing City Councillor Joe Mihevc, a former deputy chair of the TTC, and some other left-wing councillors. If Stintz was aligning with the left, we would have trouble on our hands on other fronts beyond transit.

On February 8, 2012, Toronto City Council convened for a special meeting to consider a motion put forth by Karen Stintz. The motion effectively severed the Sheppard subway plan from the rest of the transit projects previously conceived under Transit City. It reaffirmed Council's support for the previous Transit City projects, and added some clauses to include further extensions into the districts of one or two councillors in order to secure their votes. Council also directed the city manager to create an "expert advisory panel" to review the Sheppard subway plan and recommend whether to continue with it or revert to the previous LRT plan. Naturally, the "expert panel" Council put together included only members who publicly supported LRTs—plus Gordon Chong as a token attempt at balance. Council gave the panel one month to report back to a second special council meeting. The fix was in: The Sheppard line's days were numbered.

During that month, we did our best to keep the Sheppard subway alive. I knew it would all come down to funding, and Chong's study had a suggestion that I thought Rob Ford could support: a parking levy. As a special form of property tax, we could charge a levy to the owners of commercial parking spaces—spaces that are rented by the hour or month. The owner would pass that rate on to renters as part of the price of parking. My calculations suggested it would add about five dollars to the cost of a $400 monthly parking pass in a financial district building, or maybe five cents to the cost of an ice cream cone in a shopping mall with a large parking lot. Rob agreed, reluctantly.

I wrote an op-ed article for him, arguing the merits of his subway plan and vision for transit in Toronto. It ran in the February 23, 2012, *Globe and Mail*, and included an example of a "modest parking levy" that could generate over $90 million annually to help subways.

The second special council meeting was scheduled to begin at 9:30 a.m. on March 21. The entire month, we'd been working the second floor of Toronto City Hall hard. We begged, cajoled, and whipped councillors who could be moved to support the mayor's plan. We told councillors we knew the parking levy wasn't perfect—it was a placeholder plan, indicating the mayor's commitment to finding funds somewhere. We said by the time the subway was fully in development, we would likely have found another, better funding mechanism. At the same time, we were convincing die-hard right-wing councillors that the mayor wouldn't support any tax unless it was essential. By the night before the vote, we had secured twenty-six votes: three more than required to pass the mayor's plan. We were exhausted, but we had done it. I sat down with Earl and the others on the council liaison team and had a Scotch to mark the occasion. Sixteen hours later, two years of effort turned to dust.

At 8:00 a.m. on the twenty-first of March, Rob called me in and hit me with the news. "I can't support a new tax, buddy," he said. He'd been on the phone half the night with the Night Shift. They told him he'd be toast in 2014 if he voted in favor of a new tax. I argued with him, but it was no use. When Doug got in, I appealed to him, but it was clear they were aligned: Neither would vote for the parking levy. I told them that without the levy, we wouldn't get the votes we needed. Rob said he didn't mind if other councillors voted for the levy, but he couldn't. That's when I got angry.

"You think the others are going to stick their necks out for something you won't do yourself, just so you can say in 2014 that you've never supported a tax and others had? No fucking way. You have to show leadership on this. They're ready to follow you. They're in the other room ready to go."

Rob and Doug were unmoved. They were decided. They weren't going to budge. I asked the mayor to explain his decision to the councillors in the other room, but he refused. He didn't have time. There was a team of lawyers in reception waiting to see him. (It was one of a number of teams of lawyers defending the mayor against a number of actions, which I'll get into later.) I would have to deal with the councillors myself.

I was disgusted by this lack of leadership, and sickened that I'd have to defend Rob's decision as if I agreed with him. But that's the type of loyalty I'd learned in the army. In an attempt to save some of my dignity, I asked permission to give the motion I had drafted to another councillor—if anyone else was willing to move it—and Rob agreed. But I knew it was over.

So I told them—without telling them I disagreed, but without lying to them either. I said I had the motion, prepared at the mayor's request. I told them we were now down to twenty-four votes, but that my staff and I could no longer whip the council vote. I added that the mayor would not move the motion but was OK if another councillor wanted to do so.

They looked at me as if I were speaking Greek. "He wants someone else to move the motion?" someone asked. "But he's still voting for it, right?"

I took a deep breath and replied, "He will not be voting for it. Neither will his brother."

All hell broke loose. *What the fuck? Why not? What's going on?* I told them the mayor was standing on principle: no new taxes. If we can't afford a subway without a new tax, he believed we should wait until we can afford it.

They demanded to see Rob. I knocked on his door and interrupted the meeting with his lawyers to whisper in his ear. He waved me off and said he'd be there in a minute.

Back in the boardroom, Ford's team, led by the deputy mayor, was fuming. They'd agreed to back this plan, reluctantly, because they were team players. Now the mayor wouldn't even see them? The budget chief, Councillor Mike Del Grande, agreed to move the motion, but he knew it would fail the minute the councillors learned the mayor was voting against it.

More minutes ticked by. No Ford. A number of councillors threatened to barge into his office. I asked them to wait, and knocked on Ford's door again. "Excuse me, Mr. Mayor," I said in my infantry voice. "I need you in the boardroom, *right now.*" This time Rob and Doug stood and followed me.

The second they saw Rob, the councillors launched into an all-out assault. *How dare you? What the hell is going on?* Rob shrugged. "You do what you want, I don't care," he said. "But I can't support it." They kept attacking him, and when he realized they weren't going to be placated . . . he turned on us.

"What do you want me to say?" he shouted. "My staff fucked it up. I wanted to take it to Council a year ago. But they wouldn't let me. And now it's all fucked."

I thought my head would explode. I held my tongue, though. Only one person could challenge the mayor on that, in front of elected officials—his chief of staff, Amir. He did, and I'm grateful. "Mayor, that's not right," he said, from a corner of the room, standing up for his staff. "You can't put this on your staff and you know it." Rob went toe-to-toe with Amir for a few rounds, then stormed into his office and shut the door.

The council meeting lasted two days. The deputy mayor, budget chief, and a few others took turns, individually and in small groups, yelling at the mayor in the privacy of his office. Rob shrugged them off. When the bells rang to call the final vote, I stood with my staff against the upper railing of the council chamber and watched, essentially spectators, as Council voted to kill Ford's subway plan.

I was certain that Rob's backing down had permanently fractured his Blue Team coalition. But to my amazement, by the next regular meeting, a number of councillors were already asking for the mayor's guidance on various matters. However they felt about Rob Ford, they still needed a mayor and his office to coordinate their efforts. Politics as usual.

Months later, Stintz and Scarborough Councillor Glenn De Baere-maeker tried to reopen the plan to bring a subway to Scarborough. They had been taking enormous political heat from the community over kill-ing "their" subway; De Baeremaeker's own constituents were outraged and Stintz was likely thinking about running for mayor in 2014 when she'd need Scarborough support. (She did run for mayor in 2014 but dropped out before Election Day.) The two councillors proposed a complicated funding mechanism that we'd already rejected; it was nothing more than a well-hidden (but massive) property tax hike. As soon as we got wind of the plan the night before Stintz was to announce it, we pulled out all the stops and worked to give the press our spin on it. So my sole victory in the sub-way wars was a front-page article in the next day's *Toronto Sun*, describing Stintz's plan as a "Tax Attack." That poisoned the well and Council didn't support it.

Well after I was fired, Stintz and Ford worked together on another proposal to convert the Scarborough elevated train line into a subway extension of the existing Bloor-Danforth line. This plan received broad Council and provincial government support. Ford claimed victory. In the rewriting of history that victory allows, he had finally won a vote to bring a subway to Scarborough. As of this writing, the plan to build the extension has survived the 2014 municipal election, has attracted provincial and federal promises of funding support, and is working through the planning stages. I remain an ardent advocate for rapid transit in Toronto—and hopeful that the Scarborough subway will eventually get built. But, with Toronto City Council, no decision is ever truly final.

# 18 | Meet the Joneses

ROB AND DOUG Ford call each other "Jones." They started after a Deco label salesman named Jones made an impression on them when they were younger. I imagine a middle-aged expatriate Brit salesman chain-smoking cigarettes and answering the phones with a gruff "Jones!" Every phone call between the two of them—and there were easily two dozen each day, unless they were fighting—began with the same greeting: "Jones!"

To the outside world, Rob and Doug can appear as indistinguishable as their mutual nickname. In private, however, they fight almost constantly. Each maintains the other wouldn't have succeeded without him. Doug frequently says Rob wouldn't have been mayor without his help; Rob says Doug would never have made it into City Hall without his.

During Rob Ford's term as mayor, the novelist Margaret Atwood christened Doug and him the "twin Ford mayors." The perception was that Doug was the brains of the duo, and Rob was the heart. (Wrong on both counts.) I think Doug believed he and Rob were co-mayors, and enjoyed the idea that everyone on Council looked at him that way. Because they figured he was calling the shots, they treated him with respect and deference far greater than that afforded any other first-term councillor. Doug liked the sizzle at least as much as the steak, maybe even more. And Rob, who doesn't like the limelight, was fine letting Doug bask in it for him. But the truth is, Rob never saw Doug as his co-mayor.

As mentioned earlier, after Rob was elected, Doug had expected a prestigious appointment. But it didn't make sense to make him deputy mayor, or a committee chair—those perks were more useful as tools to lure others into Rob's coalition. Though Doug saw the sense of this, it was clear that being a rookie councillor and the "brother-in-chief" was not what he had in mind when he'd put his name on the ballot. At times, his disappointment erupted in anger.

"If you think I came down here just to be the councillor from Ward 2, you've got another think coming," he bellowed during one meeting with Nick and me. "I've had it. I'll just quit and go back to Chicago."

We didn't want him to quit. We needed his vote. But this friction was a constant issue for our staff. Rob almost never told Doug no—but he would tell us to say it to him. That wasn't easy. In Doug's mind, Rob's staff worked for him, too. So Rob's chief of staff had to add a line to his job description: manage Doug Ford.

Though Rob had turned down Doug's plan to cut a door between their two offices, Doug still spent almost as much time in the mayor's office as he did in his own, coming and going as he pleased. Where Rob was shy and insular, Doug was an extrovert who loved meeting with business leaders. He would meet with anybody about anything. He would frequently invite the heads of banks, real estate development companies, and other major corporations into the "Mayor's Office" for a meeting, which he would grandly conduct in Rob's boardroom. He'd sit at the head of the table, in the mayor's seat, and hold court. This meant Rob's staff frequently had to scramble to find alternative locations for our own meetings. This, as you can imagine, did not thrill us.

Often, Doug would nab one of the mayor's staffers to join his meetings, no matter what else we were supposed to be doing. Too often this was me, "the policy and strategy guy." I was usually scheduled in back-to-back from 8:00 or 9:00 a.m. through 6:00 p.m. Being dragged into one of Doug's pretend-important meetings to talk about God-knows-what kept me from getting my own work done.

Rob rarely, if ever, attended Doug's meetings. But that didn't stop Doug from parading his guests through Rob's office. Often, he would open the door—without knocking—on closed-door meetings, and barge into the middle of whatever was being discussed. Even worse, he'd march into Rob's office and drag him into the boardroom for a few minutes, "to say hi." This inevitably put Rob off-schedule and pissed off whomever Rob was already meeting—someone who'd likely waited a while to get access to the mayor, and was in the middle of a critically important discussion.

Rob complained to us that Doug kept screwing up his schedule. We told him we tried to rein Doug in, but he wouldn't listen to us. We said Rob was the only person who could do it. But he'd get all sheepish on us. "What can I do?" he'd ask. "You've got to tell him."

A year into Rob's term, some of Doug's "initiatives" started to morph from merely irritating to potentially harmful. We'd reach out to arrange a meeting between Rob and a key community stakeholder, and be turned down. Earl Provost, the master of stakeholder relationships in the mayor's office, quickly ferreted out why: Several CEOs and VIPs were pissed off with the mayor's office, they said, because they had met with the mayor, been promised action, and then nothing had happened.

We were astounded. Rob had never met with them. We had never met with them. But, we discovered, Doug had met with them—often in the mayor's office, in his very boardroom. They'd ask for something. Doug would agree. And then he'd do zip. He didn't take notes and he didn't take action. People who thought they'd met with the mayor's office had been let down. But still, Rob refused to confront his big brother.

Over time, Doug's intrusions became more brazen. Sometimes when Rob was out of the office, Doug would let himself in and sit behind his desk, making calls or meeting with his own staff. Rob was livid about this. He insisted we stop it from happening. Kia Nejatian, Rob's EA, would physically try to bar Doug from entering the mayor's office. But Doug would barge right past him.

We started locking the door. Then Doug got a key. From Rob. Who would then complain when Doug used it. It was nuts.

In August 2011, I noticed that Rob, Doug, and Amir were holding frequent closed-door meetings with senior city managers on something I wasn't involved in. Naturally I was curious, but it was none of my business. In late August, though, I was given the draft agenda for the upcoming executive committee meeting, which the mayor chaired. One item stood out.

Item EX 9.6 was a report from the city manager innocuously called "Toronto Port Lands Company—Revitalization Opportunities for the Port Lands." It was nothing less than a wholesale abandonment of the city's long-standing $1.5 billion waterfront redevelopment initiative, in favor of a completely new scheme. I was stunned; it was the first I'd heard of this scheme. When the agenda was published, it would land like a bombshell.

Angry, I called Joe Pennachetti, the city manager, to ask why I hadn't heard of this. Joe was confused. He said he'd been meeting for months with Doug Ford on this plan and, for the last few weeks, with the mayor himself, and Amir. (Aha! The secret meetings.) Joe assumed we'd been lobbying Council for support for what he described as Doug's plan.

And what a scheme! Doug was proposing a Disney-like monorail, a boat-in, five-star waterfront hotel, and—now infamously—a giant, London Eye-style Ferris wheel. This, he said, was what Toronto needed. As unimpressed as I was with the old waterfront plan, I knew Council wouldn't stand for changing it, wholesale, with no advance warning. Civil war would erupt.

I went to Rob, and told him the new plan was ridiculous—Rob hadn't campaigned on the waterfront, the waterfront was not a priority. There was no way we would get even our most loyal councillors to sign off on such a radical revision, let alone a majority. Rob agreed with me. This was Dougie's idea, he said. If I didn't like it, I should tell Dougie.

I did. Doug, not surprisingly, disagreed with me. "Buddy, you've got to relax," he said with a bright warm smile and ice-cold eyes. "Waterfront Toronto is a bunch of snakes. They've spent a billion dollars with nothing to show for it down there. It's a joke.

"They're doing it all wrong," he went on, warming to his topic. "What you have to do is get the private sector in there from the beginning. There's billions of dollars' worth of land down there going to waste and no plan to even look at it for another twenty years." It would be fine, he assured me—he'd been working the second floor. It was a slam-dunk.

Then he started flipping excitedly through architectural diagrams and artists' renderings. I listened, but I didn't believe for a minute he'd been lobbying for votes. I huddled with our staff later in the day and they reported they'd heard nothing about it from our Blue Team.

When I told Rob we should pull the report from the agenda before it went public so we could canvass the Council and work for votes, he agreed. Before I could do that, however, he and Doug "bumped into" a reporter Doug knew, and Doug launched into his "unprecedented plan" for the waterfront. When asked if he supported the plan, Rob doubled down. Absolutely. Doug's vision for the waterfront was brilliant. We were all in.

The next day, August 30, 2011, Doug did a flurry of self-orchestrated media appearances, selling his plan hard.

Not only did the "Ferris Wheel Plan" not fly—it was mercilessly mocked in the press and public as an amateurish and uneducated fantasy—for the first time, members of the mayor's own executive committee voted against him. Doug tried to bully them into agreement, but that did nothing except create a rift between him and some of the Blue Team. They didn't like Doug. Perhaps they were also jealous of the attention he got. Though they chaired important committees and he had no official appointments, he was instantly recognized anywhere in the city; he always eclipsed them. And Doug didn't like them either. For the next two months, Doug retreated to Chicago, where he managed the family business's US operations, coming to City Hall only for council meetings.

That was good news and bad news for us. Though Doug was intrusive, he was also often invaluable in helping us manage his brother. Doug is less eccentric than his brother; he was often easier to talk to and reason with. He liked to think about things and could be swayed by a good argument. He understood the importance of image, brand, and perception. When we couldn't reason with Rob on some issue or other, especially on matters of public optics or moral responsibility, we would often appeal to Doug. When Rob announced to us that he was going to skip an executive committee meeting (he was the chair!) or leave Council early to coach a high school football practice, we appealed to Doug to reel Rob back in. We didn't even have to finish the sentence. Doug got it immediately, and would go corner "Jones," badgering him into doing his job as mayor first.

When the brothers were fighting, however—which they did often, though never in public—we all backed off. Doug is a physical bully. He can be quick to anger, and, when opposed, puffs himself up and attempts direct intimidation—threatening physical violence, or some form of retribution or retaliation. I never saw or heard of him actually becoming physical with anyone, though. It was more about the bark than the bite. For example, when Councillor Josh Colle wouldn't side with the Fords on an issue, Doug's immediate reaction was to threaten to mobilize Ford Nation against Colle's father, a sitting provincial politician. I asked Doug how he'd react if someone threatened his mother. He admitted he'd rip his lungs out rather than back down. He didn't see what that had to do with the Colle issue, though.

Rob can also be a bully, but less often and in more insidious ways. When intoxicated, he acts out Doug's words—becomes physically aggressive, punching, kicking, grabbing, and shoving people around. At other times, he prefers a more psychological form of bullying, almost of torture: pitting staffers against each other and watching the office drama that unfolded.

\*\*\*

In early January 2012, Doug came up with a new off-the-wall plan: "Mayor Rob Ford's Cut the Waist Challenge." (Cut the Waist—get it?) Rob and Doug would compete to lose fifty pounds in six months, in an effort to raise money for charity and encourage others in the city to get healthy. The room let out a collective groan. We agreed it was the stupidest thing we'd heard yet. We wanted to focus on the challenging political agenda Ford had been elected to achieve. We didn't have time for a sideshow. None of us believed it would work, either: It would expose Rob to public ridicule the first time he didn't make weight. How would we select a charity? Who would manage donations?

Not to worry, Doug said—he had it all handled. He was convinced it would be good for Rob. Not only would it help him lose weight, it would also generate an upswell of public goodwill for a man struggling to lose weight. Rob didn't want to do it, but he was knuckling under Doug's passion.

Amir, too, supported the plan, which surprised me—until he took me aside and explained why. By then, we'd all realized Rob was drinking too much, and we knew it was getting worse (I'm sure that was a big part of his weight gain.) Health experts had told Amir that if Rob could lose weight, he might be empowered to get control over the rest of his life, including his drinking. I was just about convinced—and then Randy Ford showed up with a circus-style scale. Dear God.

The first official weigh-in was on Monday January 16, 2012. Newstalk 1010 radio broadcaster John Tory (who would go on to succeed Ford as mayor in 2014) was the master of ceremonies; the spectacle was broadcast live on TV and radio. It was crazy, yet for a few weeks, the plan seemed to work—citizens participated in public walks, and showed up to weigh themselves on the scale outside Rob's office. It was like Groundhog Day every Monday, the world watching to see how much weight the brothers had lost.

Like many things Ford, however, it quickly went downhill. On February 27, Rob failed to lose weight. In fact, he was up a couple of pounds. After that, he frequently skipped weigh-ins, often at the last minute. He'd phone Kia, his EA, in the morning after the TV cameras had already begun their live news hits, to tell him he wasn't coming in. It didn't win him any friends in the media, and the whole city knew he'd probably ballooned over the weekend and was afraid to show up. In April, someone released a cell phone video of him buying a big bag of fast food at a KFC, and it went viral. In May, Rob finally abandoned the plan.

Throughout, Doug publicly mocked Rob for not losing weight as fast as he was. Doug felt fine about belittling Rob, but Rob would never publicly criticize his big brother Doug.

***

On countless occasions when I worked in the mayor's office, media and political observers would wonder aloud why Rob Ford kept using his brother as his mouthpiece. Why did Rob always send Doug out to speak for him?

That drove me crazy, because the truth was, in all the time I worked with Rob at City Hall, he never once authorized Doug to speak for him. Never. But Doug did anyway. He couldn't help himself. And it invariably made things worse.

In August 2012, when I finally accepted the job as Rob's chief of staff, one of my conditions was that Doug had to stop talking for Rob—and if he messed up, we'd publicly call him out. Rob agreed. That day came less than a month later, on September 13, 2012.

Not atypically, Rob was embroiled in a controversy—this time, for using mayoral staff to help him coach his beloved high school football team. Janet Leiper, the city's integrity commissioner, was investigating and I was preparing a reply to show that the situation, though complicated, was entirely legal. Without warning, Doug stepped in to "fix" things: He told the press that the controversy was ridiculous because the staffers were volunteering. He promised to parade the junior staff before the press gallery later in the day to say so themselves.

I went ballistic. It was not the job of junior staff to defend the mayor to the media, or to be fed to the press gallery like chum. I was afraid one of them would lie about something in an attempt to protect the mayor, putting their own integrity at risk. I walked past the media gathering in front of Rob's office and closed the door behind me. This was the breaking point, I told Rob. We would not be doing what Doug said. Rob agreed. I asked him to make a statement saying that Doug doesn't speak for him. He demurred. I asked if, per our agreement, I could make that statement. He said yes.

Doug was nowhere to be found. I phoned him; no answer. I left him a voicemail telling him what I was about to do and why. Then I threw him under the bus in a statement issued to the press.

"Councillor Doug Ford speaks for Ward 2, and he's vice chair of Budget Committee and Build Toronto, among other official functions," it said. "He has insightful opinions on many issues, but he does not speak for the mayor or the mayor's office. Mayor Ford speaks for himself. When the mayor is unavailable, his press secretary may speak for him. No one else normally does."

Relations between Doug and me, always frosty, became a Cold War. And it wasn't long before Doug had wormed his way back into Rob's office, the way he always did. He'd just pester Rob mercilessly by telephone and after hours until Rob couldn't handle the stress anymore and insisted Doug be brought back inside.

\*\*\*

Doug did have some good ideas, however. One of his best occurred in late September 2012, after Rob's behavior had begun to deteriorate. Those closest to him were beginning to acknowledge that he was addicted—though we didn't yet know to what. Doug, Earl Provost, and Mike Williams, the city's general manager of economic development, put together a plan to take Ford and up to one hundred Toronto business leaders to Chicago on a trade mission. They'd travel as a group to Chicago, meet local political and business leaders, and build relationships and business opportunities.

I was opposed to it. I felt we had enough trouble keeping an addicted Rob Ford on the rails in our own city, let alone on an international adventure. But Rob wanted to go. Doug and Earl spent months planning the details with the Canadian Consulate in Chicago and with Chicago Mayor Rahm Emanuel's office. They built a list of leaders who would go along—each paying his own way to make sure it cost the taxpayers as little as possible, in true Rob Ford style.

When the trip turned out to be a success, rekindling a prosperous bilateral relationship between our two similar-sized Great Lakes cities, I apologized to Doug and told him I was happy to be wrong. Doug didn't care. During the Chicago trip, he'd fallen deeply in hate with me.

At every point in the planning, a private meeting between Rob Ford and Rahm Emanuel was on the agenda. Emanuel is arguably one of the most controversial US politicians, and the trip would mark the first time they'd meet in person. But in early September, Rob had to spend a week in court for a conflict of interest trial that came very close to kicking him out of office. It had provided the media with a number of embarrassing headlines, such as the fact that he'd never bothered to read the conflict of interest guidelines he was accused of breaching. Emanuel's office began distancing their mayor from ours. They reduced the one-on-one time and cut the other meetings down to a short, strictly controlled list of people, which was negotiated between the two sides with the fervor of a nuclear arms treaty.

Eventually, it was decided that the main meeting would happen on the second day of Rob's trip, and would include the two mayors, the two senior political staffers to the mayors, the two diplomatic representatives, and the two senior business leaders involved in the meetings. On the Toronto side, that was: Mayor Rob Ford; me as chief of staff; the Canadian Consul General Gitane De Silva; and Robert Deluce, CEO of Porter Airlines (which flew six flights to Chicago daily). Doug played an active role in planning this meeting. He knew exactly who was going to be involved. Yet when we arrived in Chicago, it became apparent to all that he expected to be in that meeting.

Our Chicago counterparts made it clear that wasn't going to happen. Not only was Rahm Emanuel not inviting his big brother to the meeting, he was not inviting any other elected representatives of Chicago's council. If Mayor Ford was going to have a councillor at the table, Mayor Emanuel would be expected to do the same. Doug Ford wasn't even the chair of economic development (that would be Councillor Michael Thompson, who was also in Chicago on the trip). He was just the councillor from Ward 2. There was absolutely no business reason for him to attend.

In order to avoid a confrontation, we didn't tell Doug where or when the meeting was taking place. He found out anyway—most likely from Rob. When we arrived for the meeting, Doug was already in the room chatting up the Chicagoans, along with a half dozen Toronto councillors he'd brought along. I eyeballed the boardroom table in the center of the room. Eight chairs. Eight name cards. None said "Doug Ford."

As the meeting time approached, we started shooing the extra people out of the room. I whispered in Doug's ear that he would have to leave. "You'll be leaving here on a stretcher before I'm leaving this room, buddy," Doug hissed, his eyes blazing, his voice angry. He stood with his back to the wall while everyone else left. As Emanuel entered, one of his staff approached me and said that Doug would have to leave.

"I've asked him, but he won't listen to me," I said. "We don't want him here either. Do you want to ask him to go?"

She walked up to Doug and spoke quietly with him for a minute. As he left, he made sure to scowl at me. Later, I learned from Earl that while the meeting took place, Doug spent the entire hour outside the door, ranting wildly about me to the other councillors. I was done, he said. I was dead. I was fired. Rob had often told me how much Dougie wanted me fired. From then on, I believed him.

*** 

Throughout Rob's mayoralty, Doug was forever horning in on his brother's photos—when a dignitary visited the mayor's office, or a major announcement was made. That irked me. I felt Doug's presence made Rob look weak, as if he needed his big brother around. The reality was, Rob made all the decisions, despite Doug's advice.

I think Doug wanted people to look at the photos and see him standing next to Rob—the taller, better dressed, slimmer, handsomer Jones, with better teeth—and think, "There's the man who should be mayor: Doug, not Rob." And I think Rob allowed Doug into the photos for a similar reason: so people would look at both Jones, smiling, and think, "Yeah, but Doug's not the mayor. Rob is. Doug just wants to be."

# PART III | THE UNRAVELING: MARCH 2012 TO MARCH 2013

# 19 | The Demons Rule St. Patrick's Day

PEOPLE ASK ME all the time to pinpoint when Rob's demons took over. The short answer is St. Patrick's Day, 2012. But I saw my first hint of trouble more than a year earlier, on January 12, 2011.

I awoke at 6:45 to breaking news on my clock radio that a Toronto police officer was being rushed to the hospital in life-threatening condition, after a wild chase with a stolen snowplow. By the time I was out of the shower, Nick Kouvalis was on the phone: Sergeant Ryan Russell had died. The information was not yet public; his wife and two-year-old son were en route to the hospital. Police Chief Bill Blair had been calling Ford for half an hour and getting no answer. I lived closest to Rob, so I raced over. I called him repeatedly on the fifteen-minute drive. No answer.

I began banging on his door at about 7:45 a.m. No response. Rob's car was in the driveway, so I began knocking on his bedroom window. After about eight minutes, the door opened. Rob, wearing a bathrobe pulled tight over sweatpants, looking exhausted and angry, stood squinting at the bright daylight behind me. Before he could complain, I stepped into the doorway to hide him from passersby and told him a police officer had been killed—he needed to call the chief and then get dressed, because that I was taking him to the hospital. It was the first time since the election I caught Rob when he was not ready to do his job. Unfortunately, it wouldn't be the last.

***

On Monday, October 24, 2011, Rob was scheduled to kick off a 9:30 a.m. council meeting in which he hoped to finalize one of his key agenda items: the contract award for the privatization of half of the city's garbage collection. He didn't answer my calls until 8:30 a.m. He said he was en route and might be on time. He also said something had gone terribly wrong at his home as he was leaving: He'd been assaulted by reporters in his driveway.

He was breathless, flustered. "What do you mean by 'assaulted'?" I asked.

He said that as he tried to get into his van, he'd been "attacked" by a man dressed up as a woman, and a camera crew. He'd called police, but left before they arrived. He didn't recognize the reporters, but thought they were carrying a microphone with "Channel 22" on it. Toronto doesn't have a Channel 22; maybe he meant CP24? Nope. 22.

Shit. For two weeks, the CBC TV comedy show *This Hour Has 22 Minutes*—sort of a half-hour version of *SNL*'s Weekend Update, complete with mock news anchors and recurring characters—had been hounding us to let them interview Rob. We'd declined. In one of their most popular routines, the actress Mary Walsh played a feisty middle-aged woman character called Marg Delahunty, Princess Warrior; she dressed in Valkyrie garb, ambushed politicians, and asked questions (not unlike Stephen Colbert did on his show). Most politicians chuckled their way through it. I asked Rob if his "attackers" could have been the *22 Minutes* crew. Though the show had been a fixture on CBC since 1993, he'd never heard of it.

By the end of the day, Rob was a laughingstock for calling 9-1-1 on a female comedian. When the CBC aired the footage, which showed Walsh on Ford's driveway, pushing herself against his car door to prevent him from closing it, we called them out for trespassing and assault. But instead of backing down, the CBC upped the ante: A few days later they ran a report, quoting unnamed sources, claiming that the mayor had raged at the female operator who took his 9-1-1 call. "You bitches!" he reportedly said. "Don't you fucking know? I'm Rob fucking Ford, the mayor of this city!"

It was one thing to overreact to a comedic ambush. It was another thing to be accused of misogyny—that trail led to past reports (all denied by Ford) of domestic abuse. We didn't need to connect those dots. We wanted to shut this down immediately, and prove that the CBC was doubling down after being caught lying about not trespassing at Ford's home.

Adrienne, Ford's press secretary at the time, and I immediately cornered Rob: What had he said? He categorically denied calling the dispatcher names, though he admitted to using "the F-word." We'd both worked with Rob through a number of crises during the campaign. We'd learned one important lesson: Don't take his word for it.

Amir, then chief of staff, wanted to issue a statement denying the charge. But we all knew a false denial would just make the situation worse. We had to know for sure what Rob had said on the 9-1-1 call. So at 9:30 a.m. on October 27, Amir, Adrienne, and I sat in Inspector Stu Eley's office at Toronto police headquarters on College Street listening to three police audio files from Monday morning.

At 08:15, Rob tells a 9-1-1 operator that there are people at his house attacking him. He's speaking clearly, at normal volume and pace, but to me he sounds scared. Mary Walsh is audible in the background, yelling, "Open the door!" The operator asks him who the people are and if they have weapons. He says they're a camera crew. I can hear a child's voice in the background—his daughter Stephanie. Rob describes a black vehicle outside his house and gives police the license plate number. He's told the police are en route.

As the 9-1-1 operator asks more questions, Rob starts to sound exasperated. He says he's never seen the people before in his life. He reports they are leaving in the black vehicle, heading east on his street. The operator repeats that police are on the way. Rob says he has to get to City Hall. The call lasts four minutes and eight seconds.

At 08:23 Rob calls back to 9-1-1 and tells the operator who answers that he has to leave. He doesn't seem to realize it's not the same operator he spoke with before. She asks for his name and he tells her Rob Ford. When she asks him to repeat it, he says, "It's Rob Ford. The mayor of Toronto." He complains that it's been "ten to fifteen minutes" since he called the first time. (In fact, the first call ended four minutes prior.) "It's a joke," he says and adds that he'll take it up with the chief. This call ends at 08:24.

Four and half minutes later, a police dispatcher (not a 9-1-1 operator) calls Rob to find out where he is; the police are at his house and he's gone. She sounds annoyed and patronizing. At this point, he's en route to City Hall. He's angry and tells her it's too late; he waited, but had to leave after "fifteen fucking minutes." He complains it's appalling how "you guys treat me."

She gets angry back. "You're language is atrocious, sir," she says. "The officers do have to drive there." Then the tape ends abruptly—so abruptly that I wondered if there had been more. The police assured me the recording was complete.

Back in our office, Adrienne and I issued a news release disputing the CBC's version of the tape. But the abrupt ending still bothered me. I was concerned the police might "find" more of the conversation for use as leverage someday. So we asked Mark Pugash, the spokesman for Police Chief Bill Blair, to have the chief issue a statement backing up ours. He was hesitant. We all agreed the tapes shouldn't be released—not only did the mayor sound rattled and scared, not the way I wanted the mayor to sound, but it would set a bad precedent that the police didn't want to set. In Canada, 9-1-1 tapes are rarely released to the public, unless they are introduced as evidence in court. Doing so, the chief feared, might cause some people to avoid calling the police for help.

We insisted the chief make a statement. We couldn't order him to do so, but Adrienne hounded Pugash and Amir leaned on the chief's office. They must issue a statement. Later that day, the chief issued one that corroborated what we'd heard on the tapes. I breathed a sigh of relief. The chief and the mayor were in it together now.

*\*\*\**

By the end of 2011, Rob was getting harder to manage. He was late for meetings—even after I started pushing them back by an hour. He was coming to City Hall less and less. When he did show, he exhibited little interest in the agenda. Or he'd insist on a meeting with someone and then cancel it with little notice. Often, he'd cancel the same meeting two or three times, leaving the staff to try to salvage whatever relationship he was wrecking.

The city manager was growing concerned. He'd had weekly sit-downs with the previous mayor; he barely saw Rob. Then there was the executive committee meeting I mentioned in an earlier chapter, where Rob had been acting so strangely that some observers on Twitter speculated he was drunk. Twitter was also full of sightings of Rob in liquor stores buying booze, often in mickeys, the serious drinkers' pocket flask.

Eventually the Twitter sightings became such an issue that Amir told Rob to stop going to liquor stores. Every time he did, the entire city knew, and it didn't look good. From then on, Rob told Amir or Kia when he wanted booze, and a staffer would buy it. When I became chief of staff in August 2012, I continued the policy. Drinking wasn't illegal. And since Kia would tell me whenever a staffer was running "an errand" for the mayor, I'd know how often he was buying. (It was often.)

In late 2011, we reached out to a key supporter of Rob's from the election campaign, an addiction counselor who was himself in recovery, and asked him to spend time with Rob. He, too, felt Rob had a problem with alcohol. For the next year, he and Rob met for private conversations.

We also felt Rob's weight was an issue. He'd tried and failed programs in the past, but Amir got them to reopen their doors to Ford. He felt that if Rob could stick with a weight-loss program, it would give him a psychological boost to deal with his alcohol consumption.

By early 2012 Rob definitely wasn't focused on running the city. After the subway debacle in March, he should have been rebuilding his council coalition. A surprising number were willing to stick with him. But Rob had checked out. Several councillors informed us they would not attend any more meetings in the mayor's office if the mayor wasn't present. Major decisions were being delayed. In the few hours Rob was working, all he wanted to do was return constituent calls. I myself had a growing list of decisions he needed to make, and was seeing him less and less.

Eventually, things were so backed up that Amir and Earl proposed that we go ahead and make decisions ourselves, to keep the business of the city moving. On the few occasions we were able to pin Rob down, he'd practically waive the decision-making anyway, with an unconcerned, "Do whatever you want. You're the boss."

I disagreed; I didn't feel we had the authority to make decisions. The people of Toronto had elected Rob Ford, not Amir or me. If he wasn't going to make the decisions, they would have to remain unmade. Or we should get another elected official to make them. I met secretly with Doug Holyday, the deputy mayor, at his golf club one weekend to tell him what was happening in the mayor's office—the demons that Rob was struggling with, and our concerns over moral authority. I felt somebody in elected office had to be kept informed.

As for the rest of the staff, much of their time was channeled into handling Ford. He'd always been a nocturnal creature, but his nightlife was a worsening headache. Junior staff reported that Rob was behaving oddly at evening events. He didn't drink in front of them, but he seemed drunk. He would stay up so late returning constituent calls that we started receiving complaints from people he'd awoken, because he called them back at midnight. Amir, Earl, and I told him dozens of times that he had to end his constituent calls at 10 p.m. He didn't understand why.

When he wasn't calling constituents, he was jawing with the Night Shift. Then he'd start calling staff. Some nights, Amir would get two or three calls between 11:00 p.m. and 4:00 a.m.. Often, the calls were Rob complaining that a young staffer hadn't returned enough constituent calls. Equally often,

Rob would order Amir to take action "first thing in the morning" on some ridiculous thing that had no doubt originated with the Night Shift.

When he'd finished haranguing Amir, he'd hang up and call Earl or Kia. In the morning, we'd compare notes and sort out which requests were legit and which were merely damage we needed to fix. Earl and I developed a theory that Rob was intentionally torturing Amir to make him resign. Amir had seen Rob at his worst (to that point, anyway), but he wasn't "inner circle," so Rob didn't trust him. He didn't really trust anyone.

I was mostly spared the calls. I'd never been his friend, and I made it clear I wouldn't be one of his menservants. I argued with him in private and frequently told him he was flat-out wrong. But I never betrayed him and always had his back in public. He'd semi-fired me a number of times for telling him the truth, but I think he respected me for it. Not that he ever said so.

I did get some calls, though. And they were cause for concern. The first was sometime in February 2012, well after 2:00 a.m. Rob, sounding inconsolable, kept repeating, rapid-fire, that he was sorry, so sorry, he'd fucked it all up. "I'm sorry, brother. I did something bad and it's over. It's all over." He said he felt bad for me, for the staff. He'd let us all down. He let everyone down. Then he "let me go" and hung up. I never found out exactly what he was talking about.

*** 

Lunchtime at Swiss Chalet, Sunday, March 18, 2012. I was eating a chicken sandwich. Rob and Doug were down the street, in the middle of their two-hour weekly radio show on Newstalk 1010. Earl, who was eating with me, was looking ill. After I learned why, I lost my appetite, too. Ford had been out the night before—St. Patrick's Day. As I heard, first from Earl, and later from the staffers who'd been present, he'd been way, way out.

Though there'd been nothing on Ford's calendar for Saturday night, Brooks Barnett, a special assistant to the mayor, was in the office, on standby in case Ford needed a body man. Just before 9:00 p.m., without warning, Rob rolled in with two guests. He was looking to party—to have, as he puts it, "a few pops" with his friends: Peter Kordas, who drove a bus Rob sometimes rented for his high school football team; and a beautiful, twenty-something blonde named Alana, who appeared to be a friend of Peter's. Brooks recognized Peter, but had never seen the woman before. The three went into Rob's office and began drinking.

At some point, Rob stuck his head out and invited Brooks to join the party. He stayed, reluctantly. He also sent a discreet PIN message to Amir, outlining the situation. Amir asked Isaac Ransom, the deputy press secretary, to go assist Brooks. When Isaac arrived, he found Rob and his guests in the mayor's office, already very drunk. Rob kept urging Brooks and Isaac to join in; they pretended to, so they could keep an eye on him.

Soon, Rob and his pals decided they wanted to go out on the town. Brooks and Isaac tried to dissuade him. Isaac called Earl, who arrived *tout de suite*, and also urged Rob to stay put and have fun in private. Rob wasn't listening—he was keen to attend a party he'd heard about on The Esplanade, a short, bar-lined street a ten-minute walk from City Hall. Then one of the guests asked to light up a joint of marijuana. Rob said yes. Earl said no. He sternly reminded Rob that he was the chief magistrate of the city and there was no goddamned way people were going to smoke drugs in the office of the mayor. Rob pouted.

Eventually, Rob, his two guests, and his two anxious staffers left City Hall and hailed a cab. Ransom remained behind to dispose of the booze bottles and glasses before the cleaners found them. During the ride to the bar, Rob directed a number of insulting racial remarks at the cab driver, calling him a "Paki" even though he clearly was not. Then he flung a handful of business cards at the driver from the back seat, telling him, "I'm Rob Ford, the mayor of Toronto. If there's anything I can do for you, call me anytime." Not quite the low profile the staff had hoped for.

At the Bier Markt bar, Earl quickly secured a private room and whisked Rob and his party inside, away from the public eye. There, the mayor and his friends partied for some time, drinking more alcohol and eating chicken wings. At some point, a young female friend of Alana's arrived; then the bar DJ and his girlfriend joined in, too. Though the press would later report that Rob snorted cocaine off the arm of one of the young women, none of his staffers corroborate that, and they insist they had eyes on him all night. I believe the staffers. Given what else occurred that night, I think they would have told me if they'd seen Rob do coke. As the night wore on, they certainly saw him do worse.

Eventually, Rob decided he wanted to go back to City Hall. On his way out of the bar, he tried to dance on the dance floor, stumbled around a bit, and fell to the ground. He was assisted up and out to a cab by his staff and bar security personnel. (Again, so much for discretion.)

Back in his office, Rob seemed to be coming down from a high. He grew morose and reminisced about his father. He broke into tears. Then he became angry, and started ragging on the "Liberal hacks" in his office. (Earl, Isaac, and Brooks are all members of Canada's Liberal party; Ford is a staunch Conservative.) Without warning, Ford became violent. He pushed Earl off a couch and onto the floor, then loomed over him with his arm cocked and fist clenched, threatening to strike him. When the others protested, Rob turned his wrath on Brooks. He charged him with his left hand out, grabbed him by the collar, and slammed him into the wall, right arm pulled back ready to punch him. The staffers got him to back off and calm down, but the atmosphere was electrically charged.

At some point (exact times are hard to pin down, but everyone agrees on what happened), Olivia Gondek, the senior policy and council liaison, who managed much of the mayor's agenda on council, arrived in Rob's office to pick something up. Sensing imminent trouble, she stayed to help the staffers. Rob, by now completely blotto, began speaking to her in a sexually harassing and inappropriate manner. He was describing in explicit detail what he'd like to do sexually with her. Olivia had been Rob's executive assistant while he was a councillor; she knew him better than most of us. She also knew how to shut him up, and was one of the few members on staff who wouldn't tolerate any crap from him. She sharply rebuked him and stopped him cold, then told him he was drunk and should go home to his wife, Renata. Rob sat down like an embarrassed little boy.

Gondek left. For a while, Rob wandered the second floor mezzanine of City Hall with an open bottle of alcohol in his hand, until his staff corralled him back into his office. Finally, at about 4:00 a.m., the party wound down; the staffers guided Rob out of the building toward a taxi.

But Rob wasn't done. First, he caused a ruckus at the security desk near the building's main entrance, because he thought his car had been stolen—until Earl reminded him he hadn't driven to work that day. Second, he made more lewd remarks, this time to the female City Hall security guard who was helping to shepherd him to a taxi. The staffers pulled him away and stuffed him into the cab. Earl got into the front seat with the driver, to see Rob home.

In the cab, Rob punched a number into his cell phone and tried to arrange to meet someone. Earl insisted the cab continue directly to the mayor's home. Angry, Rob ordered the cab to pull over; he wanted Earl to get out in the middle of nowhere. Earl refused and instructed the driver to carry on. At Rob's house, Rob and Earl both got out of the cab. While Earl was paying the driver, Rob jumped into his black Cadillac Escalade and accelerated so rapidly out of his driveway that the taxi had to squeal out of the way, and Earl had to dive for safety lest he be flattened by the mayor of Toronto.

Needless to say, I was feeling grim when I went to work the next day, Monday, March 19, 2012. During the senior staff meeting, Amir asked me for an update on our preparations for the second special council meeting about the Sheppard subway, which was scheduled for March 21. I exploded.

"Who the fuck cares?" I asked. "There is only one thing that matters right now: The mayor of Toronto is a fucking addict! And he's out of control."

Stunned silence. Many in the room suddenly took a keen interest in their notepads. Earl paled. Amir tried to calm me down, but I was having none of it.

"Have you heard what happened here Saturday night?" I went on. "Rob physically assaulted two of our staff. He sexually harassed another. He was drunk in public. He wanted to smoke a joint in his office. He's out of control.

"It doesn't matter what we do at the council meeting. It doesn't matter if we win or lose. The subway doesn't matter. The budget doesn't matter. Nothing matters until he goes to fucking rehab."

Earl cleared his throat. I wheeled on him. "You were fucking attacked by a 330-pound addict!" I cried. "So was Brooks. We can't ignore this shit. Everything else we're doing can just stop until this is dealt with."

The meeting ended. Earl, Amir, and I discussed what to do. Eventually Amir agreed to confront Rob, and I agreed to keep working on the subway file. Earl and I offered to go with Amir when he spoke to Rob; we felt there would be strength in numbers. Amir declined. "This is something for me to discuss with him alone," he said.

He was right. The chief of staff has a special relationship with the mayor, and a unique burden. He knew it would be better if Rob didn't feel we were ganging up on him. I went back to work.

Every day for the next few months, I asked what we were doing about "the addict." Amir said he'd spoken to Rob, and Rob had agreed to take some action. He wasn't going to rehab, but he would see a counselor. I suggested we speak with Doug, and with Diane, Rob's mom. Amir already had.

And for a few months, Rob got better. His behavior was less erratic. He showed up for meetings, he took a more active role in city affairs. I kept waiting for media stories about St. Patrick's Day, but it took months for them to surface. When the story that Rob had done coke in the back room finally appeared, we shrugged it off; we thought it was false. No one in the media seemed to realize that the most horrifying moments of that night had not occurred at the bar, but at City Hall, and outside the mayor's home.

The full story eventually emerged a year later. But for us on Ford's staff, St. Patrick's Day 2012 was a watershed moment. Before March 17, Ford had been a mayor who seemed to be in an increasing struggle with alcohol and troubles at home. After March 17, he was "the addict." It changed how the entire office functioned. The staff closed ranks in a bond of secrecy and struggle. We spent more and more time managing Rob, and less and less time leading the Council or the city. We started shedding policy objectives as we reassessed what was possible and what was not. We researched the major rehab centers, where they were, and how someone got in. I drew up a list of ground rules for the staff, and Amir and Earl agreed: No one would lie for Rob. No one would do anything illegal or against the rules.

The chief of staff's job became less about politics and more about protecting the staff from their mayor. It became about making sure Rob's family was safe, and trying to get the mayor to agree to treatment—or at least trying to insulate him from the consequences of his actions and addictions. It became about keeping Rob from dying.

For me, it was brutal. It must have been for Amir, too—he resigned four months later.

# 20 | The Phone Call

AFTER ST. PATRICK'S Day, things continued to worsen. In early April, Renata Ford was sick, in the hospital, and Rob asked the staff to come up with home care options for when she got out a few days later. Then on April 22, Rob didn't show up for his Sunday radio show. He didn't come in to work on Monday either. Staff scrambled to rebook meetings and make excuses for him. He wasn't answering his phone. Rob Ford was AWOL.

At Tuesday's senior staff meeting, we discussed when to sound the alarm. Rob had disappeared a few times before, usually for about twenty-four hours. He always popped back up the next day, as if nothing unusual had happened. It didn't seem to dawn on him that he was the mayor of Canada's biggest city. He was the only man in the city who could declare an emergency; he shouldn't just disappear without telling anyone. We talked about "what if." What if he didn't pop up? How long do we pretend everything's normal before . . . what? Who do you tell that the mayor is missing?

What if he was found dead somewhere? Or in jail? Both of these seemed like realistic possibilities. Neither would have surprised us. I was happy I'd spoken with the deputy mayor about what was going on. He diligently kept me apprised whenever he was out of town, so we'd know how to reach him if we needed him.

No one outside the office had noticed Rob's absence, and Renata wasn't asking about him, so we decided to give it a bit longer. At 11:00 a.m. Tuesday, Ford's body man, Isaac Shirokoff, finally got Rob on the phone. Rob was drunk and largely incoherent. Isaac spent over an hour talking to him, trying to find out his location. At last Ford gave him an address, on Scarlett Road in Etobicoke, not far from his home. The house belonged to a woman we didn't know. Isaac went to the address, with instructions to take Rob's car keys and sit on him until Doug arrived. At 2:00 p.m., Doug reported that Rob was back in his own bed, sound asleep. Renata, also at home, told Isaac she wanted Rob to stop bringing booze home. Could we help? She was trying to stay healthy.

Just over a week later, on May 2, 2012, I'd just finished dinner with my kids when my phone exploded with Twitter alerts. Dozens of people were talking about an incident at Ford's house between Rob and *Toronto Star* reporter Daniel Dale. I contacted Amir. He told me Rob had caught a reporter trespassing on his property and called the police. Our new press secretary, George Christopoulos (Adrienne Batra had left in November 2011), was on his way, but it would take at least thirty minutes for him to get there. I packed my kids into the car and headed over. There were police cars in front of Rob's house when I arrived.

I told my kids to stay in the car and walked up the driveway. As I got to the front door, it opened and a uniformed cop emerged, walking around me into the yard. I stepped into Rob's home for the second time. Inside the front door, a small dark living room opened up on the left. The curtains were drawn tight behind a plush couch pushed against the window. Rob's kids were lying on a mattress in the middle of the living room floor, which was covered with their toys and blankets, watching a large TV that dominated the space. It was a mess.

To my right was the master bedroom, ankle-deep in dirty clothes, including Rob's expensive suits. Doug and Rob came out of the kitchen straight ahead of me, and we convened at the entrance to the living room. Another police officer followed the brothers out of the kitchen and joined us. I never went further into the house.

Rob, dressed in an old blue tracksuit, was agitated and working himself into a lather. He'd clearly related the story a few times, and it was already morphing into an epic confrontation in his mind. He told me a neighbor had phoned to warn him that a stranger was taking pictures over Rob's backyard fence. (Rob's house is at the end of a street and backs onto a public park.) Rob ran out his front door, then skirted the perimeter of his yard along the outside of his fence, into the parkland behind his backyard. There, he found Dale, on his way to the street.

Dale is about thirty, five-foot-nine, slight and bespectacled, with short, brown (receding) hair and a gentle nature. Although he worked for the dreaded *Star*, Dale had always been straightforward and honest with me.

Ford confronted Dale; Dale dropped his cell phone and fled. Ford claimed the reporter was taking photos of his backyard while standing on some cinder blocks piled up against his fence. Dale claimed he was there reporting a story: Rob wanted to buy a sliver of the parkland beside his home, and Dale said he was looking at that land.

I didn't know whom to believe. I didn't trust Rob's version because he'd embellished and fabricated details in earlier crises. Also, the way Dale described Ford standing over him, ready to punch him, was nearly identical to the way Rob had threatened Earl and Brooks on St. Patrick's Day. I didn't trust Dale either because parts of his story didn't seem to add up. A version of his story was online before he showed up at Ford's house—was he researching the story after it was published? The land Ford was asking to buy wasn't behind his house; it was a small triangular slice fronting the street right beside the Ford home; there was no reason to go behind Ford's yard to see it. Dale also said he didn't take pictures with his phone, because its battery had died. Yet, while Rob, Doug, and I were talking with the police officer in the house, Dale's phone rang in the cop's hand. The battery clearly wasn't dead.

I tweeted about those inaccuracies. I didn't deny Dale's version of events, but I wanted to defend Rob with the truth I had. Some people speculated that Rob recharged Dale's phone, but I don't believe either Rob or Doug would have thought of that. I helped Rob rewind video from his security cameras to see if Dale was caught on tape; he wasn't. After George arrived, I left.

The next day, as I watched TV coverage of an impromptu press conference Rob had given on his front lawn after I'd left the night before, I recognized a man standing behind Rob: David Price. A close friend of Doug's, Price had hung around the campaign in 2010. None of us in Rob's office trusted him. I hadn't seen Price when I was there, which was a bit odd—he usually stuck to Doug like glue. But if you told me that Price had the idea to charge Dale's cell, to check it out before the cops arrived—well, that wouldn't surprise me. I stopped tweeting about the whole episode. Maybe Dale was telling the truth.

This incident supercharged the war between the Fords and the *Toronto Star*. Now it was as personal for the journalists as it had always been for Rob. Innuendo emerged from Ford Nation that Dale was a creep; Rob's kids played in the backyard where Dale was supposedly "peeping." It got ugly. Rob upped the ante in each retelling of the story: *There was video evidence!* (There wasn't.) *Dale had been in Rob's yard!* (He hadn't.) Rob began insinuating that Dale was photographing his kids. Eventually, in 2014, Dale sued Ford and forced him to admit there was no evidence whatsoever that Dale had entered Ford's yard or taken photographs of anything.

But in the immediate aftermath of the incident at Rob's place, the *Toronto Star* bureau at City Hall treated the mayor's office with open contempt. Although officially they were shunned, in the backrooms, we'd always gotten along. No longer. David Rider, the *Star* bureau chief, even refused to make eye contact with me, or acknowledge my existence when I said hello in the hallway.

*\*\*\**

I was also concerned about how Rob was handling his money. Since he was first elected councillor, he had claimed almost no expenses from the city. He boasted about this so much that other councillors complained—in fact, they passed a motion requiring him to spend some of the money allocated to his office. (That had backfired; it turned Ford into a martyr for taxpayers.)

When Rob became mayor, things got worse: He refused to let any of his staff claim their expenses. This was unfair. We weren't paying people a lot, and their costs were legitimate. Earl and I fought Rob on this so often that he begrudgingly agreed to reimburse staff expenses—out of his own pocket. Literally: someone would hand Rob a receipt, and he'd pull out a stack of $20s and peel a few off. (He usually had around $1,000 in his pocket.) The staff found this so embarrassing they ate all but the biggest work expenses. I certainly did; I never claimed anything.

But in mid-2012, Rob suddenly began paying for everything by check. His pocket cash seemed to have evaporated. He began arguing about a lot of expenses, and taking longer and longer to pay back the few he deemed worthy. Just before Christmas, I overheard Rob ask Kia to book Rob's family vacation to Florida on Kia's credit card. (Kia told me soon after that it wasn't the first time he'd put charges of Rob's on his card, and he was still waiting for repayment.) I went into Rob's office and closed the door. I told him it wasn't appropriate for him to ask staffers to cover his expenses on their credit cards, especially during the holidays. If he didn't want to use his own card, he could write a check or pay in cash at the travel agency. He conceded—or so I thought.

I wasn't sure if this cash crunch was due to the hundreds of thousands of dollars he'd spent on legal bills, or if he was burning it on his other, recreational uses.

Then this happened: A junior staffer named Chris Fickel had a minor accident in a city car. No one was hurt, appropriate reports were filed, and the matter was closed. Until weeks later, that is, when Chris asked to speak with me privately. Nervously, he admitted to me that Rob had pulled him aside, and told him that the woman whose car he'd hit had phoned him and was threatening to sue. Rob said he'd calmed her down by offering to have Chris pay her $2,000 to "make the problem go away." Rob said he'd deliver the money himself, because the woman might not want to see Chris. If he didn't pay, Rob warned, Chris could be charged and do jail time. To me, it sounded perilously close to a shakedown.

Chris, always a loyal, honest guy, agonized over sharing his story with me. I confronted Rob. He denied it at first, then went on the attack. His story was that Chris, who he called "as useless as tits on a bull," had come to him, saying he needed money to pay off the woman. I let that one go, and told him a) there was no way a staffer was paying anybody anything; and b) Rob should back off the whole thing.

When I told Chris he was off the hook, he broke down and related a slew of things that had happened between him and the mayor. One evening a few months prior, on Chris's day off, Rob had ordered him to stop by Rob's house to look at Renata's computer. When Chris got there, Rob insisted Chris join him and Renata in the basement. When Chris protested that he had a date waiting in the car, Rob told him to bring her in, too. Downstairs, Chris and his date witnessed a surreal scene: The mayor disappeared briefly, then returned with a joint of marijuana he offered around the room. No one joined him, so he smoked it alone. As soon as they could, Chris and his date hightailed it out of there.

On another occasion, Chris was riding in the backseat of Rob's Escalade; Rob was driving, with one of his assistant high school football coaches riding shotgun. They stopped briefly at a local high school and Chris watched Rob pull a 12 oz. mickey of vodka out of a paper bag and down it in about two minutes, alternating each chug with a mouthful of Gatorade. Chris was shocked. He asked the mayor to let him out at the next corner; he said he wanted to catch the bus. Chris had never told anyone, he said, because he didn't want to get fired or get the mayor in trouble. Immediately, I moved him off Rob's staff and onto mine. I also told him that he was never again to ride in a vehicle driven by the mayor.

The next morning at the senior staff meeting, I made it policy: No staffers were permitted to be in a vehicle operated by the mayor. They could ride in Rob's car if someone else drove. If Rob was driving, they were to follow him in a city car.

When Rob came in later that morning, I told him privately that I'd heard from three people who said they'd seen him driving after drinking, and in one case driving while drinking. I said "three" to protect Chris, and because it was true: Two different senior members of the Toronto Police Service had told me officers had pulled over the mayor's car late at night on multiple occasions and driven him home rather than charging him for driving under the influence.

All Rob wanted to know was who had accused him. I refused to say. "Chris!" he said. I said it didn't matter who'd told me—what mattered was that staff was no longer to ride in his car if he was driving.

He exploded. "You're saying I'm driving drunk?!"

"Are you?" I asked.

"No fucking way, buddy," he sputtered. "You're saying I'm a criminal. Why don't you call the police?"

"I'm not saying that you drive drunk," I countered, in my most level and measured voice. "I'm saying that I don't know if you're always sober when you drive, so I'm taking steps to make sure our staff—your employees—are safe."

"I can't believe you're accusing me! Prove it!"

"I don't have to prove it, Rob. It's bad enough that I don't know," I said. "Don't you see that? It's bad enough that I can't be sure you're not driving drunk."

Rob tried arguing that I didn't have the authority to order staff not to drive with him, but I pointed out that under the provincial Occupational Health and Safety Act, employers were legally responsible for ensuring a safe workplace for their employees. "I've wanted you to have a driver since we first met. So has everyone," I said. "You should have a driver—you're the mayor of Canada's largest city. So now you will." He argued some more, then he dismissed me with his standard perfunctory "You do what you want, brother. I don't care."

I did not report Chris's story to the police. It was hearsay, and it was too late. I'd arrested two drunk drivers in my life, and I knew it was essential to witness the act of driving and to have continuity of evidence through to a blood alcohol test establishing the driver over the legal limit. That didn't exist weeks after the fact. There was nothing the police could do with the information. Besides, as I mentioned, they already knew the mayor was driving drunk, and weren't doing anything about it.

***

Rob was still capable of good days. When the subway platform at Union Station, the hub of Toronto's mass transit system, flooded on June 1, Rob marched down there (a fifteen-minute walk) with a small entourage, checked out the damage, and gave a quick update to the press. He looked pulled together and in charge.

The next evening, when a gang shooting at the Eaton Centre, Toronto's most famous shopping mall, shocked the city (two people died and five more were wounded), I picked up Rob at his house and drove him to City Hall, which is a block west of the mall. After we'd waited almost an hour for Police Chief Blair to join us (he was at a fancy dinner and didn't want the mayor to beat him to the scene), Rob had had enough; we walked over to the mall's south entrance and ducked under the police tape. Again, Rob got a briefing and spoke to the press; again, he looked good.

Among the wounded was thirteen-year-old Connor Stevenson, who'd been shot in the head. Over the next few weeks, Rob made at least two private visits to the Hospital for Sick Children to see Connor and his family. We never publicized those visits, because we thought it would look opportunistic. But Rob thought it was the right thing to do, and felt comfortable doing it. (Connor made a phenomenal recovery.)

But not long after the Eaton Centre shooting, my work BlackBerry again rang in the middle of the night. 2:39 a.m. Blocked number. Uh-oh—Rob.

He's out of it, but he doesn't sound drunk. This time, he's speaking superfast. Agitated. I can barely understand half of what he says. A clear word or phrase here, then incoherence for several sentences. Gradually, I piece it together.

He says he's been arguing with Renata and wants me to witness (by phone) that he is leaving the house. I can hear Renata in the background, alternately screaming and pleading with him. Her speech is slurred and she sounds extremely agitated. I turn down the volume on my phone and slip out of the bedroom, closing my son's bedroom door as I walk down to the kitchen where I can talk without waking up my kids. I grab a pen and a pad of my kids' construction paper and start taking notes. Rob sounds like he's out of control, and I'm worried I may have to remember this conversation. It's now 2:44 a.m. "Rob, what's going on?" I ask. "Is everyone okay? Are the kids okay?"

Rob doesn't answer. I hear Renata, in the background, say, "Stop bothering me . . . Get out of this room." I hear Rob ask her, "Did I give you $200?" They both sound angry. But he's 330 pounds and tall, and she's about 120 and shorter. I'm hoping to God this doesn't get physical.

**Rob:** "Can I talk to you about what happened?" I don't know if he means me or Renata. Next he tells me he and Renata were fighting because "she was sleeping with someone else."

At this point, I am not surprised by anything outrageous coming from Rob's mouth.

**Renata:** "Get out!"

Both of them spit a string of curses at one another. I can't hear it all, but it doesn't sound good. I strain to hear the kids, but there's no indication they're there. Maybe Rob and Renata are in the basement. Maybe the kids sleep upstairs.

**Rob (to Renata):** "Can I get the money back? You have a lot of money there. What else did you shove up there?"

**Rob (to me):** "I can't live like this. She'll fuck guys right in front of me."

More outrageous Rob.

It's now 2:48.

**Rob (to Renata):** "I want to talk about what happened last night."

**Renata:** "I fucked my ex old man." I can't tell whether she's being straight or mocking him.

**Rob (to me):** "I gave her $200 for the kids. You have no idea, man . . . I swear to God I'm going to kill this woman, brother."

Fuck me. I grab my personal iPhone, which is charging on the kitchen counter. I key in 9-1-1 but don't press "Enter." Not yet. At the moment, the mayor and his wife are having a no-holds-barred screaming fest, but that's not illegal. My parents used to have those when I was a kid. No one got hurt. Not physically, anyway.

**Renata:** "Get out of my face. You're driving me nuts!"

**Rob:** "I'll rip this fucking door open!"

**Renata:** "Get out of here. Leave me alone!"

**Rob:** "Just open the door and talk to me."

**Renata:** "I'm calling Dougie." I'm hoping she means Doug Ford, Rob's brother, and not Dougie Ford, her and Rob's four-year-old son. But does this mean Renata calls Doug when Rob is out of control?

I wonder if Rob has forgotten I'm on the phone. At this point, he definitely sounds like the aggressor. Renata sounds like she's locked herself in a room. She keeps yelling at him to leave.

**Rob (to Renata, to himself, I can't quite tell):** "Don't smoke in my room . . . I catch him on video . . . What dope do you have under there? It looks like a pharmacy . . . Needle here, pills. $500 back there."

**Rob (suddenly, to me):** "She's a whore, dude. She's got $520 hidden away. They pay her to blow them or for a fuck. I catch them. Stephanie tells me these guys are coming over." Stephanie is his then-eight-year-old daughter.

I can't tell if Rob believes what he's saying or if he's making up lies to anger Renata and make me think everything is her fault.

"Where are the kids, Rob?" I ask. He doesn't answer.

I can hear him rustling around the house. I don't hear Renata anymore. I'm hoping he's moved away from her.

**Rob:** "I just found $500 in the couch and a cell phone . . ." I can hear him huffing as he searches under the sofa cushions. His speech is calming down a little bit.

**Rob:** "I'm going insane."

It's now 2:57 a.m. I'm exhausted, but I feel the adrenalin coursing through my veins. How can I shut this down? I can't drive over there and leave my own kids alone in the house. I have to do it by phone.

**Rob:** "There's $1,120 in cash in the couch, dude. You guys all knew about this and you never told me, fuckers."

He's still searching the room. I can hear him moving stuff around.

**Rob:** "I just found a big piece of blow . . . a rock." There's a long pause and I can't hear him well, as if he's put the phone down. But it sounds like he's saying, "I'll light this thing up."

His next few sentences are clearer.

**Rob:** "I just found this rock. I put a light to it and it melts."

**Rob:** "You knew this. You guys knew everything all along. She's a whore and a junkie, dude."

More lies to enrage Renata?

**Rob:** "She just took my gun upstairs."

His *what*? They have a fucking gun? It's ominously quiet in the background. I don't hear Renata or anyone else. Just Rob breathing, then speaking. His voice gets really fast again. I don't know if he's making shit up. I can't tell what's really happening from what fantasies he's spinning.

"Where are your kids, Rob?" I ask again. Again, he doesn't seem to hear me.

**Rob:** "It's quiet now. Let's go upstairs." I hear his footsteps on the stairs. I beg him to stay downstairs, to let Renata be. Don't wake up the kids. Stop arguing. Don't make the police come to the house. Again.

**Rob (to Renata):** "There's a lot of cash downstairs." I hear her muffled voice in the background. She sounds sleepy.

**Rob (to Renata), yelling:** "We've got you cornered like a rat!"

**Renata:** "Don't wake up the kids!"

**Rob:** "She's got my piece . . . She's gone . . . Get the fuck downstairs."

I wonder again, should I get in my car? Should I get someone over there?

Renata, louder now, no longer behind a door: "Are you going to leave me alone?"

**Rob:** "I'm going to give you five dollars see . . ." [ . . . . ] incoherent ". . . or I'm putting three bullets in your head. You're pinched. I'll pump you full . . ." [ . . . . ] again incoherent [ . . . . ]

Fuck. Fuck. I fumble with my iPhone again. Call now? "Do you have a gun, Rob?" I ask.

"She stole it," he answers.

Rob had once told me that his dad had had a vintage gun. I'd asked where it was, if it was legally registered, who owned it now. The last thing I wanted was a gun in Ford's house. Any gun, but especially an illegal gun. Canada has tight gun laws, which the mayor of Toronto should not break. Rob had answered that he didn't own any guns, but that Doug did.

**Rob (to Renata), mockingly:** "Let's go down and talk about what's going on." He laughs.

**Rob (to me):** "Now she's upstairs in the kids' room."

"Just let her be, Rob," I plead. "Let the kids sleep. They don't need to see their mom and dad fighting."

Too late. I hear Stephanie's voice in the background. My left thumb hovers over the "Enter" button on my iPhone, ready to summon the police. My heart is pounding. I hear blood rushing through my neck. I lean forward, mouth open, straining to hear what's going on in Rob Ford's house. It's like being back in the army, in the dark woods, straining to hear footsteps.

**Rob:** "Steph, is Mommy being bad or good?"

I can half-hear Stephanie's sleepy voice.

"Rob, leave her alone," I say, trying to sound stern but calm. Reasonable. An ally. "Let her sleep. Don't drag her into your fight."

Again, he asks his daughter whether her mommy is good or bad.

"Mommy is good," she replies, in a tired little voice. "Everyone in this house is good." More mature than either of her parents, she's trying to keep the peace. My heart cracks. It's now 3:05.

I hear Rob say, "See no monkey, hear no monkey," in the creepiest kiddie-talk voice I've ever heard. A shiver goes down my spine.

"Let her go back to sleep, Rob," I plead.

**Rob:** "I've never stolen in my life, man." That's a ninety-degree turn in his conversation, but a welcome one. It sounds like he's moving away from the kids' room. His voice speeds up again. I can't understand all of it.

**Rob:** "I've never fucked around . . . I would be a world leader . . . People say you're fucked, but you're honest and never stold [*sic*] anything."

Suddenly he's angry, this time with Doug. He rambles on about a panic rush order from Maple Leaf Foods that Deco had received. They'd paid ten times the normal invoice price. "Dougie says, 'Don't fuck this up,'" Rob babbles.

Then: "You and I are exactly the same." I don't even want to think about where that came from.

He continues talking about me, about how smart I am, but how I don't unwind, I don't have a life. He respects me. But . . .

At 3:13, out of nowhere, Renata starts yelling again in the background—I mean, really shouting.

**Renata:** "Shut the fuck up!"

Rob: "Don't put your hands on me! Don't grab my phone!"

I'm straining to hear anything that sounds like a blow, a push or a shove. I unlock my iPhone again, ready to call 9-1-1.

**Rob:** "Don't touch me!"

**Renata:** "I'll call the cops. Stay away from me! Get the hell out of my way. Get out!"

**Rob:** "Call 9-1-1! Or Dougie—you're fucking him."

Whoa, what? Suddenly Renata is talking to me—speaking over Rob as he holds the phone. "Mark, can you please get Rob out of the house?" she pleads.

I ask Rob to back off, leave Renata alone. I ask him to go to another room so he and I can talk. I'm keeping my voice low, slow, soothing. I hear him moving, I think, downstairs. Renata's voice disappears and I hear a door close.

Rob is mumbling something I can't make out, so I keep talking. I tell him I can send him a car, take him to a hotel. "You can get a good night's sleep," I say. "You don't have to fight anymore. How about it?"

It's now 3:23. Rob unleashes a blast of words at hyper-speed. I can only make out a few words here and there.

"...doobies..."

"I smoked that shit..."

"I sold that shit..."

"...heroin..."

3:30. He's still talking.

"...my dad shot this guy..."

"...after he shot my cousin..."

"...Cousin Willy died...cousin Dougie..."

"I'm doing it in the washroom. I'm snorting shit. I'm smashing shit..."

"I come out all dripping wet.."

3:35.

"Since Mikey the transvestite died..."

"...fighter..."

"...left-handed..."

Finally, at 3:57, his monologue begins to slow. I can make out a few more words and phrases. Rob says he doesn't smoke but talks about others "smoking weed in the 'man cave,'" and I remember that one of Deco's three buildings has been nicknamed "the man cave." Doug and Randy were rumored to host friends there occasionally.

Rob: "It's lonely at the top. My therapy is talking. You're a good listener, Towhey. I'm gonna give you $1,000 for listening to my shit." I tell him he doesn't need to do that, he can call me anytime. He insists. "You shouldn't have to put up with my shit," he says.

It's 4:00 a.m. He now sounds calm. As he has done on other late night calls, he begins to apologize, says he's sorry he fucked everything up. He says he'll be okay, but he's sorry for me, because I have nothing in my life. He says I'm fucked. I'm standing in my kitchen in the dark, looking at a construction paper pad full of my boss's ravings. I'm inclined to agree.

Rob: "I gotta go. I gotta go to the washroom to do another smash. I'm not a corrupt guy. Hell, maybe when it comes to getting head or drunk or doing drugs . . ."

At last, calmed down, he says he's "gotta let you go" and hangs up. It's 4:20 a.m. I've been listening to him for an hour and forty minutes. I'm emotionally spent. I plug my phones back into their chargers, take a long drink of water, and go back to bed, hoping to God my phone won't ring again that night. It doesn't. But he still owes me that $1,000.

***

Throughout the summer and into the fall of 2012, the calls from Rob keep coming. September 12, he phones at 7:54 p.m. He says he's at his friend Ron Singer's mom's house. We talk about the upcoming meeting with Chicago mayor Rahm Emanuel. Rob sounds high.

Just over ten hours later, my work phone rings at 6:12 a.m. It's Rob, but he can't hear me. I say "Hello?" five or six times, then realize it's a pocket dial. Rob is famous for them. At first, the sound is loud, chaotic—yelling voices, lots of movement. I'm worried he's in a fight. Then I hear his voice, not in distress. But what I hear freezes me.

I hear four male voices. One is Rob, speaking fast, incoherent, sounding high. The other is distorted, but Rob calls him "Ron." I wonder if it's Ron Singer, with whom he'd been the night before. Whoever Ron is, he sounds loaded. It's the other two voices that electrify me, however. Because they're stone-cold sober. I don't recognize them. I'm alarmed that Ford is wired out of his mind with people who are dead sober. Who watches someone get fucked up? And why?

Rob is talking about his wife, about offering her up to the guys he's with, about how they can "eat her pussy." I hang up.

When Kia, Rob's EA, calls him at 7:00 a.m. to begin the daily process of getting Rob up and on the grid, Kia's surprised to find Rob already awake. But he quickly realizes Rob hasn't been to bed. Rob cancels his appointments for the day. He does make it to his high school football team's afternoon practice, but doesn't do much coaching. Mostly, he stands on the sidelines looking hungover while his assistant coaches run the drills. During a break in the practice, he mumbles through an incomprehensible speech to the team, then leaves early. Chris Fickel, his body man, follows Rob home in the city car. In his driveway, Rob vomits down the outside of his Cadillac. Fickel asks Ford's cleaning lady to wash it off before someone sees it, then leaves.

By this time, the office is used to Rob's schedule changing daily. We put up with his ridiculous demands for meetings at early hours, knowing perfectly well that he won't be there. Instead, we focus on triaging the legislative and policy agenda, discarding objectives that are no longer possible with a dysfunctional mayor. We've stopped fighting the problem; we've learned to be flexible. "It is what it is" becomes our unofficial motto. Meanwhile, I talk to Rob whenever I can about his drinking—we call it that, even though I'm pretty sure there's more than one demon plaguing him—and speak often with his friend the addiction counselor for advice.

November 2, Rob calls me at 5:38 p.m. He sounds high, talking a mile a minute about some conspiracy. In the background I hear Renata, her words slurred. I can also hear kids; they sound wild, running around, yelling.

Rob tells me a Bell telephone technician is at his house. He says his computer has been hacked, it's been bugged, it's been acting strange since he caught Daniel Dale behind his house, the *Toronto Star* or somebody is tapping his Internet lines and probably his telephone lines too, he called the police, but the fuckers probably are doing it too, and he spoke to (Minister of Finance) Jim Flaherty and Stephen Harper and (Member of Parliament) Parm Gill, he called the top guy at Bell Canada who sent this technician out to the house to find the tap and fix it, it's not in the house though, they can't find it, but the computer's hacked, and that's a privacy issue, you can't just tap someone's phone and their Internet, he'll go to the media.

When he finally takes a breath, I jump in. "Let's not get the media involved in this, okay, boss?" I say. "It sounds like a Microsoft Windows error—they happen a lot, you know. Can I talk to the technician?"

The technician comes on the phone. Which means he's in Ford's house, witnessing the mayor of Toronto spinning out of control. Great.

The tech sounds more like a lineman than a computer tech. He points out the computer looks old and is running very slowly. I thank him and ask for the mayor again. I ask Rob to bring his computer to work in the morning so we can fix it. I still can't believe the technician hasn't told the world what he saw that night.

# 21 | The Kids are Alright?

AFTER ST. PATRICK'S Day, it was clear that Rob was an addict. It was less clear what he was addicted to. Alcohol was a given. But there seemed to be more. Much of his behavior didn't reconcile with what I understood to be the common effects of alcohol. He often appeared hyperactive, extremely agitated, and paranoid. He would rub his forearms repeatedly as if they were itchy and talk so fast you couldn't understand what he was saying. Other times he seemed so exhausted he could barely stand up.

One of the reasons it took us as long as it did to notice Rob's substance abuse is that he was brilliant at blaming others. In the beginning, during the campaign, he'd blame Renata, his wife, for his sleeplessness. He'd say Renata had a habit of calling 9-1-1 when she was angry or drunk. By the end of the campaign, he was so tired he could hardly function. He said he was awake all night caring for his two children, because Renata wasn't up to it. Her parents watched the kids during the day, but let them sleep all afternoon. So when Rob got home from campaigning at 10:00 or 11:00 p.m., they were wide awake. He'd then have to feed them, clean the house, and do the laundry because Renata "couldn't," Rob said. So he barely slept.

After Rob was elected, when he started showing up late for work or missing scheduled appointments altogether, he again blamed his wife. Renata was causing trouble at home, he'd say. One Christmas morning, for example, Rob was supposed to fly to Florida with Renata and the kids. But Renata hadn't made it to the airport. She was "out of it," Rob said. So he took the kids and left without her. Her parents, Polish Canadian immigrants who don't speak much English, called the police and told them Rob was abducting the children. Exactly how Renata was out of it, we could only speculate. The police had attended calls at the house before and what little we learned from them tended to corroborate Rob's version of events.

As Rob's behavior worsened, he spread the blame around. He'd blame Doug for some things. If he missed an event, he'd say that a staffer had forgotten to put the information in his events folder in his car. He'd yell at Amir or me, and we'd prove that the staffer had done his or her job perfectly. Then he'd blame someone or something else.

After Rob admitted he was drinking too much, he blamed it on Renata and Doug. They were driving him crazy: Her at home; him at work, on the phone, at Deco, everywhere.

Once we concluded Rob was an addict—or, I should say, once I'd concluded he was an addict, since no one else was willing to use that word—we began looking for ways to get him help. My preference was a residential rehab program. I thought it would be the easiest for us to manage: clean, simple, clear-cut. But he'd say he didn't need it. He had a few drinks now and then, so what? We were overreacting.

I did worry about who would take care of Rob's kids if he went into treatment. He so often told us Renata couldn't. We once asked Doug about who in the family could step in—but Doug said Renata would freak if we even suggested it; she'd think whoever it was would try to steal them. We thought that perhaps both Renata and Rob could go somewhere together, without the kids, to get whatever therapy either or both needed. Amir and I began compiling a file folder of rehab centers and addiction treatment programs. We hoped we'd be able to use it before Rob died, or some other terrible thing happened.

In the meantime, we kept leaning on the recovering addict who'd been advising Rob. He had experience coaching alcoholics and others with substance abuse problems in the community and in prisons. We'd ask his advice and find opportunities for him and Rob to spend time together whenever possible.

\*\*\*

Every few days, I'd open our morning senior staff meeting by asking, "How are the kids?" The staff, some of whom were parents themselves, would compare notes about who had seen Stephanie and Dougie last, and how they looked. We believed their parents weren't doing a great job, but that wasn't really our determination to make. Our concern was, are they safe? Although it wasn't public knowledge, we understood the Children's Aid Society of Toronto, the government's children protection services, had visited the Ford home a number of times. They appeared to conclude the kids were all right. In fact, they seem to have deemed Rob Ford to be the more competent parent. (That sobered us.)

We concluded that any solution for Rob would also have to encompass whatever issues might be affecting Renata. Rob told a lot of stories about Renata, but I have no idea what was true and what was pure, spiteful fiction. I do know that on a number of occasions, staff reported she did not look or sound well. So we added her to our regular morning check-in. "How's Renata?" I'd ask. "Who saw her last? How did she look?"

On two occasions, Renata called the office and asked for help getting treatment. (Because there are rumors about Ford allegedly being abusive toward his wife, I must point out that the treatment she sought was not for trauma, and I never saw evidence of physical abuse.) On both occasions, we provided staff to help her get there safely. The last time I saw Renata was on television, months after I'd left office, and after Rob had returned from the rehab he finally checked into in 2014. She looked, on TV, better than I'd ever seen her. Rob Ford was a challenging and often exhausting man to work for. I can only imagine what it must be like to live with him.

Safety aside, Rob's kids were an issue for his staff right from the beginning of his mayoralty. The first time Rob brought in Stephanie, then age seven (schools were closed for a professional development day), some of the staff volunteered to keep an eye on her while Rob worked. But Stephie is a true Ford, precocious and strong-willed. When she wanted to see her dad, she would see him, and no one was able to stop her barging through a closed door—straight into the TV spotlight in the Protocol Lounge where her father was in the middle of greeting the US Ambassador to Canada, David Jacobson, in a press conference. The ambassador took it in good humor and everyone got a chuckle out of it.

One day of child care we could handle. But those days piled up—first every school professional development day. Then Christmas week and spring break. Then the full summer holidays loomed. Having to care for Ford's children in the office for days at a time became a problem for the staff. They couldn't get their work done. They hadn't signed up to be babysitters. The office environment was ill-suited to young children; naturally, after hours of hanging out, they grew bored and troublesome. First Amir, then I, pushed Rob to find either a day care or a nanny. For a time, Amir was able to help him find one. But she didn't last long. Neither did the next one, or the next.

After I became chief of staff in August 2012, I told Rob—firmly—that his kids could not be in the office all month. He could find a solution, or take time off and stay home himself. Reluctantly, he hired someone again.

One day, in late August 2012, Rob was driving the family to the annual Canadian National Exhibition—Toronto's supersized version of a summer fair. While checking in by phone with Rob's body man, who was in the car with the Ford family, (this was before I'd issued the prohibition on driving with Rob) I overheard him struggling to get Dougie to sit down; the five-year-old was jumping all over the back seat.

"Isn't he in a car seat?" I asked. Ontario law required kids Dougie's age and size to use a car seat. Nope. His car seat was in Renata's car. I told the staffer to get the kids to sit down and put on their seatbelts. I also told him to make sure Rob kept the tinted windows up when he drove up to the gate where George Christopoulos, the press secretary, was waiting with a gaggle of TV cameras. We didn't need to see the kids hanging out of the car on the evening news.

The next day, I told Rob to install a car seat in his Escalade. Rob argued he didn't need one and demanded to see the law himself. So I printed off the Highway Traffic Act and highlighted the relevant sections. Rob promised to look after it, but I never found out if he did.

\*\*\*

But nothing, I mean nothing, compared to the Sandwich Run for sheer Ford absurdity. One September day in 2012, I asked Kia where everyone was. We had four special assistants and I couldn't find any of them. "Well, one is on the Sandwich Run . . ." he started to answer.

I cut him off: "I'm sorry, the what?"

Kia told me that every day since school had begun, the mayor had detailed one of his staffers to drive from City Hall, which is downtown, out to Stephanie's elementary school, which is in the far northwest corner of the city, to buy a submarine sandwich from a specific store and take it to her in time for lunch. The task took two and half hours of staff time per day. It was against every rule on the books—and also just plain stupid.

I turned on my heel and walked into Rob's office. I told him the Sandwich Run stopped that day, and reminded him how much shit he'd get in if anyone found out he was spending the taxpayers' money on this. I pointed out that a mayoral staffer in a suit showing up at a school full of unionized teachers who weren't exactly Rob's biggest fans was unlikely to go unnoticed for long. I asked why he didn't simply make her a sandwich at home and put it in a bag.

"She only likes subs from that store," he argued.

"Then buy it the night before and put it in the fridge," I said.

"It has to have tomatoes and they get soggy if it's not freshly made."

"Then give her something else for lunch," I said.

"She won't eat anything else."

I said my kids had been finicky eaters too, but if you pack them a lunch, sooner or later they'll eat it. Kids hate change, but they get used to it fast. She wasn't going to starve. He shook his head no.

"Rob," I said in my calmest voice. "You can prepay the sandwich shop and we'll get the guy to deliver. You'll pay him whatever it costs, but we can't have a staffer spend three hours a day waiting on your daughter."

"Okay," he conceded.

I walked back to my office, sat down, leaned back, and closed my eyes. If only I could have solved all of Ford's problems that easily.

# 22 | Chief of Staff

A FTER ST. PATRICK's Day, a lot of us on the mayor's staff started polishing our resumes. The only policy file that still interested me was the provincial government's announcement in March 2012 that they were looking to put a casino in the city somewhere. I thought it could be the missing piece to a concept I'd been working on for the underused Exhibition Place grounds. But that didn't seem enough to stick around for.

Amir Remtulla beat me out the door, however. In July, Earl and I heard rumors from our various networks that Amir had landed a job at Toronto 2015, the organizing committee for the upcoming Pan Am Games. We weren't surprised—he'd been booking increasing numbers of off-site breakfast and lunch meetings, obviously networking. I was a bit envious. When he came in to tell me he was leaving on July 7, 2012, I congratulated him.

Although we hadn't always gotten along and I sometimes didn't trust him, we'd been through ridiculous times together and I'd grown to like him. Often, after a particularly crazy day, Earl, Amir, and I would sit in Earl's office, just looking at each other and shaking our heads. We said, "It is what it is," so often, it should have been inscribed in Latin and painted on the wall as the office motto. Earl often joked about writing a book about our exploits after it was all over. He proposed to call it *Peaks and Valleys*. I suggested a more apt title might be *Peaks and . . . Oh, Fuck!*

But when Amir left, I realized I couldn't procrastinate any more. I was either going to take over as chief of staff, or quit. And I wasn't sure I wanted the job. As director of policy and strategic planning, I worked with city staff, implementing ideas and delivering results. As chief of staff, I would be fully occupied with the minute-to-minute crazy that was Rob Ford. Then again, the job paid a lot better than mine, about $50,000 better. And it would hurt my career if it looked like I'd been passed over.

I didn't have a lot of time to think about it, however—as soon as Amir gave Ford his notice, Rob called me into his office and offered me the job. I accepted, with conditions. We had to discuss his "drinking," and the role Doug played. And the money had to be right. Being Rob, he tried to bargain my salary down. When I stood firm, he tried to do an end run around me—make me interim chief of staff, again, while he looked for someone else. I refused that, too, and went back to my office.

A few minutes later, Earl walked in. "Rob just made me interim chief of staff," he said. "What happened? Why didn't he offer chief of staff to you?"

I filled him in. "You have to take it," Earl replied. "Tell him you will. You can work out the money later."

I told Earl I couldn't do that. I knew that if Rob didn't pay me what he'd paid Amir and Nick, there was no way he'd listen to me. I knew money was the only measure that mattered to him.

That afternoon, we issued a press release announcing Amir's departure and Earl's appointment as interim chief. As I left to head home, I bumped into a reporter who asked if I was going to be the next chief. Because I needed a little career insurance to protect my reputation, I gave him some background info: the mayor had offered it to me, but wouldn't meet my conditions. Let people speculate about what my conditions were—I'd done what I needed to protect myself.

For a couple of weeks, Earl tried to convince me to give in and take the job. Then he settled into the role, and I could see him become more of a competitor than a booster. Fair enough. In one ear, Doug kept telling me that he was my only supporter, that the councillors were telling Rob to pick someone from the outside, that they hated me. (I'm sure some of them did. Also fair enough.) In the other ear, Rob would say that Doug wanted me gone. I kept singing Rob the same song: His was the only opinion that mattered; I'd be his chief, but he had to pay me, and he had to start showing up for work—mentally and physically.

I knew I'd earn every cent. Rob was retrenching into his old habits that summer—skipping meetings, showing up late, and generally not performing. As his workday shrank, his nightlife was obviously expanding, and it seemed obvious he was drinking, a lot. Whenever he was in the office, he spent half his time in the washroom; when he emerged, his face was always flushed and he smelled of strong mouthwash and cologne. So, when a councillor suggested Rob form a search committee to interview chief of staff candidates, he agreed. Anything to avoid a decision.

It was ludicrous. The councillors were playing for power—if they could pick their own guy for the job, they'd have the keys to the kingdom. I refused to participate. They asked for a resume. I didn't provide one.

In the meantime, I continued to talk with Rob. On a number of days, we had surprisingly deep conversations. On one of those good days, I told him I was worried about him and his kids. I knew he was drinking and maybe doing drugs. He admitted he might have a problem with alcohol, but swore he didn't touch drugs. I told him about my own heart-attack scare and said maybe we could try to get in shape together, take some kind of daily exercise break.

I also reiterated the rest of my conditions: First, I wanted $185,000 but I would agree to $180,000 (which was what he'd paid me before, when I was interim chief)—if he would agree to review the salary after six months. Second, he had to show up for work. I told him a rested, sober Rob Ford could be mayor for life. I also told him, flat out, that a drunk Rob Ford was a mess who was going to die, and I didn't want any part of that. Third, we needed to do something about Doug. I outlined a plan to get Doug focused on productive things and out of Rob's hair. If Doug wanted to be chief of staff, I said he should resign his council seat and Rob could hire him.

Doug had been a problem that summer for Rob and for Earl. After a particularly brutal gang shooting on Danzig Avenue in the city's east end, Prime Minister Stephen Harper had come to Toronto to talk with the mayor about how to work together to prevent future gang violence. The prime minister's office had been adamant they didn't want Doug Ford at those meetings. Despite Earl's objections, Doug had literally pushed his way into the private session with Harper and Rob. Harper's team was unhappy, Earl was embarrassed, and Rob had looked foolish.

Some days, Rob listened to me. Other days, he got angry. He told me no one had any business telling him how to run his personal life. I countered that his drinking wasn't a personal issue because it so clearly affected his work. I also said that when he wanted real "personal time," then he had to stop dragging staff into it.

One Sunday in August, Rob called when I was driving with my kids. I told him it wasn't a good time to talk, but he ignored me and launched into another round of salary negotiations. Finally he said, "Okay. I'm okay if Dougie's okay."

"It's not Doug's decision, Rob. It's yours."

"I know, I know. Just talk to him. He's driving me nuts. He wants you gone. They all want you gone. The only one sticking up for you is me, man."

I agreed to talk to Doug, who told me Rob didn't care if I stayed or left, but that he (Doug) was in my corner. I said, if you're okay with me, I'm okay with it.

Rob also insisted that I meet with the search committee. "I know, I know what you're going to say," he said. "Just meet with them."

Two days later, I met with the search committee: Councillors Michael Thompson, Denzil Minnan-Wong, and Paul Ainslie. Paul pulled me aside beforehand and told me that he wanted me, but the other two didn't. In the room, I was a bad interviewee, contemptuous of the process, not taking it seriously. But the question I remember in crystal clear detail came from Denzil Minnan-Wong. He said the mayor's office had done a poor job of crisis management and asked, "What would you do to improve the office's ability to respond to and manage crises?"

I looked him square in the eye and leaned forward in my chair, palms down on the table. "Councillor," I said. "I've been doing crisis management for over twenty years. This office is better at crisis management than any other organization I've seen, anywhere on the planet. You have absolutely no idea how many crises you've never heard about." And that was the end of that interview.

\*\*\*

I'd known from the beginning that working with Rob Ford was like riding a bullet train through a pitch-black tunnel toward a dead end. It was a thrilling ride, but it would be important to jump clear before we hit the wall. The wall seemed very close now. Maybe it was time to jump.

But I didn't have anything else lined up, and I couldn't afford to be without an income. If Rob agreed to my terms, and if I could hang on even a little while, I could pay off a lot more of my debt and start to rebuild my pathetic financial situation. I also genuinely felt I was the best person to run the office. Someone had to protect the staff, not to mention the city. I knew I'd feel horrible if I left and something happened that I felt I could have managed. I had to admit it—I wanted the job.

But first, I had to endure the strangest, most awkward interview of my life, with Rob and his mother, Diane. It seemed inconceivable that she had come into City Hall just to be part of my interview, but she was there when Rob called me in, and she participated throughout. She asked me what my priorities for Rob would be and I laid them out, including that he and I would work together to "get him healthy again"—my euphemism for "he has to stop drinking." I felt like I was asking her for his hand in marriage.

It must have worked though, because Rob agreed to everything: He'd pay me $185,000. He'd get his drinking under control. He'd let me manage Doug. He even agreed to a "throw Doug under the bus" option if we needed it.

The office issued a press release. I ducked all media calls, and took my kids to Niagara Falls for a long weekend. When I walked into the office on Monday, August 20, 2012, I took a deep breath. I was chief of staff to Mayor Rob Ford.

\*\*\*

That day, I gathered the entire staff in the boardroom for a first meeting. I looked around at the fourteen faces, and realized I'd have to staff up. I introduced Earl as my deputy chief of staff (I had to work at that, but eventually I convinced him). And even though most people already knew my four principles, I spelled them out again:

Number one, we don't break the law, and we don't help anyone else break it. Never. And that included city rules and regulations.

Number two, we protect confidences. No discussing anything confidential, even with spouses. Unless the law required us to.

Number three, we tell the truth. Always. Most importantly, to each other. I didn't want or expect anyone to lie about anything—certainly not for the mayor. We can keep secrets, but we had to do it without lying.

Number four, we advance the mayor's agenda. We will do what it takes to help him succeed—as long as it doesn't break rules one through three.

I paused for a second and looked at each of them in turn. If someone ever wanted one of them to break a rule, I said—even the mayor—or even if something just didn't feel right, they should stall for time and call me or Kia. He and I would judge what was okay and what wasn't. I assured them they didn't have to say "no" to the mayor; I would do that for them. I could see by their faces that we all knew that latter bit would surely be put to the test.

\*\*\*

I had some big plans as chief of staff. I wanted to get Rob out to public events that would make him look better, even if he was only working three or four hours a day. I wanted to get him in shape and refocused. I wanted to work out a reduced but smart legislative agenda that we could deliver on. I even wanted to effect a rapprochement with our harshest critic, the *Toronto Star*. Rob agreed, as long as the paper would refrain from declaring victory. He didn't want a banner headline proclaiming, "Ford gives in, talks to *Star*." As soon as he said it, I realized I was being naive. They would absolutely claim victory. So we settled for putting the *Star* back onto our distribution lists and normalizing our backroom relations with them.

But despite my good intentions, Rob didn't get better. He got consistently worse. Soon after I took over as chief of staff, much of his time was swallowed up by arduous courtroom trials, on various issues and allegations that will be detailed in the next chapter. The stress of that manifested itself in his dependency issues almost immediately. He was once again sliding down the slippery slope to incapacity, gaining speed— this time taking me with him.

# 23 | The Courts

Rob's lawsuits—that's another sideshow I had to deal with as his chief of staff. In March 2012, when the subway war was at its most heated, Rob couldn't speak to his executive committee because he was tied up in his office with a team of lawyers. They were discussing one of his three—three!—cases making their way through various courts or tribunals. There was a libel suit, a compliance audit of his election finances, and a conflict of interest charge. The first one could cost him $6 million. The latter two could cost him his job. Rob was going to have to appear and testify at two of them.

It's not that uncommon for politicians to be sued during their tenure. But Rob Ford attracted legal trouble like honey draws flies. I was seriously concerned that fundamental democratic principles were at risk, because most of the cases were connected to a small cohort of activists who seemed bent on overturning the election results. If they succeeded, no elected official would ever be safe again.

Rob was a wealthy man and could afford to hire quality lawyers to defend him—but barely. He's not as wealthy as many people think he is, and the trio of lawsuits seriously hurt him financially, costing him between $500,000 and $1 million based on what I'd learned from him and Doug.

The least dangerous case was the libel case, brought against Rob during the 2010 election campaign by the owner of the Boardwalk Café. During the election campaign, in the *Toronto Sun* editorial board meeting I mentioned earlier, Rob said he wished he could tell journalists what happened in secret council meetings to award government contracts—in this case, to a lakeside restaurant—and described them as full of "corruption and skulduggery." George Foulidis, whose family owned a company called Tuggs that owned the café, launched a $6 million libel suit against Rob, claiming Rob's comments were defamatory. We assumed it was a political attack that would disappear once the election was over. It didn't. Two years of legal wrangling later, the case went to trial in November 2012.

Rob Ford was called to testify on Friday, November 16, 2012. He'd been in court listening to Foulidis testify since Tuesday. He'd originally been expected to testify Thursday, but had to coach his beloved Don Bosco Eagles high school football team in a big playoff game. The judge adjourned the proceedings while they played. (Yes, really.) They won. Now it was his turn on the stand.

Getting Rob in and out of the courthouse was a major operation. First, we were always worried he would sleep in. He wasn't a morning person to begin with, and he was drinking a lot. Court started promptly at 10:00 a.m. and it wouldn't do to attract the judge's ire by showing up late. Especially on the day he was to take the witness stand. I planned the day like a military operation and briefed the staff on the details.

There would be one body man in the city car, posted at the mayor's house from 7:30 a.m. Friday morning. He was our eyes and ears at the mayor's home. He'd tell us when the mayor was out and moving—Rob drove himself in his personal Escalade. If the mayor was late, the body man could knock on the door and wake him up. Once the mayor was moving, the body man would follow in the city car and update us on Rob's location as he went. Remember, I'd banned our staffers from riding in Rob's vehicle if he was driving—and Rob was always driving.

He'd pull his car into City Hall's underground parking garage at about 9:30, come upstairs to use the washroom and make sure he looked okay, and be back in the garage by 9:45. A staffer would drive his Escalade the 150 yards between City Hall and the courthouse with Ford in the front passenger seat and the body man and me in the back. We'd pull out of the parking garage at 9:48 and stop outside the courthouse by 9:50.

There, George Christopoulos, the press secretary, who would have been in position by 9:30 a.m., would meet us at the private entrance reserved for judges and lawyers. Because the mayor was, by tradition, the chief magistrate of the city, we'd arranged with court security to allow him to use that door. We could stop the Escalade at the curb; Ford would have a short walk to the doors. Camera crews and protesters would be all over, but we'd form a box around him to get him through. The cameras wouldn't follow him in; no cameras are allowed inside Canadian courthouses. We'd go straight through the doors, bypassing the metal detectors, up two floors by escalator, and into a private jury room where we'd wait until just before 10:00 a.m., when we'd move him into the courtroom.

We had a choice of exit options to get him back to City Hall at lunchtime and again at the end of the day. We could take him back the same way we came. We could use a long-forgotten underground tunnel connecting the courthouse to the law society building half a block away and then go by car or foot to City Hall. Once and only once, we tried walking out the emergency-exit doors on the east side of the courthouse and directly to City Hall. It was a disaster. Swarmed by about sixty media guys in a pressing scrum, Rob broke into a run and hightailed it all the way back to City Hall, with TV cameramen trying to run backward in front of him, still photographers and recorder-waving reporters sprinting on his heels. He was surprisingly fast for a man of his size; he ran like a linebacker, chin down, arms tucked in, and shoulders up. It was a sprint to keep up with him and journalists fell from the pack like lame gazelles. We're lucky no one got hurt. Also, that there were no lions.

Rob's testimony went well and court recessed until December 27, when the judge issued a written finding in Rob's favor and ordered Foulidis to pay Rob's court costs. Foulidis appealed; the Court of Appeal heard the appeal in May 2014 and on July 8 ruled for Ford again. As of this writing, Foulidis has yet to pay Ford anything. It cost Rob a fortune to defend himself, but he avoided a $6 million judgment.

*** 

The most serious case, however, began before the libel case—and finished after. It was for a conflict of interest charge that could have cost Ford his job as mayor, and ended his career in politics—all for something that began frivolously.

When Ford was still a councillor, a resident complained that he'd used a City of Toronto envelope to send out fundraising letters for his personal charity, the Rob Ford Football Foundation (RFFF), which raised money to equip Toronto high school football teams. Ford ignored the complaint; he just shook his head. But in August 2010, during his mayoral campaign, the City of Toronto's integrity commissioner decided that using the envelope violated the Council Code of Conduct (even though he had paid for the stationery, and the postage, from his own pocket). So Ford stopped using his councillor stationery for RFFF letters and had Foundation stationery printed instead.

In the course of all this ridiculousness, however, the commissioner also noted that RFFF had received $3,150 in donations from lobbyists, clients of lobbyists, and a company that had business with the city. She suggested that these donors may have felt obliged to donate to the Foundation in order to stay in good grace with a city official, and ordered Rob to pay the money back.

He refused. He hadn't received the money, he argued; his Foundation had, and the Foundation was outside her jurisdiction. Ford asked how he could possibly repay funds he'd never received. The commissioner recommended to Council that it find Ford in breach of the conduct code. Council, which at the time considered then Councillor Ford a lone wolf and an embarrassment, did so.

Ford never paid back the money. Instead, when he took office as mayor, he wrote letters to the donors asking them if they wanted the money back. I pointed out that this would simply further the concern that the donors would feel obligated to refuse. He was mayor now, I said, not just a councillor. Not surprisingly, none of the donors wanted the money back—in no small part because they'd already claimed the tax deduction and didn't want to have to redo last year's tax returns.

The integrity commissioner wasn't satisfied. She submitted a follow-up report to Council on February 7, 2012, pointing out that Rob had still not complied with Council's earlier order. But this time, Rob was mayor. I was in Council with Rob the day this came to the floor and asked if he wanted to abstain on the issue—not because I thought it was a conflict of interest but because I thought it might look bad. He said he didn't want to speak on the matter, but was planning to vote against it. It would further his image: The integrity commissioner and Council's left wing were bullying a guy for caring about disadvantaged kids.

But then Anthony Perruzza, a "leftie" Rob got along with, entreated Rob to speak about it on the floor. Just tell everyone about the Foundation and what it does, he suggested; nobody here is looking for a pound of flesh, let's just make it go away. So Rob put his name on the speakers' list.

No one in the room thought anything of it. I didn't pay any attention. Although it is solely the responsibility of each member of Council to ensure he or she is not in conflict on any item, it was routine for the city solicitor or the city clerk to point out conflicts involving the mayor, during a routine briefing before each Council meeting. No one had recognized a conflict of interest here.

So Rob told the councillors what the RFFF did and listed all the schools that had benefited from the Foundation's money. Councillor Maria Augimeri asked if he was still using Council stationery; he said no and held up a piece of RFFF letterhead. After some back and forth, Councillor Paul Ainslie stood and moved a motion to, essentially, repeal Council's previous decision. As voting began, I walked up to Rob and asked if he wanted to abstain. Instead, he voted, the motion passed, and the problem was over. Or so we thought.

One month later, a private citizen named Paul Magder filed a complaint alleging Rob Ford had violated the Municipal Conflict of Interest Act by voting on the disposition of the integrity commissioner's report about the $3,150 in Foundation donations. Magder appeared to be connected to a group of four or five individuals who generated most of the integrity commissioner and Compliance Audit Committee complaints leveled against Ford and his administration between 2010 and 2014. To us, he was a pain in the ass. But his complaint had legal legs. So on September 5, 2012, Rob Ford was back in court again. His lawyer, Alan Lenczner, was a nationally renowned expert about whose cases legal books had been written. He was expensive, but Rob grudgingly agreed to pay, because if the judge found he had violated the act, there was only one punishment available: removal from office.

Rob was on the witness stand for a long time. The opposing attorney enjoyed mocking him. The media, especially bloggers, loved it. It was hard to watch. But Ford stuck to his talking points like a burr.

Asked if he'd ever read the Councillor Handbook that "clearly outlined" the conflict of interest provisions, he said "no." Asked why, he explained that his father had been a Member of Provincial Parliament, so he knew the rules. I winced at that one. He could easily have said that as mayor, he hadn't received a councillor handbook, the *Council Briefing* book, because he wasn't a councillor. Instead, he'd received four volumes of transition books and a thirty-day briefing from city staff. Still, when the embarrassment ended, Rob's lawyers were confident they'd made their case.

On November 26, 2012, we were waiting for the judge's decision in the cushy, twenty-sixth-floor executive boardroom of the law offices of Lenczner Slaght. Far below us, the streets of downtown Toronto hummed. As the decision rolled off the fax, Lenczner's associate Andrew Parley skimmed through the pages, then said casually, "Well, we lost." The judge was ordering Ford out of office.

Rob sat at the table, utterly still. Doug sat opposite him, looking like a giant coil inside him was tightening up, readying him to spring. I immediately started taking notes. The judge had disagreed with almost all of the legal arguments Lenczner had made. He ordered Ford out of office—but gave him fourteen days to file an appeal.

"Well, he's wrong," Lenczner said. "He's just wrong." (Apparently not, I thought—you were wrong.) I asked about an appeal, how that would proceed, what that would cost. Finally, Rob spoke up. "Will they give me enough time to clean out my office?" he asked.

I kept my face neutral, but I couldn't believe it. The guy is faced with losing his mayoralty, and the thing that concerned him was getting his stuff home? I promised him that, if it came to that, it would be dignified. Back at City Hall, I left Rob alone with Doug and Earl and dashed off to write a speech. I hadn't prepared for this. That was an oversight, a bad one.

The mayor chose to appeal and was back in court the first week of January 2013. Alan Lenczner argued that the trial judge had erred in his interpretation of the law and should have agreed with Lenczner's argument that Council's order to repay the $3,150 had been unlawful in the first place. The Code of Conduct provided only two punishment options: reprimand, or forfeiture of up to ninety days' pay; repayment was not an option. Therefore, the order was invalid and shouldn't have existed—and, if it didn't exist, the later report saying the first order hadn't been complied with was nullified. And Ford couldn't possibly be found in conflict of interest for voting on a matter that legally hadn't happened. Appeal arguments wrapped up on January 7, 2013, and we waited.

In the meantime, we tried to keep it business as usual in the mayor's office. Ford remained mayor and continued with his duties, though it was an awkward time during which his foes pretended he didn't have the right to be mayor; and his allies began jockeying for position "if" he were eventually ordered out of office.

\*\*\*

On January 25, 2013, we were back at the law firm, in a smaller boardroom this time, awaiting the decision of the Superior Court on the appeal. Rob was convinced he would lose. I wasn't sure. But I made sure to prepare two speeches, A if Rob won, and B if he lost. We'd also spent a lot of time preparing for a potential, sudden-death transition—because if Rob lost, he'd cease being mayor the minute the judgment was announced. In our plan, the deputy mayor would step in until Council decided whether to call a by-election for a new mayor, or to appoint one.

We'd spent a lot of time canvassing Council members to determine which option most preferred, but there was no clear consensus. The Fords were initially insistent that only a by-election would be democratic, because it seemed likely Rob would be able to run for reelection. He'd probably have a pretty good chance of winning, too. His addiction issues were not yet well known, and voters would be pissed that they lost a mayor they'd elected over the paltry sum of $3,150—which, not incidentally, had helped disadvantaged kids in rough neighborhoods.

To take advantage of that possibility, I'd started referring whenever I could to the number 383,501. I tweeted it alone, with no explanation. I used it as a hashtag. I printed it in large font on a sheet of paper and posted it on the mayor's office window like a poster. Others in the office and in Ford Nation followed. It was quoted on the Internet and discussed on radio. Christie Blatchford, a brilliant columnist for the *National Post*, even wrote a column on the number. It was, of course, the number of votes cast for Rob Ford in the 2010 election. That's how many people would be robbed of their democratic choice if a solitary, unelected judge unseated him.

I prepared a speech for Deputy Mayor Doug Holyday in case he became the acting mayor. He said he'd keep the staff intact, which I felt relieved about. Meanwhile, the staff kept busy copying the constituent contact data we had on our computers onto discs, and backing up our emails and other files onto USB drives. The city clerk's office confirmed for me that all constituency information—including emails—belonged to Rob Ford, not to the city. If he were forced out of office, the IT department would immediately shut down database access for all of us in the office. In essence, a new office would be constituted from scratch to support the deputy mayor. But Ford could give copies of the data to the deputy mayor if he chose; we were enabling him to do that with no loss of continuity. We were ready.

***

While Rob, Doug, and I waited in the lawyer's boardroom for the decision, the mayor's staff and Doug's staff gathered in the mayor's boardroom. The second I heard, I would send a PIN message to Earl: Speech A or Speech B.

To be honest, I was hoping for Speech B, that Rob would lose the appeal. I suspect many on the mayor's staff were wishing for the same. But we didn't talk about it. The stress of working for an uncontrollable man under constant public derision, and facing near-total Council opposition was exhausting. Plan B seemed like a graceful resolution. Rob would be gone. The deputy mayor would take over. The staff would stay employed, under a man who wasn't a megalomaniacal addict. It was likely Holyday would let me go and bring in his own chief of staff, but I'd have a graceful exit without having to quit.

We waited quietly. We'd run out of things to say. I sipped coffee and scanned Twitter. I could see the media was poised, too. The expected decision time came and went. Then Parley got an email from the judge's clerk. We didn't notice him skimming through the decision until he said softly, "We won."

Rob and Doug leapt from their seats and embraced in a powerful bear hug. Doug phoned his mom, Diane. I pressed "send" on my prepared tweet:

> :)
> 383,501

I then sent Earl the PIN: "Speech A!" He responded, "What??" He'd forgotten which plan was which. I said, "We won." Earl must have repeated that out loud, because a cheer erupted in the mayor's boardroom, which the reporters outside could hear—I watched them tweet about it. When I stood to shake Rob's hand, I made sure I was smiling.

***

Though it was a bit of an anticlimax, Rob also dodged a bullet on February 25, 2013, when a tribunal investigating a compliance audit into Rob's 2010 campaign expenses also ruled in his favor. He could have been unseated as mayor had they not. Though they said Rob had breached the Municipal Elections Act on a number of counts, those breaches were minor and did not warrant prosecution. Rob Ford was three for three on legal action, cleared to continue as mayor of Toronto. The only thing left standing between him and a successful term was . . . Rob Ford.

# 24 | The Garrison Ball

"**P**UT ROB ON the phone."

My words crystallized into an icy fog as I paced back and forth outside the Garrison Ball, Toronto's annual glittering fundraiser for wounded veterans and military families.

Inside the Liberty Grand, a sprawling, Beaux-Arts event space on Toronto's waterfront, eight hundred members of the city's who's who—generals, politicians, religious leaders, captains of industry, millionaire bankers, and senior police officers—were seated at round tables of ten, set with towering silver candelabras, dozens of forks, and fine china on gold chargers, finishing their artfully sparse green salads. Police Chief Bill Blair sat at the head table, along with Minister of National Defense Peter MacKay and Vice-Admiral Paul Maddison, Commander of the Royal Canadian Navy.

I was outside, in a tuxedo, doing something that had become way too familiar: waiting in the cold and dark, trying to get Rob Ford on the phone. He was being driven by a man I didn't trust to an event I desperately didn't want him to attend.

The night should have gone like this: Ford should have arrived during the cocktail reception, shaken a few hundred hands, distributed a few hundred business cards and his trademark fridge magnets, posed for a few hundred photos with admiring fans, then slipped out of the room before the salad was served. He never liked to stay for dinner. He often had two or three events to "fly by" on an average evening and he was not comfortable making small talk at a table with strangers. He also didn't fit comfortably at a table for ten, even on the best of days. Squeeze him into a formal suit—the mayor never wore a tuxedo; it didn't suit his "average guy" image—and dinners were unbearable for him.

Instead, Ford was two hours late, and not answering his cell. That was a bad sign; Ford often turned it off to avoid my calls after he'd done something he knew was wrong. It was one of his tells.

Another bad sign: Ford was being driven there by a man named Sandro Lisi. Though I'd never met Lisi, I'd heard a lot about him. He'd been hanging out with Ford for a few months at that point. Based on the reports I'd heard from the mayor's body men, I was worried Sandro might be a drug dealer. Possibly, the mayor's drug dealer.

Ford had been in Chicago the night before, on a boys' weekend with Canada's Finance Minister, Jim Flaherty, and Rob's brother Doug. They'd gone down to watch the Toronto Maple Leafs hockey team play the Chicago Blackhawks. It was a big game in a city notorious for foul winter weather.

Not surprisingly, Ford's plane home was delayed by hours. Because I knew he hadn't wanted to attend the event in the first place, and figured he might have had a late night out on the town, I thought he'd be in a lousy mood and skip the event. I certainly hoped so, because I'd already made excuses for his lateness and set the ground for him not to attend.

At this point, I figured I had about ten minutes to manage the situation, to convince Ford to go home, before he arrived here in God knows what shape and did something politically ruinous. As I punched numbers into my cell with fingers that were fast going numb, I watched a photographer from the *Globe and Mail* leave the venue and head back to his car. At least the last of the media covering the event was gone. I moved farther away from the friendly doorman who'd let me in and out several times already. This was a private conversation.

A few minutes earlier, I'd gotten a phone call from Nico Fidani, the mayor's body man for the night, warning me the mayor had made up his mind to go to the Ball, no matter how late he was; that Lisi was driving him; and that Ford was bringing his two kids, Stephanie and Dougie. As nervous as I was about Ford showing up, I was even more concerned about the kids' being here. Why weren't they at home?

"How is he?" I'd asked Fidani. The answer I was dreading was "Not good." It was the answer I got.

Fidani also sent a text: Lisi's cell number. I punched it in. Lisi answered. I introduced myself and asked him, as calmly as I could, to give the phone to Rob. I heard Lisi fumbling the phone, and then Ford's voice: "Yeah?" He sounded rough as hell, and we were only one syllable into the conversation.

"Hi, boss, how's it going?" I asked, sounding as neutral as I could. I wanted to see how he sounded, and I wanted to ease him into the idea of turning around. The more it could be his idea, the better.

He launched a volley of words at me, ultra-fast, choppy, largely incoherent. He sounded like a tape recording played back at three times the normal speed. I cut him off.

"Hey, boss, the event here started two hours ago and everyone's already eating dinner," I said. "If you come now, it'll just be awkward. I've already made excuses for you, that your plane was delayed in Chicago. They know you're not coming. You've had a long day already, why don't you head home and take the night off with your kids?"

He wasn't having it. "I'm okay, brother, I'll be there," he said. Not good. Normally, he called me "buddy." He called everybody "buddy." That's how he wanted the world to be, a place where everyone was his pal. When he was drunk or high, I was learning, we all became "brothers."

I tried again. "Rob, I don't think you should come. You sound really rough. You're obviously tired. And there's no place here for kids, so they'll be miserable."

Out of nowhere, Ford exploded. I'd seen this movie before and knew I had to back him off the ledge quickly if I could. "What's wrong with my kids?" he screamed. "Don't you ever say shit about my kids. You're way outta line!"

Those words, at least, I could understand. "Rob, your kids are beautiful," I said, keeping my voice calm and friendly, pretending he wasn't crazy angry, so he could dial it down without having to make excuses, as if it hadn't happened. "They're great kids. I've never said anything bad about them. I'm just saying, this is a black-tie event, people have paid $150 a plate, it's very crowded, very formal. There are no other kids here. I've got kids too. They like to run around and have fun. There's no place to do that here. They'll be miserable. Why put them through that?"

"You leave my fucking kids out of this," Ford growled, followed by a long, garbled sentence I couldn't understand.

The last thing I needed was a drunk—or high—mayor crashing a high society event. The media were actively digging into Ford's past, looking for dirt to add to the court cases, the liquor store sightings, the quiet rumors about his sobriety and after-hours behavior. Since the St. Patrick's Day 2012 incident, we knew they were looking to tie Ford to alcohol, and even drugs, in a way they could report. We knew he was being regularly followed by media snoops and God knows who, wherever he went. There were mystery cars outside his house almost full time now. Doug had even started imagining an airplane was following Rob. We were all getting a bit paranoid, I thought. But with good reason, I believed. (It turned out, as I learned well after I left the mayor's office, there actually was a police airplane following Rob.)

We knew all this investigative effort by the media had turned up some dirt on the Fords—not just Rob, but Doug and the family. We just didn't know what. We knew they knew we knew. What we didn't know was what the hell Rob was doing when we weren't with him. But the indications didn't look good. He was regularly late for work, disappeared for days at a time and often slept at hotels with his kids, apparently keeping away from his wife Renata. We knew he was drinking alcohol, sometimes to excess, more and more frequently. We suspected he was using more than alcohol. I'd already confronted him about it twice.

The city was growing tired of negative stories and behavioral scandals involving Rob Ford. I didn't want him at this event if he looked as bad as he sounded on the phone. If he did, his political career would be over.

I tried pleading. "Please, Rob. I'm begging you. You sound terrible. You're obviously not well. Please, just turn around and take the night off. You deserve a night off."

"I'm good, brother," he answered, followed by more babble.

As a last resort, I tried ordering him. "Rob. Turn around and go home. You're done. The night is over. Do not come here. If you come here, your mayoralty is over. You'll be finished politically. It'll all be over. Go home."

He hung up on me.

I called right back and pleaded with Lisi to turn the car around. I explained the ballroom was full of soldiers and cops. Lisi said he'd try. I knew he wouldn't.

Nico arrived in his own car and told me Rob and Lisi had made a detour somewhere, he wasn't sure how long behind him they'd be. I left Nico at the door and went back into the dining room praying they'd turned around and gone home. I threaded my way through the round tables of VIP diners clad in ball gowns and tuxedos, or scarlet military mess dress jackets, and sat down at my table. The other guests had finished their salads and were waiting for the main course. I explained that, as I was working, I'd have to keep my phone on the table—as uncouth as that was.

Less than fifteen minutes later, my BlackBerry buzzed silently. I stood and answered it, already walking. It was Nico. "We're at the front," he said, sounding breathless and keyed up. "I need you right now."

"On my way," I replied, clicking off the phone and picking up my pace.

I made it outside the dining room and into the nearly empty foyer just as Ford burst through the doors. He looked like shit on a stick. His face was scarlet and beaded with sweat. He was arguing with Nico and his arms were flailing around like a man trying to shoo flies away. The flies were his two children, each of them dressed to the nines, running circles around Rob's tree trunk legs.

To me, he appeared to be under the influence of something. Alcohol for sure, and maybe something more. He smelled of too much aftershave. He was talking quickly and incoherently. I don't know much about drugs or alcohol, but I'd never met a drunk who speeded up. Alcohol is a depressant, not a stimulant, right?

Rob was dressed in his black formal suit with a long black tie tugged to one side. One of his shirttails was hanging out of the front of his pants and his shirt was soaked through with sweat. I walked up close to him, so I could speak quietly with him and also so my body would block his disheveled appearance from the view of anyone passing by.

"Hey Rob, you don't need to be here," I tried again.

"Fuck off. We're here and I'm going to the dinner," he insisted and tried to push me out of the way. "Dougie, Stephanie, let's go," he said to his kids, with more waving and shooing with his arms.

This was a different Rob Ford than I was used to. I'd heard of this Rob Ford—from Earl, from George, and from the junior staff who attended events with him. But I'd never seen this first hand. My God. Had he been like this before? Or was this worse than ever? Either way, I was racking my brain to figure out how I could get him out of there.

I backed up in front of him, trying to use my body to block his path to the ballroom, about twenty feet away. He kept plowing forward. "Get out of my way, Mark," he said. "I swear, I'll drop you if I have to."

By this time, he was pressed up against me. I held my left arm across his chest, trying to physically restrain him. His bloodshot eyes were mere inches from mine. His breath was on my neck. "I'll fucking drop you," he said.

I could feel his body tense up. I was keenly aware of how close we were and where his hands and arms were. I wasn't going to let him hit me, so I stepped back and opened some space between us. He glared at me and I stared back at him.

Just then, two middle-aged women in expensive gowns returned from the ladies room and walked around Ford and me. One of them looked him up and down, and said, "You should slow down and stop acting like a bull in a china shop!"

That may have helped Ford remember he was at a public event. But he repeated that he was going inside and I couldn't stop him. I took a different tack.

"Okay," I said. "But it's hot in there and the kids still have their coats on. Let's hang up their coats downstairs and get you straightened out, your tie needs straightening."

After a few minutes of debate, he finally agreed we should check the kids' coats and he could use the washroom before going into the dinner. I led them around the corner away from the ballroom. Distance was my friend.

The only problem was that the washrooms and coat check room were in the basement, down an extremely steep set of carpeted stairs. I sent Nico and the kids ahead and went down the stairs just ahead of Ford. I wasn't sure if I could catch him if he fell, but I thought I'd have to try. If I stayed close enough, I could catch him at the beginning of a stumble, before his massive body picked up momentum.

We made it down the stairs without incident, although a military officer we recognized did pass us on the stairs. He later told the media he'd prevented Rob from falling down the stairs. That's not how I remember it, and I may have been the only one at the dinner not drinking.

Once safely on the lower level, we checked the kids' coats and Rob chatted up the servers in his usual retail politics, aw-shucks style. He posed for pictures with the two women working the coat check. His chat with them became unusually familiar, almost flirtatious. He never became vulgar or suggestive, but it was unusual for him and I wasn't comfortable with it. Still, I didn't rush him along, because the longer we were downstairs, the less time we would be upstairs in the full glare of the public eye.

Still, guests were coming and going from the washrooms. I told Ford discreetly that he needed to tuck his shirt in and he looked down. He proceeded to shove his errant shirttail down the front of his pants without turning around. The coat check women chuckled.

Meanwhile, the kids were running rings around us, burning up energy. "I'm hungry!" Stephanie declared.

This allowed me an opening. I pointed out to Rob that there were no empty seats available for the kids, that the meal had already been served, and that it was food the kids wouldn't like anyway. Why didn't we send them to McDonald's with Nico—it wasn't far away.

Rob agreed. Nico reclaimed the kids' coats and ushered them upstairs and out to the mayor's car.

That was a relief. But Rob was determined to say hello to people. There was no point fighting him on this any further. "We'll go upstairs and do a once-around the room," I said, as firmly as I could. "Then we're out of here. You look terrible and sound worse. So lots of smiling and shaking hands and not so much talking, okay?"

"Okay, boss," he said.

We headed upstairs—me behind him this time, praying he didn't slip. As we entered the room, I saw that the main course had been cleared and people were mingling between the tables, talking over the dinner music from a military band on the balcony.

Almost immediately, Rob was surrounded and shaking hands. He smiled and laughed and posed for dozens of pictures. Thank God it was hot and loud. Councillor Paul Ainslie spoke with Ford for a few minutes, then came up to me and said, "If you need any help, let me know." As well, a few friends I knew in uniform, a member of Parliament, and a senior political staffer to a federal minister expressed concern for the mayor's health, asking "Is he okay?" "He's not feeling well, and he's tired after just making it back from Chicago," I said. Both statements quite true.

We'd made it halfway through the room and I was thinking we might pull this off, when the guest speaker was introduced and everyone began sitting down for the keynote speech. Ford and I were standing in the middle of the room, becoming increasingly conspicuous. I grabbed his elbow, told him we should sit during the speech, and tried to direct him to the table he was assigned to. It was in a dark back corner beside the stage, out of eyesight. Instead, Ford pulled out a chair in the middle of the room, right below the podium, and plopped himself down on it, surprising the table guests there.

"This isn't your table," I whispered into his ear. "Follow me, I'll take you to your table."

But Ford wasn't moving. The room was loud and he was borderline incoherent, yet he was talking up a storm with the woman seated next to him and her date. Sitting next to him, I urged him to be quiet during the speech. The second it ended, I got Rob back on his feet. "Okay, let's get out of here," I said.

"Did we do the whole room?" he asked.

"Yes," I lied. I guided him back to the doorway, and we made reasonably swift progress out of the building and over to the waiting Cadillac. The kids were in back, playing with Happy Meal toys. But Rob, now in a buoyant mood, didn't want to leave right away. We stood outside his car while he rambled incoherently.

I introduced myself to Sandro Lisi, who was driving Ford's Escalade, shaking his hand through the window, sizing him up. He was young, late twenties or early thirties, fit, and dressed in a casual but expensive shirt. He was sober, and looked amused by the situation. I asked him to take Rob straight home. He nodded.

Another man was also in the car. I don't know where he came from, but Nico was familiar with him. Maybe they picked him up during the "detour" en route to the event. The mayor called him "Bruno," and he hopped out of the front passenger seat to let the mayor in. He was older, mid to late fifties, a thin, nervous-looking guy with rumpled clothes. He was bent over when he stood, and avoided eye contact when he spoke.

Rob immediately started abusing him, calling him names, pretending to fight with him. Ford pushed Bruno, claimed he could beat the shit out of him, and aggressively kicked at him three or four times, coming dangerously close to connecting his massive legs with Bruno's slight frame. Bruno scampered back into the front passenger seat like a whipped dog and crawled over the seat into the back of the truck, shouting at Rob to stop it. He said he was sick of his bullying and wasn't going to stand for it anymore.

Rob laughed. Then he got wistful. This was a Rob Ford I'd heard on the phone before, late at night. Babbling on about how it was me and the staff he was really sorry for. He'd "screwed everything up," but he'd be okay, you know, because he had money. He was sorry for guys like me who didn't have anything. No wife. No money. I'd heard it before from him in more than one late-night phone call.

He talked about how great his wife was and how we should all party together. He'd get some whores for us and we'd party all night. He went on about how much fun he'd had in Chicago with his brother and Jim Flaherty. They'd partied and partied, he said. At some point, Doug and Flaherty had fucked off and left him on his own. So fuck them. He talked about whores and drugs. It was hard to tell how much of the story was true.

He went on like that. Veering from anger with the world to commiserating with me over how badly he'd fucked everything up for everyone. At one point, he said he loved me; he wrapped his meaty arm around my neck to bend my head down while he kissed the top of it. It was awkward, but it wasn't threatening. (Much later, stories would appear suggesting Rob had me in a headlock. That never happened, but I imagine the kiss may have looked like that to someone passing by.)

I kept trying to end the conversation and get him back into the car and out of there. Nico and I, along with Tom Beyer, who'd arrived after Ford was outside—I'd sent a "Calling all cavalry" text to the staff—jockeyed around him to block him from view of people who began leaving the event early.

After about twenty interminable minutes, we managed to tuck Ford back into the car and send him off with Lisi and Bruno. I thanked Nico and Tom and sent them home. I braced myself for a mess to clean up in the morning.

***

But when I woke up, to my surprise, there was nothing in the news. Had we been that effective?

Most people at the Garrison Ball hadn't actually seen the mayor. Most of those who did, did so from afar. Those who'd gotten closer had seen him in the dark, in a tightly crowded space, with lots of noise that made hearing difficult. And most in attendance had had a glass or two of wine themselves.

Soon enough, though, George Christopoulos called to tell me the sharks were circling—he had wind of reporters working a story about the Ball. They weren't exactly sure what had happened, but they knew something had.

I discussed the situation with Doug, who didn't believe it could have been as bad as I was saying. I stressed to him that I'd heard staff complaints that Rob had been "out of sorts" at events before, but this was the first time I'd seen it firsthand. He had been out of control. If I hadn't been there, it would have been a disaster, with him and his kids all over the front page. As it was, he'd almost attacked me.

Doug was unconvinced. But I insisted that I was taking evening events off Rob's schedule, and Doug nodded. There was only one major evening event coming up: the Canadian Jewish Political Affairs Committee's annual Action Party. It was a high-profile event, hosted by an influential group, another who's who of Canadian politics. The prime minister, premier, and every elected politician who could make it to Toronto were likely to make an appearance. Rob had always attended and was well-liked by the crowd.

Earl argued that Ford had to attend the CJPAC event. His absence would be noted. I disagreed. "We have no idea who'll show up after dark, Dr. Jekyll or Mr. Hyde," I said. "It's too risky."

\*\*\*

On March 7, 2013, Earl and I walked about 250 yards across City Hall's Nathan Phillips Square, across the street, and into the almost 350-year-old Hudson's Bay Company's flagship department store. It occupies an entire city block at Queen and Bay Streets. On the eighth floor was an art deco event facility called the Arcadian Court. When we stepped out of the elevator, the CJPAC Action Party was in full swing.

Dozens of Toronto's young, politically active members of the Jewish community, dressed up in evening gowns, cocktail dresses, tuxedos, and Hugo Boss suits, lined up at registration tables. We were there to represent the Office of the Mayor, since the mayor wasn't coming. We passed on Ford's regrets to an organizer and entered the buzzing venue.

Spread over two floors, the event was as glamorous as a movie set. We worked our way around the room, greeting the political movers and shakers of Toronto, Ontario, and Canada. In huddles here and there, political celebrities were surrounded by star-struck young activists. Justin Trudeau, the Liberal Party of Canada's new heartthrob leader (son of Pierre Trudeau, Canada's most venerated modern-day prime minister), had just left; people were still jazzed by his presence.

I lost Earl in the crowd and headed up to the mezzanine level. On the stairs, I passed Sarah Thomson, one of Rob Ford's opponents in the 2010 mayoral campaign. She had a brightly colored drink in her hand and was accompanied by a young woman who followed her like a bubbly puppy. I said hello and she replied pleasantly.

I made my way to the bar. As I waited for my Diet Coke, my BlackBerry buzzed with a message from the staffer assigned to Rob for the evening. He was coming. As I scanned the room for a quiet spot to make a phone call, Thomson and her puppy began to chat me up, asking me if I wanted a taste of their drinks, and if Ford was coming. I demurred and excused myself.

In a quiet corner near the elevators, I sent Earl a PIN: "Come find me. Boss is coming." Then I phoned tonight's body man, a relatively new staffer named Michael Prempeh. Apparently, Doug had mentioned the event to Rob, Rob had summoned Michael to meet him at City Hall, and now they were on their way.

I called Ford to assess his condition. His voice was a bit heavy and he slurred slightly. He sounded to me like he'd been drinking, but he didn't seem as out of it as he had the night of the Garrison Ball. He insisted on coming and I told him we'd meet him at the street level door and bring him up.

I sent out PINs to the staffers who lived downtown, asking them to put on a suit and join us at the event ASAP. I wanted as many hands on deck as I could get. I found Earl and we talked through a plan.

The mezzanine was the loudest, darkest part of the venue. We would bring Rob up in an elevator, bypassing the registration area, and entering the party space through a quiet corridor used only by the venue management company. There was even a small waiting room we could use as a green room to check Rob over and get him ready for the crowd. We'd keep him up on the mezzanine where the darkness and noise would help camouflage any signs of intoxication. It was a brilliant plan. Naturally, it didn't work out.

Instead of going first to City Hall, as he'd told Michael he was doing, Ford decided to pull up right outside the door to the Bay building. Michael, racing out of the mayor's office and across the square, called to warn me. Ford's Cadillac pulled up to the sidewalk just as Michael crossed the street and the mayor hopped out of the passenger door. Sandro Lisi was driving again. He got out too, and Ford told Michael to park the car at City Hall.

I raced down to the lobby, but I missed them. Ford and Lisi took the elevator up to the eighth floor, stepping out into the sea of people swarming the registration tables. By the time Earl and I got to him, Ford was in his element. Bright lights, dozens of people gaga at having Mayor Rob Ford in their midst. It took us ten minutes to disengage Ford from the crowd and get him back into the elevator to take him up one floor to the mezzanine. In our makeshift green room, I chatted with him to assess his sobriety. He was intoxicated, but not batshit crazy. I thought we could manage this.

"Take care of my friend Sandro," Rob insisted. "Whatever he wants, make sure he gets it, okay?"

I agreed—but frankly, Sandro was on his own. Dressed in a long-sleeve designer knit shirt with a quarter zip at the neck, and expensive chinos and shoes, he looked wealthy and casual. Underdressed for this event, but he probably wouldn't have been out of place with the attendees on a normal evening.

We escorted Ford onto the mezzanine, where he was quickly surrounded by adoring fans who wanted photos with him. We got him set up near the exit, with his back to the wall, to pose for pictures. Michael had come back, and Tom Beyer had arrived in response to my mayday call, so they, with Earl, set up around Ford, each about an arm's length away from him: one in front, one on each side. They managed the crowd moving in and out, and the one in front took pictures.

I went to the bar and got a tall glass of water and handed it through the crowd to Ford, who took a long swig and handed it back to me. I moved over to a round stand-up table about twenty feet from the mob surrounding Rob and watched. Sandro had gotten himself what looked like a Coke and stood at the table next to me. He appeared to be enjoying the show.

Since everything seemed to be under control, I took a stroll around the venue. Going down the stairs, I again passed Sarah Thomson, who asked me where the mayor was. I told her and she headed upstairs. Ten minutes later, I was back at my table; the show had grown larger.

I got a PIN from Earl—he'd been warned that Sarah Thomson was going to cause trouble. A few minutes later, I watched from twenty feet away as she and a small group of friends approached the crowd around Ford. They were laughing and giggling. Thomson stood on her toes to peer over the backs of the people surrounding Ford. She spoke briefly with her assistant, then put her drink down on the floor against the wall, and pushed her way up to Ford. She posed for a photo with him. Afterward, she rejoined her friends and walked away laughing. It seemed to me she hadn't caused any trouble after all.

After about ninety minutes of posing for pictures, Ford was tired and the crowd was thinning slightly. I worked my way in beside him and suggested it was time to call it a night. Thankfully, he agreed, and we got him out of the party the way we'd planned to get him in: quietly and uneventfully. I rode down in the elevator with him and watched him get into his car. With Sandro driving, he headed off, presumably home.

As Ford left, Ontario Premier Kathleen Wynne arrived. We chatted briefly and she asked if the mayor was upstairs. "Sorry, you just missed him," I replied as she headed up to the event. Thank God, I added to myself.

I walked back to City Hall to collect my car from the underground staff parking lot. Along the way, I checked my Twitter account and saw a bunch of hits about Rob Ford. Sarah Thomson had apparently posted something damning on her Facebook account. I pulled up her page and found a rant from her, posted just after midnight, alleging the mayor had been inappropriate with her while she posed for a picture with him. She said Rob had joked that Thomson should have come to Florida with him on a recent vacation because his wife hadn't been there.

On Facebook, Thomson said she felt Ford had been disrespectful of women, and decided to post about it because as of midnight, it was International Women's Day. Later, she added to her posts an allegation that Ford had "groped" her when he put his arm around her for the photo.

As comments piled up on her Facebook page, someone suggested that "groping" was a form of "sexual assault" and Thomson agreed, beginning to use that language in her own remarks. This was quickly getting ugly.

I sent links to the tweets and Facebook page to Earl and George, saying we needed to look at this first thing in the morning.

By the time I was driving back to work, at about 7:30 a.m., the Thomson allegations were getting full radio coverage. *Shit.* Then I heard Thomson herself, giving a live interview on Newstalk 1010's highly-rated morning show with host John Moore. Moore was not a big fan of Ford's, and Thomson was blazing with both barrels. She accused Ford of groping her and saying inappropriate things about her and his wife. She also accused him of being intoxicated. By the end of the interview, she was suggesting that Ford might have been high on cocaine. *Double shit.*

I spoke to Earl, who assured me there had been no groping when Thomson posed for pictures. He'd been right there and had been on high alert since some city councillors from nearby Richmond Hill claimed to have heard Thomson say she was going to cause trouble for Rob Ford that night. Nothing had happened. And Thomson had posed for pictures more than once.

I called George from my car and we discussed how to handle the situation. We agreed we couldn't have Ford speak directly to the accusation, because even if he were innocent of the groping and drug allegations, I knew he'd been intoxicated by something at the party and we didn't want him to answer that question if asked. We also knew the media had lots of pieces of information suggesting Ford had a drinking or drug problem and was looking for something to hold them together. That something could be as little as a Ford denial. Because even if he denied groping Thomson or being intoxicated, that would open the door to a reporter following up with, "We've heard similar unsubstantiated rumors of Ford being intoxicated before: the Garrison Ball," etc. We wanted to keep that door shut.

I decided we would issue a written statement denying the groping allegations outright and ignoring the radio comments about drinking and drugs. We were on safe ground denying the groping. We had three witnesses. Earl, Michael, and Tom had all been within an arm's reach of Ford while Thomson was posing with him. And I had seen her come and go from the scrum of people surrounding Rob.

But someone had to go on the radio to deny Thomson's allegations, at least once. That should be George. But he hadn't been there, and the media would want a firsthand account. Preferably from the mayor. We couldn't go there.

So it fell to me. I could attest firsthand to what had not happened. I asked George to set up the interview. As soon as I was in the office, I contacted all three of the staffers who'd been at the party, and asked again, "Is there any way that Rob could have groped her, without you seeing it?" In every case, the answer was no.

At 8:45 a.m. on March 8, I spoke live on air with John Moore and his roundtable panel. I kept my comments to the point: The mayor did not grope Ms. Thomson. I had three staff members within arm's length of the mayor and Ms. Thomson the whole time they were together for the picture. They all said nothing happened. I myself watched her approach and enter the group for the photo then leave with her friends. She was smiling and laughing the whole time. When asked if the mayor had been drinking at the event, I replied that the only thing he'd had to drink at the event was water—which I'd brought him myself. It was all true.

Throughout the day, we remained focused; we were vocal in denying the groping allegation, and we responded to the intoxication allegations dismissively, but truthfully, by saying he'd not had anything to drink at the event. Fortunately, for us, Thomson had established a reputation with many in the media as an unreliable attention-seeker. This, plus her frequently changing version of events, undermined her allegations. By midday, most media were treating the incident as an attempt to garner attention. To this day, I feel it was.

Troubling, though, was Thomson's escalation into accusations of drug use, cocaine. It was as if it were designed to bait Ford into a denial. Every time an interviewer pressed Thomson on the allegations, though, she backpedaled.

We were lucky. We were also smart in the way we managed it. The problem, of course, was that even though we felt we had effectively rebutted Thomson's groping allegations, Ford had been intoxicated. He shouldn't have been at a public event in that state. More correctly, it was his job to be at the event—and he should have been sober.

THE GARRISON BALL | 241

***

The CJPAC story had rekindled the media's efforts to build a case for Rob Ford having a drug or alcohol problem. And that led them back to the Garrison Ball event, where they were sure something had happened, but they couldn't say exactly what. Eventually, the *Toronto Star* went to press with a front-page story stringing together a number of anonymous, unsubstantiated allegations to paint a picture that Ford had a drinking problem. The keystone of the story was the on-the-record comments of Councillor Paul Ainslie.

Paul had attended the Garrison Ball and been one of its organizers. He was also one of the Ford administration's most stalwart defenders and trusted allies on Council. The mayor had lifted him from political obscurity and appointed him to a powerful chairmanship of the city's Government Management Committee.

By coincidence, his seat in the council chamber was right beside Doug Ford. Doug was a council rookie, prone to outbursts and procedural mistakes during council meetings. Ainslie and Doug became friends and we relied heavily on that friendship, often asking Paul to ride shotgun on Doug to help keep him out of trouble—during meetings and in general. Paul was one of the few councillors whom we trusted to help. He'd been the only one I trusted on the makeshift chief of staff selection committee that had "interviewed" me before I accepted Ford's offer.

I liked Paul. He had approached me shortly after the Garrison Ball and told me that reporters, especially Robyn Doolittle from the *Toronto Star*, were hounding him for comments about the mayor's sobriety at the event. He told me he was doing his best to downplay the story. I told him to simply ignore the questions. He replied that he couldn't say nothing. After a number of conversations, it became clear that Paul had said something to Doolittle. It seemed likely he'd been suckered into acknowledging something without necessarily intending to do so. Doolittle was genius at making that happen.

I'd had a small number of conversations with Doolittle off the record. She's a smart, attractive, and enjoyable person to talk with. In different circumstances, she'd be a great friend to hang around with. But in these circumstances, she was a highly-skilled adversary. I respected that.

Talking with Doolittle is a bit like talking with a trained interrogator. Both try to become your friend, sympathetic to your side, seeming to support your position. She'd said to me a few times, "Look, I've already talked to a bunch of people who've told me Rob has a drug/alcohol problem. I know all about that. I also know that you're trying to help him. Can you tell me, off the record, what you've done? Because I don't want to write the story and have everyone think you're just enabling him. You're a good guy."

I would just smile. I could easily understand how others might take the bait. I thought Paul had probably done just that and was having regrets, trying to get Doolittle to take his name off things. Naturally, that didn't work. On March 26, 2013, the *Star* ran a story, by Doolittle and Kevin Donovan, about the Garrison Ball across its front page, quoting Ainslie as the only named source saying "I urged the mayor's chief of staff, Mark Towhey, to have the mayor leave the event." Other, anonymous, sources said Ford "seemed either drunk, high or had a medical condition."

Paul was immediately castigated by the Ford brothers and the administration.

For the same reasons we didn't want Ford to defend himself against the Thomson allegations, we didn't want him to reply to these either. George and I agreed he couldn't deny them, we believed, without lying or getting led down a garden path to more and more revelations as he responded to more and more unsubstantiated allegations—providing each reporter with a hook to hang his or her own story on.

Our plan was for us to focus on the specifics of Ainslie's quoted statement. He'd told the *Star* that he'd urged me to have the mayor leave the event. That, of course, was not true. He had not asked me to get the mayor to leave. He had, however, offered to help me if I needed help. It was an error I would use to defend the mayor without lying. It fit through my four-point test.

We eventually responded to queries from various media outlets with a one-line reply from me: "No one asked the mayor to leave and no one asked me to ask the mayor to leave." And that's all I ever said publicly about the matter.

We didn't succeed, however, in preventing Rob from responding directly to the media inquiries. And when he did, he did it in classic over-the-top Rob Ford style. He called the report that he'd been asked to leave the Garrison Ball an "outright lie" and described the *Star* story as "just lies after lies and lies." This, of course, fanned the flames and we hunkered down for another round of media excoriation.

***

Inside the mayor's office, Rob was upset with Ainslie, but he didn't lash out at him. He shrugged it off with a *let him say what he wants, it's all lies* demeanor. But Doug went ballistic. He and Paul battled each other from that point on. A number of other members of the mayor's executive committee approached me privately, in my office, to ask what the real story was and if the mayor was going to fire Ainslie from his chairmanship. Outright betrayal like that was treason and needed swift punishment, they argued.

In every case, I replied by reiterating my statement that "no one had asked the mayor to leave" the event, which was true (save for me—but I didn't count). "Don't go too hard on Paul," I'd say. "There's more to the story. He got trapped by the reporter. He tried to put it back in the box, but he fucked up."

To this day, I think Paul believes he asked me to have the mayor leave the Garrison Ball. I know he didn't. It's a technicality, but technicalities matter. Paul never trusted me again, and Doug's battles with him drove him permanently into opposition. He began to work actively against Ford and the administration. On a number of occasions, he voted against key pieces of legislation we were working on. The calls for his head from other members of the executive committee grew louder.

Eventually, even I felt he had to go, and made that recommendation to the mayor. Rob wouldn't agree until I could map out how we would backfill Ainslie's position; then he would shoot down any plan I gave him. Even with a senior member of his inner circle leading an open revolt against him, Rob Ford somehow couldn't pull the trigger. Soon, enough time had passed that firing him became moot. So I tried to broker peace. I arranged a phone call between Doug and Paul, but that ended with Doug leaving a voicemail message on Paul's phone calling him a "political whore." I mediated a sit-down meeting; that ended in a screaming match between the two councillors.

The relationship with Ainslie became untenable. There was no way to heal the rift. Once again, I proposed he be removed and prepared a letter for the mayor's signature doing so. The mayor continued to waver. For the next month and half, I carried the letter in my suit pocket everywhere I went with the mayor, in case he decided to act. He never did. Rob Ford doesn't like to fire people. Well, most people.

# PART IV | SHOWDOWN: MARCH–MAY 2013

# 25 | Ford Folds His Cards

By early 2013, Rob was working what we, behind closed doors, called "a solid two-hour day." A sense of gallows humor was permeating the office. If Rob was invited to a breakfast event, we'd deadpan, "Maybe he'll do a flyby on his way home" from wherever he disappeared to at night. Our original governance agenda was out the window and we were running with a pared-down list of objectives: survive politically to 2014, leave Rob in some position to win. Personally, I'd made the decision that I wouldn't work on Rob's reelection campaign. If given the choice, I'd remain as chief of staff (I'd taken on that role in August 2012) and run the mayor's office while he campaigned. After the election, I'd leave. I didn't tell anyone this plan, because it seemed wiser to keep quiet about it as long as possible.

As mentioned earlier, I'd been reluctant to make decisions that Ford should have been making. But at this point, Rob was so out of control that I relented. The outside world didn't notice, but it was a low point for me. That's not how democracy is supposed to work.

The first major decision I made without Rob occurred in November 2012. Earl and I were in my office, staring down the deadline for the mayor to submit his recommendations for mid-term Council appointments. These are key appointments—who is going to do what to accomplish the mayor's agenda for the next two years—as well as the "goodies" a mayor doles out to encourage Council support. Two years before, we'd spent an entire month on this—debating options with a full transition team, interviewing councillors, making recommendations to Ford. He'd participated fully in the discussions, then made the final decisions himself. This time was different.

I'd scheduled meeting after meeting with Rob to discuss this—about fifteen in all. Every time, he'd put it off. He had to go to the bathroom. He had to get home. He had a constituent meeting we'd never heard of. He didn't have time for (crucial!) Council appointments. He only had time for demons.

So at the eleventh hour—literally (it was late in the evening the decisions were due)—Earl and I made Rob's decisions for him. We were hoping to craft a coalition that would carry out the last two years of Ford's mandate. The problem was, not many councillors wanted Ford's goodies any more. They certainly didn't want to get too close to him. We wanted to bring some of the Yellow Team "mushy middle" councillors into his handpicked executive team, and drop a couple of the troublemakers. But no one wanted the jobs.

Eventually, after asking for a couple of one-hour deadline extensions from the city clerk's office, which needed to print and distribute our plan to councillors, we cobbled together a reasonable slate that we felt was best under the circumstances. Rob wouldn't be thrilled with it, but Rob wasn't there. Some councillors wouldn't be thrilled either, but that was status quo no matter who was mayor. We filed the slate with the clerk late in the evening and went home to get a few hours' sleep.

When I showed the plan to Rob in the (late) morning the following day, he just shrugged. "You're the boss," he said. Except I wasn't.

***

If doling out council goodies wasn't a big enough decision to slough off onto his staff, Ford also allowed another file to wither for lack of his leadership. The casino file could have been one of Ford's legacies. He hadn't campaigned on it, but with proper leadership, it could have turned a 198-acre parking lot on the lake shore into a crown jewel that threw off a hundred million dollars a year. Instead, thanks to his inability to engage, it just sputtered away. He didn't seem to care.

In early 2011, I began looking closely at Exhibition Place, a fairground that sits on 198 acres of city-owned, prime downtown waterfront property. The Canadian National Exhibition, a kind of state fair on steroids, takes it over for eighteen days every August, and has done so since 1879. But on the other 347 days of the year, the site is a ghost town. Owning the most impressive waterfront property in the province cost the city about $10 million each year, for maintenance on buildings that were largely unoccupied, surrounded by acres of empty parking lot. I thought that was ridiculous.

At the same time, I was hearing a litany of issues facing businesses and tourism. Tourism and conference operators were complaining that the city's nightlife had declined. In 2005, almost a hundred large nightclubs operated in a booming downtown club district. In the decade since, many had been shuttered and converted into pricey condos. Occupants of those condos did not enjoy the flood of pukers, screamers, pissers, and brawlers that nightclubs discharged at 3:00 a.m. The clubs that hadn't already been converted into condos were being forced out of business or out of the district.

Conference organizers also complained that Toronto lacked the kind of high-end convention space that could attract big-ticket groups. Exhibition Place had a massive convention facility, but no hotels or restaurants, so it didn't get top tier bookings. To me, a logical fix for all those problems was to turn the Exhibition Place grounds into a year-round entertainment destination—build hotels, restaurants, and clubs where there were empty parking lots; add sports facilities to the extant soccer field and minor league hockey arena. If we didn't allow residential development on the property, no residents would complain; a major highway and a rail corridor separated the grounds from the rest of the city. Not only could the annual fair continue, the improvements would burnish its faded luster. Torontonians and tourists would get a year-round playground, and the city would earn enough rental income to turn the grounds from a money-pit to a profit center.

The most challenging piece, however, was the hotels. In North America, new hotels commonly are built with condo units (which, when sold, pay for the construction of the hotel), and we didn't want condos. But without hotels, the plan wouldn't gel—a major convention center needs hotels. They'd also provide customers for the restaurants and entertainment venues. Then, in March 2012, the Ontario Lottery and Gaming Corporation—the provincial government agency responsible for casinos and lotteries—announced it was planning to license a casino in Toronto. A casino at Exhibition Place, I immediately thought, could make the hotel problem moot. It would generate enough traffic to feed an entertainment district and enough cash to pay for hotels without condos. It was also a popular check-box on conference organizers' wish lists.

I knew it would be a hard sell to Council, and that the battle lines wouldn't break along traditional left-right lines. Many of Ford's right-leaning coalition members were opposed to gambling for moral reasons. Some left-leaning councillors were being pushed to support a casino by construction and hospitality unions, who wanted the estimated ten thousand permanent jobs (almost all unionized) that a destination resort-casino would create. I'd gathered enough intel to know any casino would have to generate at least $100 million in revenue annually to the city in order to get enough support to pass it through Council.

I knew that with so many self-interested factions in the mix, and billions of dollars at play, there was a real threat of corruption. But Rob and Doug loved the idea. Dollar signs danced before their eyes. Even the city manager was keen on it. So we looked for a way to make it work.

The big casino companies began showing up in Toronto and hiring consulting and lobbying firms to represent their interests. They were meeting with as many councillors as they could and they all wanted to meet the mayor. To keep things fair, Rob and I agreed he'd meet with the senior executive of each casino operator once. Many wanted to meet again, but we wanted to treat everyone equally.

Other meetings would be taken by me and Earl, together. I wanted Earl to know enough about the file in case I couldn't finish it—I was already buckling under the stress of wrangling Rob. I also wanted both of us in the room so no one could say either of us had been unduly influenced.

During the early casino meetings, Rob was still reasonably engaged in city business; he met many of the major casino players. His meetings with casino owners quickly fell into a pattern: Rob would welcome the visitors and say he was a businessman. He was pro-business. Then he'd stop talking and Doug, who was present for most of these meetings, would take over. He'd talk about how successful the family business was, drop the names of some influential US politicians or businessmen he'd met, and mention "lean manufacturing" and "Six Sigma" (a quality-improvement process he'd introduced at the family business). He'd finish with, "Rob and me want something iconic. It has to be iconic."

One of the last meetings was with US billionaire Sheldon Adelson, CEO of Las Vegas Sands Corporation and a major figure in US Republican politics. As had become standard practice, after the mayor and Doug spoke, the casino owner, in this case Adelson, and his execs gave a short pitch for their vision, then I outlined the mayor's goals—specifically, that the city needed to reap $100 million per year out of the operation. That could come as rent, as a tax or a percentage of taxes paid to the province, or as a dividend if we partnered in some way. Or as some combination of the above.

I explained that we understood an iconic building would be more expensive than just "a big box" with games inside, and that would mean the casino would have to generate high enough profits to pay back the added capital expense—which is paid for out of after-tax earnings. That meant a tax rate that didn't scrape all the profit away to government; we would support them seeking a friendly tax regime from the province to allow them to build an iconic structure.

When I finished, Adelson nodded at me. "It's nice to see you understand how business works," he said. "Mayor Ford only hires people who understand business," I replied. I guess I fibbed to one of the most powerful men in America. My bad.

But Doug, true to form, was also conducting meetings outside our official ones, particularly with the folks from the Woodbine Entertainment Group. They operated a horse racing track in his district, which leased space to an extremely profitable, government-run slots floor. WEG was actively lobbying against a downtown Toronto casino location: If Toronto was to get a casino, they wanted it on their existing racetrack property. Doug began to bend Rob's ear, supporting a Woodbine location instead of Exhibition Place or a third potential site located on Front Street—also downtown.

In addition to being distanced from work, Rob was also less and less willing (or able) to battle with his brother. He'd arrive in the morning convinced (by Doug, the night before) that the casino should be at Woodbine. Then he'd tell me to do whatever I wanted. Then, for a while, he'd stop coming in at all. He'd drop off the grid for the weekend, plus a Monday. Then two or three days at the end of a week. He'd pop up just before we became seriously worried that he might not.

In his absence, I developed a list of criteria based on what was in the best interests of the city, and was the minimum "reward" City Council would demand in order to approve a casino: at least $100 million per year to the city; iconic appearance; destination tourist draw; top-tier convention facility; maximum number of construction and ongoing jobs. Against these criteria, the city manager and I felt only a downtown location (at Exhibition Place or on Front Street) could deliver. Although I personally preferred Exhibition Place, for the reasons I've described, I wasn't about to try and steer it there.

Meanwhile, I was also working with city staff as they finished their report that would recommend a decision on the casino. I insisted on being at all their meetings, and bluntly explained why: The report would not be a promotional brochure for a casino company. I also met, off the record, with senior officials from the provincial government on behalf of the mayor. Over time they agreed that $100 million for the city was achievable, and committed to making it happen. We had a deal. That is, until the Liberal Party of Ontario elected Kathleen Wynne as their new leader in 2013, and she became the province's premier. She didn't like casinos—especially not in Toronto, where she lived. Everything began to fall apart.

One by one, Liberal Party-affiliated councillors who'd supported the idea fell away, including Peter Milczyn, a key member of the mayor's executive committee. He'd been an important ally through the subway war because he was able to walk the fence and keep the trust of those on both sides while usually finding a way to be supportive of the mayor. On the casino file, however, he let me down. Although he'd helped me whip votes at the executive committee meeting, he'd shocked me by switching his own vote to "no" at the last minute. (Soon after, the sitting Liberal Member of Provincial Parliament in his district conveniently retired and the anti-casino Wynne backed Peter to fill the spot. He lost the by-election, but won the seat in the 2014 general election. Politics.)

Thursday, May 16, 2013, was decision day. The mayor had called a special council meeting to decide the casino issue for the following Tuesday. But the provincial government still hadn't answered the city's question about what the revenue sharing formula would be: would the city get enough money to make the casino worthwhile?

Although the casino plan had passed (barely) at executive committee, we didn't have enough votes to get it through Council unless the province would guarantee the city $100 million per year from the casino. And we couldn't take it to Council and lose. Although Rob didn't care, a loss would have been devastating. We were being pushed around by the province and by the opposition on Council. We needed to seize the initiative and take back control of the issue. All along, the mayor had said he'd only support a casino if it were in the best interest of the city. Council had defined $100 million as the city's "minimum best interest." That was our go or no-go factor.

We knew the premier didn't want a casino, but it was widely understood that her government needed the money the casino (and others planned for elsewhere in Ontario) would generate for them. My talks with her ministers suggested her own cabinet was conflicted on the matter. She seemed to be looking for a way to avoid a decision by blaming it all on Toronto.

At 10:00 a.m., I called Tom Teahen, my opposite number in the premier's office. They'd been stalling on making a decision about the funding formula. I told him we were at the wire and asked him point-blank: "Tom, do you want a casino?" We needed to hit that $100 million number, or it was dead in the water. Tom said they didn't have a number yet. I thanked him and hung up, my decision made. We'd spent a year trying to make it work, but like it or not, the casino was clearly dead in the water. It was time to move on. To avoid looking like we'd lost, it was important the mayor be the one who killed it. I asked George to quietly plan a press conference for 4:00 p.m.

I tell you this story for one reason: I made the decision that Rob would kill the casino. A decision that should have been made by the mayor. I called Rob and told him what we were going to do and he agreed. But I stress: I was the one telling him. I wrote his speech; he read it verbatim.

*One year ago, the government of Ontario asked Toronto to host a new casino in its downtown area. Since then, Toronto has spent a year grappling with this issue. It now appears the premier has chosen to go in a different direction. I don't know why the government has changed its mind—that's a question for the premier. I don't know why they will not support a fair share for Toronto—and for all host cities in Ontario—that's a question for the premier. I don't know why the premier doesn't support ten thousand new good-paying, mostly union jobs in Toronto—that's a question for the premier.*

*What I do know is that I will not support a casino if it is not in the best interests of Toronto. I will not ask Council to go through a very divisive and grueling debate next week to approve a casino that the premier is no longer interested in.*

While I was waiting for the press conference to happen, I killed some time by walking around the second floor, where the councillors have their offices. I realized I should have consulted with some Blue Team members on my decision. But the offices were mostly empty, councillors having left the building for the day. It seemed to me a metaphor; they'd given up on Rob, too.

At about 3:30, Ford arrived and I watched him rehearse my speech. He had no changes; he wasn't really engaged. After he finished, I told him how I'd walked around looking for a friendly councillor to discuss the decision with, to make sure it was the right one. "And you know what?" I asked, trying to get him to look at me. "I couldn't find one," meaning physically as well as spiritually. "There's no one left, Rob." He merely grunted.

I told him to run through the speech a few more times with Isaac. I went to my office, called Paul Godfrey (the chairman of the Ontario Lottery and Gaming Corporation), and left him a message that the mayor was shutting down the casino debate. It was over. After I hung up, I sat for a few minutes listening to the media assembling in the Protocol Lounge outside my office. I felt shitty. Not about my decision—as I saw it, the casino was going to die regardless. (And the grand vision for a revitalized Exhibition Place along with it.) But this wasn't how the city was supposed to run. The city needed a working mayor.

Sighing, I got up, walked the back way to Rob's office, and stood outside his bathroom, waiting for him to finish whatever it was he had to do in order to face the cameras. When he came out, I gave him my usual once-over. He looked tired, but okay. His collar was splayed, the way it always was. His shirt was wet the way it always was. His face was flush the way it always was. He looked like Rob Ford. "Any questions?" I asked him.

"Nope," he replied.

I held the door for him as he walked into the lights, then I returned to my office to watch him on TV. My boss. The mayor of the great city of Toronto. Delivering words he hadn't written, about an issue that should have been huge—yet he could not have cared less.

I left work just before 5:00. It was my night with my kids, and I wanted to take them out to dinner. I, at least, knew what my priorities were.

# 26 | Gawker Squawks

DRIVING HOME ON Thursday, May 16, listening to my car radio: *Sources at Queen's Park say Paul Godfrey, CEO of the Ontario Lottery and Gaming Corporation, has been fired. Premier Kathleen Wynne was reportedly unhappy with the handling of plans for a Toronto casino . . .*

Damage control. That was fast. No doubt, the premier's office was pissed that we'd stolen the initiative from them and blamed her for reneging on the casino funding deal and screwing the people of Toronto. Now they were taking out the trash. Godfrey had been on the outs with Wynne from the day she became premier. As I mentioned, she was a staunch opponent of casinos in general and in Toronto in particular; she wasn't going to let one get built on her watch. Her office must have figured they could clear the decks of all gaming-related bad news by turfing him.

Godfrey was a big boy, one of the most powerful men in the city. Still, I felt bad for him. I was pretty sure Rob's press conference had precipitated Godfrey's ouster earlier than planned. I called him (the second time that day) and left a message apologizing if our announcement ending the casino debate had hastened his departure.

Before I'd even passed the Exhibition Place grounds on my drive home, my phone buzzed again—my personal one this time. It was George Christopoulos. He'd just gotten an email from an editor at a US-based website called Gawker. All I knew about the site at that point was that, a few months earlier, it had published an unflattering introduction piece about Rob Ford. Today's piece was much more attention-grabbing: Gawker was claiming it had seen a video of Rob Ford smoking crack cocaine, and wanted a comment from him before they ran their story.

By this time, claims like this no longer shocked us. A lot of media had intimated they had evidence of Rob doing drugs, but we hadn't seen any hard evidence, and we certainly weren't going to encourage their fishing expeditions. Our policy was to not respond, not even with a "no comment." We knew that without some response from us, they usually held off publishing.

My kids and I were at a Boston Pizza in Etobicoke and had just ordered when my phone burped with a Google alert. The Gawker story on Rob was out. And it was bad.

"Rob Ford, Toronto's conservative mayor, is a wild lunatic given to making bizarre racist pronouncements and randomly slapping refrigerator magnets on cars. One reason for this is that he smokes crack cocaine. I know this because I watched him do it, on a videotape. He was fucking *hiiiiigh*. It's for sale if you've got six figures."

That was just the lead paragraph. Unlike a conventional news outlet, Gawker didn't hedge its accusations with "allegedly." It flat-out stated that Ford smoked crack. In Canada, that's libelous, unless you can prove it in court.

I forwarded the link to Dennis Morris, Rob's family friend and a criminal lawyer who'd advised the Fords in the past. (He'd helped us on Rob's DUI issue during the campaign.) I asked him to send a "cease and desist" letter to Gawker that might get them to pull the story, or at least soften the allegations. Then I told my kids I needed a minute, and stepped into the vestibule for privacy.

I called George. We fully expected that the newspapers, especially the *Star*, would rush anything they had in the works on Ford and drugs into the next day's paper. The story was already picking up traction on Twitter. We agreed George should head to the mayor's house early in the morning, because it would be crawling with media by sunrise. So much for our positive headlines on the casino file.

Then I called Rob. When I told him that a story online was claiming he'd been videotaped smoking crack cocaine in an apartment with some dubious-looking people, his answer sent chills down my spine. "There's no tape, buddy," he replied. There was even a hint of a laugh in his voice.

That was not the answer I wanted to hear. I wanted to hear anger. I wanted to hear "That's fucking bullshit, because I've never smoked crack cocaine in my life and I don't hang around with criminals who do." But he didn't say that.

"Rob," I asked, clearly and slowly, "is it possible that there is a tape like that?"

"Don't worry, buddy. There's no tape."

Fuck.

I asked a few more questions, but Rob laughed me off. He sounded tired, maybe into a few beers, but not high. Coherent. I told him David Price, his new director of logistics (whom Rob had insisted I hire because he was a close friend of Doug's), would have staffers at his house to help manage the inevitable morning circus. I'd given Price responsibility for managing the mayor's special assistants who acted as body men.

Months later, after I'd been fired, and after the courts had released a blockbuster affidavit containing secret police wiretap information, I would discover that, almost immediately after hanging up with me, Ford had called Sandro Lisi. Lisi then immediately called the man who had offered to sell the video to Gawker and the *Star*.

But I didn't know that when I sent a PIN to the senior staff warning them it would be all hands on deck in the morning. I then called David Price, who decided he'd handle things at Rob's house himself.

In between bites of pizza with my kids, I checked my BlackBerry and iPhone for updates. Dennis Morris copied me on his email to Gawker. It was not what I'd hoped it would be: *Greetings; I am a lawyer, and have been contacted by Mayor Ford's office in reference to your indicating you will post a photo of Mayor Ford smoking crack cocaine. Mayor Ford denies such [event] took place, and if such posting occurs, it is false and defamatory, and you will be held legally accountable. In reference to the photo you wish to publish, Mayor Ford has his photo taken daily, sometimes with others. If the person you mention is now deceased, it is sad, regardless of his alleged background. Please govern yourself accordingly. Dennis Morris.*

This was not good. It was not factually correct. (Gawker was threatening to post a story about a video of the mayor smoking crack cocaine, not a photo.) It was not intimidating. It just fanned the flames. Sure enough, Gawker quickly updated its story with the text of the email.

I called Rob again. I suggested he retain another lawyer, perhaps Gavin Tighe, who'd been working for him on the Boardwalk Café libel case. He said he was comfortable with Dennis, but didn't want Dennis doing anything he hadn't personally authorized, or someone else would have to pay the bill. So I told Dennis he should speak directly to Rob for further instruction. I wasn't about to get saddled with Rob's legal bills.

I finished dinner with my kids, took them home, and watched the story snowball online. Before midnight, the *Star's* story was up on its electronic edition. It would fill the front page of its morning paper. As we had expected, they'd been working this story for months. It had a lot of detail that Gawker didn't have. They'd obviously been waiting for a linchpin fact to make their story publishable, something they could hang anonymous quotations and circumstantial evidence on. The Gawker story provided it.

The *Star's* piece was a story about the story. It said that Gawker had run a story about the mayor "allegedly" smoking "what appears to be" crack cocaine, and then backed up Gawker's allegations with their own facts: Their reporters Robyn Doolittle and Kevin Donovan had seen a similar video and been provided the same still photo of Rob Ford with three young black men, one of whom was apparently Anthony Smith, who had been murdered outside a Toronto nightclub. The *Star* added "allegedly" and "appeared to be" to the accusations in their story, but the shitstorm had begun.

\*\*\*

The next morning, I got into the office early and pulled together a core group—Earl, Kia, George, and Isaac Ransom, the deputy press secretary—for a full and frank discussion. The mayor was scheduled to raise the flag for a Parents, Families and Friends of Lesbians and Gays (PFLAG) event that afternoon. It was his second year doing so, and it was a big deal, because he didn't participate in the city's annual gay pride parade. Raising the flag was his compromise with us.

In 2012, getting him to raise the flag had taken a full-court press by all members of the senior staff, and a military-like operation to get him to the rooftop secretly. Even then, we'd been unsure if he'd actually do it, so we hadn't told anyone we were trying. Councillor Kristyn Wong-Tam was at the podium, ready to stand in for the mayor. When I got word that Rob was in the building, Earl and I went up to the rooftop. (A few alert tweeters noted that the mayor's staff had suddenly appeared.) A few minutes later, when I got word that Rob was actually walking out to the roof, I eased my way up to the podium just before Wong-Tam was about to raise the flag, and asked if she'd mind if the mayor did it instead. She readily agreed, but asked if she could say a few words she'd prepared. As she spoke, I watched Rob and City Hall security come around the corner, behind the assembled crowd. Wong-Tam introduced him flawlessly, and the surprised crowd applauded him for doing it.

But with the entire world reading about Ford and a possible crack video, the flag-raising this year, on May 17, 2013, was going to be chaos. The television monitor in the boardroom, tuned to CP24, Toronto's twenty-four-hour live news station, was showing an ongoing live shot of the mayor's house. Dave Price, in position there since early in the morning, told me the media was everywhere. I asked him to let me know the minute Rob showed signs of life.

The core team agreed that we should continue with the flag-raising; we felt that maintaining an appearance of normalcy could cast some doubt on the crack story. We also agreed that we needed to talk to Rob, soon, to walk through a plan for containment and response to the allegations. But we didn't want to do it at City Hall. I called Doug, who suggested we meet at his mother Diane's home. Fortress Ford was the final redoubt when the family was under attack.

Rob was still off the grid, not using his cell phone. Kia kept dialing his number every sixty seconds to try to reach him. In the meantime, I briefed the key staffers on what Rob had said to me. They were as concerned as I'd been by his response.

We broke the story into knowns and unknowns. We knew he was overdrinking and appeared to be dependent on alcohol. We suspected he was using other drugs, but didn't know what. We had reason to believe he'd used marijuana and possibly OxyContin. But his behavior when he was high didn't square with our understanding of how those drugs affected people. Might he have a chronic condition—maybe diabetes— that affected his response? Either way, we felt he had a problem. So did the media and much of the public.

In Gawker's photo, Rob was reportedly standing with Anthony Smith, a gang member who'd been murdered two months prior. But the Gawker story had reported a number of things as fact that we knew weren't exactly as represented. Even if there was a video of Ford smoking from a crack pipe, it would be impossible to prove there was crack in it. So Gawker editor John Cook's claim "he smokes crack cocaine. I know this because I watched him do it, on a videotape" was embellishment. Cook also claimed that CNN had called and tipped off the mayor's office about the crack video; we knew that hadn't happened.

**In summary:** We weren't sure if there was a video. We all believed there could be.

In my mind, it didn't matter if there was. We couldn't continue running a city this way. I led a rundown of the options as I saw them.

**Option One:** Ford resigns. There was great public and political pressure for him to step down. Resigning would alleviate that pressure immediately.

It would also ease the media circus around him and allow him to return to some semblance of a normal life. Perhaps he and his family could get whatever help they needed. If Ford got help, he could relaunch his political career at the provincial or federal level, or run again municipally in 2014.

None of us believed he'd choose this option.

**Option Two:** Deny the allegations and bulldoze forward. If what Rob said remained consistent—as long as a video never showed up—he might live through this immediate crush. All of us thought he'd favor this option. None of us thought it would work. People already believed he was an addict and the story, true or false, reinforced that. They would hound his every move. Eventually, he'd collapse under the pressure. It might literally kill him.

There was another danger. Whether there was a video or not, many people now believed there was—including, no doubt, some very nasty people. Imagine being a drug dealer, willing to use a gun over paltry $100 debts, hanging out in Rexdale, a poorer neighborhood of northwest Toronto, as distant from the vibrant club and theater districts of the downtown core as you could get and still live in the same city. Now imagine that you believe someone in one of the high-rise ghettos on your turf has a video under his pillow that's worth $200,000—the amount Gawker said they were fundraising to buy the video. Wouldn't you start looking for it? And what would you do if someone got in your way?

If someone got hurt or died, Ford's name would be in the middle of it. Somebody in a picture with Ford was already dead. There was nothing to suggest that Anthony Smith's death was related to the alleged video, nor to Rob Ford—but clearly the two men had met. No, the pressure was not going to let up, video or no video.

**The final option:** Rob goes to rehab. We had a file folder full of rehab info that we'd amassed and revisited over the past year. We knew where he could go and how he could get there. If I could convince Rob to go, I planned to spirit him away without any publicity. Once Ford was checked into a (highly discreet) facility, we would inform the city clerk and the media that he was taking a leave of absence to deal with a personal health matter. We wouldn't have to specify the details. People would understand. After rehab, when Rob returned to work sober, we'd stage a media event where he could admit he'd struggled with addiction, realized he needed help, and received it. He could say he was back, better than ever, and ready to get back to doing what he was elected to do: Stand up for the little guy.

Hell, he could even be a hero: "Rob Ford was the only politician who'd ever cared about you, the ordinary Joe. Even while running North America's fourth-largest city, he went to your front door to help you. Though he had the weight of the world on his shoulders, he returned your calls, he took on your struggles. Okay, he stumbled. But no wonder—the left wing was against him, the rich and powerful hated him, the media hounded him. Even so, he wasn't beaten. He was strong enough to get help. Now he's healed. Now he's back."

In that scenario, he'd be immune from attack. His most effective opponents were the same people who preached that addiction was a disease; that addicts were patients, not criminals. If they attacked him, they'd be hypocrites. Bonus: Anything bad he'd done up to the point of entering rehab would be voided. Even things no one knew about. Crack video? He'd been an addict. Insert offence here . . . ? He'd been sick! It was a real-world "get out of jail free" card. A rehabilitated Rob Ford could, quite possibly, be mayor for life.

**We all agreed:** Even if Rob wasn't addicted to anything, he should go to rehab, then come back strong (and immune from attack) just in time for reelection. But first we had to convince Rob.

The instant Ford came back onto the grid, Kia passed me the phone. Rob sounded hoarse and grumpy, but clearheaded. I told him there was a pile of media outside his house and that the crack video was all over town: The *Star* had it on their front page in "World War 3 Starts Now"-sized font, and radio and TV stations were doing live hits from his lawn.

"No way," he replied in wonder.

I told him Doug's plan, to muster at his mom's house. Instead, "I'm coming down to City Hall," he said. I tried to talk him out of it, but his mind was made up.

I phoned Price and asked him to meet Rob at his door to walk him out, make sure he got into his car and away without an altercation with the media. "Ummm . . . yeah," stammered Price. "That's going to be a problem." He wasn't exactly outside the house, he said. He'd pulled off because the media kept coming up to him to ask him questions. Then, to my astonishment, I heard Doug Ford in the background. Price was at Diane's.

I was furious. Now I was going to have an impatient, angry mayor storming out of his house without anyone to clear a path through the media. I thought it was going to be ugly. Watching it unfold on live TV, I was right.

\*\*\*

Forty minutes later, Rob arrived at City Hall. He stormed through the phalanx of media assembled outside his office and went straight into his bathroom. My plan was to focus exclusively on the flag-raising. Ford would read a proclamation, and would not discuss the crack video allegations until afterward.

When Ford came out of the washroom, he was flushed and had large wet circles on his shirt where he'd spilled water on himself. He sat down behind his desk and I urged him to stand back up, because we were late for the flag-raising. I also urged him to formulate one sentence for the media right outside, as a holding message. We'd address the video in more detail later.

"I'm not going to say anything," Rob protested. "It's ridiculous."

I insisted he say something, or they'd never let him get near the flag pole: "If they ask whether you've used crack cocaine, or if there's a video, just say, 'That's ridiculous.' Attack the *Star* again if you have to."

Security preceded us to hold the elevator. Rob walked out of his office to an explosion of flashbulbs and TV camera lights. He stopped halfway to the elevator and turned to face the crowd, who were shouting questions at him. He said it was ridiculous. He blamed the *Star* for everything. George cut it off and into the elevator we went.

At the flag-raising, Rob read the proclamation, then stepped back. Photographers took long shots of him looking bored while other politicians made speeches. The minute the event ended, the journalists pounced, shouting questions, which Rob ignored, as we retraced our steps back into the building. Back in his office, Rob headed into the bathroom again, while Earl, George, Isaac, and I waited in his office. People wandered in, but we shooed them away. This was a closed meeting. We didn't want spectators.

When Rob finally came out, he was immediately combative. Flushed and agitated, he laughed at everything. Whether it was a drug he'd ingested in the bathroom, or just natural nervousness at having to confront something he didn't want to deal with, I couldn't tell. He insisted the story was bullshit. We were blowing it all out of proportion and needed to relax.

I began cross-examining him. "You told me there was no video," I began. "How do you know?"

Rob folded his hands over his belly, tilted his chair back, and laughed. "There's no video."

"How do you know that, Rob?"

"Buddy . . . There's no video." He laughed again, arms waving outward. "There's no video."

Isaac, seated on the leather couch that backed onto the window overlooking Nathan Phillips Square, was getting angry. "This isn't a laughing matter, Mayor," he said. "Your entire mayoralty is on the line here."

"You guys need to chill out," Rob said, an edge showing through his now forced laughter.

Isaac, close to outright anger now, started to retort. I cut him off and asked for the room. Isaac closed his notebook and followed Earl and George outside, closing the door behind them.

I turned toward Rob and sat down in the chair facing his desk. "Rob, this is serious," I said. "We're concerned that there might be a video. We're concerned about your health."

"I'm fine," Rob protested.

"When we tell you someone says there's a video of you smoking crack cocaine, and you say, 'Don't worry, buddy, there's no video,' I worry. Because you're not saying, 'There can't be a video, because I've never used crack cocaine.'"

Rob stopped laughing. *You're saying you think I'm a drug addict?*

"Honestly, Rob, I don't know," I said. Mistake. "Honestly" was one of his favorite word traps.

"Honestly?" he pounced. "So everything else you've said up to now is a lie?"

I cut him off before he could go on. "Now you're just deflecting, Rob. You do that when you want to avoid talking about something, or when you've been caught doing something."

I told him we needed to address the story. Credible witnesses—two *Toronto Star* reporters—claimed to have watched a video of him smoking crack. People believed them. We had to do something, or his mayoralty was finished.

I also told him that the school board would have to fire him as a football coach. How could they allow him to coach when there were serious allegations that he used crack cocaine and hung around with drug dealers?

Worse, he would lose his kids. The Children's Aid Society was already aware of the situation in Rob's home and considered him the responsible parent. If he was suspected of drug abuse, it was over—they'd have to take his kids.

His face was growing scarlet. When I told him he had three options, he glared at me. "Oh, really?" he asked, leaning forward in his chair, hands flat on his desk like he was poised to lunge at me. "What are they?"

I ran through the list and told him that rehab was the only viable option. I told him how we'd manage his exit and his comeback and how it would set him up for a win in 2014. I told him there were still hundreds of thousands of people in the city who loved him and would support him if he needed help. Everyone in the office was ready to walk over hot coals to help him get well. But he had to make the decision. He had to want to get better. It was time.

He laughed. "Oh, this is hilarious!" he said, picking up a pen and jotting down the options. "I've got to tell Renata about this." He stabbed the speaker button on the desk phone and dialed his home number. As it began to ring, I stood up.

"Rob, it's my job to tell you the truth and give you my best advice," I said. "I'm not going to stand here while you ridicule me to your wife."

"I'm not going to ridicule you, I just think she'd get a kick out of this," he replied. Renata didn't answer, so he left a voicemail telling her she was *not going to believe this. Mark says I have three choices. I can quit. I can go to rehab. Or I can lose.* He hung up the phone and looked down at his notes. He drew a line through each of the three options. "I'm not quitting," he said. "I'm not losing. And I'm not going to rehab."

"What do you want to do then?" I asked.

"Nothing," he answered. "It's all bullshit. I'm just going to keep going on the ground game. I'm going to keep returning phone calls." As I left the room, he was already dialing a number from his call list.

I found Earl, George, and Isaac in the boardroom. They asked which option he'd chosen. "Option four," I said. "Do nothing."

\*\*\*

The mayor had heard my advice and declined to take it. I thought his decision was stupid and doomed to fail. But ignoring reality wasn't illegal. We could still help him to pretend everything was normal. I called the entire staff together in the boardroom and told them that when I'd asked

Ford point-blank if there was a video, he'd said no. So that's what we were going with. I warned them the controversy would likely get worse before it got better, and thanked them for continuing to do their jobs despite the stress. Constituents still needed help with their problems. Councillors still needed advice on policy. We still had committee meetings to prepare for. It would be business as usual. They were clearly shaken by the news, but the fact that it didn't change their day-to-day duties seemed to give them some solid ground to stand on.

After the staff meeting, I went into David Price's office, closed the door, and reamed him out for leaving the mayor's house that morning. He told me Doug had asked him to go to Diane's. I told him that he didn't work for Doug, he worked for Rob—which meant he worked for me. I told him if he ever fucked up like that again, I'd fire his ass. He was seething as I left.

But later that night, he phoned as I was driving home. "Hypothetically speaking," Price began, "what if I told you that an informant had told me he knew where this video was?"

I asked him to cut the bullshit and tell me what he knew. He claimed he'd spent some of the morning doing a little "investigating," which was partly why he left Rob's. I thought he was making up an excuse for his fuck-up. Then he dropped a bomb: He told me someone he knew—and believed—knew where the video was.

I was in the middle of thinking that we didn't want to prove that our boss was lying about being a crackhead, and that he should ignore what he'd heard, when Price added that his "source" had told him the video might be why Anthony Smith was killed.

*Fuck me.* I pulled over. "Be clear," I said. "Did *they say* the video might be connected to a murder, or do *you think* it might be connected to a murder?"

"They said it," Price replied.

*Shit.* It was one thing to ignore evidence that may or may not be real, that a video may or may not exist, suggesting the mayor may or may not be a liar and a drug user. It was another, however, to ignore information that might be evidence in a murder investigation. According to my four-point guiding principles, that was out of bounds. Despite my nagging feeling that Price was bullshitting to compensate for screwing up, I told him we had to take that information to the police. He seemed surprised by my response, but he didn't waver or protest about going to the police.

He asked if the cops would be okay with his not revealing his source. *For fuck's sake.* "No, Dave," I replied, as calmly as I could. "I don't think they would be okay with that." I told him I would call my contact at the police and if they were interested, they'd get in touch with him.

"Do not tell the mayor where the video is, or that you know where it is," I told Price. "We do not want him to know that. That just puts him at risk." I didn't know if the video was real. I didn't know what would happen next. But I did know there were a million things that could happen to and around that video and I didn't want the mayor anywhere near it. Price said he understood.

I sat there for a while and thought this through. What the fuck was Rob involved in? What the fuck was Price involved in that he knew people who knew about murders? They'd both grown up in the area, and Rob had gone to a tough school—but he'd come from a privileged family. I didn't know Price's history. No matter how I looked at it, though, there was only one right thing to do. I dialed the cell phone number for Inspector Stu Eley, the police chief's executive officer, who was our contact for most official matters. I reached him on vacation at a summer cottage north of the city.

I explained that this was an awkward predicament, but I needed to pass on some information I had received from a staffer that might be useful to the police. I stressed that I had good reason to believe it might not be true. After I told him Price's story, he asked a few questions and said he'd pass it on to the investigators. If they wanted to talk, they'd contact me.

The next day, I got a call from Detective Sergeant Gary Giroux, one of Toronto's most experienced homicide investigators. We met at police headquarters in downtown Toronto later that afternoon. On my drive there, I got a PIN message from a staffer: He'd heard the video was in one of two apartments at 320 Dixon Road.

Giroux and Detective Sergeant Joyce Schertzer interviewed me under oath, on videotape. I was cautioned that it was an offense to lie under oath. (I was pleased to note that I was not cautioned as a suspect. Always good to know.) Before I answered their questions, I stressed that everything I was going to tell them was hearsay. I relayed Price's story, along with the information I'd received about two units on the seventeenth floor at 320 Dixon Road. They asked a few questions and I answered them honestly— though somewhat guardedly when it came to the mayor's behavior. I was still Ford's chief of staff, and he didn't know I was speaking to police.

The media horde camped outside the mayor's office was big on Monday, and bigger on Tuesday. There were cameras and crews from every Canadian TV and radio network, English and French, as well as every major newspaper in the country. There were print journalists from the *New York Times, Guardian*, and *Wall Street Journal*. There were TV crews from CNN, ABC, NBC, CBS, BBC, and Al Jazeera, plus English, French, German, and, I think, Australian networks. There were easily fifty sweaty bodies pressed together on the narrow mezzanine floor between the mayor's office and the elevator. All waiting for Ford to do . . . something. Anything. For a few days, that elevator became the most famous one in the world. There were live video feeds of anyone who came out of it. It even had its own Twitter account.

We'd been under intense media scrutiny before, but this was a whole new order of magnitude. When I'd step out of the elevator, it would be into the hot glare of two dozen TV camera lights, everyone hoping I was the mayor. "It's not him," I'd hear, and some of the lights would go dark. But not all—our every move was being live-streamed around the world. It was serious "game face" time. That, and we used the side door a lot more.

On Tuesday morning, May 21, 2013, Price told me that he'd heard the video problem "was being taken care of . . . as we speak, maybe." He wouldn't tell me how he knew, just alluded to his mysterious sources. I asked how he knew people who knew those things, and he replied, "It's a small neighborhood." That didn't reassure me. As far as I knew, Price hadn't lived in Rexdale in years.

Meanwhile, Ford worked his ground game. He went to constituents' homes. He returned phone calls. His mood was intense, serious, focused on calls, working hard to pretend nothing was unusual. Coming and going to his office, he simply ignored the gauntlet of reporters. They didn't exist.

On Wednesday morning, we received a letter from the Toronto Catholic District School Board informing Ford that he'd been terminated as coach of the Don Bosco Eagles high school football team. I'd predicted it on Friday, but I knew it was going to gut Rob. I wanted to be the person to break the news to him, in a controlled way, so he wouldn't lose control and so I could assess how he was taking it.

But I was too late. He called and told me that someone from the board had called him with the news. He was sobbing. I tried to reassure him that it would be okay—he could focus for a while on his family and his job, and then, when things calmed down, he could get another coaching gig. He cried for four or five minutes, while I listened and tried to console him. I'd only heard him cry like that once before, as we drove to his father's gravesite during the campaign in 2010. As much as I knew that he and he alone was at fault, I felt sorry for him.

Soon after Rob hung up, Doug strode into my office to talk about a plan to clear Rob's name. He mentioned that he'd been out with some cops the night before, and they'd told him about a shooting in his district—at 320 Dixon Road. On the seventeenth floor. An electric tingle ran down my spine.

Shaking, I got up and closed my door. I told Doug that was the address where I'd been told the video might be hidden, and I told him what Price had said the day before; how he'd confidently told me the problem with the video was being taken care of, "as we speak, maybe." I asked Doug how the hell he knew David Price. He said they went to high school together. *Great guy.*

For the next half-hour, and for the first time since the Chicago trade mission, Doug and I spoke as allies, not competitors, about Rob's problems. I asked him to check on his brother because he was distraught about losing the football team. I told him I feared the video was real, and asked if he or Rob had received blackmail threats. He said no, and I believed him. He admitted Rob drank too much and said he hadn't realized it was a problem until the last few days. He clearly didn't want to believe Rob was using crack. He asked if there a test he could take to prove he wasn't?

I turned to my computer to Google that, then stopped cold. "Maybe I shouldn't search this on my work computer," I said to Doug. Then I realized that was ridiculous. We had bigger problems to worry about.

I read about how cocaine leaves the body quickly, and most tests can only detect it for up to four days after use. Testing hair samples provided the longest detection period, but even they would only detect use within ninety days. The media seemed to the think the video had been made in February, three months ago. A negative hair test wouldn't prove anything. I joked if Rob shows up for work with a shaved head, we'll have our answer, and Doug and I laughed. I saw my opening, and went for it: Rob needed rehab, here's the research we've done about it, here's how it could work. Doug promised to talk it over with the family, and left—realizing, I think for the first time, that his little brother was in big trouble: he was using alcohol and probably drugs and was out of control, with his mayoralty in dire jeopardy.

Soon after Doug left, I had another fire to put out: Chris Fickel told me Rob wanted his football players to go to his house that night for a pizza party. Terrible idea. I called Rob to head him off. Over the phone, his words were fast and clipped. He sounded like he was on something. I told him the football party was a bad idea, and he demanded to know why. I explained that the board had asked him not to communicate with the students. If he did, they could get a restraining order against him and he didn't need any more legal headaches. I also said it wasn't fair to drag students through the media circus outside his house. But he just got more and more angry.

"Rob, right now I've got our staff in your office, being paid for with tax dollars, working on a pizza party at your house for football students the school board told you not to talk to. We don't need that grief, boss. It's against the rules and we can't do it.

"And you don't need this extra grief right now," I added. "You need to relax. You need to think about what we talked about, and you need to go away and get well."

He told me to fuck off. He was going to have the party in his fucking house. His house was his business. What he did with his team was none of my fucking business.

I told him I wouldn't let him take the junior staff down with him. "You do what you want, but the office staff works for me, and I won't let them help you." He hung up on me.

I stepped out of the office to tell Chris to shut down the party preparations. Immediately, his cell buzzed. "Yes, Mayor?" he asked. I could hear Rob yelling, ordering him to invite the students to the party. Chris, helpless, looked at me.

I could refuse to order the junior staff to plan Rob's party. But they couldn't refuse him, and he knew it. I reached out and took Chris's phone from him. I reiterated that the staff would not help with the party, and that he needed to focus on his health.

He'd yelled at me before. This time, though, he was screaming. His words were fast, getting stuck together in his mouth. So loud, the phone couldn't seem to transmit them properly. I could understand barely half of what he said. But I got the gist. I took a deep breath. "Rob, I can hardly understand you," I said. "You sound like you're on something. Are you high right now?"

He exploded. Who the fuck was I? Who did I think I was to accuse him? I repeated, as calmly as I could, that he needed to go away and get better. There were lots of people here to help him, who cared about him, but rehab was the only choice he had left.

"Get the fuck out," he hissed. "Get the fuck out of my office. Go home. And don't come back."

I said okay. "Do you know what I'm saying?" Ford screamed. "Do you?"

I said I did. I ended the call and handed the phone back to Chris. He was pale. I told him to turn off his phone and leave it off for the night. I told him to go home and relax, and under no circumstances was he to talk to the mayor. I couldn't have Ford undoing what I was trying to do. I needed to protect my staff.

I walked around the office and gave everyone there the same instructions. Then I sent an email to everyone who wasn't there. I chose email because I knew it would be archived; someday someone would ask for it under the Freedom of Information legislation, and I wanted the staff to have a record of my order so they wouldn't get in shit. As it happened, *Toronto Sun* reporter Don Peat published a copy of my email on June 3, 2013:

> *Subject: Direct order*
> *Do not answer calls from the mayor tonight.*
> *Take the night off.*
> *Will explain in the AM.*
> *Earl, George, David—call me when you can.*

And then, shaken, I went home.

# 27 | I Did Not Resign

I WOKE AT 6:30 a.m. with a gnawing, churning sensation in my gut. That wasn't unusual—in fact, it had become common over the last three years. I downed an extra-strength Zantac, a handful of vitamins, plus two extra-strength ibuprofen. (Breakfast of champions.) My short hair was not entirely dry by the time I stepped out of the shower, so I made a mental note to get a haircut.

I didn't have to look in the mirror to know that the stress was gnawing at me. I wasn't eating. I wasn't sleeping. I was having nightmares about work. I was having nightmares about my kids. Since the early days of transition, I'd described working with Rob Ford as akin to riding a speeding train in the dark. I'd joked that the challenge was hanging on long enough to enjoy the thrill, but getting off before the train hit the inevitable wall. Now I could feel the train shuddering under my feet, and I knew the dead end I'd feared was rushing closer.

At this point, I believed Rob was doing drugs. It also seemed like he was deeply involved with suspicious characters. His staff and I were way beyond our professional obligation to protect his confidences. I was comfortable that we had done the right thing—morally and legally— up to this point. But I wasn't sure about moving forward. We were way beyond masking the misadventures of alcoholism, which was a tough medical condition, but not illegal. Now there were credible allegations he was doing hard drugs. With criminals. I'd already gone to the police with information that might be evidence linked to a fucking murder. I was not comfortable helping him any further. I was no longer confident that we, his staff, were doing the right thing.

For the last week, I had been pushing Rob on the phone. Though I'd offered him three options the Friday morning after the Gawker story was published, I was now just talking about one. Rehab. It was the only way he could salvage his mayoralty and save his political career. It was the only way he would survive. And it was the only way I could continue to work with him. I wouldn't work for a criminal.

The way I figured it, Rob would either agree to go to rehab, or fire me. Either outcome was better than where I was now. I knew it was a matter of days, or maybe hours. In fact, maybe he'd already fired me. I was about fifty percent convinced that today would be my last day. Then again, with Rob, you could never be sure. He'd "fired" me more than once, and I was still there. Either way, I didn't feel any great sense of urgency to race in. I had a coffee date with a trusted friend to discuss my career prospects. I planned to arrive at City Hall just after noon, so I'd be there when the mayor arrived for an event scheduled at 1:00.

At 8:00 a.m., I drove my kids to school—a rare treat for all of us. I dropped them off at their two different schools, conveniently located in opposite directions from the house, and stopped at a Shoppers Drug Mart to pick up four daily newspapers—yes, even *that* one. I then drove to my favorite diner, the Dundas Street Grille, slid into an empty booth, and ordered a supremely unhealthy breakfast. Small pleasures.

One bottomless cup of coffee and four newspapers later, I could feel a little caffeine twitch in my hands as I popped back in my car and headed downtown to meet my friend. I didn't need more coffee. I needed backup.

Halfway to the meeting, my phone chirped with a message from the office. The city manager and director of council support services, who handled human resources issues for the politicians, had been at the mayor's office first thing in the morning, and were wondering when he'd be in and if he still needed them. Huh. Ford must have called them last night and asked them to come in first thing. I bet that was a colorful conversation. Unfortunately for them, he was at a morning meeting in Etobicoke.

Stopped at a red light, I messaged back: "Understood. I know what it's about." Eighty percent certain now.

I pulled into the underground City Hall parking lot just before 1:00 and walked up the stairs to the office. I knew the front hallway would be a media circus, and I didn't feel like walking that gauntlet. I went in the side entrance, unlocked my office, dropped my briefcase on the desk, and hung up my coat. My acting EA, Chris Fickel, told me a number of parents of the football kids had called to complain about the mayor's pizza party the night before. Some were livid. They alleged that Ford had brought the kids into the basement rec room at his mother's place and told them, "You can drink anything you want in here, but if you want to smoke dope you have to do that outside in the backyard." Fabulous.

I thanked Chris for the info and told him to sit tight for a bit. I then walked through the Protocol Lounge to the desk in front of the mayor's private office. Rob's door was closed. "Is he in?" I asked Kia, Rob's long-suffering EA.

"Yes, he's in with a constituent," Kia said. "He asked me to call Joe and Winnie down." That was city manager Joe Pennachetti, the city's top bureaucrat, and Winnie Li, the director of council support services. Ford must have called both last night in his fit of rage. The only possible topic of conversation was me. This was it. "Okay, let me know when he's free," I said.

Kia shot me a look that suggested he knew there was much more going on than he was being told. He had one of the most stressful jobs in the city, and always handled it with diligence and without complaint. By this point I hated working close to Rob, and didn't spend any more time with him than necessary. Poor Kia, however, had no escape.

I slipped back out the side door of the mayor's office suite and walked toward the circular hallway that provided access to the forty-four councillors' offices. For a brief moment, I was visible to the reporters and TV camera people gathered outside the glass wall at the entrance to the suite. Out of the corner of my eye, I recognized the press gallery regulars, who knew the layout of the building like the backs of their hands. They were well positioned, just outside that glass security door, to see the mayor whether he arrived via the elevator in front of his office, or popped in through the side door as I had done. I saw some of them begin to move toward the door, which their security passes could open. I didn't turn my head or slow down. Steady pace. Unhurried, but purposeful. And then I was hidden in the hallway again.

Around the corner and out of sight of the media was a long, curved wall that formed the back wall of the office area where the rest of the mayor's staff worked. The front of this office suite was made of glass walls on three sides, facing the mezzanine, where members of the public and the media could see directly into the workspace. Inside, four low-walled cubicles, for special assistants working on constituent issues, and an oval-shaped wooden meeting table were in plain view. Along the back walls and sides, there was a small meeting room and six offices for my deputy chief of staff, the press secretary, assistant press secretary, and three senior policy and council liaison staff. The offices were private, but everyone outside the glass wall could watch the comings and goings.

We called the area the Fish Bowl—which was apt, because Rob had insisted we put a sad-looking fish tank in the glass-walled front corner. We had initially named the fish after staff members, but it had soon become a macabre exercise. They never lived very long.

The Fish Bowl would shortly become famous, when TV cameras outside the glass walls followed Rob as he visited the offices of staffers who quit and interrogated those who remained about their intentions. But that would come later.

I fanned my wallet, which contained my security pass, in front of the card reader and slipped through the backdoor into the Fish Bowl. The churning mass of reporters began to slide toward the glass wall to watch me. I could see TV cameras swiveling my way. It was a test of will to ignore them. Game face.

I walked around the cubicles toward Earl Provost's office. As deputy chief of staff, he was my second in command, and the weight of the mayor's office was about to fall squarely on his shoulders. He was on the phone, so I spoke with George Christopolous, Rob's press secretary, and Sunny Petrujkic, the director of council affairs, responsible for our liaison efforts with councillors, who were chatting in George's office across from Earl's.

I explained what had happened the night before, and what was about to happen. I told George he might need to prepare a brief statement—just the facts—if the mayor wanted to issue one. "No longer works here. Thank him for his service. Best of luck in his future endeavors, etc."

When Earl was off the phone, I sat down in front of his desk. I helped myself to a handful of the jellybeans that were always present in a glass candy jar next to his vintage pen set. "I hope you're ready," I said. "Because you're going to have to keep this place going."

He was baffled. "The mayor is going to fire me this afternoon," I said.

Earl denied it. "He absolutely is," I insisted. "He's got Joe P. and Winnie Li in his office, and I'm heading over there in a minute. I'm done."

"He can't do that," Earl protested.

"It's happening," I said. I told him what went down the night before, and I mentioned a few things he would need to do in the next forty-eight hours.

As I headed back over to the mayor's suite, Kia burst out of the door. He told me the mayor was looking for me and for Earl. "I figured," I said. "Earl's in his office." Kia continued on to fetch him and I walked back into the main suite.

I was tense, but strangely calm. I knew exactly what was coming and, although I wasn't happy about it, I was as ready as I could be. I was pissed with Ford, yet relieved that the nightmare of trying to manage him was about to end. I was proud of the work I'd done, and felt that the performance of my staff—I thought of them as my team, not Rob's—had been outstanding under circumstances that were so difficult, no one would believe me if I told them.

Councillor Frances Nunziata was waiting for me just outside my office, hoping to discuss a change we were considering in the executive committee slate. I knew Ford was waiting, but I chatted a few minutes longer with her than I needed to, because, well . . . fuck him. Let him wait for me for once. And for the last time. Finally I excused myself, saying the mayor was waiting to fire me.

She laughed. Then she looked at me oddly and said, "What do you mean?" I just smiled and said I really shouldn't keep him waiting any longer.

Ford's door was closed. I had expected to stop before entering, to take a deep breath and calm my nerves. I could feel the arteries in my neck throbbing, my pulse racing. But as I reached the door, I didn't even pause. It was done. I knocked and entered, closing the door behind me.

My office, and those of all the mayor's staffers, was an interior one with no windows. It was easy to lose track of what time of day it was, or what the weather was like, when you worked twelve-, sixteen-, even twenty-four-hour days. But the mayor's office was large and had floor-to-ceiling windows facing the square outside. It was sunny that day, a beautiful afternoon. I could see tourists wandering in Nathan Phillips Square. Kids were playing around the new fountains, which had recently been turned on. They shot water straight up into the air from the concrete decking, and kids were running in and out of the spray. I smiled at the memory of how I'd joked with the city manager that I'd wanted him to install a switch inside the mayor's office, so we could activate the fountains whenever the square was full of protesters. I was mostly kidding.

Ford was at his desk, fiddling with some papers. He looked much like he had the first day I'd met him in his council office before the campaign had started, back in March 2010, but he was heavier now, sweatier, redder in the face. Joe and Winnie stood near the desk looking like they'd rather be at Guantanamo Bay. Yusuf Kassam, the chief of security, was also present, looking equally uncomfortable.

"Good afternoon, Mr. Mayor," I said as I walked up to the desk, without breaking my stride. I stopped behind one of the two high-backed guest chairs facing his desk and rested my hands on it.

"Morning," Ford said—still looking at his papers. Not looking at me. "Winnie has a letter for you. We've decided to go in a different direction."

"I understand," I said. "Thank you for the opportunity. It's been an honor and a privilege to be your chief of staff." I was conscious of the other people in the room. But I had to try one more time.

"My advice still stands," I said. "If you get help, you can make it through this thing. If you don't, well . . . you know."

"Thanks," he said, still shuffling his papers.

I stepped around the chair and stuck out my hand. He seemed genuinely surprised. But he looked up at me and shook my hand for the last time ever. His eyes met mine. "Good luck," I said.

I knew what was coming when I walked into the room, but still, a powerful wave of emotion rolled through me. We had come so far. Worked so hard. Gotten so much done. He'd had so much potential to do more. And he had fucked it all up. I was livid with him, for being so . . . to this day I don't know what the right words are. He was an idiot. He was ignorant. Refused to listen to reason. An addict. A son of a bitch. And he'd just fired me. Fuck.

I was pissed at myself, too, for running out of ideas. I just couldn't figure out how to steer the ship without bringing him back in line. I'd failed at that.

I could feel my eyes beginning to water as I turned to shake hands with Joe Pennachetti. He looked pale. I told him it had been a real pleasure working with him. We'd had disagreements, and a few heated arguments, but I had enormous respect for him. I knew we had routinely pushed him into difficult corners, and he'd always been a pro.

I also shook hands with Winnie and Yusuf, then walked out of Rob's office for the last time. Winnie and I went into my office, where we went through the usual administrative formalities. I turned in my BlackBerry and security pass. I cleared my cash and my fountain pen out of my desk and asked Winnie if she wanted me to go now, or if I could say goodbye to the staff. Politely, professionally, she said I should leave now. She said Yusuf would accompany me off the property and suggested I might want to take the stairs to avoid the media.

She looked mildly concerned when I said, "No thanks, I'll go out the front door." I'd arrived through the front door in 2010, and I was leaving with nothing to hide and nothing to be ashamed of.

\*\*\*

Yusuf Kassam, my security escort, was the sergeant at arms in Council and the most senior uniformed security officer at City Hall. He was always professional, discreet, and effective. I'd developed a friendship of sorts with him and his staff over the time I'd been at City Hall. We demanded a lot of them and the mayor had tried their patience many times, in some ways that I wasn't yet aware of.

He and I stepped out of the Protocol Lounge and into the glass-walled reception area. I could see the mass of media hovering outside. Like a school of sharks responding to a bucket of chum thrown into the water, they turned as one and approached the doors. I didn't think they realized what had just happened to me, but every day brought them a bevy of new stories to feed a growing international appetite for Ford's follies, so I knew they'd pounce as soon as we opened the doors. Tom Beyer, sitting at the reception desk, talking on his telephone headset to a constituent, looked at me curiously. I started to move toward him, to shake his hand and say goodbye, but could feel the camera lights outside the glass turning my way. "I'll call you later," I mouthed. Tom looked confused.

I opened the door and stepped into the maelstrom. A crush of reporters closed around me. They'd been camped there for days and the fug of unwashed bodies was thick in the air. The flashbulbs were blinding. The cameras were everywhere. Microphones reached out from every direction, and fifty voices at once began yelling questions. It was overwhelming. If I hadn't been through this gauntlet countless times before with the mayor, I think it would have stopped me in my tracks. But for both Yusuf and me, it had become freakishly routine. We didn't even slow down.

Ten paces to the elevator. Yusuf pressed the button. Overlapping voices behind us called out, "What's going on? Will the mayor make a statement? Are you resigning?"

"I don't have anything to say, guys," I answered. By some miracle, the elevator arrived the instant we reached it, and Yusuf and I stepped in. We could hear the whir of cameras clicking even after the doors closed.

Safely in the elevator, I could feel my emotions building. My vision blurred as my eyes watered. I tried to talk to Yusuf, to distract myself and maintain a professional air, but my voice caught in my throat. All I could say was "Take care of our boy. He's in trouble."

The elevator stopped at the ground floor to pick someone up, but Yusuf waved him off and we rode down to the basement in silence. As we stepped out of the elevator and walked down the short hallway toward the underground parking garage, we could hear thunderous footsteps coming down the stairs behind us. It sounded like a herd of elephants. They must have raced from the second floor, halfway around the rotunda, and down the stairs to the basement. Impressive speed, actually.

Yusuf, always protective, asked if I wanted to talk to them. I didn't. But it was too late. They were there. "Mark—are you still the chief of staff?" someone shouted.

"Did you resign?" another yelled.

My blood was in the water. I knew they would follow me all the way to the car if I didn't give them something to feed on. So I told Yusuf it was okay, stopped at the entrance to the garage, and turned to face them. Yusuf tucked himself alongside me to keep the horde from jostling.

More shouts: "Why are you leaving?" "Are you done as chief of staff?" "Why are you resigning?"

"I'll wait until you all get here," I said. "But I don't have much to say."

The camera lights were blinding and the tiny space between the stairs and the doorway to the underground parking garage quickly filled with bodies. They'd brought their odor with them. Microphones and iPhones reached out past the front row of reporters to record my every breath. The TV cameras loomed high overhead. Still photographers pushed to the front. The sound of footsteps on the stairs gradually diminished as the crowd thickened. One of the gallery reporters craned his neck to see if everyone was here, then turned to ask a question. A quick chorus of questions filled the air. I held up my hand.

I kept it straight. "It's been a great time working with you guys," I said. "It's been an honor and a privilege working with the staff in the mayor's office. They're outstanding professionals. They've done great work and I hope to work with them again sometime. That's all I really have to say."

"Why are you leaving?" they called out. "Why are you resigning, Mark?" "I am no longer the chief of staff," I said. "I did not resign."

I thanked them again and began walking to my car, flanked by Yusuf and another security guard who'd appeared out of nowhere. My "feed 'em then leave 'em" theory hadn't been as brilliant as I'd hoped. They were just hungrier now.

Another barrage of questions: Was I fired? Why won't the mayor listen to his staff? Have you tried? (That was a good one.)

"I've given the mayor my advice," I replied. "He can choose to take it or not take it."

They asked me, "What advice?" I said it was for Ford alone. My silence was mostly about managing my reputation. I was emotional and it wasn't the right time to say anything. Also, my advice to the mayor was no one else's business. Finally, if I walked out of the office and spilled my guts, I would never be a trusted advisor again.

They asked if Ford had a substance abuse problem, if I'd urged him to seek help. I had, of course, but I just repeated that my advice for the mayor was advice for the mayor. It was confidential.

"Did you ask Ford about the tape? What did he tell you?" they shouted. I didn't answer. It was important to me that people not see me as angry, disgruntled, or beaten up. Better for me to look like I was somehow still in control, although I hardly felt that way.

They asked if my leaving was a sign that Ford was at his end. I just said, "It's a sign that I'm leaving."

They asked if the mayor should step down, if I'd urged him to step down. They asked, "Did this come as a shock to you?" I answered that one: "No," I said. I'd definitely seen it coming, though that didn't make it feel any better.

I thanked the security guys for having my back. I unlocked my car and tossed my briefcase into the passenger's seat. I asked the press to step back, so I could pull out without killing anyone. They obliged, and I drove to the garage gate. The bar lifted. I waved at the camera and left the building.

I pulled over in the first spot I saw. I took off my suit jacket and hung it up in the back seat. Then I sat in the driver's seat for about five minutes, listening to my heart pound and willing it to slow down. Wow.

My iPhone pinged with notifications of tweets mentioning me. Dozens of them were already up, linking to the breaking news that I'd been fired. Or resigned. Nobody really knew why, but I was out. Again, I felt it was important that I not look beaten. *Toronto Sun* reporter Don Peat had tweeted a picture of me driving out of the parking lot in my red SUV. I retweeted it, saying, "Very happy now that I remembered to wash my car yesterday." When in doubt, gallows humor.

As a soldier I'd learned that even on the darkest days, humor was the one weapon that could keep the wolves at bay a little longer. And invariably, just a little longer would turn out to be long enough. That little truth is likely the reason there are no unfunny soldiers.

It was 2:00 p.m. and I was unemployed. *What the hell do I do now?* I wondered.

\*\*\*

I drove out of downtown and returned, by instinct, to the diner where I'd eaten just hours earlier. I felt like I'd shed a hundred pounds since then. I first went there before I was married, with my then-fiancée. We went again when she was pregnant and just weeks after Hunter, my first son, was born. Now divorced with two kids (Jonathan came along five years later), it had become even homier than my new apartment. I sat in a corner booth, by the window, with my back to the wall. I ordered my standby lunch. My phone rang.

It was my father, calling from British Columbia, on Canada's west coast, three time zones behind Toronto. He'd seen the news. Already. I looked at my watch. Less than thirty minutes had passed since I'd left City Hall.

My iPhone chimed all night on my bedside table. I'd started the day as chief of staff to the mayor of Toronto, with just over one thousand followers on Twitter. That night, another one thousand joined them. Reporters throughout Canada and the United States wanted interviews. At 5:00 a.m., morning radio producers started leaving pleading messages. I finally turned the phone off and caught two hours' sleep before I had to get the kids up for school—because really, what was there to say? They all wanted to know if the mayor of Toronto was a crack addict. They wanted to know if the video was real and if I knew where it was. They wanted to know everything that I didn't know or couldn't tell them. The Fords could afford to sue me, and my net worth was less than zero. I had no money in the bank, no assets to my name, about $50,000 in debt with collection agents and lawyers looking for my hide. And now I was unemployed with zero income and maybe about $15,000 coming in severance.

Still, as the morning wore on, I found myself being drawn into a world of narcissism. Twitter, news sites, TV and radio shows—they were all talking about me. It was impossible to not watch, read, or listen. I bought newspapers with me on the cover. Embarrassed, I slid them across the counter to the cashier as if they were porn. She scanned them without glancing at the picture or me. Her world wasn't centered around local politics. Around me. Patrons at my diner recognized me, though. The manager even bought my lunch. It was very kind. I had become a newly-famous failure.

It went on like this for a couple of weeks, me chasing an endless loop of myself around the Internet. It was awful. I'm one of those guys who get swallowed up in their work. Without a job, I had no life. I had known, intellectually, that as soon as I was gone, it would be like I never was. The city, the office, and the mayor would keep moving without me. I knew that people who once called regularly—to ask for advice, to go to lunch, to curry favor—would forget my number. I knew that invitations to events would cease, because they were always about inviting the office, not the person. I knew that it would be difficult to be on the outside looking at the world passing me by, rather than be at the center, helping shape the city. I knew it would hurt like hell. And it did.

# PART V | FROM THE SIDELINES: JUNE 2013–OCTOBER 2014

# 28 | The Office Disintegrates

I WAS FIRED on Thursday, but I remained connected to the mayor's office for some time. I had projects I needed to hand off to Earl, and as the situation in the office fell further into chaos, sources kept me informed about what was happening inside. That continued until Rob left office on November 30, 2014.

That first Friday, six members of Ford's executive committee signed a joint letter asking the mayor to address the media allegation that he had a substance abuse problem, and that there was a video of him smoking crack cocaine. The letter read in part, "We ask the mayor to definitively address the allegations before him. The allegations need to be addressed openly and transparently. We are encouraging the mayor to address this matter so that we can continue to focus on serving the people of Toronto."

The first signature belonged to Deputy Mayor Doug Holyday, perhaps the only member of Council whose opinion Rob truly respected. Later that afternoon, Holyday would stand beside Rob as he finally addressed the issue in a prepared statement delivered at a hastily arranged press conference. On Ford's other flank was his brother Doug, looking tired in an open-collared dress shirt under a dark business suit.

"I'd like to take this opportunity to address a number of issues that have circulated in the media over the last few days," Ford began, leaning heavily on the podium. His straight arms framed his chest, and his massive hands tightly gripped the podium's edges. "There has been a serious accusation from the *Toronto Star* that I use crack cocaine.

"I do not use crack cocaine, nor am I an addict of crack cocaine. As for a video, I cannot comment on a video that I have never seen or does not exist. It is most unfortunate, very unfortunate, that my colleagues and the great people of this city have been exposed to the fact that I have been judged by the media without any evidence."

A number of media members and legal pundits spent days trying to parse the phrase, "I do not use crack cocaine, nor am I an addict of crack cocaine." They theorized that Ford's use of present tense implied he may have used crack in the past, or that the specificity of the phrase "crack cocaine" left open the option that he had used other drugs, perhaps just regular cocaine.

To me, neither case seemed likely. Why would Ford craft a carefully constructed "non-lie" when it would be easier just to flat-out lie? I didn't believe the quasi-legal and entirely unnatural phrasing was an attempt to carefully sidestep the truth. I believe it was a combination of an amateur speechwriter, a man and his family in deep denial and trying to be their own legal counsel, and Rob simply misreading the script. With the walls collapsing around the mayor, the Fords retrenched into old habits. None of the remaining staff were trusted enough, so the family turned its back and relied on themselves.

Unfortunately for George Christopoulos and Isaac Ransom, Ford's press secretary and his deputy, many people assumed they'd crafted the speech and were developing Ford's messaging. But those people were wrong. The statement Rob read was not the one his communication advisors had prepared. It may have been written by his family, possibly Doug, or Doug's assistant Amin Massoudi. Diane Ford, Rob's mom, had often written speeches for him when he was a councillor; it was rumored that her fingerprints were on it. Certainly, the staff didn't know where the speech came from. They were frozen out.

Because they no longer had any ability to shape the messages coming out of Ford's mouth, and because they were unwilling to lie for him, both George and Isaac feared for their professional reputations. They quietly cleared out their offices over the weekend and resigned formally to Rob's new chief of staff, Earl, on Monday, May 27, 2013. They left letters in the office for the mayor.

The minute Rob heard the news, he stormed over to the Fish Bowl and inspected their offices himself, with Earl and City Hall security close on his heels. He couldn't believe they'd really gone. Maybe he even hoped to catch them, to have them shamefully marched out of the building, so he could regain the upper hand by embarrassing them. But he was robbed of his moment of revenge. They were gone.

I watched all of this on live TV from my apartment, glued to my screen, with Twitter running on my cell phone at the same time. A few days earlier, I was at the center of this maelstrom. By Monday, I had joined the voyeurs. It was an odd, out-of-body experience. I knew the characters intimately, but I no longer knew the script. I confess it made me feel good to watch them leave, as if I had somehow been vindicated, or that my absence made a difference.

While his two communication professionals were secretly clearing out their offices, Rob was on the air with Doug, hosting their weekly two-hour radio show on Toronto's Newstalk 1010. When a caller asked if it was Rob in the video, Rob doubled down on his message: "Number one, there is no video. You can't comment on something that doesn't exist." For months afterward, people would speculate about whether he had somehow secured the destruction of the video—having gone from "have never seen or does not exist" on Friday to "doesn't exist" on Sunday. I believed it was just Rob, painting an increasingly black-and-white world that he wanted to be true.

On Thursday, May 30, Ford's stalwart EA Kia Nejatian also resigned. He met privately with Earl, then left quietly out the side door, away from the cameras. Rob wasn't in.

When Ford arrived, he called all remaining staffers into his office, one by one, to ask their intentions—perhaps to intimidate them into declaring their loyalty to him. Brian Johnston—a policy and council liaison staffer who'd worked his way up from an entry-level job in the office, and earned Ford's trust by being ever cheerful and volunteering to manage the mayor's numerous football and hockey pools—admitted he wanted out. Ford told him to go immediately, and had him marched out of the building by security, with media in tow. The spectacle was a repeat of my departure, but Brian didn't even have a car to get into. He walked through Toronto's underground maze of shops to the subway. Watching his departure on live TV, I was afraid the pack of reporters would stay with him all the way home. Mercifully, they let him go at the exit from the underground parking garage.

The next day, a fifth staffer resigned, special assistant Michael Prempeh, who'd been baptized by fire at the CJPAC Action Party in March, where Sarah Thomson had accused Ford of groping her.

Watching all these departures from home, I was angry that none of the departing staffers were thanked for their service by a mayor who had leaned heavily on them, depended on their discretion and professionalism, and ultimately abused their loyalty. Earl couldn't, because it would have contravened Ford's instructions. So I tried—I tweeted farewells and plaudits for each of them as I learned of their departures. I felt some small satisfaction when the news media picked up my comments and included them in their stories.

But even losing half his staff in a matter of days didn't deter Ford—he flatly denied media suggestions of trouble in his office. "I've always said I would never stand in the way of an opportunity for any employee," he explained. It was a pretty thin spin, since Brian had been marched out like a criminal. Then again, Rob didn't literally stand in Brian's way on the way out.

Hurriedly, Ford hired a handful of novices—some from the football team he'd coached—whom he described to the media as "movers and shakers." Not only had none of them apparently worked in politics before, few might have ever held a full-time job before. I knew he liked their youth and inexperience, though. They were more likely to be compliant and not complain.

Ford rewarded staff that stuck by him with hefty raises of $5,000 per year. Critics described these increases as evidence that Ford had abandoned his "respect for taxpayers" mantra to save his own neck. As far as I was concerned, the raises were deserved. Ford had always woefully underpaid his staff, knowing they would work for the thrill and the experience. I had pushed, every day of my tenure as chief of staff, to boost salaries—especially when there was a disparity (there were a number of them) where individuals whom Ford liked were paid more, sometimes tens of thousands of dollars more, than others doing the same work. He'd always refused. So even if his motives were suspect, I applauded the result.

Earl Provost, though, had a mess on his hands and a moral struggle in his heart. On the one hand, he was finally the chief of staff to a major political leader—a role he'd been preparing for his entire life. On the other hand, he was receiving dozens of calls and emails from friends and supporters urging him to abandon ship. They felt his reputation would be destroyed if he stayed with the "crackhead" mayor. I felt for him. I knew what Earl's friends did not.

Earl is a professional political operative, loyal to a fault. Loyal to a mayor who'd sworn to him he hadn't smoked crack and there was no video. Loyal to the Office of the Mayor, which needed a steady hand at the helm regardless of the mayor's condition. Most of all, loyal to the young staffers who needed someone to lead and protect them. He was now their only protection from the rage and craziness that was Rob Ford.

It's a strange anomaly, difficult for anyone who's worked in other governments to understand, that the City of Toronto operates largely without a professional political staff. Councillors have one or two staffers who are, by and large, personal assistants, providing scheduling and customer service. This puts a heavy burden on the mayor's staff, who play an important role as a conduit between the politicians—all of them—and the civil service.

Even when Rob Ford was neutered, first by circumstance and later by Council, the Office of the Mayor continued to play a liaison role. Without a functioning mayor's office, the city doesn't run as it was designed. Earl knew that. Earl was stuck.

The second weekend after I was fired, I arranged with Earl to come into the office and clean out my stuff. He met me at the door (I'd been stripped of my security pass). My office was untouched. I spent an hour cleaning out my personal items and going through a few files that had been "chief of staff only."

From a locked drawer in my former desk, I handed Earl an innocuous manila folder. Letter-sized, it contained pages of information about every major drug and alcohol rehabilitation clinic we'd researched. It was a personal file—not something related to city business, not releasable under a Freedom of Information request. Amir Remtulla had given it to me; I'd added the names and numbers of some resources we'd used at one of the nearby clinics; and now I was passing it to Earl. It was his challenge now.

I also walked through an update on major files I'd been working. The sad reality was, with the mayor in the state he was in, and the office in the state it was in, there wasn't a lot of policy to do. Many of our goals during the first two years of Rob's term had been completed or launched. The rest were impossible, given the current situation. So Earl's job was essentially babysitting: protect the staff from the mayor; try to keep the mayor alive to the end of the term; don't let anyone do anything against the law; and see if he could rehabilitate Ford's image, if not the man himself, and position him for reelection in 2014. It was going to be a hell of a challenge. Better him than me, I thought.

But strangely, my concern for the mayor's policy agenda continued for a long time after I left. After the Ontario government had announced it was going ahead with a plan to extend Toronto's Bloor–Danforth subway line along an elevated platform to the Scarborough Town Centre in the city's eastern borough, I called Earl to remind him that the plan was virtually identical to what Rob had promised during the campaign. I didn't want Ford to react badly to this unexpected commitment from a government he'd often railed against. After my call, I noticed that Ford pointed to the Scarborough subway plan as a "promise kept." Don't ask me why I cared. It's politics.

# 29 | Ford's World Dissolves

TRUE TO FORM, at the beginning of June, Rob Ford was on his best behavior. Sure, he was dodging all press questions relating to the video or allegations of his drug and alcohol abuse. Yes, on June 1, a few hundred people protested in the public square outside City Hall, demanding he resign. But he was busy that day. To raise funds for Toronto's Hospital for Sick Children, he was serving ice cream at a Baskin-Robbins.

That same day, KiSS 92.5 FM radio host Maurie Sherman phoned Rob to ask why he was refusing to answer questions about the video. "I was told by my lawyers not to say a word and I'm listening to my lawyers," Ford explained. "So I'm moving on. I've had five, I think six, press conferences in the past week."

At the first of those press conferences, when the media threw out questions about his drug use, Ford looked at them, jaw clenched, and asked, "Anything else?" But there was nothing else the reporters—and everyone else in the city, the country, and the world—wanted to know; they had to keep asking drug-related questions. Ford calmly turned and walked out of the room.

As the week went on, Ford played his ground game. Returning phone calls. Home visits to constituents with problems. A new addition to his routine, though, was a daily media availability, often with something mundane to announce. At each press conference, he'd make a brief announcement; there would be a few questions about the announcement; then reporters would return to the drug questions.

"Anything else?" Ford would ask, repeatedly. Then he'd do his calm exit. Reporters were frustrated. Critics were furious. But after a few of these performances, the media stopped asking drug questions. Rob's strategy seemed to be working. Behind the scenes, however, rumors were swirling: A major police operation was looming. Ford might be arrested.

On June 14, Ford's "calm" strategy became moot. Toronto awoke to news that police had executed a massive pre-dawn raid, dubbed Project Traveller, to root out guns and gangs at thirty different locations in the city and across the province. Twenty-eight people had been arrested in the morning raids that concluded a year-long investigation producing a total of forty-three arrests and hundreds of charges. Forty firearms— none of them owned legally—were seized, along with $3 million worth of narcotics and $572,000 in cash. Forty search warrants had been issued; media lawyers went into immediate overdrive to have them released to the public.

One of the key locations of the raid was the high-rise housing complex at 320 Dixon Road in Rexdale—in Ward 2, represented by first Rob, then Doug Ford—the same address I had passed on to police as a possible location for the crack video. It was also where *Toronto Star* reporters Robyn Doolittle and Kevin Donovan had met the anonymous source who tried to sell them the crack video. The same source had provided them with the now-infamous photo of a grinning, very drunk-looking Rob Ford standing with his arms around three young, tough-looking men.

The three men in the photo were Anthony Smith, Muhammad Khattak, and Monir Kassim, and the photo was taken outside a blue-collar brick bungalow at 15 Windsor Road in North Etobicoke. The photo couldn't have been snapped long before Smith was shot dead and Khattak was wounded in a gangland-style shooting outside a Toronto nightclub on March 28, 2013. (It was Dave Price's tip that the crack video might have been the motive for Smith's murder that had led me to contact the police.) The two surviving men from the photo, Khattak (who had recovered) and Kassim, were arrested in the raids at 320 Dixon Road. Another link between Ford, the video, and alleged gangsters.

According to one newspaper, a woman at 320 Dixon Road had demanded to know why her building was being overrun by police. An anonymous police officer had told her, "You can blame your buddy Rob Ford for this."

\*\*\*

On Thursday, June 20, I received a call from Toronto police asking me to meet Detective Sergeant Gary Giroux and Detective Joyce Schertzer for a second interview at 3:00 p.m. at the headquarters for 51 Division, on Parliament Street in downtown Toronto. Again, I swore an oath, and we went over much of the same territory we'd covered in the first interview. But this time the police had many more detailed questions about the mayor, and the mayor's staff. I told the truth in both interviews, but was more forthcoming in the second; I felt more comfortable venturing beyond provable facts and discussing what I believed to be true, even if I couldn't prove it.

The police asked me about the house at 15 Windsor Road, which was the location of the photo of Ford with Smith, Khattak, and Kassim—although I didn't know that at the time. (Good investigative work by reporters uncovered that address later.) The house, apparently, is home to the Basso family, and the police asked me if I knew any of them. I did not. Many months later, I read a newspaper story mentioning one of the Basso sons, Enzo, worked at the Ford family business. The penny dropped: Enzo was the ever-grinning handyman Rob used to bellow for at Deco, whenever a menial task needed doing. Apparently his brother, Fabbio Basso, had gone to high school with Rob and now lived in the house at 15 Windsor Road with his mother and sister.

As I sat in my car replaying the interview in my head, I realized I was comfortable with everything I'd said in the interview—except for one thing I already regretted. The two detectives took a surprising interest in Tom Beyer, the receptionist in the mayor's office. They wanted to know why he always answered the mayor's phone. I explained that was his job. The cops probed further: Tom was one of the older staffers. He'd been with the mayor as long as I had. Why wasn't he in a more senior role? They seemed to think there was something nefarious about it. There wasn't. I pointed out that answering calls was a top priority for Rob Ford. I said that Tom was really good at dealing with the public, and he didn't really have the skills we needed elsewhere.

That bit about Tom's skills is the part I regret. It sounded like I meant he didn't have skills, which is not what I meant. I was concerned if Tom heard it out of context, he would be hurt by it. I really hoped my statement didn't become public.

\*\*\*

Rob Ford was able to stay out of trouble for almost two months. On August 9, he was scheduled to attend Taste of the Danforth, an annual three-day street festival that draws about 1.3 million visitors to restaurants on Danforth Avenue, Toronto's Greek business district. He was supposed to work the crowd—Mayor 101 stuff. Instead, he was recorded on a cell phone video, drunk.

Rob's staff was in position sometime after 7:30 p.m., waiting for him at one end of the two-kilometer-long street. Rob, who'd insisted on driving himself as usual, was a no-show. He wasn't answering his phone, either. Finally, around 9:30 p.m., he picked up. He'd just arrived, but at the wrong end of the street, was out walking on his own, and didn't know where he was. He sounded drunk.

Ford sightings started popping up on Twitter. Some of the staff made their way forward through the one hundred thousand-plus-person crowd toward him. Others hopped on the subway to get to the far end of the street; they'd work backward to find him.

Then a cell phone video was posted to the Internet. In near-real time, much of Toronto watched their mayor wander drunkenly through a sea of people. Some asked him to pose with them for selfies. Others openly mocked him. He didn't look bad, in a blue suit with a clean white shirt and tie. But in some of the videos he could be heard talking quickly and calling everyone "brother." I recognized the speech pattern from my own late-night interactions with him. By the time his staff, along with a handful of police, caught up to him and helped move him through the crowd, it was too late. Ford was a spectacle, again.

Once again councillors—including Jaye Robinson, a member of Ford's own executive committee—called for him to step down. Ford's response didn't ease their minds. "Did I have a couple of beers?" he said. "Absolutely, I had a couple of beers. But you know what, I had a good time."

***

By the end of August, the police investigation that spawned the June raids at 320 Dixon Road had grown tentacles that were beginning to reach Ford. A new investigation called Project Brazen II seemed to be centered on the mayor himself. The media, through the courts, was pressing the police to release information. It was only a matter of time before they would.

I, meanwhile, began appearing on Newstalk 1010 (the radio station that hosted Rob Ford's show) as a regular Thursday panelist on the morning show hosted by John Moore. It was awkward at times, since I was both in the news about Ford (whenever information was revealed about the time I worked for him) and commenting on it (as a freshly fired private citizen). But I dealt with it by avoiding involvement in the Ford story when possible and, when that wasn't possible, by answering those questions I could answer with honesty and by explaining why I couldn't answer when I had to protect a confidence.

At the end of October, the press won a major battle: A judge agreed that a 474-page document related to Project Brazen II—called an Information to Obtain Search Warrant, or ITO—was in the public interest. Brazen II was the project name for the Project Traveler spin-off investigation that centered on the mayor. The judge decreed that the document would be released on October 31, 2013, albeit with a large portion blacked out to protect evidence that could be used later at trial, or might reveal police techniques or sources.

As the documents were released online, I could feel the entire Canadian media establishment reading it along with me. I was in the Newstalk 1010 radio studio with John Tory (who would eventually succeed Ford as mayor) and a number of other pundits, waiting to comment on the release. Live on air, we were passing pages around as fast as the station's printers could pump them out.

It was soon clear that the police affidavit was more than just information to obtain a search warrant for a dry cleaner's premises suspected of fronting an illegal drug dealing operation—which is what it had ostensibly been submitted for. It was an extensive information dump of everything the Toronto Police Service knew about the shadowy activities of Rob Ford. It drew extensively from the interviews they'd conducted with me and the other mayoral staff, as well as from redacted sources of intelligence that apparently included wiretaps. It seemed that, unable to lay charges against the mayor, the police service had decided the next best thing was to throw Ford under the bus.

I was relieved to see most of my interview had not been included in the document, though some looked like it had been blacked out.

While everyone digested the ITO information, Toronto was also holding its breath, waiting for Police Chief Bill Blair to comment on the ITO at a press conference that afternoon. We expected the standard deflection, that he couldn't say anything at this time. Instead, he electrified us.

"As a result of the evidence that was seized on June 13th at the conclusion of Project Traveller, a number of electronic devices, computers, telephones, and hard drives were seized . . ." I looked at John Tory and mouthed, "They found the video!" He nodded.

Blair continued, ". . . we are now in possession of a recovered digital video file relevant to the investigations that have been conducted. That file contains video images which appear to be those images which were previously reported in the press with respect to events that took place we believe at a house on Windsor Road in Etobicoke . . . I think it's fair to say the mayor does appear in that video."

Boom!

Until that very moment, I still wasn't sure if there was a video of Rob Ford smoking crack, or if it would ever be found. But now it was real. And the police had it. Wow.

***

On November 3, the Sunday after Blair's bombshell announcement, Rob and Doug returned to Newstalk 1010 for their weekly show from 1:00–3:00 p.m. It was memorable for me, for three reasons.

First, Rob called on Blair to release the video to the public so everyone, including him, could see it. He also acknowledged the sections of the Project Brazen II ITO that included staff interviews related to St. Patrick's Day 2012. He admitted he'd gotten "a little out of control" and needed to "maybe slow down on my drinking."

Second, I had been tapped to guest-host the radio show that followed the Fords' for the entire month of November. This was my first day—and I hadn't seen Rob since he fired me. As I was prepping my show in one office, with the Fords in the studio just down the hall, my phone rang. It was Earl. He said Rob was in a bad mood. He didn't want Rob to see me; could I please stay out of sight?

My anxiety level, already high, rose higher. There was a six-minute gap between the Fords' show and mine. It took Rob and Doug a few minutes to exit the studio, and when they did, they had to pass the office I was in. I stood back from the door, where they wouldn't see me as they rushed by. They were moving fast. Just a blur of blue suits and the thump of footsteps falling hard on the industrial carpet.

When I thought they were safely past, I stepped into the narrow hallway—and was nearly bowled over by a stream of photographers and TV camera people trailing the Fords. I made it into the studio with just over sixty seconds to spare. I sat down in a chair still warm from Rob Ford's bulk. I pulled on a pair of headphones that had just come off his head. It was surreal.

The final reason that day was memorable: It turned out to be the Fords' last radio show. Following revelations Rob would make on November 5,

Newstalk 1010 decided to cancel the program. The next Sunday, I was asked to host three hours—two to cover the Fords' cancelled show, and the hour following. At the end of November, I took over Rob Ford's time slot permanently. Since the summer of 2014, the first hour of the show is simulcast on a number of BellMedia radio stations across Ontario. In homage to Rob Ford, however, I always start the second (Toronto-only) hour of the show with the same theme song: "Video Killed the Radio Star," by the Buggles. Call it karma.

***

On November 5, an impromptu media scrum outside Ford's office caught Earl Provost, Rob's chief of staff, off guard. As had become routine, a large media horde was camped outside the mayor's office when Ford arrived on the elevator. He pushed his way through the crowd to the glass door, then stopped. And turned around. Unaccompanied, unprompted, Rob faced the reporters and started to answer a question about the crack video. Then he stopped himself and said, "You guys have asked me a question . . . You asked me a question back in May and you can repeat that question." The reporters' faces quickly turn from bored to confused to thrilled as a Global News TV reporter shouted out, "Do you smoke crack cocaine?"

"Exactly," Ford said. "Yes, I have smoked crack cocaine . . . but no . . . do I? Am I an addict? No. Have I tried it? Um, probably in one of my drunken stupors, probably approximately about a year ago. I answered your question. You ask the question properly, I'll answer it."

Earl knew the mayor had wanted to make a statement to the press, but he'd planned for Ford to do it later, in the Protocol Lounge, after Earl had reviewed it. Instead, Rob just appeared in his doorway and blurted out the most memorable line of his, and possibly any politician's, career. (His career to that date that is. Proving that only Ford can top Ford, he would best his own record a few weeks later.)

Maybe the pressure had finally gotten to him. He was still Rob—he tried to sit on his high horse, lecturing to reporters that his dissembling was their fault for not asking the right question. I was shocked that he'd admitted it. But, watching him on TV, I could almost see the weight of the lie lifted from his shoulders as he said it. Maybe, just maybe, he'd finally get help.

Instead, forty-eight hours later on November 7, another bomb was dropped by the *Toronto Star*: they'd purchased a new video of an agitated

Rob Ford, seemingly intoxicated, pacing around in a blandly-decorated living/dining room, talking theatrically about killing someone. "I'm telling you, it's first-degree murder," he says in it.

A year after I was fired, I learned more about this video from two witnesses who were there, whose stories agree. Neither of them wishes to be named for fear of reprisal. The house where the video was taken belongs to one of Ford's assistant football coaches. Rob had arrived, unannounced and unexpected, and began inviting friends over for an impromptu party. (The homeowner wasn't happy about it.) He wears a blue long-sleeve shirt with the sleeves pushed up to the elbows. He looks red-faced and sweaty. At one point, he sits down at the family's piano and begins pounding the keys as if he can play. He can't. "Duh-nuh-nuh-nuhhh . . ." he bellows.

According to the witnesses, Ford had ranted about several people that evening. One, they say, was Justin Trudeau, the leader of the Liberal Party of Canada and son of (revered) former Prime Minister Pierre Elliott Trudeau. Ford, who despises Justin, railed on about a charity boxing match in which Trudeau bested Conservative party senator Patrick Brazeau.

Ford also talked about Mike Tyson that night. Ford wanted to meet Tyson, and one of the people at the party knew someone who knew Tyson's publicist. Ford, puffed up, kept asking who was tougher, him or Tyson?

As well, Ford talked about the wrestling stars Hulk Hogan and the Iron Sheik. At one point, Ford wanted to phone the Iron Sheik and invite him to the party.

(Weirdly, on August 23, 2013, Ford actually did arm-wrestle Hulk Hogan in a publicity stunt for the opening of Fan Expo Canada. A year later, on September 9, 2014—a month and a half before the 2014 election, and just three days before Rob withdrew from the race to battle cancer— Mike Tyson visited Ford in his office at City Hall and endorsed him to the hovering media as "the best mayor in Toronto's history." You can't make this stuff up.)

According to my sources, the November 7 video shows an almost incoherent and violently aggressive Rob Ford role-playing an imaginary encounter with Trudeau and Tyson and/or Hogan. (At the point the video is recorded, it's not clear that Ford himself knows who he's talking about. The witnesses don't agree.) He's standing up, weight shifting from left foot to right. His arms are bent, elbows pinned to his sides. He looks like a T. rex. When he's not shoving his sleeves higher up his arms and scratching himself, his hands wave and clap frantically. For seventy-seven seconds, he speaks near-gibberish.

"Cause I'm gonna kill that fucking guy," Ford says. "I'm telling you, it's first-degree murder." (In the background, someone yells, "Mike Tyson!")

"But I'll fight him," Ford continues. ". . . No holds barred, brother. He dies or I die, brother . . . I'm telling you . . . no . . . Brother, you've never seen me fucking go . . . When he's down I'll rip his fucking throat out. I'll poke his eyes out . . . I'll . . . fuck when he's dead, oh, I'll make sure that motherfucker's dead. I need fucking ten minutes to make sure he's dead."

The Rob Ford we see in this video is the same Rob Ford who wanted to smoke dope in City Hall on St. Patrick's Day 2012, then attacked two members of his own staff, the same Rob Ford who appalled attendees of the Garrison Ball in February 2013. This Rob Ford is scary.

At one point, my sources told me, Rob called Bruno—whom I'd seen in Ford's Cadillac at the Garrison Ball—to come over to the house. When Bruno arrived at the door, Rob answered it—and, it's alleged, cold-cocked Bruno in the face, knocking him to the ground. Rob then allegedly grabbed him and dragged him into the house and through the living room. All hail the chief.

\*\*\*

On November 13, the court cleared most of the blacked-out sections of the Project Brazen II ITO for release to the media. The night before, I began to worry that my statement would be included. I called Detective Sergeant Giroux and left a voicemail asking if he could tell me what parts, if any, of my statement was included. He never responded.

In the morning, to my dismay, I read that I was all over the ITO. I got angry. Angrier than I'd been in years. Angry at Ford. Angry at the police. Angry at myself for talking to the police and encouraging my staff to do so too. Most of my interview was completely irrelevant to the purpose of the ITO. It was confidential information. Our opinions. The same can be said for the interviews of my former staff. The police were dumping information that could never be used in court, simply to screw over Rob Ford. And in the process, we were getting screwed too.

Just as I was starting to get my life back together, I felt Rob Ford sucking me back into the muck. My voicemail filled up within fifteen minutes of the document being released. I turned the phone off. I spent the day curled up on my sofa, ignoring the outside world.

The next day, I realized that if I put something on the record in selected media appearances, I could thereafter ignore other requests. I accepted invitations to speak on the record to Newstalk 1010 as well as CP24 and CBC News Network.

All three posed similar questions. They asked me to comment on details of my statement to the police. I answered that I spoke to the police under oath and in confidence, that everything I'd told them was true, and that much of what I'd said—though out of context and incomplete—was exposed in the ITO. However, I wasn't going to reiterate it for the media. They could read it themselves and I would keep my counsel.

They asked if I thought Rob was a drug addict. I deflected the question by saying that it didn't matter what I thought—it only mattered what Rob thought. I wished him well. They asked what my advice for him would be, and I answered, honestly, that I hoped he would take the weekend, put aside his responsibilities as mayor, think about his kids, his family, and his health, and decide what was best for them. Then we talked about Rob's chances for reelection and the upcoming campaign, safer ground for me to provide expert commentary.

I hated every minute of it.

But the newly released ITO did have a positive effect. Reading it, I could begin to fill in some of the empty spaces in the puzzle that had been the last two years of my life. For example, on the night Gawker broke the crack video story, I spoke to Rob twice. Right after I told him about the video, he'd hung up the phone with me and called his friend Sandro Lisi, who'd driven him to both the Garrison Ball and the CJPAC event. According to the ITO, which included telephone logs of Lisi's phone, Sandro had then immediately called the guy who just happened to have offered the video for sale to Gawker and the *Toronto Star*.

Dave Price had told me Anthony Smith, the deceased gang member in the photo with Ford, may have been murdered over the crack video. He'd gotten that information from his mysterious source, he said. But reading the ITO, I realized one had nothing to do with the other. The police information in the document stated that this theory had been disproven by evidence that remained blacked out. That was a relief.

***

On November 14, 2013, I'd just finished a roundtable panel on Newstalk 1010 and was talking with Britt Aharoni, one of the senior producers at the station, when someone yelled from the newsroom at me, "Hey, Mark, you're being sued!" We walked into the room just in time to watch Rob

Ford, sporting his personalized "Mayor Ford" Toronto Argonauts football team jersey, announce outside his office—on live TV—that the ITO contained outright lies and he would be suing me and a number of the other staffers interviewed by police. He then paused and turned back to the cameras before uttering what became his most jaw-dropping comment in a long list of jaw-droppers.

"Oh, and Olivia Gondek," he added, referring to the staffer he'd sexually harassed in his office on St. Patrick's Day 2012. "It said I want to eat her pussy. I've never said that in my life to her. I would never do that. I'm happily married. I've got more than enough to eat at home."

Britt squealed and shoved me hard into the wall with a "Get out!" that would do Elaine Benes of *Seinfeld* proud. Otherwise, there was a stunned silence in the newsroom as everyone else tried to process the words that had just issued from Mayor Rob Ford's mouth. Like everyone, CP24 reporter Katie Simpson was clearly stunned by what had just happened, but she had to deal with a live TV feed.

"I know we're live right now, but I don't know if we can . . . I, uh . . . Mayor Ford speaking as Mayor Ford does . . . very plainly," Simpson said. "As he said in council yesterday, he 'effed up,' and now using language that I don't think we can broadcast on TV, but we just broadcast that on TV . . ." She then gamely wrapped up and threw to her newsroom ". . . because I don't think there are words for what just happened." Later that night on *The Daily Show*, Jon Stewart would play the tape and then reel back in his chair, repeatedly yelling, "What?! What?!"

Through it all, I guess my expression stayed neutral because Britt, incredulous, asked me, "How can you not react to that?"

"It's Rob," I replied, shrugging. "It's what he does." After three years of it, I was finally immune.

\*\*\*

After that, there really was no going forward with Rob. Councillors lined up to be interviewed about how they couldn't get anything done while Ford remained in office. (Behind the scenes, of course, the city continued to function—water kept flowing; sewage continued to be treated; garbage got picked up; building permits were issued; the police, fire, and ambulance corps responded to calls as usual—but that story wasn't sexy.) Legally, the councillors were in a quandary. Toronto has no process of impeachment for mayors. Unless one quits or dies, or is convicted of a serious offense, he or she will remain mayor and head of Council until the term expires. But the premier of Ontario announced that her government was prepared to intervene in the Ford situation if Toronto's Council requested it.

Things never reached that point. Instead, councillors called a series of special meetings to strip Ford of all the mayoral powers that are delegated by Council. (For example, they voted to "undelegate" his power to make appointments.) Council assigned the stripped-away powers to the deputy mayor, Councillor Norm Kelly. They also voted to slash Ford's budget, leaving him enough money for only three or four staffers; the rest were transferred, along with the bulk of the mayor's budget, to Kelly. Rob remained mayor, but in name only.

I reached out to Kelly to offer advice; we'd spoke on the phone a few times and had a couple of lunches. In our first call, he told me the staff he'd inherited didn't seem to be performing well, and that he couldn't reach them after hours. I explained why: They likely had something akin to PTSD. For the past two years, they'd been hostage to Ford. They were exhausted, physically and emotionally. Now that they felt "safe," they probably passed out cold every night. I suggested that if he treated them with kid gloves for a few days, they'd come around. I also suggested he thank them from time to time. Ford had never done that. When Kelly did, they responded quickly to his much-different leadership style.

In December, Canada's media voted Rob Ford the Newsmaker of the Year. It was the least surprising story of his term.

# 30 | The Comeback?

ON JANUARY 2, 2014, Rob Ford was first in line when the city's elections office opened on the first working day of the year to register candidates for the election to be held ten months later on October 27. Throughout his term as mayor, whenever he was asked if he would run for reelection, Ford had always said the same thing: he'd be first to register when the time came. And he was—the campaign was on.

To the world, Ford was a laughingstock—at best, a punch line; at worst, a drug addict who associated with known criminal gangs and, possibly, murderers. He was the subject of an ongoing police investigation. The courts and a sheaf of Freedom of Information requests were unearthing a steady drip of embarrassing secrets about his behavior. He had been humiliated by a City Council that had stripped him of most of his powers. He was the world's most notorious mayor but, by God, he was running for reelection. And he was favored by many to win.

Even at their mayor's lowest, the hard-core citizens of Ford Nation had not turned their back on him. He might be a drug addict, but he was their drug addict. Stripped of most of his powers as mayor, he was still playing his ground game: returning scores of telephone calls every day, visiting constituents at their homes, and touring low-income housing complexes across the city.

Plus, Mother Nature had delivered an unexpected Christmas present to Rob in late December. A major winter ice storm had knocked out power to much of the city, leaving thousands of residents in the dark and cold for days—and for some, weeks. It was terrible news for the citizens of Toronto, but good fortune for a hands-on mayor looking to prove himself in a crisis. There's not much for a mayor to do in a disaster except show up, appear in control, sound calm, and stay out of the way of the people doing the actual work. Rob did it well.

It also helped that Deputy Mayor Norm Kelly, who was officially overseeing the city's response to the crisis, couldn't match Ford on showmanship. Once the cleanup was underway, he decamped to Florida for a brief, long-planned vacation. Ford swooped in, and his political capital went up.

For his reelection bid, Ford didn't seem to have a professional campaign team. Doug was his campaign manager. He didn't seem to think he needed more. His early challengers were a motley lot: a self-admitted policy wonk (David Soknacki) and Rob's sometime nemesis on Council (Karen Stintz). Neither were serious contenders. But soon a solid but uninspiring member of Parliament for the New Democratic Party (Olivia Chow, who was still benefitting from the public's affection for her late husband, Jack Layton, a former federal NDP leader) and a Newstalk 1010 radio personality (John Tory, who had run for mayor and lost in 2003) made it an interesting race.

None of them inspired much love, even among their supporters. Rob had a real advantage: Despite his personal woes, he was running on a fairly solid record. Circus aside, the Ford years had been good for most Torontonians' pocketbooks.

So when another video of a drunken Rob Ford surfaced in late January, Ford Nation shrugged it off. This time he was in a dingy restaurant called Steak Queen, in the city's low-income northwest corner. He was with his friend Sandro Lisi, and—inexplicably—he was speaking in a rapid, often crass Jamaican patois. But instead of turning their backs on Ford, his supporters blamed the media for picking on him.

There was a running battle of words between the Fords and Toronto's police chief, with Doug accusing Chief Bill Blair of conducting a politically motivated witch hunt against the mayor. Rob piled on, daring the chief to arrest him—in language eerily similar to what he'd said in Florida while being arrested for DUI in 1999. Back then, it was "Go ahead. Take me to jail." In 2014, Rob said, "If he's going to arrest me, arrest me." Ford Nation ate it up.

And when, on a family trip to Vancouver in February, Rob was cited for jaywalking outside his hotel, and then spent the night in a local pub, carousing with the locals; when he purportedly spent an hour in the bathroom there and emerged speaking rapidly and incoherently; when he stayed well past closing time—well, that was just Ford business as usual. "What he does on his time off is his business" was a common refrain inside Ford Nation.

For months, late-night comedians around the world were getting laughs just by saying, "Today, Rob Ford . . ." He was the infamous Crack

Mayor of Toronto. But in March, Jimmy Kimmel invited Ford himself to be a guest on his ABC show. Incredibly, Rob accepted. He wore a black suit, a black shirt, and a fire-engine red tie. Kimmel's opening question— "Why are you dressed like a magician?"—set the tone. He mocked Ford mercilessly, disguising it as affection. At one point, he even daubed the sweat off Ford's face. Most people watching squirmed for him, and most people would have been humiliated. But Rob seemed to enjoy it. The shy guy who avoided the spotlight was suddenly a globe-trotting celebrity. If he was a joke, he was determined to be in on it.

\*\*\*

In the first televised mayoral debate, on March 26, 2014, Ford easily bested the other four candidates. He had simple messages, and he stuck to them. But the glow didn't last. On April 30, a second video of him smoking crack cocaine surfaced. This time, he was in the basement of his sister, Kathy Ford. (She later confirmed to police that it was Rob, and it was crack.) Even Rob Ford had a last straw, and this was it.

The next day, May 1, Rob got into a car driven by his nephew Michael Ford and went to rehab. Finally. He intended to go to a facility in Chicago, but ended up back in Canada. The media speculated he'd been turned back at O'Hare Airport because of his drug use confessions, but nothing was ever confirmed. Back in Ontario, he checked into the GreeneStone clinic, located in cottage country a few hours north of Toronto. Rumors abounded: He wasn't really in rehab. He was seeing prostitutes. He was playing golf. But he almost certainly was there, although not in a fully sequestered program. On June 30, tanned, he returned to Toronto and resumed his campaign.

"He's had a real eye-opener on life and self and things that may have triggered his addiction before," big brother Doug told CBC News. (I think it was the first time Doug had used the word "addiction.") "It's going to be a new Rob Ford."

Rob's first post-rehab words to the public were cloaked in therapy-speak. "For a long, long time, I resisted the idea of getting help," he told reporters. "I was in complete denial. I had become my own worst enemy . . . I can proudly say I have begun the process of taking control of my life." Polls immediately put him in second place in the mayor's race, behind Olivia Chow, but running strongly.

\*\*\*

I'm not sure how many political lives Rob Ford has, but he's used up more than a cat's share. In September, however, he arrived at what may be his final one. On the 10th, the day after boxer Mike Tyson endorsed him as Toronto's best mayor ever, Twitter was alive with reports that Rob had checked into Humber River Regional Hospital, not far from his home.

He'd been to that hospital before. The last time, in August 2012, he was admitted for a breathing ailment that was officially diagnosed as asthma-related, but which his staff suspected was related to his substance abuse. Back then, I'd brought him a letter to sign, appointing Norm Kelly as acting deputy mayor in the event that Rob was incapacitated. (Deputy Mayor Doug Holyday was out of town.) Rob signed it while sitting up in his hospital bed, wearing a blue patient's gown. I photographed him doing it, then had George tweet the photo to show Toronto that Rob was working hard, even in hospital.

This latest hospital visit was graver. I first heard it through my grapevine, and the media confirmed it: Rob Ford had a large tumor in his abdomen, almost certainly cancerous. The prognosis was not good.

Two days later, September 12, was the deadline for nominations in October's mayoral election—the last day to add a name to, or remove one from, the ballot. Rob was still in the hospital, but pundits, including me, were predicting that he'd continue to run. So we were stunned to hear that three things had happened in well-coordinated succession.

First, Rob's nephew Michael, who had registered to run for Rob's old council seat in Ward 2, slipped unnoticed into the elections office and withdrew from the race; he filed to run for school board trustee instead. Then Rob's campaign agent filed papers withdrawing Ford from the mayoral race, and filed papers for him to run in the Ward 2 council race. Finally, Doug Ford registered to run for mayor. There was a brief moment of uncertainty because Doug didn't have the full registration fee on him: the cost to register for the mayoral race is $200, not the $100 that it costs to register for a council race. Fortunately, John Nunziata, a friend who was also running for council, was in the elections office, and lent Doug the extra $100.

The Fords, true to form, had closed ranks. On my radio show, I joked that they'd pulled off "a three-Ford monte." But privately I believed there was only one possible reason Rob Ford would take his name off the mayor's ballot: he was dying.

Over that weekend, I left a number of voicemail and text messages for Doug. On Sunday evening I connected with him—the first time I'd spoken to him since I was fired. He told me Rob's cancer was bad. Very bad. I asked if I could visit, but he told me Rob couldn't have visitors yet. He said when Rob was ready, I was welcome.

Honestly, I wasn't sure I wanted to visit him. I didn't know what I wanted to say. I didn't know if I was ready to pretend he hadn't screwed me over. But, I thought, he's dying. As much as I wanted to hate Rob, the truth was I didn't. Part of me still felt sorry for him. The Ford magic is strong. Making peace with a dying foe seemed the right thing to do.

On September 17, in a press conference at Toronto's Mount Sinai Hospital, Dr. Zane Cohen announced that Rob's was a "difficult and very rare type of tumor." It was a malignant liposarcoma, four inches in diameter, in his abdomen—and it was aggressive. Rob began chemotherapy immediately and underwent a number of rounds. His skin looked gray and he was visibly weak when he voted in the October 2014 advance polls, but his strength seemed to return as he finished chemo.

As of this writing, Rob has completed chemo, along with follow-up radiation, and on May 11, 2015, underwent extensive surgery to remove the tumor. After convalescing in hospital for two weeks, he was released to recuperate at home. Instead, he went directly to City Hall to check in with his office and to speak with the media, appearing on TV news in a bright red T-shirt, black shorts, and bedroom slippers.

"I was going crazy. I wanted to come down and make couple of calls and touch base with a couple of people."

He's back. And he's the same. Always spoiling for a fight with the new mayor, he shows up at City Council meetings seemingly looking for opportunities to annoy and pester Mayor John Tory. And to remind Ford Nation that Tory and his new City Council aren't going to look after their hard-earned pennies without Rob Ford on hand to make them.

\*\*\*

*October 27, 2014*

For me, 2014's mayoral election day started with a 7:45 a.m. roundtable discussion at Newstalk 1010. I predicted John Tory would win, but Doug Ford would finish surprisingly strong. However, election chatter was eclipsed by a scandal that, this time at least, had nothing to do with Rob Ford. CBC radio host Jian Ghomeshi, who was popular across Canada and the United States for his love of the arts and his liberalism, had been accused of sexually assaulting a number of women. In a rambling Facebook post, he defended his sex practices as consensual, but CBC wasn't buying it; they'd fired him. The crack stories were old news; stolid, well-behaved Toronto had a sex scandal. And not just any kind of sex, but *kinky* sex. Where was this kind of news when I was struggling to keep Rob's misdemeanors off the front page?

It was strange for me to watch Doug Ford go through the standard election day rituals—breakfast with supporters, then a visit to the polling station accompanied by his wife Karla. He'd run a short, sharp campaign. Like Rob in his aborted reelection effort, Doug hadn't built a professional campaign team. He relied on Ford Nation to turn out in strength for him of their own accord. He'd stunned the pundits, and even surprised me, in his first debate as a candidate, when he caught the ever-polished and silver-tongued John Tory flat-footed with some off-the-cuff questions Tory couldn't answer. Doug Ford was a serious contender.

The switcheroo, I suspect, had been an eye-opener for the Fords. Doug had always acted as if he'd been elected mayor alongside Rob in 2010. They behaved as if the political offices they'd won were family property—to be inherited by a Ford-approved heir. It seems when Doug replaced Rob on the mayor's ticket, he assumed he'd inherit Rob's campaign office and bank account. But election laws don't work that way. The shocking reality was, as far as the law was concerned, Rob and Doug Ford were two different people.

Would the Nation see it that way too? Would Doug Ford suffer because he didn't have Rob's political experience and natural charisma? Or could he profit from the fact that many people had assumed he was the brains of the Ford operation, without the drugs?

Deciding how to vote was a challenge. I knew Doug Ford better than most people casting ballots that day. I felt that his platform ideas—keep costs down, focus on rapid transit—made the most sense. But I knew that Doug would not be able to lead Council better than his brother had. Not yet, anyway.

Doug was no Rob. When sober, Rob was able to get things done at City Hall. He relied heavily on staff and other councillors to do the heavy lifting, yes—but he was willing to stand up in a corner of the council chamber, in front of the media, and take body blow after bruising blow. Even—maybe especially—if he knew ahead of time that he'd be the only one on his side of the vote, he'd stuck to his guns until his opponents had exhausted themselves, then shrugged his shoulders and continued on. It was political rope-a-dope that would make Muhammad Ali proud. Sober Rob Ford infuriated all of his opponents and many of his allies. But his inherent likeability was almost inescapable.

Doug, on the other hand, didn't mind having enemies. He liked fighting, maybe even more than he liked winning. Given a choice between fighting an impossible battle at City Hall or sidestepping the fray and achieving victory in a less confrontational way, he usually chose the fight. I didn't believe he'd be able to rally Council around him. A Doug Ford administration seemed likely to be hung from the get-go.

On the other hand, John Tory personified everything Toronto wanted in a mayor. He was handsome, articulate, well-dressed, thoughtful, positive, never openly mean-spirited—and sane, which meant a lot to Torontonians exhausted and embarrassed by Ford. Also, he didn't smoke crack. But I feared that his promise of consensus on Council would come at a cost—quid pro quo votes that would hurt taxpayers. My struggle, I know, was shared by thousands of small "c" conservatives across the city. In the end, though, it was clear to most that John Tory was better equipped to lead Toronto.

The whole city turned out to vote in the election, which was broadly accepted as a referendum on Rob Ford. In 2010, just over 50 percent of eligible voters had cast ballots in the Toronto mayor's race. That had been a record turnout, but it was shattered in 2014. This time, a stunning 64 percent of eligible voters turned up, more than 980,000 of them.

At 8:00 p.m. the polls closed. Twelve minutes later, John Tory was declared Toronto's sixty-fifth mayor. The Ford era was over. (At least for now.) In absolute numbers, Tory earned more votes than Rob Ford had four years prior, though his popular vote, 40.3 percent, was lower than Ford's 47.1 percent.

Ward 2 overwhelmingly reelected Rob Ford as their city councillor, with over 59 percent of the vote—though he didn't even campaign. In his victory speech carried live on TV, Rob vowed that the Ford family would "never, ever, ever give up," and that he would definitely be running for mayor in 2018. Once again, the scrapper from Etobicoke was dreaming big about becoming the next mayor of North America's fourth-largest city.

*\*\**

What legacy did Rob Ford leave as mayor of Toronto? Is it the end of the $60 vehicle registration tax, or the fact the Toronto Transit Commission is now a designated essential service—an all but irreversible designation? Is it the practice of completing Toronto budgets two months sooner than they were before, giving Council more control over spending and saving taxpayer dollars? Will it be the Scarborough Subway—if that's ever completed? Perhaps it's a renewed sense of what Toronto is and isn't. Ford wasn't old guard, dignified, WASPy, dull. Neither is Toronto, not anymore.

Given his health, it seems unlikely Rob will run for mayor in 2018. It seems unimaginable that he could win. For those two reasons alone, I wouldn't bet against him.

# 31 | Manifest Ford

Way back in the first month of the campaign, as Rob and I were driving home after a debate, I pointed out something I wanted him to change. He'd said the same thing at three different events, and it was problematic. The media hadn't reported it yet, and I didn't want them to.

"There's a line you say a lot, that I want you to stop saying," I told him. "I know what you mean, but it sounds bad. When you're talking about your father and why you got into politics, why you want to be mayor, you say, 'Many are called, but few are chosen.'"

"What's wrong with that?" Ford asked.

Rob and I talked often back then about why he got into politics. He'd told me many times about driving around with his father when Doug Sr. was a provincial politician. When Doug Sr.'s constituents had problems, he'd go directly to their doors to help them. That was how you sold labels, Rob's father taught him, and that was how you served constituents. Customer service. At their doorstep.

Doug Sr. had explained to young Rob that the Fords had been lucky. He hadn't been born with much, but he'd been blessed with an opportunity to succeed. Most people didn't get that, and that's why the Ford family had to give back to their community. And then he'd say it: "Many people were called, but few were chosen."

To Rob, that sentence meant that many people were called to serve their community, but few were chosen to lead. The Ford family had been chosen to lead. He had been chosen. Public service wasn't an option, for him or his family. It was their duty. It was their destiny.

I explained to Rob that, since the phrase originated in the Bible, people to whom he said it might assume he believed he was God's choice to be their mayor. (Which is, of course, exactly what I believe it meant to him.) They might think that was arrogant.

"Oh," he grunted. He never said it again.

***

During Rob's campaign, Doug Ford often seemed to think he too was running for mayor. He would introduce Rob at campaign events, often speaking longer than Rob did, firing up the crowd with what "we" will do when he and Rob run City Hall. He was nominally the campaign manager, but spoke often to the media—something good campaign managers rarely do. Late in August, just before the September 10, 2010, cutoff for nominations, he decided he'd run in Ward 2 for Rob's Council seat. He felt he needed to be in City Hall to help his brother muscle through "their" agenda.

Naturally, this was a point of contention between Doug and Nick, who was Rob's actual campaign manager. Nick and Doug argued regularly when Doug overshadowed his brother. I remember a few of those disagreements. We tried to explain that people were voting for Rob, so it was Rob who needed to shine.

"That's where you're wrong, buddy," Doug said, his face glowing red with anger. "People are voting for the Ford family. That's what they want."

Once Rob was elected, Doug made it clear that he expected to be named deputy mayor. When that didn't happen, and he was excluded entirely from the executive committee as the transition team awarded choice appointments in order to buy support and form a coalition, I suspect Doug's ego was a bit bruised. Yet he continued to act as if "we" were mayor. He wanted that private doorway installed between his councillor's office and the mayor's office. Rob did not agree. He wanted some space from his older brother. But as I said, he rarely confronted Doug on issues unless his back was to the wall.

Nick and I argued the door would make Rob look weak, as if he needed his older brother around to make decisions. Doug didn't see it that way. I pointed out that, because the door led into the boardroom, it would be a problem during meetings. It would also piss off the other councillors who, obviously, wouldn't have their own private door into the mayor's boardroom. Finally, I asked what would happen in the future, when there was a different mayor and councillor from Ward 2? Would it be sealed off? How much would that cost? All I got was blank stares from both Doug and Rob, as if they couldn't imagine a future where there wouldn't be a Ford on both sides of that door.

It turned out that unionized city workers would have to install the door, at an exorbitant cost. That provided Rob with a way out. He didn't approve the expense. Doug was disappointed, but couldn't argue the point. Respect for taxpayers.

According to Nick, in the last days of the campaign, Doug had asked Nick what would happen if Rob died in office. Doug thought he should replace him. I looked at Nick, stunned. "Are you serious?" Perhaps Doug was joking, but it rang true. If the Ford family had been elected mayor, as Doug believed, naturally the throne would pass to family if Rob died.

Early in Rob's term of office, it became clear that Doug was bored with his councillor duties and aspired to higher office. The Progressive Conservative Party of Ontario (the party for whom Doug Ford Sr. had been a backbencher) was at this time led by Tim Hudak, a tall, gangly, and uncomfortable-looking politician from Niagara who'd been a minor cabinet minister in the last PC government. In the 2011 provincial election, which many people believed would be a "gimme" for him and his party, the PC Party lost badly, and the knives were out for Hudak's job.

Doug Ford held one of the knives. He very much wanted to be the leader of his father's old political party, and to one-up both his dad and his younger brother by becoming premier of Ontario.

This one-upmanship seemed to drive both brothers. I often felt like Rob and Doug were in a race to capture the flag their father had planted by being a member of provincial parliament. By becoming mayor of Canada's largest city, Rob had clearly outstripped his father's political importance. For Doug to best Rob, he would have to become, at the very least, a provincial cabinet minister. Being premier of the province, however, would be a clear win. Then the only way Rob could top Premier Doug would be to become prime minister of Canada.

Which is exactly what Rob intended to become.

In a newspaper interview at the dawn of his political career, Rob confessed that his ultimate goal was to become prime minister. Early in his 2010 mayoral campaign, he said the same thing. Both Nick and I jumped on him and told him to stop talking about future goals, and to focus, humbly, on winning the support of the people of Toronto as mayor. But his ambition didn't go away.

In August 2012, Rob decided to take a family vacation to Alberta— Canada's conservative heartland and the epicenter of its oil industry. If Canada has a Texas, Alberta is it. Rob had never traveled out west. In fact, he'd never traveled much at all. He'd been to Guadalajara in 2011, after considerable coercion, to attend the Pan Am Games as the mayor of the next host city. He'd travelled to Florida often, where his family owned some condos, and to Chicago, where the family business had an office. He'd been to China once, with his father on Deco business, when he was younger. Other than that, he spent his life in and around Toronto.

The Alberta trip was purely recreational: Rob wanted to see a Canadian Football League game in Edmonton and Calgary, the two Alberta cities with franchises. We spoke with the mayors' offices in both cities to let them know Rob was coming, since he generates a media whirlwind wherever he goes. The mayors of both cities were planning to be away on holidays at the time of Rob's visit, so we briefed Rob on that. He wasn't concerned. It was a family trip. With football.

Of course, as soon as the media learned Rob was going to Alberta, they asked him why. He told them, off the cuff, that it was a "working vacation." He has a compulsive need to be thought of as always working. Once he was in Edmonton, he decided on the spur of the moment to visit the mayor—just to prove he was working. Of course, the mayor wasn't in; we'd told Rob that a dozen times. Nevertheless, he barged unannounced into Edmonton City Hall, after bumming a ride with a citizen who found him looking lost on a side street in the city's downtown. Not surprisingly, great embarrassment ensued, followed by unnecessary headlines.

Then he pulled the same stunt in Calgary.

Rob loved Alberta. He gushed about it. He loved it so much, he insisted on writing an open letter to the province to be sent to the major newspapers in Alberta, thanking the people for their hospitality and friendliness. I saw the draft letter written by Isaac Ransom, who was then our issues management specialist, and went in to speak with Rob about it.

"Why are you doing this?" I asked him.

"Don't worry about it," Rob said.

"I am worried about it," I explained. "I'm your chief of staff, I'm worried about everything you do and how it affects our ability to get things done, your chances for reelection, everything. I don't understand this. It will just highlight your trip and the fact that you tried to visit people you knew weren't there. It's another day of negative headlines we don't need. It doesn't make sense to me."

"It's fine."

"Rob, I don't understand this. If there's more to the story that I don't know, tell me and I'll shut up. But if there's nothing else than what I see, this is a bad idea."

Rob explained there was more to the story, but he wasn't comfortable telling me the details. Visiting Alberta was part of a bigger plan: He wanted to build Ford Nation across Canada. I took the letter back to Ransom and suggested some edits. It went out the same day.

The next year, after I was fired, Rob went to Vancouver on a similar trip. It earned him even more notoriety. He was ticketed by police for jaywalking and drinking well after closing time in a pub full of people. Expanding Ford Nation.

Meanwhile, Doug Ford was jockeying to run in the 2014 provincial election, and was considered a star candidate by the Progressive Conservative Party of Ontario—so much so that the party held a district open for him to represent until late in the pre-campaign period. But when the time came to declare, Doug's political stock had plummeted. He'd spent too much time at Rob's side, defending him, arguing lies as if he believed them, when Rob's addiction was plain enough for all to see. Though Hudak lost the 2014 provincial election and resigned as leader of the PC Party, leaving the position open, Doug had become as politically toxic as his brother, and missed his chance.

Doug had no interest in returning to City Hall in his brother's shadow—or, worse, working with another mayor. He vowed he was through with politics. The family drafted Kathy's son Michael Ford, Rob and Doug's nephew, to run in Ward 2, the Fords' dynastic homeland. Michael's a nice, humble kid. I'm not convinced he wanted to run for the seat. But Doug declared, "There will be a Ford on the ballot in Ward 2," and Michael stepped up.

On September 12, 2014, Toronto witnessed the three-Ford monte. Doug stepped into the mayoralty race as if it were a tag-team wrestling match and he would just take over where his brother left off. In the US, the concept of manifest destiny presumed that Canada would eventually, inevitably, become part of the United States. In the Ford family, the belief in their own manifest destiny presumes that a Ford will run the city of Toronto, the province of Ontario, and the country. It's their duty—and more than that, they were chosen to do it. They may not have an overt plan to achieve this goal, but the idea of it seems to influence every political decision they make. There are a number of young Fords being groomed for greatness. When they're old enough to join the family business, it will be interesting to see which one they choose: the label company, or politics.

To many outside Toronto, the Fords' dream sounds crazy. But in the Toronto municipal election on October 27, 2014, it proved anything but.

Michael Ford won his school district seat. Rob won back his seat in Ward 2. Doug Ford did not win the mayoralty, but he came close—the winner, John Tory, had 395,124 votes, and Doug had 331,006. Most of the city's political establishment was stunned by those numbers, but not me. I know that Ford Nation remains alive and well.

Three of Doug's daughters will be of electable age before the next city election. And Rob's own children, Stephanie and Dougie, may follow in their father's footsteps. If they inherit their father's magical likeability while avoiding his devastating addictions, Manifest Ford could be realized.

Meanwhile, in a quiet cemetery off Royal York road in Northern Etobicoke, a short drive from Diane Ford's house, Doug Ford Sr.'s gravestone sits surrounded by carefully tended, colorful flowers. The polished red granite stone is inscribed with the following words:

*In loving memory of Douglas Bruce Ford.*
*Feb. 27, 1933–Sept. 22, 2006*
*Cherished Father and Beloved Husband of Ruth Diane Campbell.*
*"Of those who are called, few are chosen."*

# 32 | The Toll it Took

Working for Rob Ford was, without doubt, the most challenging professional assignment I've ever had. From the very first day on the campaign, it was an immersive experience that I struggle to describe. In some ways, it was like being on a military operation; it was a twenty-four-hour-a-day, seven-day-a-week job with occasional time off to sleep when you were lucky. In that, it was much like any other political job. But Rob Ford was not like any other politician.

At no point did I ever feel confident I'd still be around at the end of the week. I didn't even hang pictures on my office wall until mid-2012. A few months later, I was promoted and moved offices. A few months after that, I was gone. We lived life on the edge the entire time. On the edge of failure. On the edge of discovery—discovery of something we could sense was terribly wrong, but couldn't yet understand ourselves.

By the end of 2011, we were living like characters in a murder mystery. Something was wrong. Things were happening that shouldn't have been happening, and things that should have been happening, weren't. None of us were entirely sure who we could trust and who might turn out to be the "murderer." We were, physically and emotionally, under siege.

As we began to piece together some of what was going on around us—some of the puzzle pieces fit for sure, others we were less certain about—the picture that emerged was scary. Our suspicions that Rob was abusing alcohol solidified as fact. We weren't certain he was addicted to it, but we had grave concerns as addiction seemed to be one of the few possibilities that explained most of his behavior. I expressed my concerns openly—first to Amir, then, after he left, to Rob. Many times.

I've never had more difficult conversations than those. Even thinking about having one, my gut would churn and I could taste acid at the back of my throat. Never before have I had to look someone in the eye and tell him

I believed he was addicted to drugs or alcohol. That it was a problem that was affecting his work performance. That it was a problem that was going to cost him his career, his family, his life.

My stress, in such sustained duration, was unequalled by any other experience I've ever had, including military service. I lived the job and nothing else. My rare moments with my kids were interrupted by calls from work about one crisis or another, or from an enraged and unrealistic mayor demanding an immediate and impossible fix. One night, for example, he decided at the last minute to go to a U2 concert at the Rogers Centre with one of his mystery buddies. He'd be there in ten minutes and demanded a staffer meet him on the sidewalk to park his car, then bring it to him at the end of the show. I patiently explained this was impossible. I didn't have people pre-positioned all over the city in case he decided to drop in somewhere and wanted a personal valet. He'd just have to park it and walk across the street like everyone else. Or take a taxi. Not a happy mayor.

Every morning I'd wake up around 5:30, feeling more tired than I'd been when I fell asleep. I was routinely in such a zombified state that it would take me over an hour to get out of my small apartment. By the time I pulled into the underground parking lot at City Hall, I'd feel like I was wearing two of the lead vests they lay over you during a dental x-ray. I'd park, shake them off, pull on my jacket and straighten my tie, then walk into the building through what felt like a field of wet cement. Each step a gargantuan effort.

Once I got to my office, whether as director of policy and strategic planning or later as chief of staff, though, the adrenaline would kick in. From there, the events of the day just washed over me, and the hours would pass in a blur. Meeting after meeting, exhausting and intoxicating at the same time. Working twenty, even thirty, major policy files at a time required a mental agility I hadn't exercised in years, but it was tiring. I don't eat breakfast and there was rarely time for lunch. But coffee—there was always time for that. By the time I left the building, after 8:00 p.m. on a normal day, I was running on fumes. Driving home became a concern. More than once, I found myself zoning out at stoplights, roused back to the task of driving by the honking of horns behind me, well after the light had turned green. I resolved to get more sleep. I never did.

By the time I closed the door to my apartment behind me, it would be 9:00 p.m. at the earliest. I'd undress as soon I entered, flop down on the couch, and fall asleep. Many nights, I landed face down, fully clothed, on my bed, fast asleep until the alarm went off in the morning.

Those hours aren't unusual for a political office or a corporate executive. What was unusual, and debilitating, was my level of wariness. I couldn't trust the man I worked for, and I found that tremendously taxing. As Rob's condition got worse, we gave up on many of our objectives and focused on survival. Our own. And his—first we worried about his reelection. Then we worried about him surviving his term, politically. Soon we worried about him surviving it at all.

Everyone felt the same. Many people working in the Office of the Mayor, and in Doug Ford's office, saw their health deteriorate. At least two young staffers developed cancer. I got off relatively easy: I developed an aggressive form of cataracts that began robbing me of sight by the time I was chief of staff. I don't know if stress contributed to our conditions, but I know it prevented us from finding time to see a doctor.

But the truth is, looking back, I'd do it again. Like my time overseas with the military and with international NGOs, working in high-pressure environments, doing work I felt was important, was exhilarating. Addictive, in its own way.

My main concerns were for my energetic young staffers. They did their jobs as well as they knew how, despite what many may describe as an abusive relationship with a man who demanded, belittled, and hectored them, and utterly failed to recognize their efforts with even a thank-you unless prompted. The staff adhered to my four rules and behaved with professionalism. They've been criticized for enabling an addict and helping to cover up criminality, but that's unjustified. They did not enable an addict. They enabled the function of government. At every opportunity, they tried to steer Ford back to a healthy course. They also never hid or assisted any criminal wrongdoing. When they had concerns, they brought them to Amir or to me. It was our job to handle them, and we tried to do it. My staffers can look back at their performance with clear consciences. Though that doesn't make their experience any easier to recover from.

After I was fired, many staff members quit and at least one went on stress leave. Most quit without securing another job first. Some resigned on principle; some because they simply couldn't survive staying any longer. Few got jobs quickly—I believe, because they were emotionally, physically, and mentally spent.

Many who stayed had no choice. Every time some pundit or Twitter twit would demand that they quit on principle, I would fume. People working in that office have a responsibility to the mayor and to the people who elected him, regardless of the mayor's behavior, and they are the only effective conduit between the city's civil service and its politicians. Without competent people in the mayor's office, the functioning of city government breaks down.

There are also economic realities. Political staff spend a year campaigning for their candidate—virtually for free. They accrue debts and work in lower-paying jobs to get by between elections. When they are fortunate enough to work with a winning candidate and land a staff job in an administration, much of their salary goes to paying off debts. No one gets rich. Few can afford to quit.

As for me, I was paid well. Most of my staff weren't, despite my best attempts. When I was fired, I went from an income of $185,000 per year to zero in an instant. I never signed back the "I won't sue you" waiver of liability to the city, so I didn't receive my severance—which added up to only about $14,000 anyway. My final pay, vacation pay included, deposited about $15,000 in my bank account. I'd been poor before, so I knew I could live cheap.

To find a new job at a senior level would normally take eighteen months. I could stretch the $15 grand to cover six. But two days after I got the $15,000, my bank account was down to $3,000. One of my larger creditors had gotten a court order to garnish my bank account. I had a pile of mail inside my front door going back almost a year—another casualty of my hours. I hadn't read the collection notices, and they'd scooped my money. It was an expensive lesson.

It's hard to network when you can't afford gas or a cell phone. It's hard to afford a dentist when you break a tooth—so I lived with a jagged one for a year. It's hard to stay informed if you can't afford newspapers, cable TV, or Internet. Still, I was far luckier than tens of thousands of others in the region who live like this all the time with little hope of improvement. My eyesight grew worse and I couldn't afford the gas anyway, so I left my car parked for a few weeks. What money I earned selling op-ed columns to newspapers and appearing on radio roundtables I saved to pay for surgery on one eye. I could see again out of it, but it wasn't quite as good as hoped. I lived with the other eye cloudy for almost a year before I could afford the second surgery.

I fell into a depression that I couldn't get out of. I'd been depressed before, once for a period of years. But I'd never admitted to anyone except my ex-wife that I was suffering, and her only after our relationship ended. I understood intellectually that depression is an illness, not a weakness. But in my shame, I felt it was an illness only the weak suffer from.

I'd been able to pull myself out of depression before by staying busy and having a sense of purpose. On the campaign, and in the mayor's office, I felt like I was contributing to society, so depression wasn't a problem. Until I took a rare day off. As exhausted as I was, I could feel myself circling the bowl again, slowly being sucked down the funnel into a funk. So I went back to work early and grew more tired. It was a trap.

After I was fired, I couldn't stay busy. I developed some job leads, but couldn't find it in myself to pursue them. And there was always a fresh batch of Rob Ford news to drive me deeper into my bed. At one point, my bank account was down to just over $7.00. I stopped seeing my kids for a long time, because I couldn't afford to do anything with them. (But hey, on the plus side, I was losing weight.)

On the rare occasion that I'd work up the fortitude to schedule a coffee date with a friend, I'd find a clean shirt and venture out.

"How are you?"

"Peachy."

I figured I was hiding the truth pretty well.

By Christmas 2013, I was bringing in enough cash from radio work to pay my rent and feed myself. But I was a radio host who couldn't listen to his own station because he didn't have a working radio in his ten-year-old car. I couldn't muster the energy to even send invoices until it was desperate. A great friend suggested I see a doctor, but I just joked that I didn't want to be diagnosed with anything I couldn't afford the drugs for.

So I got worse. Days would go by without my leaving my 800-square-foot apartment. Then weeks. Eventually, I admitted defeat and decided to ask for help.

The irony is not lost on me. I'd pushed Rob Ford for months to admit he needed help and that all he had to do was ask. I was livid with him for his inability to do something as easy as say, "I need help." He'd fired me instead of admitting it to me. Or to himself. I don't know which of us was stronger, and which of us was stupider.

After months of false starts, I mustered up the courage to talk to a doctor about my depression. It finally dawned on me that it didn't matter who knew I was having problems if I couldn't get work again—and I wouldn't get work again if I couldn't get better. That led to a prescription for an antidepressant and appointments with a psychiatrist. I'm not completely back to where I want to be, but it seems to be working. I feel much better.

I was shocked, and still am, at how profoundly stories about Rob Ford affect me. Every time he hits the news, my new normal gets derailed for a day. For a long time, each new Ford revelation resulted in an onslaught of media inquiries for interviews—wanting me to tell the inside story or to interpret the latest news from the Ford universe. I avoided those, because I did not—do not—want to be "the Ford whisperer" for the rest of my life. And each time I did media left me hiding at home for a little while longer.

I want to be angry at Rob. I really do. But I'm not. (I'm a bit angry with myself because of that.) I still have an enormous amount of sympathy for the man. As much as everything that's happened to him is his own fault—save his cancer, of course—I can't escape the impression that he's also a victim of bullies who hate him for what he is: an "undereducated," over-privileged fat kid from the 'burbs.

This book is part of my personal reconciliation with myself. I needed to sort through the experience, share my side of the story, and face it all at once. There have been so many questions, so many accusations—none of which can be answered in a 140-character tweet, or a 650-word essay, or a five-minute radio interview. They all demand a longer form. This book, I decided, would be that telling. But every time I sat down to write, I had to force myself. I didn't want to relive it. But I needed to.

As of this writing, there are still one or two former staff members from Rob's office who haven't found permanent work, or who are again unemployed after the jobs they landed in didn't last. I don't know if they're dealing with demons of their own. I haven't had the courage to ask them. Maybe I will now.